The Fundamental Teachings

OF

Quran and Hadith

Compiled & Edited By

NISAR AHMED

KITAB BHAVAN

New Delhi-110002

KITAB BHAVAN
Publishers, Distributors, Exporters & Importers
1784, Kalan Mahal, Darya Ganj,
New Delhi - 1100 02 (India)

Phones : (91-11) 23277392/93, 23274686, 32906494
Fax : (91-11) 23263383
Website : www.kitabbhavan.com
Email : nasri@vsnl.com
: nusrat@bol.net.in

First Published in India ... 1974
4th Edition 2009

ISBN : 81-7151-050-7
Book Code No. : F00035

Printed & Published in India by :
Nusrat Ali Nasri for KITAB BHAVAN
1784, Kalan Mahal, Darya Ganj,
New Delhi - 1100 02 [India]

PREFACE

The Qur'an and Hadith are both complementary to each other. One is the word of God Himself, presenting Islam directly from the Divine source, while the other consists of the sayings of the Holy Prophet who is next to God the most authentic source of Islmic teachings, principles and practices. Together they make one whole and contain all that is needed for and guidance of humanity.

If, therefore, we want to comprise all essential aspects of Islam, we need only refer to these two sources and pick out the various significant points in their proper order, the basic articles of faith coming first and the other correlevant ideas and practices following them.

The principal purpose of this book is nothing else than this. The fundamental conceptions of Islam have been clearly set forth in the Qur'an . I mean such matters of basic nature as the Unity of Good, Prophethood. Prayer, Fasting, etc. These give a gerneral idea of the diverse aspects and problems of Faith and of human life which the divine revelation seeks to direct.

The Traditions come next.These record the sayings and actions of the prophet himself, and as such are of unquestionable validity regarding the profession and practice of the Faith. That being so the Qur'an has naturally been given the first position in preparing this handbook of Islamic principles and laws. This has been followed by selected traditions of the Holy Prophet which are in the nature of a commentary or an exposition of the Quranic text. To elucidate them further, general remarks have been added; the translations and comments being both drawn from the writings of scholars and writers of established repute. Whatever has been said in these remarks is based totally on the above mentioned basic and unalterable sources of Islamic thought and action i.e. the Qur'an and Hadith. This enables the book to be an honest and simple exposition of what Islam stands for and what it demands from its followers. It also serves to introduce Islam to those who do not subscribe to it but to whom its call is equally addressed as members of the great Brotherhood of men.

The first part of the compilation contains the most important aricles of faith, practices and social teachings of Islam the second consist of matters bearing upon state, administration, political affairs, legal system, economics, labour, and ethics. The third further deals with the ethical system and other matters of moment. The verses of the Qur'an and the sayings of the Holy Prophet are so many luminous lamps lighted for us and I have put them down here so that any one can move forward in their light without fear of being lost.

For purposes of translating Quranic verses, the standard works of M.M. Pickthall, Allama Abudullah Yousuf Ali, Maulana A. Majid Daryabadi and M. Mohd. Ali have been used. As regards *Ahadith* and remarks thereon, the English translation of Mishkat by Maulana Fazlul Karim has been freely consulted at every step. Other books used for occasional references have been mentioned separately.

It is with genuine gratitude that I acknowledge my indebtedness to Dr. Amir Hasan Siddiqi without whose help it would not have been possible for me to carry this work through.

I would be failing in my duty if I do not acknowledge the labourious attention bestowed upon this book by my friend Mr. Rafiq Khawar, in first editing it and then preparing it for a regular publication. His selfless devotion to such unrewarding works is his greatest reward.

With these few lines I am presenting my humble efforts before the readers. I believe they would find it use ful as the previous ones in spotlighting the matters under consideration.

NISAR AHMED

Dedicated to

my respected teacher

Late DR. AMIR HASAN SIDDIQI

B. A. (Hon.), Ph. D. (Lond.)

as a token of my regard for him

&

in appreciation of his love for Islam.

FOREWORD

Mr. Nisar Ahmed who has made this collection of Quranic verses and the Traditions according with them, has long been in the field as one who has made a deep study of Islam and is well versed in the literature bearing upon it. His writings which touch various aspects of the Islamic faith, are read with keen interest for he has the knack of bringing home significant maters to his readers in a clear and lucid manner. He has the rare gift of matching expression to thought.

The light of Islam has been there for centuries but it is in constant need of fresh presentation so that the common man could grasp its essentials and translate them into practice. Mr. Ahmed has fulfilled this need by a judicious selection of suitable verses from the Qur'an together with appropriate traditions so that one can see at a glance what Islam stands for and how it should be practised. The selections fall into a well determined pattern. The first part comprising this volume, comprehends the fundamental tenets of Islam and the social pattern of life emerging from them, to be followed by others on political and economic matters. The triology thus covers the whole range of matters concerning Islam. Prove a handy manual for those who want to know and understand Islam.

AMIR HASAN SIDDIQI

CONTENTS

بسم الله الرحمن الرحيم

In the name of Allah, the Beneficent, the Merciful.

توحيد

ONENESS OF GOD

QURAN:

وإلهكم إله واحد لا إله إلا هو الرحمن الرحيم

1. And your God is one God! There is no God save Him, the Beneficient, the Marciful. (2 : 163)

إن في خلق السماوات والأرض واختلاف الليل والنهار والفلك التي تجري في البحر بما
ينفع الناس وما أنزل الله من السماء من ماء فأحيا به الأرض بعد موتها وبث فيها من
كل دابة وتصريف الرياح والسحاب المسخر بين السماء والأرض لآيات لقوم يعقلون

2. Most surely in the creation of the heavens and the earth and the alternation of the night and the day, and the ships that run in the sea with that which is of use to men, and the water that Allah sends down from the sky, thereby reviving the earth after its death and spreading in it all (kinds of) animals, and the changing of the winds and the clouds made subservient between the heaven and the earth, there are signs for a people who understand. (2 : 164)

الله لا إله إلا هو الحي القيوم لا تأخذه سنة ولا نوم له ما في السماوات وما في الأرض
من ذا الذي يشفع عنده إلا بإذنه يعلم ما بين أيديهم وما خلفهم ولا يحيطون بشيء
من علمه إلا بما شاء وسع كرسيه السماوات والأرض ولا يؤوده حفظهما وهو العلي العظيم

3. Allah! there is no God save Him, the Alive, the Eternal. Neither slumber nor sleep overtaketh Him. Unto Him belongeth whatsoever

is in the heavens and whatsoever is in the earth. Who is he that intercedeth with Him save by His leave? He knoweth that which is in front of them and that which is behind them, while they encompass nothing of His knowledge save what He will. His throne includeth the heavens and the earth and He is never weary of preserving them. He is the Sublime, the Tremendous. (2 : 255)

قُلْ اَىُّ شَىْءٍ اَكْبَرُ شَهَادَةً ؕ قُلِ اللّٰهُ ۙ شَهِيْدٌۢ بَيْنِىْ وَبَيْنَكُمْ ۚ وَاُوْحِىَ اِلَىَّ هٰذَا الْقُرْاٰنُ لِاُنْذِرَكُمْ بِهٖ وَمَنْۢ بَلَغَ ؕ اَئِنَّكُمْ لَتَشْهَدُوْنَ اَنَّ مَعَ اللّٰهِ اٰلِهَةً اُخْرٰى ؕ قُلْ لَّاۤ اَشْهَدُ ۚ قُلْ اِنَّمَا هُوَ اِلٰهٌ وَّاحِدٌ وَّ اِنَّنِىْ بَرِىْٓءٌ مِّمَّا تُشْرِكُوْنَ ۘ

4. Say: what thing is of most weight in testimony? Say: Allah is Witness beween me and you. And this Quran hath been inspired in me, that I may warn therewith you and whosoever it may reach. Do ye in sooth bear witness that there are gods beside Allah? Say: I bear no such witness. Say: He is only One God. Lo! I am innocent of that which ye associate (with Him). (6 : 19)

قُلْ هُوَ اللّٰهُ اَحَدٌ ۚ اَللّٰهُ الصَّمَدُ ۚ لَمْ يَلِدْ ۙ وَلَمْ يُوْلَدْ ۙ وَلَمْ يَكُنْ لَّهٗ كُفُوًا اَحَدٌ

5. Say: He is Allah, the One! Allah, the eternally besought of all! He begetteth not, nor was begotten. And there is none comparable to Him. (112).

لَوْ كَانَ فِيْهِمَاۤ اٰلِهَةٌ اِلَّا اللّٰهُ لَفَسَدَتَا ۚ فَسُبْحٰنَ اللّٰهِ رَبِّ الْعَرْشِ عَمَّا يَصِفُوْنَ

6. If there were therein gods beside Allah, then verily both (the heavens and the earth) had been disordered. Glorified be Allah, the Lord of the Throne, from all that they ascribe (unto Him). (21 : 22)

قُلْ اِنَّمَاۤ اَنَا بَشَرٌ مِّثْلُكُمْ يُوْحٰۤى اِلَىَّ اَنَّمَاۤ اِلٰهُكُمْ اِلٰهٌ وَّاحِدٌ

7. Say: I am only a mortal like you. My Lord inspireth in me that your God is only One God. (18 : 110).

HADIS:

(١) عن ابن عمر رضى الله عنه، قال: قال رسول الله صلي الله عليه وسلم: بني الاسلام على خمس: شهادة ان لااله الاالله و ان محمداً عبده و رسوله، و اقام الصلاة، و ايتاء الزكاة، والحج، وصوم رمضان (متفق عليه)

(1) Ibn-Omer reported that the Holy Prophet said: Islam is built on five things—to bear witness that there is no deity but Allah and that Muhammad (P.H.) is His servant and His messenger, to keep up prayer, to pay zakat, to take pilgrimage and to keep fast in the Ramazan. (Bukhari, Muslim)

(٢) عن عبادة بن الصامت رضى الله عنه، قال: سمعت، سول الله صلى الله عليه وسلم يقول: من شهد ان لااله الا الله و ان محمداً رسول الله، حرم الله عليه النار (مسلم)

(2) Ubada bin es-Samit said: I heard Allah's Messenger say, "If any one testifies that there is no god but Allah and that Muhammad (P.H.) is Allah's messenger, Allah will keep him from going to hell." (Muslim)

(٣) وعن عثمان رضى الله عنه، قال: قال رسول الله صلى الله عليه وسلم: من مات وهو يعلم انه لااله الا الله دخل الجنة (مسلم)

(3) Uthman bin Affan reported Allah's Messenger as saying, "Whosoever dies knowing that there is no god but Allah, will enter paradise." (Muslim)

(٤) وعن معاذ رضى الله عنه، قال: كنت ردف رسول الله صلى الله عليه وسلم على حمار، ليس بينى وبينه الا موخرة الرحل، فقال: يا معاذ! هل تدرى ما حق الله على عباده؟ وما حق العباد على الله؟ قلت:

الله و رسوله اعلم . قال: فان حق الله على العباد ان يعبدوه ولا
يشركوا به شيئاً ، و حق العباد على الله ان لايعذب من لا يشرك
به شيئاً ـ فقلت : يا رسول الله ! افلا ابشربه الناس؟ قال : لاتبشرهم
فيتكلوا ـ (متفق عليه)

(4) Mu'adh said: I was riding behind the Prophet on an ass with nothing between him and me but the rear part of the saddle, when he said, "Do you know, Mua'dh, what Allah has the right to expect from His servants, and what His servants have the right to expect from Allah?" I replied, "Allah and His Messenger know best." He said, "What God has the right to expect from His servants is that they should serve Him without associating anything with Him; what the servants have the right to expect from Allah is that He should not punish one who does not associate anything with Him."
(Bukhari, Muslim)

(٥) وعن معاذ بن جبل رضى الله عنه، قال : قال لى رسول الله صلى الله
عليه وسلم : مفاتيح الجنة، شهادة ان لا اله الا الله (احمد)

(5) Mu'adh bin Jabal reported that Allah's Messenger said to him, "The keys to paradise lie in testifying that there is no god but Allah."
(Ahmad)

(٦) وعن معاذ بن جبل رضى الله عنه، قال : سمعت رسول الله يقول
من لقى الله لايشرك به شيئاً، و يصلى الخمس، و يصوم رمضان،
غفر له ـ قلت:افلا أبشرهم يا رسول الله، قال: دعهم يعملوا (احمد)

(6) Mu'adh bin Jabal said that he heard Allah's Messenger say, "He who met his Lord having not associated anything with Him, having observed the five times of prayer, and fasting during the Ramazan, will be forgiven".
(Ahmad)

Remarks:

Belief in the unity of God is the most fundamental and important teaching of the Quran and Hadith. It is the foundation of the entire faith.

The confession of this faith is the gate-way to Islam. It is expressed in the primary Kalimah of Islam : لااله الاالله محمد رسول الله The first part of this Kalimah contains the affirmation of the Oneness of God. It means that no one except the Almighty is worthy of worship and obedience, and homage should be paid to Him alone because He and no one else is our Lord and Creator, Nourisher, Sustainer and the Dispenser of Life after Death.

God is One, though He is capable of doing all sorts of things. Hence the multipilicity of His attributes. God is not only the Creator, but also the master of all : He rules over the heavens and the earth; nothing moves without His knowledge and His permission The Prophet Muhammad has said that God has ninety-nine "most beautiful names", for ninety-nine principle attributes: He is the Creator, the essence of the existence of all, wise, just, merciful, omnipresent, omnipotent, omniscient, determinant of everything, to Whom belongs life, death, resurrection, etc. etc,

God has given us the organs and faculties which we possess, and every gift implies a particular obligation. To worship God, to be thankful to him, to obey him, to shun all that does not suit His universal Divinity-all these constitute the individual duties of everyone, for which each one shall be personally responsible.

رسالت

PROPHETHOOD

QURAN:

الله أعلم حيث يجعل رسالته

1. **Allah knoweth best with whom to place His message. (6:124)**

وما أرسلنا من قبلك إلا رجالا نوحي إليهم فاسألوا أهل الذكر إن كنتم لا تعلمون

2. **And We sent not (as Our messenger) berfore thee other than men whom We inspired—Ask the followers of the Remembrance if ye know not. (16:43)**

ولكل أمة رسول

3. **And for every nation there is a messenger. (10 : 47)**

ولقد بعثنا في كل أمة رسولا أن اعبدوا الله واجتنبوا الطاغوت

4. **And verily we have raised in every nation a messenger, (Proclaiming) : Serve Allah and shun false gods. (16 : 36)**

إن الذين يكفرون بالله ورسله ويريدون أن يفرقوا بين الله ورسله ويقولون نؤمن ببعض ونكفر ببعض
ويريدون أن يتخذوا بين ذلك سبيلا أولئك هم الكافرون حقا وأعتدنا للكافرين عذابا مهينا

5. **Lo ! those who disbelieve in Allah and His messengers, and seek to make distinctsion between Allah and His messengers and say : We believe in some and disbelieve in others, and seek to choose a course in between ; such are disbelievers in truth ; and for disbelievers We prepare a shameful doom.**

(4 : 150—151)

وما أرسلنا من رسول إلا ليطاع بإذن الله (نساء-٦٤)

6. **We sent no messenger save that he should be obeyed by Allah's leave. (4:64)**

ما كان محمد ابا احد من رجالكم ولكن رسول الله وخاتم النبيين وكان الله بكل شيء عليما (احزاب)

7. **Muhammad is not the father of any man among you, but he is the Messenger of Allah and the Seal of the Prophets ; and Allah is ever Aware of all things. (33 : 40)**

وما ارسلنك الا كافة للناس بشيرا ونذيرا ولكن اكثر الناس لا يعلمون (السباء ٢٨)

8. **And we have not sent thee (O Muhammad) save as a bringer of good tidings and a warner unto all mankind ; but most of mankind know not. (34 : 28)**

وما اتكم الرسول فخذوه وما نهكم عنه فانتهوا

9. **And whatsoever the Messenger giveth you, take it and whatsoever he forbiddeth, abstain (from it). (59 : 7)**

HADIS :

١ ـ عن ابن عمر رضى الله عنه، قال : قال رسول الله صلى الله عليه وسلم : بنى الاسلام على خمس . شهادة ان لا اله الاالله و ان محمداً عبده و رسوله ، و اقام الصلاة ، و ايتاء الزكاة ، و الحج ، و صوم رمضان (متفق عليه)

1. **Ibn Omer reported that the Holy Prophe said : Islam is built on five things—to bear witness that there is no deity but Allah and that Muhammad (P. H.) is His servant and His Messenger, to keep up prayer, to pay zakat, to make pilgrimage and to keep fast in Ramazan. (Bukhari, Muslim)**

٢ ـ عن عبادة بن الصامت رضى الله عنه ، قال : سمعت رسول الله صلى الله عليه وسلم يقول : من شهد ان لا اله الاالله وان محمداً رسول الله، حرم الله عليه النار ـ (مسلم)

2. Ubada bin as Samit said, "I heard Allah's Messenger say, "If any one testifies that there is no god but Allah and that Muhammad is Allah's Messenger, Allah will keep him from going to hell." (Muslim)

٣ ـ وعن العباس بن عبد المطلب، قال: قال رسول الله صلى الله عليه وسلم: ذاق طعم الايمان من رضي بالله رباً، و بالاسلام ديناً، وبمحمد رسولاً (مسلم)

3. Al-Abbas bin Abdul Muttalib reported Allah's Messenger as saying, "He who is well pleased with Allah as Lord, with Islam as Religion, and with Muhammad as Messenger, will experience the flavour of faith." (Muslim)

٤ ـ وعن عبد الله بن عمرو، قال: قال رسول الله صلى الله عليه وسلم: لا يومن احدكم حتى يكون هواه تبعاً لما جئتُ به. (مشكواة)

4. Abdulla bin Amr reported Allah's Messenger as saying, "None of you is a believer until his desire bows to what I have brought." (Mishkat)

٥ ـ وعن ابى هريرة، قال. قال رسول الله صلى الله عليه وسلم: كل امتي يدخلون الجنة الا من أبى قيل: ومن أبى؟ قال: من اطاعنى دخل الجنة، ومن عصانى فقد أبى ـ (بخارى)

5. Abu Huraira reported Allah's Messenger as saying, "All my people will enter paradise except those who refused." On being asked as to who refused, he replied, "He who obeys me will enter paradise, and he who disobeys me has refused." (Bukhari).

٦ ـ وعن انس رضى الله عنه، قال قال رسول الله صلى الله عليه وسلم ـ لا يومن احدكم حتى اكون احب اليه من والده و ولده والناس اجمعين (متفق عليه)

6. Anas reported Allah's Messenger as saying. "None of you believes until I am dearer to him than his father, his child and all mankind." (Bukhari, Muslim)

٧ - قال رسول الله صلى الله عليه و سلم: انى آخر الانبياء و ان مسجدى آخر المساجد
(مسلم)

7. The Prophet of Allah said, "I am the last of prophets and my mosque is the last of mosques." (Muslim)

٨ - قال رسول الله صلى الله عليه وسلم: لا نبي بعدى ولا امة بعد امتى
(بيهقى)

8. The Prophet of Allah said, "There would be no prophet after me, and there would be no Ummah after my Ummah. (Beheqi).

Remarks.

* A prophet is defined as a human being chosen by God to reveal and impart His message and guidance to His servants and entrusted with responsibilities of a spiritual and temporal leader.
* Prophethood is hundred percent a Divine gift and not an acquirement.
* The long line of prophets began with the begining of the human race. Ever since man started his career on earth, God, as the universal Cherisher and Sustainer, has been ministering to his spiritual needs as He has been to his physical needs.
* No nation, no people have been left without a Divine Messenger having been sent to them. All prophets have been men of great piety and models of good behaviour.
* The concept of prophethood is rendered meaningless as soon as Prophets are taken to be gods, sons of God, gods incarnate or angels.
* The only Right Path for man is the one which the Prophet declares to be so and the correct way of life only that which he informs us to be from God.
* Muhammad (Peace be upon him) is the last Prophet of God, and every Muslim is required to obey him in all matters of life.

آخرت

THE HEREAFTER

QURAN :

وَبِالْآخِرَةِ هُمْ يُوقِنُونَ ۝

1. **... and are certain of the Hereafter. (2 : 4)**

إِنَّ الَّذِينَ آمَنُوا وَالَّذِينَ هَادُوا وَالصَّابِئُونَ وَالنَّصَارَىٰ مَنْ آمَنَ بِاللَّهِ وَالْيَوْمِ الْآخِرِ وَعَمِلَ صَالِحًا فَلَا خَوْفٌ
عَلَيْهِمْ وَلَا هُمْ يَحْزَنُونَ ۝

2. **Lo ! Those who believe, and those who are Jews, and Sabaeans, and Christians—Whosoever believeth in Allah and the Last Day and—doeth right—there shall no fear come upon them neither shall they grieve. (5 : 69).**

إِلَٰهُكُمْ إِلَٰهٌ وَاحِدٌ ۚ فَالَّذِينَ لَا يُؤْمِنُونَ بِالْآخِرَةِ قُلُوبُهُمْ مُنْكِرَةٌ وَهُمْ مُسْتَكْبِرُونَ ۝

3. **Your God is One God. But as for those who believe not in the Hereafter their hearts refuse to know, for they are proud. (16 : 22)**

وَأَنَّ الَّذِينَ لَا يُؤْمِنُونَ بِالْآخِرَةِ أَعْتَدْنَا لَهُمْ عَذَابًا أَلِيمًا ۝

4. **And that those who believe not in the Hereafter, for them We have prepared a parinful doom. (17 : 10).**

قَدْ خَسِرَ الَّذِينَ كَذَّبُوا بِلِقَاءِ اللَّهِ ۖ حَتَّىٰ إِذَا جَاءَتْهُمُ السَّاعَةُ بَغْتَةً قَالُوا يَا حَسْرَتَنَا عَلَىٰ مَا فَرَّطْنَا فِيهَا وَهُمْ يَحْمِلُونَ أَوْزَارَهُمْ
عَلَىٰ ظُهُورِهِمْ ۚ أَلَا سَاءَ مَا يَزِرُونَ ۝ وَمَا الْحَيَاةُ الدُّنْيَا إِلَّا لَعِبٌ وَلَهْوٌ ۖ وَلَلدَّارُ الْآخِرَةُ خَيْرٌ لِلَّذِينَ يَتَّقُونَ ۚ أَفَلَا تَعْقِلُونَ ۝

5. **Lost indeed are they who treat it as a falsehood that they must meet God,—until on a sudden the hour is on them, and they say : "Ah ! Woe unto us that we took no thought of it"; for they bear their burdens on their backs, and evil indeed**

are the burdens that they bear ! What is the life of this world but play and amusement ? But best is the Home in the Hereafter, for those who are righteous. Will ye not then understand ? (6 : 31,32).

اِعْلَمُوْٓا اَنَّمَا الْحَيٰوةُ الدُّنْيَا لَعِبٌ وَّلَهْوٌ وَّزِيْنَةٌ وَّتَفَاخُرٌ بَيْنَكُمْ وَتَكَاثُرٌ فِي الْاَمْوَالِ وَالْاَوْلَادِ كَمَثَلِ غَيْثٍ اَعْجَبَ
الْكُفَّارَ نَبَاتُهٗ ثُمَّ يَهِيْجُ فَتَرٰىهُ مُصْفَرًّا ثُمَّ يَكُوْنُ حُطٰمًا ۭ وَفِي الْاٰخِرَةِ عَذَابٌ شَدِيْدٌ ۙ وَّمَغْفِرَةٌ مِّنَ اللّٰهِ وَرِضْوَانٌ ۭ
مَا الْحَيٰوةُ الدُّنْيَآ اِلَّا مَتَاعُ الْغُرُوْرِ ۝

6. Know that the life of the world is only play, and idle talk, and pageantry, and boasting among you, and rivalry in respect of wealth and children ; as the likeness of vegetation after rain, whereof the growth is pleasing to the husbandman, but afterward it drieth up and thou seest it turning yellow, then it becometh straw. And in the Hereafter there is grievous punishment, and (also) forgiveness from Allah and His good pleasure, whereas the life of the world is but a matter of illusion. (57 : 20).

يٰٓاَيُّهَا النَّاسُ اِنْ كُنْتُمْ فِيْ رَيْبٍ مِّنَ الْبَعْثِ فَاِنَّا خَلَقْنٰكُمْ مِّنْ تُرَابٍ ثُمَّ مِنْ نُّطْفَةٍ ثُمَّ مِنْ عَلَقَةٍ ثُمَّ مِنْ مُّضْغَةٍ
مُّخَلَّقَةٍ وَّغَيْرِ مُخَلَّقَةٍ لِّنُبَيِّنَ لَكُمْ ۭ وَنُقِرُّ فِي الْاَرْحَامِ مَا نَشَاۗءُ اِلٰٓى اَجَلٍ مُّسَمًّى ثُمَّ نُخْرِجُكُمْ طِفْلًا ثُمَّ لِتَبْلُغُوْٓا اَشُدَّكُمْ
وَمِنْكُمْ مَّنْ يُّتَوَفّٰى وَمِنْكُمْ مَّنْ يُّرَدُّ اِلٰٓى اَرْذَلِ الْعُمُرِ لِكَيْلَا يَعْلَمَ مِنْ بَعْدِ عِلْمٍ شَيْـًٔا ۭ وَتَرَى الْاَرْضَ هَامِدَةً فَاِذَآ
اَنْزَلْنَا عَلَيْهَا الْمَاۗءَ اهْتَزَّتْ وَرَبَتْ وَاَنْبَتَتْ مِنْ كُلِّ زَوْجٍ بَهِيْجٍ ۝ ذٰلِكَ بِاَنَّ اللّٰهَ هُوَ الْحَقُّ وَاَنَّهٗ يُحْيِ الْمَوْتٰى وَاَنَّهٗ
عَلٰى كُلِّ شَيْءٍ قَدِيْرٌ ۝ وَّاَنَّ السَّاعَةَ اٰتِيَةٌ لَّا رَيْبَ فِيْهَا ۙ وَاَنَّ اللّٰهَ يَبْعَثُ مَنْ فِي الْقُبُوْرِ ۝

7. O Mankind: if ye have a doubt about the Resurrection, (consider) that We created you out of dust, then out of sperm, then out of a leach-like clot, then out of a morsal of flesh, partly formed and partly unformed, in order that We may manifest (Our Power) to you ; and We cause whom We will to rest in the wombs for an appointed term, then do We bring you out as babes, then (foster you) that ye may reach your age of full strength. And some of you are called to die, and some are sent back to the feablest old age, so that they know nothing after having known (much). And (further), thou seest the earth barren and lifeless, but when We pour down rain on it, it is stirred (to life), it swells, and it puts forth every kind of beautiful

growth (in pairs). This is so because God is the Reality : it is He Who gives life to the dead, and it is He Who has Power over all things. (22 : 5,6)

وَاتَّقُوا يَوْمًا تُرْجَعُونَ فِيهِ إِلَى اللَّهِ ثُمَّ تُوَفَّى كُلُّ نَفْسٍ مَا كَسَبَتْ وَهُمْ لَا يُظْلَمُونَ

8. And fear the Day when ye shall be brought back to Allah. Then shall every soul be paid what it earned ; and none shall be dealt with unjustly. (2 : 281)

HADIS :

١ - عن ابي هريرة ، قال : قال رسول الله صلى الله عليه وسلم :
يقبض الله الارض يوم القيامة ، و يطوي السماء بيمينه ، ثم يقول :
انا الملك ، اين ملوك الأرض؟ (متفق عليه)

1. Abu Hurairah reported that the Messenger of Allah said : Allah will hold up the earth on the Resurrection Day, and He will roll up heaven to His right side and then say : I am the king, where are the kings of the world ?" (Bukhari, Muslim)

٢ - عن ابي رزين العقيلي ، قال : قلت يا رسول الله ! كيف يعيد الله
الخلق ، و ما آية ذلك فى خلقه؟ قال : اما مررت بوادي قومك
جدباً ثم مررت به يهتز خضراً؟ قلت : نعم - قال : فتلك آية
الله فى خلقه ، كذلك يحى الله الموتى . (مشكواة)

2. Abu Razin-al-Oqaile reported : I asked : O Messenger of Allah ! how will Allah reproduce creation and what is the sign of that in His Creation ? He said : Have you not passed by the valley of your people at the time of drought and then passed by it while it is luxuriant with greens ? 'Yes,' I replied. He said : that is the sign of Allah in his Creation ; likewise Allah brings the dead to life. (Mishkat)

٣ - عن سهل بن سعد ، قال : قال رسول الله صلى الله عليه و سلم :
يحشر الناس يوم القيامة على ارض بيضاء عفراء ، كقرصة النقي ليس
فيها علم لأحد . (متفق عليه)

3. Sahl bin Sa'ad reported that the Messenger of Allah said: "People will be brought together on the Resurrection Day on a whitened ground like a spotless round piece of bread. There will be no sign therein for anybody." (Bukhari, Muslim)

٤ - عن ابى هريرة، قال: قال رسول الله صلى الله عليه وسلم: يحشر الناس يوم القيامة ثلثة اصناف: صنفاً مشاة، و صنفاً ركباناً و صنفاً على وجوههم. قيل: يا رسول الله! و كيف يمشون على وجوههم؟ قال: ان الذى امشاهم على اقدامهم قادر على ان يمشيهم على وجوههم، اما انهم يتقون بوجوههم كل حدب و شوك (الترمذى)

4. Abu-Hurairah reported that the Messenger of Allah said: "People will be gathered together on the Resurrection Day in three divisions; the footmen being one division, the riders one divison and those (who will walk) on their faces one division. It was asked: O Messenger of Allah! and how will they walk with their faces? He said: verily He who causes them to walk with their feet is powerful to cause them to walk upon their faces. Behold! they will certainly guard with their faces every lofty place and thorn. (Tirmizi)

٥ - عن ابى هريرة، قال: قال رسول الله صلى الله عليه وسلم: قال الله تعالى: اعددت لعبادى الصالحين ما لا عين رأت، ولا اذن سمعت، ولا خطر على قلب بشر، و اقرؤوا ان شئتم: فلا تعلم نفس ما اخفى لهم من قرة اعين. (متفق عليه)

5. Abu-Hurairah reported that the Messenger of Allah said: "The Almighty Allah said: I have prepared for my righteous servants which no eye hath seen, and no ear hath heard, and no heart of man hath conceived. And read if you like: "Now no person knows what delights of the eye are kept hidden." (Bukhari, Muslim)

٦ - عن ابى هريرة، قال: قال رسول الله صلى الله عليه وسلم: من يدخل الجنة ينعم ولا يباس، ولا تبلى ثيابه، ولا يفنى شبابه. (مسلم)

6. Abu-Hurairah reported that the Messenger of Allah said: "Whosoever enters Paradise shall be in joy and not in want, and neither his clothes will get old, nor his youth will end." (Muslim)]

٧ ـ عن ابي هريرة، ان رسول الله صلى الله عليه وسلم قال: ناركم جزء من سبعين جزء من نار جهنم ـ قيل: يا رسول الله! ان كانت لكافية ـ قال: فضلت عليهن بتسعة وستين جزءا كلهن مثل حرها. (متفق عليه)

7. Abu-Hurairah reported that the Messenger of Allah said: "Your fire is a portion out of seventy portions of the fire of Hell." It was asked, "O Messenger of Allah! they are certainly sufficient." He said: "They were given excellence by sixty-nine portions, each of them being like their heat." (Bukhari, Muslim)

٨ ـ عن النعمان بن بشير، قال: قال رسول الله صلى الله عليه وسلم: ان اهون اهل النار عذاباً من له نعلان وشراكان من نار، يغلى منها دماغه كما يغلى المرجل، ما يرى ان احداً اشد منه عذاباً وانه لاهونهم عذاباً ـ (متفق عليه)

8. Nu'man bin Bashir reported that the Messenger of Allah said: "Verily the easiest of the inmates of fire in punishment will be one who will have a pair of shoes and laces of fire. His brain will boil up on their account as the kettle boils up. No body will be seen to suffer heavier punishment than he, but he will be the easiest of them in punishment." (Bukhari, Muslim)

Remarks:

—. As the belief in life after death has always been a part and parcel of the teachings of the prophets, the Last Prophet, Muhammad (Peace & Blessings of Allah be on him) has also directed us to believe in Resurrection and in the Day of Judgment.

—. This has always been an essential condition of being a Muslim, because the denial of this belief makes other beliefs meaningless. This denial also destroys the very sanction for good life, and man is driven to a life of ignorance and disbelief; it becomes absolutely impossible for him to fashion his life as suggested by Islam.

The essential ingredients of this belief are as follows :—

1. That the life of this world and of all that is in it, will come to an end on an appointed day. Every thing will be annihilated. That day is called Qayamah, i. e., The Last Day.

2. That all the human beings who had lived in the world since its inception will then be restored to life and will be presented before God who will sit in Court on that day. This is called Hashr (Resurrection).

3. That the entire record of every man and woman — a complete record of all their deeds and misdeeds — will be presented before God for final judgment.

4. That God shall finally adjudge the record of every person. He shall weigh everyone's good and bad deeds. One who excels in goodness will be accorded a good reward ; one whose evils and wrongs outweigh his good deeds, will be punished.

5. That the reward and punishment will be administered judiciously. Those who emerge successful in this judgment, will go to Paradise and doors of eternal bliss will be opened to them; those who are condemned and deserve punishment, will be sent to Hell — the abode of fire and torture.*

—. The gist of this belief is that at the end of this mortal life, there is to come another life and another world in which men will be requited for the good or evil they might have done during their earthly sojourn.*

—. Now the only authentic knowledge available to us about the world of Requital, is that supplied by the Last Prophet of Allah.

—. The concept of the Hereafter plays a powerful role in the reformation of our lives.

* Towards Understanding Islam, —Maududi.

صلاة

SALAT (NAMAZ OR PRAYER)

QURAN :

اِنَّنِیْۤ اَنَا اللّٰهُ لَاۤ اِلٰهَ اِلَّاۤ اَنَا فَاعْبُدْنِیْ وَاَقِمِ الصَّلٰوةَ لِذِكْرِیْ

1. **Lo! I, even I, am Allah. There is no God save Me. So serve Me and establish worship for My rememberance. (20: 14)**

ذٰلِكَ الدِّیْنُ الْقَیِّمُ وَلٰكِنَّ اَكْثَرَ النَّاسِ لَا یَعْلَمُوْنَ مُنِیْبِیْنَ اِلَیْهِ وَاتَّقُوْهُ وَاَقِیْمُوا الصَّلٰوةَ وَلَا تَكُوْنُوْا مِنَ الْمُشْرِكِیْنَ

2. **That is the right religion, but most men know not — Turning unto Him (only) ; and be careful of your duty unto Him, and establish worship, and be not of those who ascribe partners (unto Him). (30 : 30)**

فَاَقِیْمُوا الصَّلٰوةَ اِنَّ الصَّلٰوةَ كَانَتْ عَلَى الْمُؤْمِنِیْنَ كِتٰبًا مَّوْقُوْتًا

3. **Set up regular prayers : for such prayers are enjoined on believers at stated times. (4 : 103)**

اُتْلُ مَاۤ اُوْحِیَ اِلَیْكَ مِنَ الْكِتٰبِ وَاَقِمِ الصَّلٰوةَ اِنَّ الصَّلٰوةَ تَنْهٰى عَنِ الْفَحْشَآءِ وَالْمُنْكَرِ وَلَذِكْرُ اللّٰهِ اَكْبَرُ

4. **Recite what is sent of the Book by inspiration to thee, and establish regular prayer ; for prayer restrain from shameful and unjust deeds, and rememberance of Allah is the greatest. (29 : 45)**

كُلُّ نَفْسٍ بِمَا كَسَبَتْ رَهِیْنَةٌ اِلَّاۤ اَصْحٰبَ الْیَمِیْنِ فِیْ جَنّٰتٍ یَتَسَآءَلُوْنَ عَنِ الْمُجْرِمِیْنَ مَا سَلَكَكُمْ فِیْ سَقَرَ قَالُوْا لَمْ نَكُ مِنَ الْمُصَلِّیْنَ

5. **Every soul will be held in pledge for its deeds, except the Companions of the Right Hand. (They will be) in Gardens (of delight) : they will question each other and (ask) of the**

Sinners: "What led you into Hell-fire?" They will say, "We were not of those who prayed." (74 : 38—43)

وَأَقِمِ الصَّلٰوةَ طَرَفَيِ النَّهَارِ وَزُلَفًا مِّنَ الَّيْلِ إِنَّ الْحَسَنٰتِ يُذْهِبْنَ السَّيِّاٰتِ ذٰلِكَ ذِكْرٰى لِلذّٰكِرِيْنَ ۝

6. And establish regular prayers at the two ends of the day and at the approaches of the night: for those things that are good remove those that are evil. Be that the word of remembrance for those who remember. (11 : 114)

أَقِمِ الصَّلٰوةَ لِدُلُوْكِ الشَّمْسِ إِلٰى غَسَقِ الَّيْلِ وَقُرْاٰنَ الْفَجْرِ

7. Establish regular prayers at the sun's decline till the darkness of the night and the morning recitation. (17 : 78)

وَارْكَعُوْا مَعَ الرّٰكِعِيْنَ ۝

8. And bow down with those who bow down. (2 : 43)

يٰٓأَيُّهَا الَّذِيْنَ اٰمَنُوْٓا إِذَا نُوْدِيَ لِلصَّلٰوةِ مِنْ يَّوْمِ الْجُمُعَةِ فَاسْعَوْا إِلٰى ذِكْرِ اللّٰهِ وَذَرُوا الْبَيْعَ

9. O ye who believe! When the call is proclaimed to prayer on Friday, hasten earnestly to the remembrance of Allah and leave off business. (62 : 9)

يٰٓأَيُّهَا الَّذِيْنَ اٰمَنُوْٓا إِذَا قُمْتُمْ إِلَى الصَّلٰوةِ فَاغْسِلُوْا وُجُوْهَكُمْ وَأَيْدِيَكُمْ إِلَى الْمَرَافِقِ وَامْسَحُوْا بِرُءُوْسِكُمْ وَأَرْجُلَكُمْ
إِلَى الْكَعْبَيْنِ

10. O ye who believe: when ye prepare for prayer, wash your faces and your hands (and arms) to the elbows, and rub your heads (with water) and (wash) your feet to the ankles. (5 : 7)

حٰفِظُوْا عَلَى الصَّلَوٰتِ وَالصَّلٰوةِ الْوُسْطٰى وَقُوْمُوْا لِلّٰهِ قٰنِتِيْنَ ۝

11. Guard strictly your (habit of) prayers, especially the Middle prayer, and stand up truly obedient to Allah. (2 : 238)

قَدْ أَفْلَحَ الْمُؤْمِنُوْنَ ۝ الَّذِيْنَ هُمْ فِيْ صَلَاتِهِمْ خٰشِعُوْنَ ۝

12. Successful indeed are the believers who humble themselves in their prayers. (23 : 1)

HADIS :

١ ـ عن ابن عمر رضى الله عنه، قال : قال رسول الله صلى الله عليه وسلم : بنى الاسلام على خمس : شهادة ان لا اله الا الله و ان محمداً عبده و رسوله، واقام الصلاة، وايتاء الزكاة، والحج، وصوم رمضان (متفق عليه)

1. Abdullah bin Umar reported Allah's Messenger as saying: "Islam is founded on five pillars: bearing witness that there is no God but Allah and Muhammad is His Servant and Apostle; establishment of *Salat*; paying of *Zakat*; performance of *Hajj* and fasting in Ramadhan". (Bukhari, Muslim)

٢ عن ابى هريرة، قال : قال رسول الله صلى الله عليه وسلم : لا سهم فى الاسلام لمن لا صلاة له ولا صلاة لمن لا وضوء له .

(البزار، حاكم)

2. Abu Hurairah reported Allah's Messenger as saying: "There is no portion in Islam for a person who does not say his *Salat* and there is no *Salat* wihtout *Wadhu.*" (Al-Bazzar, Hakim)

٣ ـ عن بريدة، قال : قال رسول الله صلى الله عليه وسلم : العهد الذي بيننا و بينهم الصلاة، فمن تركها فقد كفر .

(احمد، ترمذى، نسائى، ابن ماجه)

3. Buraida reported Allah's Messenger as saying: "The covenant between us and them is prayer; so if anyone abandons it he has become an infidel". (Ahmed, Tirmizi, Nasai, Ibn Majah)

٤ ـ عن ابى هريرة، قال : سمعت رسول الله صلى الله عليه وسلم يقول : اريتم لو ان نهراً بباب احدكم يغسل فيه كل يوم خمس مرات، هل يبقى من درنه شئ ؟ قالوا لا يبقى من درنه شئ ـ قال :

فكذلك مثل الصلوات الخمس، يمحو الله بهن الخطايا .

(بخاری ، مسلم ، ترمذی ، ابن ماجه)

4. Abu Hurairah narrates that: Once he heard the Prophet (*Sallallaho Alahiwasallam*) ask his companions "Do you believe that dirt can remain on a person bathing five times a day in a brook running in front of his doors?" "No", replied the companions, "No dirt can remain on his body." The Prophet remarked: "So exactly similar is the effect of *Salat* offered five times a day. With the Grace of Allah, it washes away all the sins."

(Bukhari, Muslim, Tirmizi, Ibn Majah)

٥ - عن عبادة بن الصامت، قال : قال رسول الله صلى الله عليه وسلم : خمس صلوات افترضهن الله تعالي، من احسن وضوءهن، وصلاهن لوقتهن، واتم ركوعهن وخشوعهن ، كان له على الله عهد ان يغفرله، ومن لم يفعل فليس له على الله عهد ان شاء غفرله، وان شاء عذبه . (احمد- ابوداؤد- مالك- نسائی)

5. Ubada bin as-Samit reported Allah's Messenger as saying, "Five times of prayer have been prescribed by God. If any one performs the ablution for them well, observes them at their proper time, and perfectly performs the bowing and showing of submissiveness during them, he has a covenant from God to forgive him, but if any one does not do so, he has no covenant. If He wills He may forgive him, and if He wills He may punish him." (Ahmad, Abu Dawood, Malik, Nasai)

٦ - عن ابی ذر : ان النبي صلى الله عليه وسلم خرج زمن الشتاء ، والورق يتهافت، فاخذ بغصنين من شجرة قال : فجعل ذلك الورق يتهافت قال: . فقال يا اباذر ! قلت : لبيك يا رسول الله! قال: ان العبد المسلم ليصلى الصلاة يريد بها وجه الله فتهافت عنه ذنوبه، كما تهافت هذا الورق عن هذه الشجرة . (احمد)

6. Abu Dharr said that the Prophet went out in winter time when the leaves were falling, and took two branches of a tree whose leaves began to fall. He then addressed Abu Dharr who replied, "At your service, Messenger of God." He said, "A Muslim observes prayer for God's sake and his sins fall from him as these leaves fall from this tree." (Ahmad)

٧ - عن عبدالله بن قرط، قال: قال رسول الله صلى الله عليه وسلم:
اول ما يحاسب به العبد يوم القيمة الصلاة فان صلحت صلح سائر
عمله وان فسدت فسد سائر عمله. (الطبرانى)

7. Abdullah bin Qart reported the Messenger of Allah as saying. "The first thing a person shall have to give account of on the Day of Judgement will be *Salat*. If it is found correct, all his deeds will be correct; and if it is found wanting, all his deeds are rotten." (Tabarani)

٨ - عن ابن عمر، ان رسول الله صلى الله عليه وسلم قال: صلاة الجماعة
تفضل صلاة الفذ بسبع و عشرين درجة. (متفق عليه)

8. Abdullah bin Umar reported Allah's Messenger as saying: "A *Salat* with Jamaat is twenty-seven times superior to *Salat* performed individually." (Bukhari, Muslim)

٩ - عن ابى هريرة، قال: قال رسول الله صلى الله عليه وسلم: لقد
هممت ان آمر فتيتى فيجمعوا لى حزماً من حطب ثم الى قوماً
يصلون فى بيوتهم ليست بهم علة فاحرقها عليهم. (مسلم)

9. Abu Hurairah reported Allah's Messenger as saying, "I wish I would ask the boys to collect a huge quantity of firewood for me and then I would go about and set fire to the dwellings of those who offer the *Salat* at their own houses without any excuse." (Muslim)

١٠ - عن عمرو بن شعيب عن ابيه، عن جده، قال: قال رسول الله

صلی اللہ علیہ وسلم: مروا اولادکم بالصلاۃ و ھم ابناء سبع سنین، و اضربوھم علیھا و ھم ابناء عشر سنین و فرقوا بینھم فی المضاجع.
(ابو داؤد)

10. Amr bin Shuaib said on his father's authority that his grand-father reported Allah's Messenger as saying, "Command your children to observe prayer when they are seven years old, and beat them for (not observing) it when they are ten years old, and do not let them sleep together." (Abu Dawood)

Remarks :

1. There can be no better course of moral and spiritual training than the prayer. It is this which makes one a perfect Muslim. It reminds him of his Covenant with God, refreshes his faith in Him and keeps the belief in the Day of udgment alive and ever present before his mind's eye. It makes him follow the Prophet, and trains him in the observance of his duties.

2. Daily prayers strengthen the foundation of faith, prepare for the observance of a life of virtue and obedience to God and refresh that belief from which spring courage, sincerity, purposefulness, purity of heart, advancement of soul and enrichment of morals.

3. Every Muslim must say his prayers in congregation, especially the Friday and Eid prayers. This creates among the Muslims a bond of love and mutual understanding, sense of collective unity, national fraternity and deep feeling of brotherhood. Prayers are also a symbol of equality, for the poor and the rich, the low and the high, the rulers and the ruled, the educated and the un-lettered, the black and the white all stand in one row and prostrate before their Lord. They also inculcate in them a strong sense of discipline and obedience to the elected leader. In short, prayers train them in all those virtues which make possible the development of a rich individual and collective life.*

* "Towards Understanding Islam"!

4. **The prayer in Islam is collective. Although individual prayer is permitted, it is by no means encouraged. The prophet expressed great resentment at those able-bodied and healthy Muslims who prayed at home, while they had a mosque nearby.**

5. **There are numerous conditions to be fulfilled at the time of offering *Salat*, e. g., the cleanliness of body. dress and ground on which it is offered, and *Wadhu* (ablution).**

6. **This brief study tells us that *Salat* exerts its influence over all the departments of life and transforms the entire existence of a person into one of virtue and godliness.**

الذكاة والصدقات

ZAKAT AND SADAQAH (TAXES AND ALMS)

QURAN:

وانفقوا في سبيل الله ولا تلقوا بايديكم الى التهلكة وأحسنوا ان الله يحب المحسنين

1. **And Spend of your substance in the cause of Allah and cast not yourselves to perdition with your own hands and do good (to others). Surely Allah loves the doers of good. (2 : 195)**

انما وليكم الله ورسوله والذين امنوا الذين يقيمون الصلوة ويؤتون الزكوة وهم راكعون

2. **Your real friends are (no less than) Allah and His Messenger and those who believe, who establish worship and pay the poor-due, and bow down (in prayer) (5 : 58)**

ذلك الكتب لا ريب فيه هدى للمتقين الذين يؤمنون بالغيب ويقيمون الصلوة ومما رزقنهم ينفقون

3. **This is the Scripture whereof there is no doubt, a guidance unto those who ward off (evil). Who believe in the Unseen and establish worship, and spend of that we have bestowed upon them. (2 : 2-3)**

خذ من اموالهم صدقة تطهرهم وتزكيهم بها

4. **Take alms of their wealth, wherewith thou mayst purify them and mayst make them grow. (9 : 103)**

واقيموا الصلوة واتوا الزكوة وما تقدموا لانفسكم من خير تجدوه عند الله ان الله بما تعملون بصير

5. **Establish worship, and pay the poor-due, and whatever of good ye send before (you) for your souls, ye will find it with Allah, Lo! Allah is Seer of what ye do. (2 : 110)**

فَأَقِيمُوا الصَّلَوٰةَ وَآتُوا الزَّكَوٰةَ وَاعْتَصِمُوا بِاللَّهِ هُوَ مَوْلَاكُمْ ۚ

6. So establish worship and pay the poor - due, and hold fast to Allah. (22 : 78)

مَثَلُ الَّذِينَ يُنفِقُونَ أَمْوَالَهُمْ فِي سَبِيلِ اللَّهِ كَمَثَلِ حَبَّةٍ أَنبَتَتْ سَبْعَ سَنَابِلَ فِي كُلِّ سُنبُلَةٍ مِّائَةُ حَبَّةٍ ۗ وَاللَّهُ
يُضَاعِفُ لِمَن يَشَاءُ ۗ وَاللَّهُ وَاسِعٌ عَلِيمٌ ۝ الَّذِينَ يُنفِقُونَ أَمْوَالَهُمْ فِي سَبِيلِ اللَّهِ ثُمَّ لَا يُتْبِعُونَ مَا أَنفَقُوا مَنًّا وَ
لَا أَذًى ۙ لَّهُمْ أَجْرُهُمْ عِندَ رَبِّهِمْ وَلَا خَوْفٌ عَلَيْهِمْ وَلَا هُمْ يَحْزَنُونَ ۝ قَوْلٌ مَّعْرُوفٌ وَمَغْفِرَةٌ خَيْرٌ مِّن
صَدَقَةٍ يَتْبَعُهَا أَذًى ۗ وَاللَّهُ غَنِيٌّ حَلِيمٌ ۝ يَا أَيُّهَا الَّذِينَ آمَنُوا لَا تُبْطِلُوا صَدَقَاتِكُم بِالْمَنِّ وَالْأَذَىٰ

7. The liknees of those who spend their wealth in Allah's way is as the likeness of a grain which groweth seven ears, in every ear a hundred grains. And Allah giveth increase manifold to whom He will. And Allah is all embracing, all knowing. Those who spend their wealth for the cause of Allah, and after that make not reproach and injury to follow that which they have spent, their reward is with their Lord, and they shall have no fear come upon them, nor shall they grieve. A kind word with forgiveness is better than alms-giving followed by injury. Allah is Absolute, Clement. O ye, who believe! Render not vain your alms giving by reproach and injury. (2 : 261-264)

إِنَّ الَّذِينَ يَتْلُونَ كِتَابَ اللَّهِ وَأَقَامُوا الصَّلَوٰةَ وَأَنفَقُوا مِمَّا رَزَقْنَاهُمْ سِرًّا وَعَلَانِيَةً يَرْجُونَ تِجَارَةً لَّن تَبُورَ ۝ لِيُوَفِّيَهُمْ
أُجُورَهُمْ وَيَزِيدَهُم مِّن فَضْلِهِ ۚ إِنَّهُ غَفُورٌ شَكُورٌ ۝

8. Lo! Those who read the Scripture of Allah and establish worship, and spend of that which we have bestowed on them secretly and openly, they look forward to imperishable gain. That He will pay them their wages and increase them of His grace. Lo! He is Forgiving, Responsive. (35 : 29-30)

وَالَّذِينَ يَكْنِزُونَ الذَّهَبَ وَالْفِضَّةَ وَلَا يُنفِقُونَهَا فِي سَبِيلِ اللَّهِ فَبَشِّرْهُم بِعَذَابٍ أَلِيمٍ ۝ يَوْمَ يُحْمَىٰ عَلَيْهَا
فِي نَارِ جَهَنَّمَ فَتُكْوَىٰ بِهَا جِبَاهُهُمْ وَجُنُوبُهُمْ وَظُهُورُهُمْ ۖ هَٰذَا مَا كَنَزْتُمْ لِأَنفُسِكُمْ فَذُوقُوا مَا كُنتُمْ تَكْنِزُونَ ۝

9. And those who hoard up gold and silver and spend it not in the way of Allah unto them give tidings (O. Muhammad) of a painful

doom. On the day when it will (all) be heated in the fire of hell, and their fore-heads and their flanks and their backs will be branded therewith. Here is that which ye hoarded up for yourselves. Now taste what ye used to hoard. (9 : 34-35)

إِنَّمَا الصَّدَقٰتُ لِلْفُقَرَاءِ وَالْمَسٰكِينِ وَالْعٰمِلِينَ عَلَيْهَا وَالْمُؤَلَّفَةِ قُلُوبُهُمْ وَفِي الرِّقَابِ وَالْغٰرِمِينَ وَفِي سَبِيلِ اللّٰهِ
وَابْنِ السَّبِيلِ فَرِيضَةً مِّنَ اللّٰهِ وَاللّٰهُ عَلِيمٌ حَكِيمٌ ۝ (توبه-٦٠)

10. The alms are only for the poor and the needy and those who collect them and those whose hearts are to be reconciled, and to free the captives and the debtors, and for the cause of Allah and for the way-farer, a duty imposed by Allah. And Allah is Knower, Wise.

HADIS :

١ ـ عن جابر وحذيفة، قالا: قال رسول الله صلى الله عليه وسلم: كل معروف صدقة ـ (متفق عليه)

1. Jaber and Huzaifah reported that the Messenger of Allah said; "Every good deed is charity." (Bukhari, Muslim)

٢ ـ عن انس، قال: قال رسول الله صلى الله عليه وسلم: ان الصدقة لتطفى غضب الرب وتدفع ميتة السوء ـ (الترمذي)

2. Anas reported that the Messenger of Allah said, "Verily charity appeases wrath of the Lord and removes pangs of death." (Tirmizi).

٣ ـ عن ابى سعيد، قال: قال رسول الله صلى الله عليه وسلم: لأن يتصدق المرء فى حياته بدرهم خير له من أن يتصدق بمائة عند موته ـ (ابو داؤد)

3. Abu Saeed reported that the Messenger of Allah said, "The charity of a silver coin in one's lifetime is better for him than his charity of one hundred silver coins at the time of his death." (Abu Daud).

٤ ـ عن ابن عباس ، أن رسول الله صلى الله عليه وسلم بعث معاذاً إلى أليمن، فقال : إنك تأتى قوماً أهل كتاب، فادعهم إلى شهادة أن لا إله الا الله وان محمداً رسول الله. فإن هم أطاعوا لذلك، فأعلمهم أن الله قد فرض عليهم خمس صلوات فى اليوم والليلة فإن هم أطاعوا لذلك، فأعلمهم أن الله قد فرض عليهم صدقةً تؤخذ من أغنيائهم فترد على فقرآئهم. فإن هم أطاعوا لذلك، فإياك وكرائم أموالهم، واتق دعوة المظلوم، فإنه ليس بينها و بين الله حجاب ـ (متفق عليه)

4. Ibn - Abbas reported that the Holy Prophet sent Mu'az to Yemen saying: "Certainly you will come across a people, the people of the Book. Call them to bear witness that there is no God but Allah and that Mohammad is the Messenger of Allah. If they submit to that, teach them that verily Allah has made obligatory upon them prayer for five times a day and a night. If they submit to that, teach them that verily Allah has made obligatory over them Zakat which will be taken from the rich and will be given to the poor among them. If they then obey that, it will be your duty to take care of their lawful properties; and fear the invocation of the oppressed, because between it and Allah, there is no screen."
(Bukhari, Muslim)

٥ ـ عن ابى هريره قال: قال رسول الله صلى الله عليه وسلم : من آتاه الله مالا فلم يؤد ذكاته، مثل له ماله يوم القيامة شجاعاً أقرع له زبيبتان، يطوقه يوم القيامة، ثم يأخذ بلهزمتيه، يعنى شدقيه، ثم يقول: أنا مالك، أنا كنزك ثم تلا : (ولا يحسبن الذين يبخلون) الآية ـ (البخارى)

5. Abu Hurairah reported that the Messenger of Allah said, "Whomsoever Allah gives wealth but who does not pay its Zakat, his wealth will be likened for him on the resurrection

day to a huge bald snake having two fangs. It will bite him round his neck on the resurrection day and then take hold of him with its two fangs, meaning its two jaws. Afterwards it will say: I am your wealth, I am your hidden treasure:" Then he recited: "And let not those think who are niggardly," the verse. (Bukhari).

٦ ـ عن ابن عمر، قال: قال رسول الله صلى الله عليه وسلم: من استفاد مالاً فلا زكاة فيه حتى يحول عليه الحول (ترمذى)

6. Ibn Omar reported that the Messenger of Allah said, "who-ever acquires wealth, there is no Zakat therefor until a year passes over it." (Tirmizi).

٧ ـ عن عائشه، قالت: سمعت رسول الله صلى الله عليه وسلم يقول: ما خالطت الذكاة مالاً قط إلا اهلكه (شافعى، بخارى)

7. Ayesha reported: I heard the Messenger of Allah say, "Zakat never mixes with a property but to destory it." (Shafeyi. Bukhari)

٨ - عن على رضى الله عنه، قال: قال رسول الله صلى الله عليه وسلم: قد عفوت عن الخيل و الرقيق، فهاتوا صدقة الرقة: من كل اربعين درهما درهم، وليس فى تسعين ومائة شئ، فإذا بلغت مائتين، ففيها خمسة دراهم ـ (ترمذى ـ ابو داؤد)

8. Ali reported that the Messenger of Allah said, "I have exempted horses and asses (from Zakat). So take Zakat of silver, one dirham from every forty dirham. There is no Zakat for 190 dirhams. When they reach 200 (dirhams) then there are 5 dirham Zakat therefor." (Tirmizi, Abu Daud).

٩ - عن على، أن النبى صلى الله عليه وسلم قال "ليس فى الخضراوات صدقه، ولا فى العرايا صدقة، ولا فى اقل من خمسة اوسق صدقة، ولا فى العوامل صدقة، ولا في الجبهة". قال الصقر: الجهة الخيل و البغال و العبيد (دارقطنى)

9. Ali reported that the Messenger of Allah said, "There is no Zakat for vegetables, nor there is Zakat for cultivated plants, nor there is Zakat for less than five "wasaqs", nor there is Zakat for animals of labour, nor there is Zakat for "Jabha". (Saqr said : Jabha is horse, mule and servants.) (Darqutni)

١٠ ـ عن ابن عمر، قال: فرض رسول الله صلى الله عليه وسلم زكاة الفطر صاعاً من تمر أو صاعاً من شعير، على العبد، و الحر، و الذكر، والأنثى، و الصغير، و الكبير من المسلمين ـ وأمر بها أن تؤدى قبل خروج الناس إلى الصلاة (متفق عليه)

10. Ibn Omar reported that the Messenger of Allah made obligatory the charity of 'Fitr,—One Sa'a of dates or one Sa'a of barley upon the slave and the free, male and female, young and old from among the Muslims. He directed its payment before the people go out for the prayer. (Bukhari, Muslim).

Remarks :

1. Zakat is a fundamental obligation, and a great pillar on which the structure of Islam stands.
2. Zakat is often mentioned in the Holy Quran simultaneously with Salat (Prayer), which shows that it is almost equal to the latter in importance in the Islamic organisation of worship. It may also be noted that Salat and Zakat are spoken of together as the basic ordinances of the religion of every Prophet
3. The most frequently recurring words for charity are infaq—(means spending benevolently)—Ihsan—(the doing of good)—Zakat — (growth and purification) and Sadaqah, which is derived from the root Sidq, meaning truth, and comes to signify a charitable deed. [1]
4. In Islam charity has been given a very wide meaning. It means any benefit done to any person (or animal), economic, spiritual, moral or consolatory.
5. Beside the compulsory charity namely Zakat, Islam also enjoins optional charities by various denominations, such

---

1. The Religion of Islam. Mohd. Ali.

as infaq, ihsan, and sadaqat. These words connote charity in a broad sense. It has, however, promised great reward for optional charities.[1]

6. Charity, in the sense of giving away one's wealth, is of two kinds, voluntary and obligatory. Voluntary charity is generaly mentioned in the Holy Quran as infaq or ihsan or sadaqah. Obligatory charity is generally mentioned under the name Zakat, but it is sometime called a sadaqah, specially in Hadith.

   The word Zakat is derived from Zaka, which means: it (a plant) grew. The other derivatives of the word, as used in the Holy Quran, carry the sense of purification from sins.

7. Zakat is an annual charge on property which remained in the possession of a person for a whole year, when its value reached a certain limit, called the "nisab". Nisab differs with different kinds of property but generally it is levied at almost a uniform state, being 2½ percent on the accumulated wealth.[2]

8. Zakat is levied not merely on the cash-balance. It is also charged on gold, silver, merchandise, cattle and other valuables.

9. It fosters in us the qualities of sacrifice and rids us of selfishness and plutocracy. It is also beneficial for lowly-placed persons in the society and poor brethren.

10. Zakat is not simply obligatory charity, it is a state institution, or where there is no Muslim State, a national institution.

11. The Holy Prophet has forbidden his own kith and kin from taking zakat. Though it is obligatory on them to pay, but they cannot receive it even when they are poor and needy.

---

1. Eg: Tras of Miskat by Fazlul Karim.
2. The Religion of Islam.

الصوم

SAUM (ROZA OR FAST)

QURAN:

يٰأَيُّهَا الَّذِيْنَ اٰمَنُوْا كُتِبَ عَلَيْكُمُ الصِّيَامُ كَمَا كُتِبَ عَلَى الَّذِيْنَ مِنْ قَبْلِكُمْ لَعَلَّكُمْ تَتَّقُوْنَ ۙ اَيَّامًا مَّعْدُوْدٰتٍ ؕ
فَمَنْ كَانَ مِنْكُمْ مَّرِيْضًا اَوْ عَلٰى سَفَرٍ فَعِدَّةٌ مِّنْ اَيَّامٍ اُخَرَ ؕ وَعَلَى الَّذِيْنَ يُطِيْقُوْنَهٗ فِدْيَةٌ طَعَامُ مِسْكِيْنٍ ؕ فَمَنْ
تَطَوَّعَ خَيْرًا فَهُوَ خَيْرٌ لَّهٗ ؕ وَاَنْ تَصُوْمُوْا خَيْرٌ لَّكُمْ اِنْ كُنْتُمْ تَعْلَمُوْنَ ۝ شَهْرُ رَمَضَانَ الَّذِيْٓ اُنْزِلَ فِيْهِ الْقُرْاٰنُ هُدًى
لِّلنَّاسِ وَبَيِّنٰتٍ مِّنَ الْهُدٰى وَالْفُرْقَانِ ۚ فَمَنْ شَهِدَ مِنْكُمُ الشَّهْرَ فَلْيَصُمْهُ ؕ وَمَنْ كَانَ مَرِيْضًا اَوْ عَلٰى سَفَرٍ فَعِدَّةٌ
مِّنْ اَيَّامٍ اُخَرَ ؕ يُرِيْدُ اللّٰهُ بِكُمُ الْيُسْرَ وَلَا يُرِيْدُ بِكُمُ الْعُسْرَ وَلِتُكْمِلُوا الْعِدَّةَ وَلِتُكَبِّرُوا اللّٰهَ عَلٰى مَا هَدٰىكُمْ وَلَعَلَّكُمْ
تَشْكُرُوْنَ ۝ وَاِذَا سَاَلَكَ عِبَادِيْ عَنِّيْ فَاِنِّيْ قَرِيْبٌ ؕ اُجِيْبُ دَعْوَةَ الدَّاعِ اِذَا دَعَانِ فَلْيَسْتَجِيْبُوْا لِيْ وَلْيُؤْمِنُوْا بِيْ لَعَلَّهُمْ
يَرْشُدُوْنَ ۝ اُحِلَّ لَكُمْ لَيْلَةَ الصِّيَامِ الرَّفَثُ اِلٰى نِسَآئِكُمْ ؕ هُنَّ لِبَاسٌ لَّكُمْ وَاَنْتُمْ لِبَاسٌ لَّهُنَّ ؕ عَلِمَ اللّٰهُ اَنَّكُمْ
كُنْتُمْ تَخْتَانُوْنَ اَنْفُسَكُمْ فَتَابَ عَلَيْكُمْ وَعَفَا عَنْكُمْ ۚ فَالْـٰٔنَ بَاشِرُوْهُنَّ وَابْتَغُوْا مَا كَتَبَ اللّٰهُ لَكُمْ وَكُلُوْا وَاشْرَبُوْا
حَتّٰى يَتَبَيَّنَ لَكُمُ الْخَيْطُ الْاَبْيَضُ مِنَ الْخَيْطِ الْاَسْوَدِ مِنَ الْفَجْرِ ثُمَّ اَتِمُّوا الصِّيَامَ اِلَى الَّيْلِ ۚ وَلَا تُبَاشِرُوْهُنَّ وَ
اَنْتُمْ عٰكِفُوْنَ فِي الْمَسٰجِدِ ؕ تِلْكَ حُدُوْدُ اللّٰهِ فَلَا تَقْرَبُوْهَا ؕ كَذٰلِكَ يُبَيِّنُ اللّٰهُ اٰيٰتِهٖ لِلنَّاسِ لَعَلَّهُمْ يَتَّقُوْنَ ۝

1. O ye who believe! Fasting is prescribed for you, even as it was prescribed for those before you, that you may ward off evil. (Fast) a certain number of days, and for him who is sick among you or on a journey, (the same) number of other days; and for those who can afford it there is a ransom: the feeding of a man in need. But who so doeth good of his own accord it is better for him; and that ye fast is better for you if ye did but know. The month of Ramadan in which was revealed the Quran, a guidance for mankind, and clear proofs of the guidance, and the Criterion (of right and wrong). And whosoever of you is present, let him fast the month, and

whosoever of you is sick or on journey, (let him fast the same) number of other days. Allah desireth for your ease; He desireth not hardship for you, and (He desireth) that ye should complete the period, and that ye should magnify Allah for having guided you, and that peradventure ye may be thankful. And when My servants question thee concerning Me, then surely I am nigh. I answer the prayer of the suppliant when he crieth unto Me, so let them hear My call and let them trust in Me in order that they may be led right. It is made lawful for you to go unto your wives on the night of the fast. They are raiment for you and ye are raiment for them. Allah is Aware that ye were deceiving yourselves in this respect and He hath turned in mercy toward you and relieved you. So hold intercourse with them and seek that which Allah hath ordained for you, and eat and drink until the white thread becometh distinct to you from the black thread of the dawn. Then strictly observe the fast till nightfall and touch them not, but be at your devotions in the mosques. These are the limits imposed by Allah, so approach them not. Thus Allah expoundeth His revelations to mankind that they may ward off (evil). (2: 183-187).

حٰمٓ ۝ وَالْكِتٰبِ الْمُبِيْنِ ۝ اِنَّآ اَنْزَلْنٰهُ فِيْ لَيْلَةٍ مُّبٰرَكَةٍ اِنَّا كُنَّا مُنْذِرِيْنَ ۝ فِيْهَا يُفْرَقُ كُلُّ اَمْرٍ حَكِيْمٍ ۝ اَمْرًا مِّنْ عِنْدِنَا ۗ اِنَّا كُنَّا
مُرْسِلِيْنَ ۝

2. Ha Mim ! By the Scripture that maketh plain. Lo ! We revealed it on a blessed night— Lo ! We are ever warning— whereon every wise command is made clear—A command from our presence— Lo ! we are ever sending (messengers). (44: 1-5)

اِنَّآ اَنْزَلْنٰهُ فِيْ لَيْلَةِ الْقَدْرِ ۝ وَمَآ اَدْرٰىكَ مَا لَيْلَةُ الْقَدْرِ ۝ لَيْلَةُ الْقَدْرِ ۙ خَيْرٌ مِّنْ اَلْفِ شَهْرٍ ۝ تَنَزَّلُ الْمَلٰٓئِكَةُ وَالرُّوْحُ فِيْهَا
بِاِذْنِ رَبِّهِمْ ۚ مِنْ كُلِّ اَمْرٍ ۝ سَلٰمٌ ۛ هِيَ حَتّٰى مَطْلَعِ الْفَجْرِ ۝

3. Lo ! We revealad it on the Night of Power. Ah, what will convey unto thee what the Night of Power is ! The Night of Power is better than a thousand months. The Angels and the Spirit descend therein, by the permission of their Lord, with all decrees. (That night is) Peace until rising of the dawn. (97: 1-5).

HADIS:

عن ابى هريرة، قال: قال رسول الله صلى الله عليه وسلم: اتاكم رمضان شهر مبارك، فرض الله عليكم صيامه، تفتح فيه ابواب السماء، و تغلق فيه ابواب الجحيم و تغل فيه مردة الشياطين، لله فيه ليلة خير من الف شهر، من حرم خيرها فقد حرم۔ (احمد، نسائى)

1. Abu Hurairah reported that the Messenger of Allah said, "There came to you Ramadan, a blessed month. Its fasting Allah made obligatory on you. The doors of Heaven are opened up therein, and the doors of Hell are shut up therein and the mischievous devils are put in chains. For Allah there is a night therein which is better than one thousand months. Whoso is deprived of its good, is deprived of all good."
(Ahmad, Nasai)

عن عبد الله بن عمرو: ان رسول الله صلى الله عليه وسلم قال: الصيام و القرآن يشفعان للعبد، يقول الصيام: أي رب! انى منعته الطعام والشهوات بالنهار فشفعنى فيه، ويقول القرآن: منعته النوم بالليل فشفعنى فيه، فيشفعان (البيهقى)

2. Abdullah-Ibn-Amr reported that the Messenger of Allah said, "Fasting and the Quran will intercede for a man. Fasting will say: O Lord! I denied him food and sexual satisfaction during day-time. So make me an intercessor for him. And the Quran will say: I denied him sleep during night. So make me an intercessor for him. So both of them will be allowed to intercede."
(Baihaqi)

عن أبى هريرة، قال: قال رسول الله صلى الله عليه وسلم: صوموا لرويته وافطروا لرويته، فإن غم عليكم فاكملوا عدة شعبان ثلاثين.
(متفق عليه)

3. Abu Hurairah reported that the Messenger of Allah said, "Fast at the sight of it and break it at the sight of it; if there is cloud over you, then complete the number of Sha'ban thirty. (Bukhari, Muslim)

عن ابی هريرة، قال: قال رسول الله صلى الله عليه وسلم: من صام رمضان ايماناً واحتساباً غفر له ما تقدم من ذنبه، ومن قام رمضان ايماناً واحتساباً غفر له ما تقدم من ذنبه، ومن قام ليلة القدر ايماناً واحتساباً غفر له ما تقدم من ذنبه. (متفق عليه)

4. Abu Hurairah reported that the Messenger of Allah said, "Whoso fasts Ramadan out of faith and hopeful of rewards, all his past sins will be forgiven; and whoso stands up (in prayer) in Ramadan out of faith and hopeful of reward, all his past sins will be forgiven and whoso stands up (in prayer) at the Night of Power out of faith and hopeful of reward, all his past sins will be forgiven." (Bukhari, Muslim)

وعنه، قال: قال رسول الله صلى الله عليه وسلم: كل عمل ابن آدم يضاعف الحسنة بعشر امثالها الى سبع مائة ضعف، قال الله تعالى: الا الصوم فانه لى وانا اجزي به، يدع شهوته وطعامه من اجلى، للصائم فرحتان: فرحة عند فطره، وفرحة عند لقاء ربه، ولخلوف فم الصائم اطيب عند الله من ريح المسك، والصيام جنة، فاذا كان يوم صوم احدكم فلا يرفث ولا يصخب فان سابه احد او قاتله فليقل: إني أمرؤ صائم. (متفق عليه)

5. The same reported that the Messenger of Allah said, "Every good action of the son of Adam shall be multiplied with ten of its likes upto seven hundred times. The Almighty Allah said : except fasting, because it is for Me, and I shall Myself compensate it, for he gives up his passions and food for Me. For a fasting man, there are two rejoicings; one rejoicing at the time of his breaking fast and one at the time of meeting his Lord, and certainly the fragrance of the mouth of a fasting man is more pleasant to

Allah than the smell of musk. And fasting is a shield. So when the fasting of some one of you comes up, he shall not utter foul words, nor shall he cry hoarse. If then any body rebukes him or fights with him, let him say: I am a man observing fast."

(Bukhari, Muslim(

عن سهل بن سعد، قال: قال رسول الله صلى الله عليه وسلم: فى الجنة ثمانية ابواب، منها باب يسمى الريان لايدخله الا الصائمون. (متفق عليه)

6. Sahl-Ben-Sa'ad reported that the Messenger of Allah said, "In paradise, there are eight doors of which there is a door named Rayyan. None but those who fast will enter it."

(Bukhari, Muslim)

عن انس رضى الله عنه، قال: قال رسول الله صلى الله عليه وسلم: تسحروا فإن السحور بركة. (متفق عليه)

7. Anas reported that the Messenger of Allah said, "Take tiffin before dawn, because in this tiffin there is blessing."

(Bukhari, Muslim)

عن أبي هريرة رضى الله عنه، قال: قال رسول الله صلي الله عليه وسلم: قال الله تعالى: احب عبادي إلى أعجلهم فطراً. (الترمذي)

8. Abu Hurairah reported that the Messenger of Allah said, "The Almighty Allah said: The dearest of My servants in My sight are those that hasten in breaking fast." (Tirmizi)

عن سلمان بن عامر، قال: قال رسول الله صلى الله عليه وسلم: اذا افطر احدكم فليفطر على تمر، فانه بركة فان لم يجد فليفطر على ماء، فانه طهور. (احمد، ترمذى، ابو داؤد، ابن ماجه)

9. Salman-bin-Amer reported that the Messenger of Allah said, "When one of you breaks fast, let him breakfast with date

because it is a blessing; if he does not find it, let him breakfast with water, because it is pure."

(Ahmed, Tirmizi, Abu Daud, Ibn-Majah)

عن ابى هريرة رضى الله عنه، قال: قال رسول الله صلى الله عليه وسلم: من لم يدع قول الزور والعمل به، فليس لله حاجة فى أن يدع طعامه وشرابه . (البخارى)

10. Abu Hurairah reported that the messenger of Allah said, "Whosoever does not give up false talk and action according to it, then Allah has no need that he should give up his food and drink." (Bukhari)

عن ابى هريرة ، رضى الله عنه ، قال : قال رسول الله صلى الله عليه وسلم : من نسى وهو صائم فاكل أو شرب، فليتم صومه، فانما أطعمه الله و سقاه . (متفق عليه)

11. Abu Hurairah reported that the Messenger of Allah said, "Whosoever forgot while he was fasting and then ate or drank, let him complete his fast because Allah fed him and gave him drink." (Bukhari, Muslim)

عن أبى هريرة، قال . قال رسول الله صلى الله عليه وسلم: من افطر يوماً من رمضان من غير رخصة ولامرض لم يقض عنه صوم الدهر كله وإن صامه (احمد، ترمذى، ابن ماجه، ابوداؤد، دارمى)

12. Abu Hurairah reported that the Messenger of Allah said, "Whosoever breaks fast of one day of Ramdan without excuse and illness, the fasting of his whole age will not compensate it even if he keeps fast for it."

(Ahmed, Tirmizi, Ibn-Majah, Abu Daud, Darmi)

عن عائشه رضى الله عنها ، قالت : قال رسول الله صلى الله عليه وسلم : تحروا ليلة القدر فى الوتر من العشر الاواخر من رمضان (البخاري)

13. **Ayesha reported that the Messenger of Allah said, "Search for the Night of Power in an odd (night) among the last ten (nights) of Ramadan." (Bukhari)**

عن عائشة، قالت، قلت: يا رسول الله! أرأيت ان علمت أي ليلة ليلة القدر، ما اقول فيها؟ قال: قولى. اللهم انك عفو تحب العفو فاعف عنى. (احمد، ابن ماجه، ترمذى)

14. **Ayesha reported: I asked: O Messenger of Allah! inform me that if I can recognise my night as the Night of Power, what should I say therein? He said, "Say: O Allah! Thou art forgiving, thou loveth forgiving, so forgive me." (Ahmad, Ibn Majah, Tirmizi)**

عن عائشة، ان النبى صلى الله عليه وسلم كان يعتكف العشر الاواخر من رمضان حتى توفاه الله، ثم اعتكف ازواجه من بعده (متفق عليه)

15. **Ayesha reported that the Messenger of Allah used to seclude himself for the last ten (nights) of Ramadan until Allah took him away Afterwards his wives secluded themselves after him. (Bukhari, Muslim)**

Remarks

(1) Fasting is one of the five fundamental obligations upon which Islam stands. It is obligatory on every adult Muslim.

(2) It is a universal institution, inasmuch as all the religions of the world and all the great religious personalities adopted fasting though the same stress is not laid and the forms and motives vary.

In Islam fasting is made a permanent spiritual, moral and physical discipline of the highest order. The institution of fasting was introduced after the institution of prayer and was made obligatory in the second year of Hijra at Madina.

(3) Fasting commences with the new moon of Ramadan and ends on the appearance of the moon of Shawwal. The fast begins with

the appearance of dim light on the eastern horizon before the early dawn till the setting of the sun. Before beginning the fast some light food or tiffin should be taken. After that the following declaration (نيت) for fast may also be made : نويت ان اصوم غدا من شهر رمضان (I have willed to keep fast of this day in the month of Ramadan). Immediately after the setting of the sun, the fast should be broken with the following invocation :—

اللهم انى لك صمت وبك آمنت وعليك توكلت وعلى رزقك افطرت .

(O, Lord ! For thee did I fast, in Thee do I believe, in Thee do I put trust, and with Thy plenty do I break fast).

(4) In addition to the compulsory (فرض) fasts in Ramadan, every Muslim is allowed to keep voluntary fasts—expiatory fasts, compensatory fasts, and fasts in fulfilment of a vow, on any day he likes except the Id days and the three days of Tashriq (*i.e.* 11, 12, 13 Zil Hij).

(5) "Itikaf" means to stay in a place As a religious practice it signifies total seclusion from wordly duties and staying in a mosque for a certain number of days, specially in the last ten days in the month of Ramadhan for whole-time divine service.[1]

(6) Results obtained by fasting :—

(1) Fasting brings passion under control. Passion is the root of all evils and this can be regulated by abstaining from bodily desires.

(2) It purifies the soul and makes it sublime.

(3) It affords concentration in prayer.

(4) It checks false notions of pride and prestige.

(5) It greatly contributes to the preservation of health. The rest given to the digestive organs for a whole month gives additional strength.

---

1. Tr. Mishkat. Fazlul Karim, p. 558 Vol. II.

(6) It accustoms a man to face the hardships of life. It also increases the power of endurance.

(7) It has a social value. It is the signal for a mass movement towards equality which is not limited to one vicinity or even one country but affects the whole Muslim world. Fasting brings the rich and poor on the same level. Both are allowed to take only two meals a day. This also awakens sympathy for the poor in the hearts of the rich.

(8) It keeps our faith in God as a living force.

الحج

HAJJ OR PILGRIMAGE

QURAN :

إِنَّ أَوَّلَ بَيْتٍ وُضِعَ لِلنَّاسِ لَلَّذِي بِبَكَّةَ مُبَارَكًا وَهُدًى لِّلْعَالَمِينَ ۝ فِيهِ آيَاتٌ بَيِّنَاتٌ مَّقَامُ
إِبْرَاهِيمَ ۖ وَمَن دَخَلَهُ كَانَ آمِنًا ۗ وَلِلَّهِ عَلَى النَّاسِ حِجُّ الْبَيْتِ مَنِ اسْتَطَاعَ إِلَيْهِ سَبِيلًا ۚ وَمَن كَفَرَ فَإِنَّ اللَّهَ
غَنِيٌّ عَنِ الْعَالَمِينَ ۝

Certainly for men the First House is the one at Bakkah, (MACCAH) blessed and a guidance for the nations. In it are clear signs: (It is) the place of Abraham; and whoever enters it is safe; and pilgrimage to the House is a duty which men owe to Allah—whoever can find a way to it. And whoever disbelieves, surely Allah is above need of the worlds.
(3 : 96, 97)

وَإِذْ قَالَ إِبْرَاهِيمُ رَبِّ اجْعَلْ هَٰذَا الْبَلَدَ آمِنًا وَاجْنُبْنِي وَبَنِيَّ أَن نَّعْبُدَ الْأَصْنَامَ ۝ رَبِّ إِنَّهُنَّ
أَضْلَلْنَ كَثِيرًا مِّنَ النَّاسِ ۖ فَمَن تَبِعَنِي فَإِنَّهُ مِنِّي ۖ وَمَنْ عَصَانِي فَإِنَّكَ غَفُورٌ رَّحِيمٌ ۝ رَبَّنَا إِنِّي أَسْكَنتُ مِن ذُرِّيَّتِي
بِوَادٍ غَيْرِ ذِي زَرْعٍ عِندَ بَيْتِكَ الْمُحَرَّمِ رَبَّنَا لِيُقِيمُوا الصَّلَاةَ فَاجْعَلْ أَفْئِدَةً مِّنَ النَّاسِ تَهْوِي إِلَيْهِمْ وَارْزُقْهُم مِّنَ
الثَّمَرَاتِ لَعَلَّهُمْ يَشْكُرُونَ ۝

And when Abraham said: My Lord, make this city secure, and preserve me and my sons from worshipping idols. My Lord, surely they have led many men astray. So whoever follows me, he is surely of me; and whoever disobeys me, thou surely art Forgiving, Merciful. Our Lord, I have settled a part of my offspring in a valley un-productive of fruit near Thy Sacred House. Our Lord, that they may keep up prayer; so make the hearts of some people yearn towards them, and provide them with fruit; so that they may be grateful. (14 : 35-37)

وَإِذْ بَوَّأْنَا لِإِبْرَاهِيمَ مَكَانَ الْبَيْتِ أَن لَّا تُشْرِكْ بِي شَيْئًا وَطَهِّرْ بَيْتِيَ لِلطَّائِفِينَ وَ
الْقَائِمِينَ وَالرُّكَّعِ السُّجُودِ ۝ وَأَذِّن فِي النَّاسِ بِالْحَجِّ يَأْتُوكَ رِجَالًا وَعَلَىٰ كُلِّ ضَامِرٍ يَأْتِينَ مِن كُلِّ فَجٍّ عَمِيقٍ ۝
لِّيَشْهَدُوا مَنَافِعَ لَهُمْ وَيَذْكُرُوا اسْمَ اللَّهِ فِي أَيَّامٍ مَّعْلُومَاتٍ عَلَىٰ مَا رَزَقَهُم مِّن بَهِيمَةِ الْأَنْعَامِ ۖ فَكُلُوا مِنْهَا وَأَطْعِمُوا
الْبَائِسَ الْفَقِيرَ ۝ ثُمَّ لْيَقْضُوا تَفَثَهُمْ وَلْيُوفُوا نُذُورَهُمْ وَلْيَطَّوَّفُوا بِالْبَيْتِ الْعَتِيقِ ۝ ذَٰلِكَ وَمَن يُعَظِّمْ حُرُمَاتِ اللَّهِ
فَهُوَ خَيْرٌ لَّهُ عِندَ رَبِّهِ ۗ وَأُحِلَّتْ لَكُمُ الْأَنْعَامُ إِلَّا مَا يُتْلَىٰ عَلَيْكُمْ ۖ فَاجْتَنِبُوا الرِّجْسَ مِنَ الْأَوْثَانِ وَاجْتَنِبُوا قَوْلَ
الزُّورِ ۝ حُنَفَاءَ لِلَّهِ غَيْرَ مُشْرِكِينَ بِهِ ۚ وَمَن يُشْرِكْ بِاللَّهِ فَكَأَنَّمَا خَرَّ مِنَ السَّمَاءِ فَتَخْطَفُهُ الطَّيْرُ أَوْ تَهْوِي بِهِ الرِّيحُ فِي
مَكَانٍ سَحِيقٍ ۝ ذَٰلِكَ وَمَن يُعَظِّمْ شَعَائِرَ اللَّهِ فَإِنَّهَا مِن تَقْوَى الْقُلُوبِ ۝ لَكُمْ فِيهَا مَنَافِعُ إِلَىٰ أَجَلٍ مُّسَمًّى ثُمَّ
مَحِلُّهَا إِلَى الْبَيْتِ الْعَتِيقِ ۝

And when We pointed to Abraham the place of the House, saying: Associate naught with Me, and purify My House for those who make circuits and stand to pray and bow and prostrate themselves. And proclaim to men the Pilgrimage: they will come to thee on foot and on every lean camel, coming from every remote path. That they may witness benefits (provided) for them, and mention the name of Allah on appointed days over what He has given them of the cattle quadrupeds; then eat of them and feed the distressed ones, the needy. Then let them complete their rites prescribed for them, and let them fulfil their vows and go round the Ancient House. That (shall be so). And whosoever respects the sacred ordinances of Allah, it is good for him in the sight of his Lord. And the cattle are made lawful for you, except that which is mentioned to you, so shun the filth of the idols and shun false words, being upright for Allah, not associating aught with Him. And whosoever associates (aught) with Allah, it is as if he had fallen from heaven, then the birds had snatched him away, or the wind had carried him off to a distant place. That (shall be so). And whoever respects the ordinances of Allah, this is surely from the piety of hearts. Therein are benefits for you for a term appointed, then their place of sacrifice is near the Ancient House. (22 : 26—33)

وأتموا الحج والعمرة لله فإن أحصرتم فما استيسر من الهدي ولا تحلقوا رءوسكم حتى يبلغ الهدي محله
فمن كان منكم مريضا أو به أذى من رأسه ففدية من صيام أو صدقة أو نسك فإذا أمنتم فمن تمتع
بالعمرة إلى الحج فما استيسر من الهدي فمن لم يجد فصيام ثلاثة أيام في الحج وسبعة إذا رجعتم تلك
عشرة كاملة ذلك لمن لم يكن أهله حاضري المسجد الحرام واتقوا الله واعلموا أن الله شديد العقاب ۝ الحج
أشهر معلومات فمن فرض فيهن الحج فلا رفث ولا فسوق ولا جدال في الحج وما تفعلوا من خير يعلمه الله
وتزودوا فإن خير الزاد التقوى واتقون يا أولي الألباب ۝ ليس عليكم جناح أن تبتغوا فضلا من ربكم
فإذا أفضتم من عرفات فاذكروا الله عند المشعر الحرام واذكروه كما هداكم وإن كنتم من قبله لمن
الضالين ۝ ثم أفيضوا من حيث أفاض الناس واستغفروا الله إن الله غفور رحيم ۝ فإذا قضيتم مناسككم
فاذكروا الله كذكركم آباءكم أو أشد ذكرا فمن الناس من يقول ربنا آتنا في الدنيا وما له في الآخرة من خلاق ۝
ومنهم من يقول ربنا آتنا في الدنيا حسنة وفي الآخرة حسنة وقنا عذاب النار ۝ أولئك لهم نصيب مما كسبوا
والله سريع الحساب ۝ واذكروا الله في أيام معدودات فمن تعجل في يومين فلا إثم عليه ومن تأخر فلا إثم عليه
لمن اتقى واتقوا الله واعلموا أنكم إليه تحشرون ۝

And complete the Hajj or Umra. But if you are prevented, (send) whatever offering is easy to obtain; and shave not your heads until the offering reaches its destination. Then whoever among you is sick or has an ailment of the head, he (may effect) a compensation by fasting or alms or sacrificing. And when you are secure, whoever profits by combining the visit with the pilgrimage (should take) whatever offering is easy to obtain. But he who cannot find (an offering) should fast for three days during the pilgrimage and for seven days when you return. These are ten (days) complete. This is for him whose family is not present in the Sacred Mosque. And keep your duty to Allah, and know that Allah is severe in requiting (evil). The months of the pilgrimage are well known, so whoever determines to perform pilgrimage therein there shall have no immodest speech, nor abusing, nor altercation in the pilgrimage. And whatever good you do, Allah knows it. And make provision for yourselves, the best provision being to keep one's duty. And keep your duty to Me, O men of understanding. It is no sin for you that you seek the bounty of your Lord. So when you press on from 'Arafat, remember Allah near the Holy Monument, and remember Him as He has guided you, though before that you were certainly of the erring ones. Then hasten on from where the people hasten on, and ask the forgiveness of Allah. Surely Allah is Forgiving, Merciful. And when you have performed your devotions, laud Allah as you lauded your fathers, rather a more hearty lauding. But there are some people who say, Our Lord, give us in the world. And for such there is no portion in the Hereafter. And there are some among them who say : Our Lord, grant us good in this world and good in the Hereafter, and save us from the chastisement of the Fire. For those there is a portion on account of what they have earned. And Allah is swift in reckoning. And remember Allah during the appointed days, but if any one hastens to leave in two days, there is no blame on him and if anyone stays on, there is no blame on him, if he aims to do right. And keep your duty to Allah, and know that you will be gathered together to Him. (2:196—203)

HADIS :

١ ـ عن ابى هريرة، قال: قال رسول الله صلى الله عليه وسلم: من حج لله فلم يرفث ولم يفسق رجع كيوم ولدته امه (متفق عليه)

Abu-Hurairah reported that the Messenger of Allah said, "Whosoever made pilgrimage for Allah while he did not indulge in sex nor did anything foul, he would return as on the day on which his mother gave birth to him." (Bukhari, Muslim)

٢ ـ وعنه، قال: قال رسول الله صل الله عليه وسلم: العمرة الى العمرة كفارة لما بينهما، والحج المبرور ليس له جزاء الا الجنة (متفق عليه)

The same reported that the Messenger of Allah said, "One Umrah upto (another) Umrah makes amends for what (sin) is between them, and an accepted Pilgrimage has got no reward except Paradise." (Bukhari, Muslim)

٣ ـ عن ابن عباس، قال: قال رسول الله صلى الله عليه وسلم: لا يخلون رجل بامرأة، ولا تسافرن امرأة الا ومعها محرم فقال رجل: يا رسول الله! اكتتبت في غزوة كذا و كذا و خرجت امرأتي حاجة قال: اذهب فا حجج مع امرأتك (متفق عليه)

Ibn-e-Abbas reported that the Messenger of Allah said: No man shall remain alone with a woman, nor shall a woman make journey except with a relative within the prohibited degrees. A man asked: O Messenger of Allah! I have been enrolled for such and such a battle, but my wife has left for Pilgrimage. He said: Go! then make pilgrimage with your wife. (Bukhari, Muslim)

٤ ـ عن ابن عباس، قال: قال رسول الله صلى الله عليه وسلم: يا ايها الناس إن الله كتب عليكم الحج فقام الاقرع ابن

حابس فقال: افی کل عام یا رسول الله؟ قال : لو قلتها نعم ،
اوجبت، ولو وجبت لم تعملوا بها، ولم تسطيعوا، و الحج مرة
فمن زاد فتطوع (احمد - نسائی - دارمی)

Ibn-e-Abbas reported that the Messenger of Allah said, "O men! Verily Allah prescribed Pilgrimage for you." Aqra'a-bin Habes got up and said, "Is it in every year O Messenger of Allah?" He said, "If I were to say "yes," it would become obligatory; and if it were made compulsory, you would not act upon it, nor would you be able to. And pilgrmiage is (obligatory) once only and whoever observes (it) more, it is optional." (Ahmad, Nasai, Darmi)

٥ - عن ابن عمر، قال : جاء رجل الى النبي صل الله عليه وسلم
فقال: يا رسول الله، ما يوجب الحج ؟ فقال : الزاد و الراحلة
(ترمذی - ابن ماجه)

Ibn Omar reported that a man came to the Prophet and asked, "O Apostle of Allah! What makes the Pilgrimage compulsory? He replied, "Means and conveyance." (Tirmizi, Ibn Majah)

٦ - عن ابن عمر، قال سمعت رسول الله صلى الله عليه وسلم يهلُّ
ملبدآ يقول: لبيك، اللهم لبيك لا شريك لك لبيك، ان الحمد
والنعمة لك والملك، لاشريك لك - لايزيد على هؤلاء الكلمات
(متفق عليه)

Ibn Omar reported, I heard the Messenger of Allah proclaiming Talbiyah with a loud voice with his hair matted and saying, "Present to Thee, O Allah. Present to Thee! Present to Thee! No partner for Thee! Present to Thee! Verily all praise and all grace are Thine and also dominion. Thou hast no partner." He was not adding anything to these words. (Bukhari, Muslim)

٧ - عن عائشه ، قالت : خرجنا مع رسول الله صلى الله عليه وسلم
عام حجة الوداع ، فمنا من اهل بعمرة ، و منآ من اهل بحج

وعمرة، ومنّا من اهل بالحج، واهل رسول الله صلى الله
عليه وسلم بالحج، فاما من اهل بعمرة فحل، واما من اهل
بالحج او جمع الحج والعمرة فلم يحلوا حتى كان يوم النحر
(متفق عليه)

Ayesha reported, "We came out with the Messenger of Allah in the year of the Ferewell Pilgrimage. There were some amongst us who made Talbiah for Umrah, and there were some amongst us who made Talbiyah for Hajj and Umrah, and there were some amongst us who made Talbiyah for Hajj. As for those who made Talbiyah for Umrah, they broke Ihram; and as for those who made Talbiah only for Hajj or combined Hajj and Umrah, they did not break Ihram till the day of sacrifice." (Bukhari, Muslim)

٨ - عن ابن عمر، قال: تمتع رسول الله صلى الله عليه وسلم فى حجة
الوداع بالعمرة الى الحج، بدأ فاهل بالعمرة ثم اهل بالحج
(متفق عليه)

Ibn Omar reported that the Messenger of Allah enjoyed in the Farewell Pilgrimage Umrah along with Hajj. He began Talbiyah first for Umrah and then for Hajj. (Bukhari, Muslim)

Remarks :

(1) The word Hajj literally means designedly visiting القصدوالزيارة a place; in the legal sense repairing to the House of Allah كعبه بيت الله for necessary Devotion.

(2) This is an old institution which existed even before Islam. It was ordained as one of the five fundamental articles of Islam in 9 A.H. The Prophet of Allah introduced new meaning to it beside adding method and regularity.

(3) Hajj is obligatory on every adult once in his life, and its performance afterwards is voluntary. The following five conditions make Hajj compulsory for a Muslim:—

1. He should be free and not a slave.
2. ,, ,, ,, a major (adult) person.
3. ,, ,, ,, sane.
4. ,, ,, have a sound body and
5. Ability to undertake a journey to Mecca.

(4) Mecca today stands at the site of a small house which the Prophet Abraham (God's blessing be upon him) built for the worship of Allah Who rewarded him by calling it His own House and making it the centre which all must face when saying prayers. He also made it incumbent upon those who can afford to visit the place at least once in life-time.

(5) *Farz in Hajj.*

1. To observe Ihram (احرام)
2. To Stay at Arafat. (وقوف عرافات)
3. To make Tawaf round the Ka'bah, and (طواف)
4. To observe the duties in prescribed order.

If any of these is given up, the Hajj becomes void.

(6) *Wajeb in Hajj.*

(1) To run between Safa and Merwa.
(2) To stay at Muzdalefah on the 10th night of Zil Hajj.
(3) To throw stones at Jamrahs.
(4) To shave or cut the hair of head, and
(5) To make Tawaf at the time of leaving the city of Mecca.

If anybody breaks one of these duties, he does not thereby render his Hajj void but only invalid. He shall then have to make amends by the sacrifice of at least a goat.

(7) Hajj may be performed in either of the following three modes.—

(a) Hajj-e-Ifrad is the best method of Hajj. Therein Ihram is made for Hajj and it continues upto the day of Sacrifice. Then the pilgrim goes outside Mecca and makes Ihram again for Umrah.

(b) Hajj-e-Qeran, in which Ihram for both Umrah and Hajj is made at a time and it does not end till both are performed. For such a pilgrim, it is wajeb to sacrifice a goat. If he does not find it, he shall have to observe ten days of fasting, three days before Zil Hajj and seven days at home.

(c) Hajj-e-Tamattu حج تمتع. In this Hajj, Ihram is made first for Umrah and then for Hajj during the days of Hajj. There are therefore two distinct Ihrams in the pilgrimage. This is called حج تمتع or Hajj of enjoyment because between the two Ihrams, one is allowed to enjoy everything like a non-pilgrim.

8. *General procedure of Hajj* :—

Starting from home a pilgrim shall enter into Ihram at least at Miqat ميقات. When reaching Mecca, he shall make Tawaf seven times and run سعی between Safa and Marwa seven times. If the Ihram ends there, he shall shave or cut the hair of his head. Then with a fresh Ihram on the 8th or 9th Zil Hajj, he shall start for Arafat and reach there for waiting at noon. In the evening of the same day he will return to Muzdalafah and spend the night there. In the early dawn of 10th Zil Hajj, he shall start for Mina (منی) reaching there at noon and instantly proceed to throw stones at Jamrah-e-Aqabah. Finishing there, he shall return to Mina and after shaving shall offer one or more animals for sacrifice. On the 11th and 12th Zil Hajj, he will remain at Mina throwing seven stones in the after-noon of each day at the Jamrahs. Then he may remain at Mina on the 13th or return to Mecca on the 12th evening. After returning, he shall proceed to make Tawaf and Sayee. When leaving, he shall make final Tawaf.

(9) *Some Arabic words in Hajj defined* :—

1. Al-Hajj – One who makes Hajj (Pilgrimage).

2. Hajj-Pilgrimage to the Ka'bah at Mecca at the fixed time from 8th to 13th Zil Hajj of which the necessary rituals and devotions are called Manasik.

3. Umrah—visit to the Holy Ka'bah at any time. In Umrah, waiting at Arafat and and sacrifice of animals are dispenced with.

4. Ihram—the state in which a pilgrim performing Hajj or Umrah is required to remain and observe particular fixed rules for passing it. A man observing Ihram is called Muhrim.

5. Talbiyah—To recite in loud voice. "Present to Thee, O Allah, present to Thee! Present to Thee! No partner for Thee! Present to Thee. Verily all praise and all grace are Thine and also dominion. Thou hast no partner."

6. Miqat—It is the fixed place near Mecca from which Ihram is to begin.

7. Tawaf—Circumabulation round the Ka'bah with devotional recitation.

8. Aqabah—The last place of throwing stones.

9. Jamrah—The place of throwing stones.

10. Arafat—Arafat is the name of the plain surrounded on three sides by mountains. It is so called because pilgrims go there to *know* God.

10. *Chief object and benefits of Hajj*:—

1. The Pilgrimage is in a way the biggest of all "Ibadat". For unless a man really loves God be would never undertake a long journey leaving all his near and dear ones behind him. Then the pilgrimage is unlike any other journey. Here one's thoughts are concentrated on Allah. One's very heing vibrates with the spirit of intense devotion. When a man reaches the holy place, he finds the atmosphere laden with piety and Godliness. He visits places which bear witness to the glory of Islam and all this leaves an idelible impression on his mind, which he carries to his last breath.

2. It is the perfection of faith and true surrender to the Almighty.

3. It is the highest training for spiritual advancement.

4. It fosters a spirit of brotherly love and affection among the Muslims of different countries and climes. It is the highest manifestation of Islamic brotherhood and democracy.

5. A pilgrim is a guest of God when he goes to make the pilgrimage. If he dies on the way, he gets the reward of a Ghazi.

6. Hajj is practically jihad and brings the reward of jihad.

7. He who dies without performing Hajj, though it was incumbent upon him, dies as a Jew or a Christian.

جهاد

JIHAD OR THE HOLY WAR

QURAN :

أُذِنَ لِلَّذِينَ يُقَاتَلُونَ بِأَنَّهُمْ ظُلِمُوا ۚ وَإِنَّ اللَّهَ عَلَىٰ نَصْرِهِمْ لَقَدِيرٌ

Permission (to fight) is given to those on whom war is made because they are oppressed. And surely Allah is able to assist them.

(22 : 39)

وَجَاهِدُوا فِي اللَّهِ حَقَّ جِهَادِهِ

And strive hard for Allah with due striving. (22 : 78)

وَقَاتِلُوا فِي سَبِيلِ اللَّهِ الَّذِينَ يُقَاتِلُونَكُمْ وَلَا تَعْتَدُوا ۚ إِنَّ اللَّهَ لَا يُحِبُّ الْمُعْتَدِينَ

And fight in the way of Allah against those who fight against you but be not aggressive. Surely Allah loves not the aggressors. (2 : 190)

وَقَاتِلُوهُمْ حَتَّىٰ لَا تَكُونَ فِتْنَةٌ وَيَكُونَ الدِّينُ لِلَّهِ ۖ فَإِنِ انْتَهَوْا فَلَا عُدْوَانَ إِلَّا عَلَى الظَّالِمِينَ

And fight them until there is no persecution and faith prevails only for Allah. But if they desist, there should be no hostillty except against the oppressors. (2 : 193)

كُتِبَ عَلَيْكُمُ الْقِتَالُ وَهُوَ كُرْهٌ لَكُمْ ۖ وَعَسَىٰ أَنْ تَكْرَهُوا شَيْئًا وَهُوَ خَيْرٌ لَكُمْ ۖ وَعَسَىٰ أَنْ تُحِبُّوا شَيْئًا وَهُوَ شَرٌّ لَكُمْ

وَاللَّهُ يَعْلَمُ وَأَنْتُمْ لَا تَعْلَمُونَ

Fighting is enjoined on you, though it is disliked by you, and it may be that you dislike a thing while it is good for you ; and Allah knows while you know not- (2 : 216)

إِنَّ الَّذِينَ آمَنُوا وَالَّذِينَ هَاجَرُوا وَجَاهَدُوا فِي سَبِيلِ اللَّهِ أُولَٰئِكَ يَرْجُونَ رَحْمَتَ اللَّهِ وَاللَّهُ غَفُورٌ رَحِيمٌ ۝

Those who believed and thoso who quitted (their homes) and strove hard in Allah's way—these surely hope for the mercy of Allah. And Allah is Forgiving, Merciful. (2 : 218)

وَلَا تَحْسَبَنَّ الَّذِينَ قُتِلُوا فِي سَبِيلِ اللَّهِ أَمْوَاتًا بَلْ أَحْيَاءٌ عِنْدَ رَبِّهِمْ يُرْزَقُونَ ۝ فَرِحِينَ بِمَا آتَاهُمُ اللَّهُ مِنْ فَضْلِهِ
وَيَسْتَبْشِرُونَ بِالَّذِينَ لَمْ يَلْحَقُوا بِهِمْ مِنْ خَلْفِهِمْ أَلَّا خَوْفٌ عَلَيْهِمْ وَلَا هُمْ يَحْزَنُونَ ۝

Think not of those who are slain in Allah's way as dead. Nay, they live, finding their sustenance, in the presence of their Lord, rejoicing in what Allah has given them out of His grace, and they rejoice for the sake of those who, (being left) behind them, have not yet joined them, that they have no fear, nor shall they grieve. (3 : 169, 170)

لَا يَسْتَوِي الْقَاعِدُونَ مِنَ الْمُؤْمِنِينَ غَيْرُ أُولِي الضَّرَرِ وَالْمُجَاهِدُونَ فِي سَبِيلِ اللَّهِ بِأَمْوَالِهِمْ وَأَنْفُسِهِمْ
فَضَّلَ اللَّهُ الْمُجَاهِدِينَ بِأَمْوَالِهِمْ وَأَنْفُسِهِمْ عَلَى الْقَاعِدِينَ دَرَجَةً وَكُلًّا وَعَدَ اللَّهُ الْحُسْنَىٰ وَفَضَّلَ اللَّهُ الْمُجَاهِدِينَ
عَلَى الْقَاعِدِينَ أَجْرًا عَظِيمًا ۝ دَرَجَاتٍ مِنْهُ وَمَغْفِرَةً وَرَحْمَةً وَكَانَ اللَّهُ غَفُورًا رَحِيمًا ۝

The holders-back from among the believers not disabled by injury, and those who strive hard in Allah's way with their property and their persons, are not equal. Allah has made the strivers with their property and their persons to excel the holders-back in a (high) degree. And to each Allah has promised good. And Allah has granted to the strivers above the holders-back a mighty reward—(high) degrees from Him, and protection and mercy. And Allah is ever Forgiving, Merciful. (4 : 95,96)

وَالَّذِينَ آمَنُوا وَهَاجَرُوا وَجَاهَدُوا فِي سَبِيلِ اللَّهِ وَالَّذِينَ آوَوا وَّنَصَرُوا أُولَٰئِكَ هُمُ الْمُؤْمِنُونَ حَقًّا
لَّهُم مَّغْفِرَةٌ وَرِزْقٌ كَرِيمٌ

And those who belived and adopted exile and struggled hard in Allah's way, and those who gave shelter and helped—these are the believers truly. For them is forgiveness and an honourable provision. (8:74)

الَّذِينَ آمَنُوا وَهَاجَرُوا وَجَاهَدُوا فِي سَبِيلِ اللَّهِ بِأَمْوَالِهِمْ وَأَنفُسِهِمْ أَعْظَمُ دَرَجَةً عِندَ اللَّهِ وَأُولَٰئِكَ
هُمُ الْفَائِزُونَ

Those who believed and adopted exile, and strove hard in Allah's way with their wealth and their lives, are much higher in rank with Allah. And it is these that shall triumph. (9:20)

قُلْ إِن كَانَ آبَاؤُكُمْ وَأَبْنَاؤُكُمْ وَإِخْوَانُكُمْ وَأَزْوَاجُكُمْ وَعَشِيرَتُكُمْ وَأَمْوَالٌ اقْتَرَفْتُمُوهَا وَتِجَارَةٌ تَخْشَوْنَ
كَسَادَهَا وَمَسَاكِنُ تَرْضَوْنَهَا أَحَبَّ إِلَيْكُم مِّنَ اللَّهِ وَرَسُولِهِ وَجِهَادٍ فِي سَبِيلِهِ فَتَرَبَّصُوا حَتَّىٰ يَأْتِيَ اللَّهُ بِأَمْرِهِ
وَاللَّهُ لَا يَهْدِي الْقَوْمَ الْفَاسِقِينَ

If your fathers and your sons and your brethren and your wives and your kinsfolk and the wealth you have acquired, and trade whose dullness you fear, and dwellings you love, are dearer to you than Allah and His Messenger and striving in His way, then wait until Allah brings His decision to pass. And Allah guides not the transgressing people. (9:24)

يَا أَيُّهَا النَّبِيُّ جَاهِدِ الْكُفَّارَ وَالْمُنَافِقِينَ وَاغْلُظْ عَلَيْهِمْ وَمَأْوَاهُمْ جَهَنَّمُ وَبِئْسَ الْمَصِيرُ

O Prophet, strive hard against the disbelievers, the hypocrites, and be firm against them. And their abode is hell, and evil is that destination. (9:73)

وَمَن جَاهَدَ فَإِنَّمَا يُجَاهِدُ لِنَفْسِهِ ۚ إِنَّ اللَّهَ لَغَنِيٌّ عَنِ الْعَالَمِينَ ○

And whoever strives hard, strives for himself. Surely Allah is free of all needs from all creation. (29:6)

وَالَّذِينَ جَاهَدُوا فِينَا لَنَهْدِيَنَّهُمْ سُبُلَنَا ۚ وَإِنَّ اللَّهَ لَمَعَ الْمُحْسِنِينَ ○

And those who strive hard for us. We shall certainly guide them in our ways. And Allah is surely with the doers of good. (29:69)

وَلَنَبْلُوَنَّكُمْ حَتَّىٰ نَعْلَمَ الْمُجَاهِدِينَ مِنكُمْ وَالصَّابِرِينَ وَنَبْلُوَ أَخْبَارَكُمْ ○

And certainly We shall try you, till We know those among you who strive hard, and the steadfast, and We shall try your reported (mettle). (47:31)

HADIS:

١ - عن ابي هريرة، قال : قال رسول الله صلى الله عليه وسلم : مثل المجاهد فى سبيل الله كمثل الصائم القائم القانت بآيات الله، لايفتر من صيام ولاصلاة حتى يرجع المجاهد فى سبيل الله .

(متفق عليه)

Abu Hurairah reported that the Messenger of Allah said, "The example of a fighter in the way of Allah is the one who fasts, stands up (in prayer) and obeys the verses of Allah without any break of fast and prayer until the fighter in the way of Allah returns." (Bukhari, Muslim)

٢ - عن ابى هريرة، قال : قال رسول الله صلى الله عليه وسلم :...... والذى نفسى بيده لوددت ان أقتل فى سبيل الله ، ثم أحيى ، ثم اقتل، ثم أحيى، ثم أقتل، ثم أحيى، ثم أقتل - (متفق عليه)

2. Abu Hurairah reported that the Holy Prophet said........."By Him in whose hand there is my life, how much do I like that I should be killed in the way of Allah and then be brought back to life, and then be killed and then be brought back to life, and then be killed and then be brought back to life, and then be killed." (Bukhari, Muslim)

٣ ـ عن سهل بن سعد ، قال : قال رسول الله صلى الله عليه وسلم :
رباط يوم فى سبيل الله خير من الدينا وما عليها ـ (متفق عليه)

3. Sahl bin Sa'ad reported that the Messenger of Allah said, "Guarding for a day in the way of Allah is better than the world and what is therein." (Bukhari, Muslim)

٤ ـ عن ابى عبس، قال . قال رسول الله صلى الله عليه وسلم: ما اغبرت
قدما عبد فى سبيل الله فتمسه النار ـ (البخاري)

4. Abi 'Abs reported that the Messenger of Allah said, "No feet of a servant are covered with dust in the way of Allah to touch Hell-fire." (Bukhari)

٥ ـ عن عبد الله بن عمرو، ان النبي صلى الله عليه وسلم قال . القتل
فى سبيل الله يكفر كل شى الا الدين ـ (مسلم)

5. Abdullah bin Amr reported that the Holy Prophet said, "To be killed in the way of Allah atones for everything except debt." (Muslim)

٦ ـ عن ابي هريرة، قال: قال رسول الله صلى الله عليه وسلم: من
مات ولم يغز ولم يحدث به نفسه ، مات على شعبة من نفاق ـ
(مسلم)

6. Abu Hurairah reported that the Messenger of Allah said, 'Whosoever dies without fighting (holy war) and without consulting himself about it, dies on a branch of hypocrisy." (Muslim)

٧ ـ عن ابى موسى ، قال : جاء رجل الى النبي صلى الله عليه وسلم ،
فقال الرجل يقاتل للمغنم، والرجل يقاتل للذكر ، والرجل يقاتل

لبري مكانه، فمن فى سبيل الله؟ قال: من قاتل لتكون كلمة الله هى العليا، فهو فى سبيل الله - (متفق عليه)

7. Abu Musa reported that a man came to the Messenger of Allah and enquired, "A man fights for booty, a man fights for fame, and a man fights that his position may be known—who then (fights) in the way of Allah?" He said, "Whosoever fights to raise highest thereby the word of Allah, is in the way of Allah." (Bukhari, Muslim)

٨ - عن انس عن النبى صلى الله عليه و سلم، قال: جاهدوا المشركين باموالكم، وانفسكم، والسنتكم - (ابو داؤد و النسائى والدارمى)

8. Anas reported from the Holy Prophet who said, "Fight against the polytheists with your properties, your lives and your tongues." (Abu Daud, Nasai, Darmi)

٩ - عن جابر، قال: قال رجل للنبي صلى الله عليه وسلم يوم احد: ارأيت ان قتلت فاين انا؟ قال: فى الجنة، فالقى تمرات فى يده ثم قاتل حتى قتل - (متفق عليه)

9. Jaber reported that a man asked the Messenger of Allah on the Day of Uhud, "Inform me where I shall be if I am killed." "In Paradise", said he. He then threw away the dates in his hand and fought till he was killed. (Bukhari, Muslim)

١٠ - عن جابر، قال: قال رسول الله صلى الله عليه وسلم: الحرب خدعة - (متفق عليه)

10. Jaber reported that the Messenger of Allah said, "War is a deception." (Bukhari, Muslim)

١١ - عن انس، ان رسول الله صلى الله عليه وسلم قال: انطلقوا بسم الله، وبالله وعلى ملة رسول الله، لاتقتلوا شيخا فانياً، ولا طفلاً صغيراً، ولاامراةً، ولا تغلوا، وضموا غنائمكم، واصلحوا، واحسنوا فان الله يحب المحسنين - (ابو داؤد)

11. Anas reported that the Messenger of Allah said, "March in the name of Allah, and with the succour of Allah and over the religion of the Messenger of Allah ! Kill not the emaciated old, nor the young children, nor the women, and deceive not; collect your booty, do good and show kindness, because Allah loves those who do good to others." (Abu Daud).

١٢ - عن ابى هريرة، عن رسول الله صلى الله عليه وسلم قال: فلم تحل الغنائم لاحد من قبلنا، ذلك بان الله راى ضعفنا وعجزنا فطيبها لنا۔

(متفق عليه)

12. Abu Huraira reported that the Messenger of Allah said, "Booty was not lawful for anybody previous to us. That was because Allah saw our weakness and helplessness, and so He made it lawful for us. (Bukhari, Muslim)

Remarks:—

1. The word "Jihad" is derived from Juhd (جهد) or Jahad meaning ability, exertion or power, and Jihad (جهاد) and Mujahida (مجاهده) mean the exerting one's power in repelling the enemy.

Technically it means exerting one's power in repelling the enemy to the extent of one's ability whether by word (قول) or by deed (فعل). It also means a war undertaken for a just cause (in the way of Allah) and for the defence of Islam. A man who exerts himself physically or mentally, or spends his wealth in the way of Allah is indeed engaged in Jihad.

2. Jihad is of three kinds; viz., the carrying on of a struggle :— 1. against a visible enemy; 2. against the devil and 3. against the self (نفس).

Jihad is, therefore, far from being synonymous with war, while the meaning of "war undertaken for the propagation of Islam", which is supposed by European writers to be the significance of Jihad, is unknown equally to the Arabic language, and the teachings of the Holy Quran. Even in Hadis litrature, the word jihad is not used exclusively for fighting (قتال). For example, hajj is called a Jihad (Bukhari. 25 : 4). The greatest Jihad, "says the Prophet," is the fight against the evil passions of one's self (نفس) — (4: 193 w) because these are the enemies of the soul working secretly to undermine the most vital qualities of a man. The great tussle which ensues in the mind between the good and evil forces of a man is called the greatest fight.

3. The propagation of Islam is no doubt a religious duty of every true Muslim who must follow the example of the Holy Prophet, but "the spread of Islam by force". is a thing of which no trace can be found in the Holy Quran or Hadis.

4. The fight must be against aggressors who create disturbance in the world and destroy the houses of God of all faiths.

5. Jihad is one of the most meritorious acts in Islam and is the best source of earning eternal bliss, but it must be under taken for self-defence and in the way of Allah.

6. Jihad is the best action of a Muslim (23 : 19). A great reward has been promised for supplying even arms and ammunition, to the warriors (33 : 80). There are innumerable traditions relating to the mertis of Jihad.

7. The Holy Prophet introduced many reforms in military organisation and inculcated strict rules about morality and religious duties among soldiers. For example, drinking, debauchery, looting, plundering and thousands of other things were prohibited (4 : 12). Even in actual warfare, prayer had to be performed on the battlefield on the thick of fight.[1]

1· Remarks have been compiled &ith the help ef the religion of Islam (Md. Ali), English translation of Mishkwat (Fazal Karim), A Dictionary of Islam (Hughes) and Towards Understanding Islam (Abdul Ala) etc. (N.A).

From Darkness Unto Light

معاشرة

Social Life

1. Nikah or Marriage

Quran :

وَلَقَدْ أَرْسَلْنَا رُسُلًا مِّن قَبْلِكَ وَجَعَلْنَا لَهُمْ أَزْوَاجًا وَذُرِّيَّةً

And certainly we sent messengers before thee and appointed for them wives and children. (13:38)

وَكَيْفَ تَأْخُذُونَهُ وَقَدْ أَفْضَىٰ بَعْضُكُمْ إِلَىٰ بَعْضٍ وَأَخَذْنَ مِنكُم مِّيثَاقًا غَلِيظًا

And how can you take it when one of you has already gone unto the other and they have taken from you a strong covenant. (4:21)

وَأَنكِحُوا الْأَيَامَىٰ مِنكُمْ وَالصَّالِحِينَ مِنْ عِبَادِكُمْ وَإِمَائِكُمْ إِن يَكُونُوا فُقَرَاءَ يُغْنِهِمُ اللَّهُ مِن فَضْلِهِ
وَاللَّهُ وَاسِعٌ عَلِيمٌ

Any marry those among you who are single, and those who are fit among your male slaves and your female slaves; if they are needy, Allah will make them free from want out of His grace. And Allah is Ample-giving, Knowing. (24 : 32).

يَا أَيُّهَا النَّاسُ اتَّقُوا رَبَّكُمُ الَّذِي خَلَقَكُم مِّن نَّفْسٍ وَاحِدَةٍ وَخَلَقَ مِنْهَا زَوْجَهَا وَبَثَّ مِنْهُمَا
رِجَالًا كَثِيرًا وَنِسَاءً

O people, keep your duty to your Lord, Who created you from a single being and created its mate of the same (kind) and spread from these two many men and women. (4:1)

الْخَبِيثَاتُ لِلْخَبِيثِينَ وَالْخَبِيثُونَ لِلْخَبِيثَاتِ ۖ وَالطَّيِّبَاتُ لِلطَّيِّبِينَ وَالطَّيِّبُونَ لِلطَّيِّبَاتِ ۚ
أُولَٰئِكَ مُبَرَّءُونَ مِمَّا يَقُولُونَ ۖ لَهُمْ مَغْفِرَةٌ وَرِزْقٌ كَرِيمٌ

Impure women are for impure men, and impure men are for impure women. And women of purity are for men of purity and men of purity are for women of purity. These are not affected by what people say. For them there is forgiveness and a provision honourable. (24:26)

حُرِّمَتْ عَلَيْكُمْ أُمَّهَاتُكُمْ وَبَنَاتُكُمْ وَأَخَوَاتُكُمْ وَعَمَّاتُكُمْ وَخَالَاتُكُمْ وَبَنَاتُ الْأَخِ وَبَنَاتُ الْأُخْتِ وَأُمَّهَاتُكُمُ اللَّاتِي أَرْضَعْنَكُمْ
وَأَخَوَاتُكُمْ مِنَ الرَّضَاعَةِ وَأُمَّهَاتُ نِسَائِكُمْ وَرَبَائِبُكُمُ اللَّاتِي فِي حُجُورِكُمْ مِنْ نِسَائِكُمُ اللَّاتِي دَخَلْتُمْ بِهِنَّ فَإِنْ لَمْ تَكُونُوا
دَخَلْتُمْ بِهِنَّ فَلَا جُنَاحَ عَلَيْكُمْ وَحَلَائِلُ أَبْنَائِكُمُ الَّذِينَ مِنْ أَصْلَابِكُمْ وَأَنْ تَجْمَعُوا بَيْنَ الْأُخْتَيْنِ
إِلَّا مَا قَدْ سَلَفَ ۗ إِنَّ اللَّهَ كَانَ غَفُورًا رَحِيمًا

Forbidden to you are your mothers and your daughters, and your sisters, and your paternal aunts, and your maternal aunts, and brother's daughters and sister's daughters, and your mothers that have suckled you and your foster sisters, and mothers of your wives, and your step daughters who are in guardianship (born) of your wives to whom you have gone in; but if you have not gone in to them, there is no blame on you, and the wives of your sons who are of your own loins: and that you should have two sisters together, except what has already passed. Surely Allah is ever Forgiving, Merciful. (4 : 23)

وَالْمُحْصَنَاتُ مِنَ النِّسَاءِ إِلَّا مَا مَلَكَتْ أَيْمَانُكُمْ ۖ كِتَابَ اللَّهِ عَلَيْكُمْ ۚ وَأُحِلَّ لَكُمْ مَا وَرَاءَ ذَٰلِكُمْ
أَنْ تَبْتَغُوا بِأَمْوَالِكُمْ مُحْصِنِينَ غَيْرَ مُسَافِحِينَ ۚ فَمَا اسْتَمْتَعْتُمْ بِهِ مِنْهُنَّ فَآتُوهُنَّ أُجُورَهُنَّ فَرِيضَةً

And all married women except those whom your right hands possess (are forbidden); (this is) Allah's ordinance to you. And lawful for you are (all women) besides those, provided that you seek (them) with your property, taking (them) in marriage, not committing fornication. Then as to those whom you profit (by marrying), give them their dowries as appointed. (4 : 24).

وَلَهُنَّ مِثْلُ الَّذِي عَلَيْهِنَّ بِالْمَعْرُوفِ ۚ وَلِلرِّجَالِ عَلَيْهِنَّ دَرَجَةٌ

And women have rights similar to the rights against them in a just manner, and men are a degree above them. (2 : 228).

اَلرِّجَالُ قَوّٰامُوْنَ عَلَى النِّسَآءِ بِمَا فَضَّلَ اللّٰهُ بَعْضَهُمْ عَلٰى بَعْضٍ وَّبِمَآ اَنْفَقُوْا مِنْ اَمْوَالِهِمْ

Men are the maintainers of women, with what Allah has made some of them to excel others and with what they spend out of their wealth. (4:34)

يٰۤاَيُّهَا الَّذِيْنَ اٰمَنُوْا لَا يَحِلُّ لَكُمْ اَنْ تَرِثُوا النِّسَآءَ كَرْهًا ؕ وَلَا تَعْضُلُوْهُنَّ لِتَذْهَبُوْا بِبَعْضِ مَآ اٰتَيْتُمُوْهُنَّ
اِلَّاۤ اَنْ يَّاْتِيْنَ بِفَاحِشَةٍ مُّبَيِّنَةٍ ۚ وَعَاشِرُوْهُنَّ بِالْمَعْرُوْفِ ۚ فَاِنْ كَرِهْتُمُوْهُنَّ فَعَسٰۤى اَنْ تَكْرَهُوْا شَيْــًٔا وَّيَجْعَلَ اللّٰهُ
فِيْهِ خَيْرًا كَثِيْرًا ۝

O you who believe, it is not lawful for you to take women as heritage against (their) will. Nor should you straiten them by taking part of what you have given them, unless they are guilty of manifest indecency. And treat them kindly. Then if you dislike them it may be that you dislike a thing while Allah has placed abundant good in it. (4 : 19).

فَالصّٰلِحٰتُ قٰنِتٰتٌ حٰفِظٰتٌ لِّلْغَيْبِ بِمَا حَفِظَ اللّٰهُ

So the good women are obedient, guarding the unseen as Allah has guarded. (4 : 34).

وَاِنْ خِفْتُمْ شِقَاقَ بَيْنِهِمَا فَابْعَثُوْا حَكَمًا مِّنْ اَهْلِهٖ وَحَكَمًا مِّنْ اَهْلِهَا ۚ
اِنْ يُّرِيْدَاۤ اِصْلَاحًا يُّوَفِّقِ اللّٰهُ بَيْنَهُمَا

And if you fear a breach between the two, appoint an arbiter from his people and an arbiter from her people; if they both desire agreement, Allah will effect harmony between them. (4 : 35).

Hadis :

١ - عن انس ، قال . قال رسول الله صلى الله عليه وسلم : إذا تزوج العبد فقد استكمل نصف الدين ، فليتق الله فى النصف الباقى -

(بيهقى)

Anas reported that the Messenger of Allah said, "When a man has married, he has indeed made his religion half perfect. Then let him fear Allah for the remaining half." (Baihaqi)

٢ ـ عن أبي سعيد و ابن عباس، قالا : قال رسول الله صلى الله عليه وسلم : من ولد له ولد فليحسن إسمه وادبه، فاذا بلغ فايزوجه، فان بلغ ولم يزوجه فأصاب إثما، فإنما إثمه على ابيه ـ (بيهقى)

Abu Saeed and Ibn Abbas reported that the Messenger of Allah said, "Whoso has got a son born unto him, let him give him a good name and good manners. When he attains maturity, get him be married. If he attains maturity and he does not get him married and then he commits sin, his sin will fall upon his father." (Baihaqi).

٣ ـ عن ابي هريرة، قال : قال رسول الله صلى الله عليه وسلم : إذا خطب اليكم من ترضون دينه وخلقه فزوجوه، ان لاتفعلوه تكن فتنة فى الارض وفساد عريض ـ (ترمذى)

Abu Hurairah reported that the Messenger of Allah said, "When you are sought in marriage by one whom you are pleased with for his religion and for his character, get yourself married to him. If you do not do it, there will be distress in the world and wide-spread dissension." (Tirmizi).

٤ ـ عن ابي هريرة، ان رسول الله صلى الله عليه وسلم نهى أن تنكح المرأة على عمتها والعمة على بنت اخيها و المرأة على خالتها او الخالة على بنت اختها لاتنكح الصغرى على الكبرى ولاالكبرى على الصغرى ـ (ترمذى، ابوداؤد، نسائى)

Abu Hurairah reported that the Messenger of Allah prohibited: Marriage of a woman over her aunt, or of an aunt over the daughter of her brother, or of a woman over her maternal aunt, of a maternal aunt over a daughter of her sister. The younger (sister) should not be given in marriage over the older (sister), nor the elder (sister) over the younger (sister)." (Tirmizi, Abu Daud, Nasai).

٥ ـ عن جابر، قال : قال رسول الله صلى الله عليه وسلم : اذا خطب احدكم المرأة فان استطاع ان ينظر الى مايدعوه الى نكاحها فليفعل ـ (ابو داؤد)

Jaber reported that the Messenger of Allah said, "When one of you seeks a woman in marriage, and then if he is able to have a look at her whom he wishes to marry, let him do." (Abu Daud)

٦- عن ابى هريرة ، قال : قال رسول الله صلى الله عليه وسلم لاتزوج المرأة المرأة، ولاتزوج المرأة نفسها، فان الزانية هى التي تزوج نفسها - (ابن ماجه)

Abu Hurairah reported that the Messenger of Allah said, "No woman shall give a woman in marriage nor a woman shall give herself in marriage. Verily the fornicatress is she who marries by herself." (Ibn Majah)

٧ - عن محمد بن حاطب الجمحي ، عن النبى صلى الله عليه وسلم قال : فصل ما بين الحلال والحرام : الصوت والدف في النكاح - (احمد، ترمذى، نسائي، ابن ماجه)

Mohammad bin Hatib al-Jamahiy reported from the Messenger of Allah who said, "The demarcation between lawful and unlawful things in marriage is proclamation and Daf." (Ahmad, Tirmizi, Nasai, Ibn Majah).

٨ - عن جابر، ان النبي صلى الله عليه وسلم قال : من اعطى فى صداق امرأته ملء كفيه سويقاً او تمراً فقد استحل - (ابوداؤد)

Jaber reported that the Messenger of Allah said, "Whoso gives two handfuls of barley or dates as dower of his wife has rendered (her) lawful." (Abu Daud)

٩ - عن ابى هريرة ، قال: قال رسول الله صلى الله عليه وسلم: شرّ الطعام طعام الوليمة يدعى لها الاغنياء ويترك الفقراء، ومن ترك الدعوة فقد عصى الله ورسوله - (متفق عليه)

Abu Hurairah reported that the Messenger of Allah said, "The worsts of feasts is a feast of marriage where the rich are invited and the poor are omitted. Whoso does not attend the invitation, disobeys Allah and His Prophet." (Bukhari, Muslim)

١٠ ـ عن معقل ابن يسار، قال . قال رسول الله صلى الله عليه وسلم :
تزوجوا الودود الولود، فانى مكاثر بكم الامم (ابو داؤد ـ نسائى)

Ma'qal bin Yasar reported that the Apostle of Allah said, "Marry such women as are affectionate, child producing, and verily I would wish increase in your numbers among the nations." (Abu Daud, Nasai).

١١ ـ عن عائشه قالت: قال رسول الله صلى الله عليه وسلم : يحرم من
الرضاعة ما يحرم من الولادة ـ (بخاري)

Ayesha reported that the Apostle of Allah said, "What is unlawful by reason of consanguinity is unlawful by reason of fosterage". (Bukhari).

١٢ ـ عن ابى هريرة ، قال : قال رسول الله صلى الله عليه وسلم :
اليتيمة تستأمر فى نفسها، فان صمتت فهو اذنها، وان ابت فلا جواز
عليها ـ (ترمذى ـ ابوداؤد ـ نسائى)

Abu Hurairah reported that the Prophet said, "A grown-up girl shall be asked permission about herself. If she is silent, it is her permission; and if she declines, there shall be no compulsion on her." (Tirmizi, Abu Daud, Nasai).

Remarks :

(1) Marriage is the union of two souls for love and two bodies for procreation and legalising of children. It is a civil contract based on mutual consent of the bride and the bridegroom.

(2) The real, natural and first unit of human civilization is family, and there can be no family if there is no marriage. To break up family is to break up social life, for no more natural unit can be substituted in its place.

In Islam marriage has been very much emphasised. The jurists say that when the sexual passion is so strong that there is every chance of a man falling into sin, marriage then becomes binding. When the sexual passion is very strong marriage is Wajeb. When the passion remains in normal degree, it is Sunnat-e-Muakkadah. Marriage becomes

Makruh, (مکروہ) when there are no means for maintenance and when no suitable match is found. Marriage may be delayed for two reasons, for not finding a suitable match and for finding nò means wherewith to maintain the wife.

(3) Marriage has got several advantages and contributes to many-sided progress of man. Marriage is the best cure for certain kinds of diseases in grown-up men and women and enhances the physical beauty of the married couple. It gives peace of mind. It creates a family, creates society. Marriage gives impetus to social virtues. It is a check-upon the sexual passions. It contributes to moral and spiritual welfare of individuals, families and societies and ultimately leads to a "Blessed Life". A man is forbidden from taking in marraige: 1. Mothers. 2. Daughters. 3. Sisters. 4. Paternal aunts. 5. Maternal aunts. 6. Brother's daughters. 7. Sister's daughters. 8. Mothers that have suckled you. 9. Foster sisters. 10. Mothers of your wives. 11. Step daughters who are in your guardianship born of your wives to whom you have gone in. 12. Wives of your sons who are of your own loins. 13. Two sisters together. 14. All married women except those whom your right hand possess.

Jurists have expounded these prohibitions and classed them into three groups: Prohibition owing to (i) Consanguinity (ii) fosterage, and (iii) affinity.

(5) The foremost qualification of a bride is, as the Quran says (4:3), that the bride-groom and the bride's mutual choice has got the greatest consideration. According to traditions, a bride should be (i) a Muslim (2) chaste (3) virgin (4) beautiful (5) accomplished, (6) having sweet tongue and good manners (7) Possessing property (8) having child-bearing capacity and affectionate nature, and (9) equal respectability.

According to Hanafi, Law, equality is an important condition of marriage in points of family, religion, freedom, character, fortune and profession.

A Muslim can not marry an idolatress. The women of the people of the Book (اهل کتاب) can lawfully be taken in marriage, but no Muslim women can be given in marriage to a man from the people of the Book.

6. Marriage is a contract, therefore it can be performed by those who are capable of entering into a contract. In a contract of marriage at least two witnesses are essential. They must be free, sane, major and Muslims.

(7) The proclamation of marriage within moderate and lawful limits, and holding marriage feasts (ولیمہ) have been encouraged by the Holy Prophet.

(8) Dower is a consideration of the ocntract of marriage. It is essentail to the validity of a marriage. No hard and fast rule has been laid down by Quran about the amount of dower. It is to be adjusted according to the social position of the parties, their wealth, their personal qualifications and condition of the human society.

The latter jurists divided dowry into two portions: One payable on demand called Mahr Mu'ajjal (مہر معجل) and the other payable at death or dissolution of marriage by divorce called Mahr Muajjal (مہرموجل)

There is no such clear distinction either in Quran or Hadith. Where no dower has been fixed, it is to be adjudged according to the amount in one's family and the condition of the husband. This is called Mahr Misal (مہر مثل) or customary dower.

طلاق

2. Talaq or Divorce

Quran:

وَالْمُطَلَّقٰتُ يَتَرَبَّصْنَ بِاَنْفُسِهِنَّ ثَلٰثَةَ قُرُوْٓءٍ ؕ وَلَا يَحِلُّ لَهُنَّ اَنْ يَّكْتُمْنَ مَا خَلَقَ اللّٰهُ فِىْٓ اَرْحَامِهِنَّ
اِنْ كُنَّ يُؤْمِنَّ بِاللّٰهِ وَالْيَوْمِ الْاٰخِرِ ؕ وَبُعُوْلَتُهُنَّ اَحَقُّ بِرَدِّهِنَّ فِىْ ذٰلِكَ اِنْ اَرَادُوْٓا اِصْلَاحًا ؕ وَلَهُنَّ مِثْلُ
الَّذِىْ عَلَيْهِنَّ بِالْمَعْرُوْفِ وَلِلرِّجَالِ عَلَيْهِنَّ دَرَجَةٌ ؕ وَاللّٰهُ عَزِيْزٌ حَكِيْمٌ ۝ اَلطَّلَاقُ مَرَّتٰنِ فَاِمْسَاكٌۢ بِمَعْرُوْفٍ
اَوْ تَسْرِيْحٌۢ بِاِحْسَانٍ ؕ وَلَا يَحِلُّ لَكُمْ اَنْ تَاْخُذُوْا مِمَّآ اٰتَيْتُمُوْهُنَّ شَيْـًٔا اِلَّآ اَنْ يَّخَافَآ اَلَّا يُقِيْمَا حُدُوْدَ اللّٰهِ ؕ
فَاِنْ خِفْتُمْ اَلَّا يُقِيْمَا حُدُوْدَ اللّٰهِ ۙ فَلَا جُنَاحَ عَلَيْهِمَا فِيْمَا افْتَدَتْ بِهٖ ؕ تِلْكَ حُدُوْدُ اللّٰهِ فَلَا تَعْتَدُوْهَا ۚ
وَمَنْ يَّتَعَدَّ حُدُوْدَ اللّٰهِ فَاُولٰٓئِكَ هُمُ الظّٰلِمُوْنَ ۝ فَاِنْ طَلَّقَهَا فَلَا تَحِلُّ لَهٗ مِنْۢ بَعْدُ حَتّٰى تَنْكِحَ زَوْجًا
غَيْرَهٗ ؕ فَاِنْ طَلَّقَهَا فَلَا جُنَاحَ عَلَيْهِمَآ اَنْ يَّتَرَاجَعَآ اِنْ ظَنَّآ اَنْ يُّقِيْمَا حُدُوْدَ اللّٰهِ ؕ وَتِلْكَ حُدُوْدُ اللّٰهِ يُبَيِّنُهَا
لِقَوْمٍ يَّعْلَمُوْنَ ۝ وَاِذَا طَلَّقْتُمُ النِّسَآءَ فَبَلَغْنَ اَجَلَهُنَّ فَاَمْسِكُوْهُنَّ بِمَعْرُوْفٍ اَوْ سَرِّحُوْهُنَّ بِمَعْرُوْفٍ
وَلَا تُمْسِكُوْهُنَّ ضِرَارًا لِّتَعْتَدُوْا ۚ وَمَنْ يَّفْعَلْ ذٰلِكَ فَقَدْ ظَلَمَ نَفْسَهٗ ؕ وَلَا تَتَّخِذُوْٓا اٰيٰتِ اللّٰهِ هُزُوًا وَّاذْكُرُوْا
نِعْمَتَ اللّٰهِ عَلَيْكُمْ وَمَآ اَنْزَلَ عَلَيْكُمْ مِّنَ الْكِتٰبِ وَالْحِكْمَةِ يَعِظُكُمْ بِهٖ ؕ وَاتَّقُوا اللّٰهَ وَاعْلَمُوْٓا اَنَّ اللّٰهَ بِكُلِّ شَىْءٍ
عَلِيْمٌ ۝ وَاِذَا طَلَّقْتُمُ النِّسَآءَ فَبَلَغْنَ اَجَلَهُنَّ فَلَا تَعْضُلُوْهُنَّ اَنْ يَّنْكِحْنَ اَزْوَاجَهُنَّ اِذَا تَرَاضَوْا بَيْنَهُمْ
بِالْمَعْرُوْفِ ؕ ذٰلِكَ يُوْعَظُ بِهٖ مَنْ كَانَ مِنْكُمْ يُؤْمِنُ بِاللّٰهِ وَالْيَوْمِ الْاٰخِرِ ؕ ذٰلِكُمْ اَزْكٰى لَكُمْ وَاَطْهَرُ ؕ وَاللّٰهُ
يَعْلَمُ وَاَنْتُمْ لَا تَعْلَمُوْنَ ۝

1. Divorced women should keep themselves in waiting for three courses. And it is not lawful for them to hide what Allah has created in their wombs, if they have faith in God and the Last Day. And their husbands have a better right to take them back in the meanwhile if they wish for reconciliation. And women have rights similar to those against them in a just manner, and men have a degree (of advantage) over them And God is Exalted in Power, Wise. A divorce is only permissible twice; after that the parties should either hold together on equitable terms, or separate with kindness. And it is not lawful for you to take any part of

what you have given them, unless both fear that they can not keep within the limits of Allah. Then if you fear that they can not keep within the limits of Allah, there is no blame on either of them if she give something for her freedom. These are the limits of Allah. So do not transgress them. For whoso transgresseth Allah's limits such are wrong doers. And if he hath divorced her (the third time) then she is not lawful unto him thereafter until she hath wedded another husband. Then if he divorces her it is no sin for both of them that they come together again if they consider that they are able to observe the limits of Allah. These are the limits of Allah, which He makes clear to those who understand. And when you divorce women and they fulfil the term (of their Iddat), then retain them in kindness or set them free with kindness and retain them not for injury so that you exceed the limits. And whoever does this, he indeed wrongs his own soul. And take not Allah's messages for a mockery, and remember Allah's favour to you, and that which He has revealed to you of the Book and the Wisdom, for your instruction. And Fear God, and know that Allah is well acquainted with all things. And when you divorce women and they fulfil the term (of their Iddat), do not prevent them from marrying their (former) husbands, if they mutually agree on equitable terms. This instruction is for all among you, who believe in God and the Last Day. This is more profitable for you and purer. And Allah knows while you know not. (2 : 228 – 232)

وَالَّذِينَ يُتَوَفَّوْنَ مِنكُمْ وَيَذَرُونَ أَزْوَاجًا يَتَرَبَّصْنَ بِأَنفُسِهِنَّ أَرْبَعَةَ أَشْهُرٍ وَعَشْرًا ۖ فَإِذَا بَلَغْنَ أَجَلَهُنَّ
فَلَا جُنَاحَ عَلَيْكُمْ فِيمَا فَعَلْنَ فِي أَنفُسِهِنَّ بِالْمَعْرُوفِ ۗ وَاللَّهُ بِمَا تَعْمَلُونَ خَبِيرٌ ۝

2. And (as for) those of you who die and leave wives behind, such women should keep themselves in waiting for four months and ten days. When they reach their term, there is no blame on you for what they do for themselves in a lawful manner. And Allah is aware of what you do. (2 : 234)

لَّا جُنَاحَ عَلَيْكُمْ إِن طَلَّقْتُمُ النِّسَاءَ مَا لَمْ تَمَسُّوهُنَّ أَوْ تَفْرِضُوا لَهُنَّ فَرِيضَةً ۚ وَمَتِّعُوهُنَّ
عَلَى الْمُوسِعِ قَدَرُهُ وَعَلَى الْمُقْتِرِ قَدَرُهُ مَتَاعًا بِالْمَعْرُوفِ ۖ حَقًّا عَلَى الْمُحْسِنِينَ ۝ وَإِن طَلَّقْتُمُوهُنَّ مِن
قَبْلِ أَن تَمَسُّوهُنَّ وَقَدْ فَرَضْتُمْ لَهُنَّ فَرِيضَةً فَنِصْفُ مَا فَرَضْتُمْ إِلَّا أَن يَعْفُونَ أَوْ يَعْفُوَ الَّذِي بِيَدِهِ
عُقْدَةُ النِّكَاحِ ۚ وَأَن تَعْفُوا أَقْرَبُ لِلتَّقْوَىٰ ۚ وَلَا تَنسَوُا الْفَضْلَ بَيْنَكُمْ ۚ إِنَّ اللَّهَ بِمَا تَعْمَلُونَ بَصِيرٌ ۝

3. There is no blame on you if you divorce women before consummation or the fixation of their dower, and provide for, the wealthy according to his means and the strained according to his means, a provision according to usage. (This is) a duty on the doers of good. And if you divorce them before consummation, but after the fixation of a dower for them, then the half of the dower (is due to them), unless they remit it, or (the man's half) is remitted by him in whose hands is the marriage tie and the remission (of the man's half) is the nearest to righteousness. And do not forget liberality between yourselves. Surely Allah sees well all that you do. (2 : 236,237)

وَالَّذِينَ يُتَوَفَّوْنَ مِنكُمْ وَيَذَرُونَ أَزْوَاجًا وَصِيَّةً لِّأَزْوَاجِهِم مَّتَاعًا إِلَى الْحَوْلِ غَيْرَ إِخْرَاجٍ فَإِنْ خَرَجْنَ
فَلَا جُنَاحَ عَلَيْكُمْ فِي مَا فَعَلْنَ فِي أَنفُسِهِنَّ مِن مَّعْرُوفٍ وَاللَّهُ عَزِيزٌ حَكِيمٌ ۝ وَلِلْمُطَلَّقَاتِ مَتَاعٌ بِالْمَعْرُوفِ
حَقًّا عَلَى الْمُتَّقِينَ ۝

4. And those of you who die and leave wives behind, should make a bequest in favour of their wives of maintenance for the year without turning (them) out. Then if they themselves go away (and leave the residence), there is no blame on you for what they do with themselves, provided it is reasonable. And God is Exalted in Power, Wise. For divorced women maintenance (should be provided) on a reasonable (scale). This is a duty on the righteous. (2 : 240,241)

وَإِنْ خِفْتُمْ شِقَاقَ بَيْنِهِمَا فَابْعَثُوا حَكَمًا مِّنْ أَهْلِهِ وَحَكَمًا مِّنْ أَهْلِهَا إِن يُرِيدَا إِصْلَاحًا يُوَفِّقِ
اللَّهُ بَيْنَهُمَا إِنَّ اللَّهَ كَانَ عَلِيمًا خَبِيرًا ۝

5. And if you fear a breach between the two, appoint one arbiter from his family, and one from her's. If they both desire agreement, Allah will effect harmony between them. Surely Allah is ever Knowing, Aware. (4 . 35)

يَا أَيُّهَا الَّذِينَ آمَنُوا إِذَا نَكَحْتُمُ الْمُؤْمِنَاتِ ثُمَّ طَلَّقْتُمُوهُنَّ مِن قَبْلِ أَن تَمَسُّوهُنَّ فَمَا لَكُمْ عَلَيْهِنَّ مِنْ عِدَّةٍ تَعْتَدُّونَهَا
فَمَتِّعُوهُنَّ وَسَرِّحُوهُنَّ سَرَاحًا جَمِيلًا ۝

6. O you who believe, when you marry believing woman, then divorce them before you touch them; you have in their case no term which you should reckon. But make provision for them and set them free in a goodly manner. (33 : 49)

يٰٓاَيُّهَا النَّبِيُّ اِذَا طَلَّقْتُمُ النِّسَآءَ فَطَلِّقُوْهُنَّ لِعِدَّتِهِنَّ وَاَحْصُوا الْعِدَّةَ ۚ وَاتَّقُوا اللّٰهَ رَبَّكُمْ ۚ لَا تُخْرِجُوْهُنَّ مِنْۢ بُيُوْتِهِنَّ وَلَا يَخْرُجْنَ اِلَّآ اَنْ يَّاْتِيْنَ بِفَاحِشَةٍ مُّبَيِّنَةٍ ۗ وَتِلْكَ حُدُوْدُ اللّٰهِ ۗ وَمَنْ يَّتَعَدَّ حُدُوْدَ اللّٰهِ فَقَدْ ظَلَمَ نَفْسَهٗ ۗ لَا تَدْرِيْ لَعَلَّ اللّٰهَ يُحْدِثُ بَعْدَ ذٰلِكَ اَمْرًا ۝ فَاِذَا بَلَغْنَ اَجَلَهُنَّ فَاَمْسِكُوْهُنَّ بِمَعْرُوْفٍ اَوْ فَارِقُوْهُنَّ بِمَعْرُوْفٍ وَّاَشْهِدُوْا ذَوَيْ عَدْلٍ مِّنْكُمْ وَاَقِيْمُوا الشَّهَادَةَ لِلّٰهِ ۗ ذٰلِكُمْ يُوْعَظُ بِهٖ مَنْ كَانَ يُؤْمِنُ بِاللّٰهِ وَالْيَوْمِ الْاٰخِرِ ۬

7. O Prophet, when you divorce women, divorce them for their prescribed period, and calculate the period, and keep your duty to Allah, your Lord. Turn them not out of their houses, nor should they themselves go forth, unless they commit an open indecency. And these are the limits of Allah. And whosoever goes beyond the limits of Allah, he indeed wrongs his own soul. Thou knowest not that Allah may after that bring about an event. So when they have reached their prescribed time, retain them with kindness or dismiss them with kindness, and call to witness two just ones from among you and give upright testimony for Allah. With that is admonished he who believes in Allah and the Latter Day. (65; 1,2)

وَالّٰٓـِٔيْ يَئِسْنَ مِنَ الْمَحِيْضِ مِنْ نِّسَآئِكُمْ اِنِ ارْتَبْتُمْ فَعِدَّتُهُنَّ ثَلٰثَةُ اَشْهُرٍ ۙ وَّالّٰٓـِٔيْ لَمْ يَحِضْنَ ۗ وَاُولَاتُ الْاَحْمَالِ اَجَلُهُنَّ اَنْ يَّضَعْنَ حَمْلَهُنَّ ۗ

8. And those of your women who despair of menstruation, if you have a doubt, then prescribed time is three months, and of those too who have not had their courses. And the pregnant women, their prescribed time is that they lay down their burden. (65 : 4)

Hadis:

عن ثوبان، قال: قال رسول الله صلى الله عليه وسلم: ايما إمرأة سألت زوجها طلاقاً فى غير ما بأس، فحرام عليها رائحة الجنة.

(احمد و ترمذي)

Saoban reported that the Messenger of Allah said, "Whichever woman asks her husband for divorce without fault, the fragrance of Paradise is forbidden to her". (Ahmad, Tirmizi)

عن ابن عمر، أن النبي صلى الله عليه وسلم قال: ابغض الحلال إلى الله الطلاق. (ابو داؤد)

Ibn Omer reported that the Messenger of Allah said, "The most detestable of lawful things near Allah is divorce." (Abu Daud)

عن عبدالله بن عمر: أنه طلق امرأة له وهى حائض، فذكر عمر لرسول الله صلي الله عليه وسلم، فتغيظ فيه رسول الله صلى الله عليه وسلم ثم قال: ليراجعها ثم يمسكها حتى تطهر، ثم تحيض فتطهر فإن بدا له أن يطلقها فليطلقها طاهراً قبل أن يمسها فتلك العدة التى امر الله أن تطلق لها النسأء. (متفق عليه)

Abdullah bin Omar reported that he divorced his wife while she was under menstruation. Omer mentioned it to the Prophet. The Prophet became enraged at it and said, "Take her back and keep her till she becomes clean and then menstruates and then becomes clean. If it appears to him to divorce her afterwards, let him divorce her while she is clean before he touches her. This is the period of waiting which Allah enjoins for the divorce of women." (Bukhari, Muslim)

عن عائشة، قالت: سمعت رسول الله صلى الله عليه وسلم يقول: لاطلاق ولاعتاق فى اغلاق. (ابو داؤد وابن ماجه)

Ayesha reported I heard the Messenger of Allah saying, "There is no divorce and no emancipation by force." (Abu Daud, Ibn Majah)

عن ابن عباس، قال: جاء رجل الى النبى صلى الله عليه وسلم فقال: أن لى امرأة لا ترد يد لامس، فقال النبى صلى الله عليه وسلم: طلقها فقال: انى احبها قال: امسكها اذاً. (ابو داؤد نسائى)

Ibn-Abbas reported that a man came to the Prophet and said: "I have got a wife who never rejects anyone who contacts (for my money). The Prophet said, "Divorce her!" The man said, "But I love her." He said, "Keep her in that case."

(Abu Daud, Nasai)

عن محمود بن لبيد قال: أخبر رسول الله صلى الله عليه وسلم عن رجل طلق امرأته ثلث تطليقا جميعا، فقام غضبان، ثم قال: ايلعب بكتاب الله عز و جل و انا بين اظهركم؟ (نسائی)

Mahamud bin Labeed reported that the Messenger of Allah was informed about a man who gave three divorces at a time to his wife. Then he got up enraged and said, "Is the Book of the Almighty and Glorious Allah being made a Plaything while I am still among you?"

(Nasai)

عن معاذ بن جبل، قال: قال لی رسول الله صلى الله عليه و سلم: يا معاذ! ما خلق الله شيا على وجه الارض احب اليه من العتاق، ولا خلق الله شيئاً علي وجه الارض ابغض اليه من الطلاق. (دارقطنی)

Muaz bin Jabal reported : the Messenger of Allah said to me ; "O Muaz ! God created nothing on the face of the earth more dear to Him than emancipation (of Slaves) and God created nothing on the face of the earth more dislikable to Him than divorces."

(Darqutni)

عن علی، عن النبی صلى الله عليه و سلم قال: لاطلاق قبل نكاح، ولاعتاق الابعد ملك، ولا وصال فی صيام، ولايتم بعد احتلام، ولارضاع بعد فطام، ولاصمت يوم إلى الليل. (مشكواة)

Ali reported from the Prophet who said, "There is no divorce before marriage, and no emancipation but after possession, and no coition in fasting, and no orphanage after maturity and no suckling after weaning, and no silence of one day up to night."

(Mishkat)

عن سعيد بن المسيب ، قال : قال عمر بن الخطاب ايما امراة طلقت فحاضت حيضة او حيضتين ، ثم رفعتها حيضتها ، فانها تنتظر تسعة اشهر ، فان بان بها حمل فذلك ، و الا اعتدت بعد التسعة الاشهر ثلثة اشهر ، ثم حلت. (مالك)

Sayeed bin al-Musayyab reported that Omar bin al-Khattab said, "Whoso woman had been divorced and then she had one or two menstrual discharges, and then the menstruation stopped, she should waite for nine months. If pregnancy is disclosed therein, that is (to complete), and if not, she would wait for three months after nine months and then she is lawful (for others)."

(Malik)

عن المسور بن مخرمة: ان سبيعة الاسلمية نفست بعد وفات زوجها بليال ، فجاءت النبى صلى الله عليه وسلم ، فا ستاذ نته ان تنكح ، فاذن لها ، فنكحت. (بخارى)

Meswar bin Makhramah reported that Sabaia' a al Aslamiyah was delivered of a child a few nights after the death of her husband. She came to the Prophet and sought his permission to get married. He permitted her and then she wedded (Bukhari).

Remarks

1. The Arabic word Talaq literaly means freeing or the undoing of a knot. Legally, Talaq is a means of dissolving the contract of marriage in abnormal circumstances. This dissolution is only possible in contractual form of marriage, because it is a natural law that the dissatified couple should be separated from the marrage tie for the welfare of the house-hold, children and society.

2. Talaq or Divorce is an ancient institution and all nations except Hindus had adopted it in marital relations. Islam reformed all the forms of divorce and gave it a new and most complete shape. Islam affords certain rights both to man and woman, which were not given by any religion or legislator. At the same time it puts a check on divorce by

saying: of all the thirgs allowed, the most abominable to to Allah is divorce. Thus the holy Propet declared divorce to be the most hateful of all things he permitted. And it is due to this that divorce takes place rarely among the Muslims, compared with the large number of divorces in other nations. Thus the Muslims are mentally trained to face the difficulties of married life along with its comforts, and to avoid the disruption of family relations as long as possible, turning to divorce only as a last resort.

3. The right of wife to claim Talaq is recognized by the Holy Quran and Hadith. The wife's right to divorce by returning her dowry is called Khula (خلع). This is a right of divorce given by the husband to to a wife on the occurrence of a contingency If contingency arises the wife may choose to dissolve the marriage.

4. Divorce may be given orally, or in writing, but it must take place it the presence of witnesses. Whatever the words actually used, they must expressly convey the intention that the marriage tie is being dissolved.

5. There are three principal forms of divorce as recognised by the jurists i.e. (i) Talaq-e-Ahsan طلاق احسن (ii) Talaq-e-Hasan طلاق حسن and (iii)Talaq-e-Bidat طلاق بدعه.

6. Every divorce must be followed by a period of waiting called iddat عدت. The Iddat period among others serves the purpose of affording the parties a chance of reconciliation. In case of a consummated marriage the period of waiting after divorce is three courses. In absence of this incident of menses as in the case of young girls and old women, the iddat is three months after divorce. In case of a pregnant woman, Iddat is upto the time of delivery. If there is no consummation of marriage, there is no Iddat.

7. Divorce can not be effected during the period of menstruation, because in the menstrual period there is no change of conjugal relationship. It can be done at the time of Tohar (طہر) or the period of purity.*

*These remarks have been compiled with the help of the English translation of Miskhat by M. Fazlul Karim, and the Religion of Islam by Md Ali (N A)

RIGHTS AND DUTIES

(i) Husband & Wife

QURAN:

وَلَهُنَّ مِثْلُ الَّذِي عَلَيْهِنَّ بِالْمَعْرُوفِ وَلِلرِّجَالِ عَلَيْهِنَّ دَرَجَةٌ

1. And women shall have rights similar to the rights against them, according to what is equitable. But men have a degree (of advantage) over them. (2 : 228)

أُحِلَّ لَكُمْ لَيْلَةَ الصِّيَامِ الرَّفَثُ إِلَىٰ نِسَائِكُمْ هُنَّ لِبَاسٌ لَّكُمْ وَأَنتُمْ لِبَاسٌ لَّهُنَّ عَلِمَ اللَّهُ
أَنَّكُمْ كُنتُمْ تَخْتَانُونَ أَنفُسَكُمْ فَتَابَ عَلَيْكُمْ وَعَفَا عَنكُمْ فَالْآنَ بَاشِرُوهُنَّ وَابْتَغُوا مَا كَتَبَ اللَّهُ لَكُمْ

2. Permitted to you on the night of the fasts is the approach to your wives. They are your garments and you are their garment. God knows what you used to do secretly among yourselves. But He turned to you and forgave you; so now associate with them. And seek what God has ordained for you. (2 : 187)

وَآتُوا النِّسَاءَ صَدُقَاتِهِنَّ نِحْلَةً فَإِن طِبْنَ لَكُمْ عَن شَيْءٍ مِّنْهُ نَفْسًا فَكُلُوهُ هَنِيئًا مَّرِيئًا ۝

3. And give the women (on marriage) their dower as a free gift; but if they, of their own good pleasure, remit any part of it to you, take it andenjoy it wtth right good cheer. (4 : 4)

لِّلرِّجَالِ نَصِيبٌ مِّمَّا تَرَكَ الْوَالِدَانِ وَالْأَقْرَبُونَ وَلِلنِّسَاءِ نَصِيبٌ مِّمَّا تَرَكَ الْوَالِدَانِ
وَالْأَقْرَبُونَ مِمَّا قَلَّ مِنْهُ أَوْ كَثُرَ نَصِيبًا مَّفْرُوضًا

4. From what is left by parents and those nearest related there is a share for man and a share for woman, whether the property be small or large, a determinate share. (4 : 7)

يا أيها الذين آمنوا لا يحل لكم أن ترثوا النساء كرها ولا تعضلوهن لتذهبوا ببعض ما آتيتموهن
إلا أن يأتين بفاحشة مبينة وعاشروهن بالمعروف فإن كرهتموهن فعسى أن تكرهوا شيئا ويجعل الله
فيه خيرا كثيرا

5. O you who believe! you are forbidden to inherit women against their will. Nor should you treat them with harshness, that you may take away part of the dower you have given them, except where they have been guilty of open lewdness; on the contrary live with them on a footing of kindness and equity. If you take a dislike to them, it may be that you dislike a thing and God brings about through it a great deal of good. (4 : 19)

الرجال قوامون على النساء بما فضل الله بعضهم على بعض وبما أنفقوا من أموالهم
فالصالحات قانتات حافظات للغيب بما حفظ الله واللاتي تخافون نشوزهن فعظوهن واهجروهن في
المضاجع واضربوهن فإن أطعنكم فلا تبغوا عليهن سبيلا

6. Men are the protectors and maintainers of women, because God has given the one more (strength) than the other, and because they support them from their means. Therefore the righteous women are devoutly obedient, and guard in (the husband's) absence what God would have them guard. As to those women on whose part you fear disloyalty and ill-conduct, admonish them (first), (next) refuse to share their beds (and last) beat then (lightly); but if they return to obedience, seek not against them means (of annoyance). (4 : 34)

هو الذي خلقكم من نفس واحدة وجعل منها زوجها ليسكن إليها

7. It is He who created you from a single person, and made his mate of like nature, in order that he might take rest in her (in love). (7 : 189)

ومن آياته أن خلق لكم من أنفسكم أزواجا لتسكنوا إليها وجعل بينكم مودة ورحمة

8. And of His signs is this, that He created mates for you from yourselves that you might take rest in them, and He ordained between you love and compassion. (30 : 21)

أَسْكِنُوهُنَّ مِنْ حَيْثُ سَكَنتُم مِّن وُجْدِكُمْ وَلَا تُضَارُّوهُنَّ لِتُضَيِّقُوا عَلَيْهِنَّ وَإِن كُنَّ
أُولَاتِ حَمْلٍ فَأَنفِقُوا عَلَيْهِنَّ حَتَّىٰ يَضَعْنَ حَمْلَهُنَّ

9. Lodge them where you live according to your means, and injure them not to straiten them. And if they are pregnant, spend on them until they lay down their burden. (65 : 6)

مَنْ عَمِلَ صَالِحًا مِّن ذَكَرٍ أَوْ أُنثَىٰ وَهُوَ مُؤْمِنٌ فَلَنُحْيِيَنَّهُ حَيَاةً طَيِّبَةً وَلَنَجْزِيَنَّهُمْ أَجْرَهُم بِأَحْسَنِ
مَا كَانُوا يَعْمَلُونَ

10. Whoever does good, whether male or female, and is a believer we shall certainly make him live a good life, and we shall certainly give them their reward for the best of what they did. (16 : 97)

HADIS :

عن عائشة ، قالت : قال رسول الله صلى الله عليه وسلم : خيركم
خيركم لاهله ، و أنا خيركم لاهلي ، وإذا مات صاحبكم فدعوه .
(ترمذي ، دارمي)

Ayesha reported that the Messenger of Allah said, "The best of you is he who is best of you to his family, and I am the best of you to my family; and when your companion dies, desist from (descrbiing his short comings)." (Tirmizi, Darmi)

عن ابى مسعود ، قال : قال رسول الله صلى الله عليه وسلم : إذا
نفق المسلم نفقة على اهله وهو يحتسبها كانت له صدقة . (متفق عليه)

Abu Mas'ud reported that the Messenger of Allah said, "Whenever a Muslim spends something over his family hoping for its (reward), there is an act of charity for him." (Bukhari, Muslim)

عن أبى أمامة، عن النبى صلى الله عليه وسلم انه يقول: ما استفاد المومن بعد تقوي الله خيراً له من زوجة صالحة، إن امرها اطاعته، و إن نظر إليها سرته، و إن اقسم عليها ابر ته و إن غاب عنها نصحته فى نفسها و ماله. (ابن ماجه)

Abu Omamah reported from the Messenger of Allah who used to say, "Next to fear of Allah the believer finds nothing good for him than a virtuous wife. If he bids her, she obeys him; if he looks at her, she gives him pleasure; if he gives her a promise, she fulfils it, and if he is absent from her, she guards herself and his property."

(Ibn Majah)

عن عبدالله بن زمعة، قال: قال رسول الله صلى الله عليه وسلم: لايجلد احدكم امراته جلد العبد ثم يجامعها فى آخر اليوم. (متفق عليه)

Abdullah-bin-Zam'ah reported that the Messenger of Allah said, "None of you shall whip his wife the whipping of a slave, and afterwards cohabit with her at the end of the day." (Bukhari, Muslim)

عن أبي هريرة، قال: قال رسول الله صلى الله عليه وسلم: إذا دعا الرجل إمراته إلى فراشه فابت، فبات غضبان، لعنتها الملائكة حتى تصبح، و فى رواية لهما قال: والذى نفسى بيده ما من رجل يدعو إمراته إلى فراشه فتابى عليه، إلا كان الذي فى السماء ساخطاً عليها حتى يرضى عنها. (متفق عليه)

Abu Hurairah reported that the Messenger of Allah said, "Whenever a man calls his wife to his bed and she refuses, and then he passes the night in an angry mood, the angels curse her till she gets up at dawn. According to another report (quoted by Bukhari and Muslim) he said "By Him in Whose Hand there stands my life, there is no man who calls his wife to his bed and she turns away from him, except that He Who is in heaven is displeased with her, till he becomes pleased with her."

(Bukhari, Muslim)

عن أبي هريرة، قال : قال رسول الله صلى الله عليه وسلم :
لوكنت آمر احداً أن يسجد لأحد، لأمرت المراة أن تسجد لزوجها.
(ترمذى)

Abu Hurairah reported that the Massenger of Allah said, "Had I enjoined anybody to make prostration to anybody, I would have enjoined a woman to prostrate before her husband." (Tirmizi)

عن حكيم بن معاوية، عن ابيه، قال: قلت: يا رسول الله ما حق
زوجة أحدنا عليه؟ قال: أن تطعمها إذا طعمت، وتكسوها إذا اكتسيت:
ولاتضرب الوجه، ولاتقبح، ولاتهجر إلاّ في البيت.
(احمد، أبوداؤد، ابن ماجه)

Hakim-bin-Muawiyah from his father reported : I asked, "O Messenger of Allah ! what rights has the wife of one among us got over him?" He said, "It is that you shall feed her while feeding yourslef, that you shall clothe her when you clothe yourself, that you shall not slap (her) on the face, nor revile (her), nor leave (her) alone except within the house." (Ahmad, Abu Daud, Ibn Majah)

عن أبي هريرة، قال: قال رسول الله صلى الله عليه وسلم: ليس
منا من خبب امرأة على زوجها، أو عبداً على سيده . (أبوداؤد)

Abu Hurrairah reported that the Messenger of Allah said. "He is not of us who poisons the mind of a woman against her husband, or a slave against his master." (Abu Daud)

(2) PARENTS AND CHILDREN

QURAN:

وإذ أخذنا ميثاق بني إسرائيل لا تعبدون إلا الله وبالوالدين إحسانا

1. And remember we took covenant from the children of Israel (to this effect) that you shall serve none but Allah, and treat with kindness your parents. (2 : 83)

قل تعالوا أتل ما حرم ربكم عليكم ألا تشركوا به شيئا وبالوالدين إحسانا ولا تقتلوا أولادكم من إملاق نحن
نرزقكم وإياهم

2. Say : "Come I will rehearse what Allah has (really) prohibited you from : join not anything as equal with Him; be good to your parents; kill not your children on a plea of want;—we provide sustenance for you and for them." (6 : 151)

ووصينا الإنسان بوالديه إحسانا حملته أمه كرها ووضعته كرها وحمله وفصاله ثلاثون شهرا حتى إذا بلغ
أشده وبلغ أربعين سنة قال رب أوزعني أن أشكر نعمتك التي أنعمت علي وعلى والدي وأن أعمل
صالحا ترضاه وأصلح لي في ذريتي إني تبت إليك وإني من المسلمين ۝ أولئك الذين نتقبل عنهم أحسن
ما عملوا ونتجاوز عن سيئاتهم في أصحاب الجنة وعد الصدق الذي كانوا يوعدون ۝

3. And We have enjoined on man kindness to his parents. His mother bore him with trouble and she brought him forth in pain. And the bearing of him and the weaning of him is thirty months. At length when he attains his maturity and reaches forty years, he says: My Lord, grant me that I may give thanks for Thy favour, which Thou hast bestowed on me and on both my parents, and that I may do good acceptable to Thee, and be gracisum to me in respect of my off spring. Truly I turn to Thee, and truly I am of those whose who submit. Such are they from whom We shall accept the best of what they do and pass

by their ill deeds — among the owners of the Garden. A promise of truth, which they were promised. (46:15,16).

وَوَصَّيْنَا الْاِنْسَانَ بِوَالِدَيْهِ حَمَلَتْهُ اُمُّهٗ وَهْنًا عَلٰى وَهْنٍ وَّفِصٰلُهٗ فِيْ عَامَيْنِ اَنِ اشْكُرْ لِيْ وَلِوَالِدَيْكَ اِلَيَّ الْمَصِيْرُ ۝

4. And We have enjoined on man concerning his parents — his mother bore him with travail upon travail and his weaning took two years—saying : Give thanks to Me and to your parents. To Me is the eventual comming. (31-14).

يٰٓاَيُّهَا الَّذِيْنَ اٰمَنُوْا لَا تَتَّخِذُوْٓا اٰبَآءَكُمْ وَاِخْوَانَكُمْ اَوْلِيَآءَ اِنِ اسْتَحَبُّوا الْكُفْرَ عَلَى الْاِيْمَانِ ۭ وَمَنْ يَّتَوَلَّهُمْ مِّنْكُمْ
فَاُولٰٓئِكَ هُمُ الظّٰلِمُوْنَ ۝ قُلْ اِنْ كَانَ اٰبَآؤُكُمْ وَاَبْنَآؤُكُمْ وَاِخْوَانُكُمْ وَاَزْوَاجُكُمْ وَعَشِيْرَتُكُمْ وَاَمْوَالُ اقْتَرَفْتُمُوْهَا
وَتِجَارَةٌ تَخْشَوْنَ كَسَادَهَا وَمَسٰكِنُ تَرْضَوْنَهَآ اَحَبَّ اِلَيْكُمْ مِّنَ اللّٰهِ وَرَسُوْلِهٖ وَجِهَادٍ فِيْ سَبِيْلِهٖ فَتَرَبَّصُوْا حَتّٰى
يَاْتِيَ اللّٰهُ بِاَمْرِهٖ ۭ وَاللّٰهُ لَا يَهْدِي الْقَوْمَ الْفٰسِقِيْنَ ۝

5. O you who believe ! Take not for protectors your fathers an your brothers if they love Infidelity above Faith : If any of you do so, they do wrong. Say : If it be that your fathers, your sons, your brothsers, your mates or your kindred; and the wealth you have gained and the commerce in which you fear a decline; and the dwellings in which you delight—are dearer to you than God, or His Apostle, or the striving in His cause;—then wait until God brings about His decision; and Allah guides not the rebellious. (9:23, 24).

وَقَضٰى رَبُّكَ اَلَّا تَعْبُدُوْٓا اِلَّآ اِيَّاهُ وَبِالْوَالِدَيْنِ اِحْسَانًا ۭ اِمَّا يَبْلُغَنَّ عِنْدَكَ الْكِبَرَ اَحَدُهُمَآ اَوْ كِلٰهُمَا فَلَا تَقُلْ لَّهُمَآ
اُفٍّ وَّلَا تَنْهَرْهُمَا وَقُلْ لَّهُمَا قَوْلًا كَرِيْمًا ۝ وَاخْفِضْ لَهُمَا جَنَاحَ الذُّلِّ مِنَ الرَّحْمَةِ وَقُلْ رَّبِّ ارْحَمْهُمَا كَمَا
رَبَّيٰنِيْ صَغِيْرًا ۝

6. And they Lord hath decreed that ye serve none but Him, and that ye be kind to parents. If either or both of them reach old age with thee, say not "Fie" to them, nor chide them, and speak to them a generous word. And lower to them the wing of humility out of mercy, and say; My Lord, have mercy on them, as they brought me up (when I was) little. (17:23, 24).

يَسْأَلُونَكَ مَاذَا يُنْفِقُونَ قُلْ مَا أَنْفَقْتُمْ مِنْ خَيْرٍ فَلِلْوَالِدَيْنِ

7. They ask thee what they should spend (in Charity). Say: Whatfever you spend that is good, is for parents. (2:215).

وَإِذَا قِيلَ لَهُمُ اتَّبِعُوا مَا أَنْزَلَ اللهُ قَالُوا بَلْ نَتَّبِعُ مَا أَلْفَيْنَا عَلَيْهِ آبَاءَنَا
أَوَلَوْ كَانَ آبَاؤُهُمْ لَا يَعْقِلُونَ شَيْئًا وَلَا يَهْتَدُونَ

8. When it is said to them: "Follow what God has revealed"; they say, "Nay ! we shall follow the ways of our fathers". What ! even though their fathers were void of wisdom and guidence. (2:170).

وَوَصَّيْنَا الْإِنْسَانَ بِوَالِدَيْهِ حُسْنًا وَإِنْ جَاهَدَاكَ لِتُشْرِكَ بِي مَا لَيْسَ لَكَ بِهِ عِلْمٌ فَلَا تُطِعْهُمَا

9. And we have enjoined on man kindness to his parents. But if they contend with thee to associate (others) with Me, of which thou hast no knowledge, obey them not. (29:8).

يَا أَيُّهَا الَّذِينَ آمَنُوا قُوا أَنْفُسَكُمْ وَأَهْلِيكُمْ نَارًا وَقُودُهَا النَّاسُ وَالْحِجَارَةُ

10. O you who believe ! save your families from a Fire whose fuel is men and stones- (66:6).

وَالْوَالِدَاتُ يُرْضِعْنَ أَوْلَادَهُنَّ حَوْلَيْنِ كَامِلَيْنِ لِمَنْ أَرَادَ أَنْ يُتِمَّ الرَّضَاعَةَ وَعَلَى الْمَوْلُودِ لَهُ رِزْقُهُنَّ وَكِسْوَتُهُنَّ
بِالْمَعْرُوفِ لَا تُكَلَّفُ نَفْسٌ إِلَّا وُسْعَهَا لَا تُضَارَّ وَالِدَةٌ بِوَلَدِهَا وَلَا مَوْلُودٌ لَهُ بِوَلَدِهِ وَعَلَى الْوَارِثِ مِثْلُ ذَٰلِكَ
فَإِنْ أَرَادَا فِصَالًا عَنْ تَرَاضٍ مِنْهُمَا وَتَشَاوُرٍ فَلَا جُنَاحَ عَلَيْهِمَا وَإِنْ أَرَدْتُمْ أَنْ تَسْتَرْضِعُوا أَوْلَادَكُمْ فَلَا جُنَاحَ
عَلَيْكُمْ إِذَا سَلَّمْتُمْ مَا آتَيْتُمْ بِالْمَعْرُوفِ

11. The mothers shall give suck to their offsprings for two whole years, if the father desires to complete the term. But he shall bear the cost of their food and clothing on equitable terms. No so ul shall have a burden laid on it greater than it can bear. No mother shall be treated unfairly on acconnt of her child, nor father on account of his child. An heir shall be chargable in the same way. If they both decide on weaning, by mutual consent, and after due consulation, there is no blame on

them. If ye decide on a foster-mother for your offspring, there is no blame on you provided ye pay (the mother) what ye offered, on equitable terms. (2:233).

وَإِذَا الْمَوْءُدَةُ سُئِلَتْ ۞ بِأَيِّ ذَنْبٍ قُتِلَتْ ۞

12. And when the one buried alive is asked for what sin she was killed. (81:8, 9).

Hadis :

عن أبي هريرة، قال: قال رجل: يا رسول الله : من أحق بحسن صحابتي؟ قال: امك، قال: ثم من؟ قال: امك، قال: ثم من؟ قال: امك، قال: ثم من؟ قال: أبوك، وفي رواية قال: امك ثم امك ثم اباك ثم ادناك ادناك. (متفق عليه)

Abu Hurairah reported that a man enquired, "O Apostle of Allah! Who is the most proper person for my good associatson?" "Thy mother", replied he. Then he asked who was next? "Thy mother", replied he. Then he asked who was next? 'Thy mother", he replied. He enquired: Who was next? "Thy father", he said. In another narration, he replied, "Thy mother, then thy mother, then thy mother, and then thy father and then thy nearest relatives and then thy nearer relatives."

(Bukhari, Muslim)

عن عبدالله بن عمرو، قال: قال: رسول الله صلى الله عليه وسلم: من الكبائر شتم الرجل والديه، قالوا: يا رسول الله! وهل يشتم الرجل والديه؟ قال: نعم، يسب أبا الرجل فيسب اباه و يسب امه فيسب امه.

(متفق عليه)

Abdullah bin Amr reported that the Messenger of Allah said, "Of the greatest sins there is a man's abusing his parents." They enquired, "O Apostle of Allah! does any man abuse his parents? "Yes", said he,

"He abuses the father of a man who abuses his father (in return), and he abuses the father of a man who abusus his mother (in return)."
(Bukhari, Muslim).

عن عبدالله بن عمرو، قال: رسول الله صلى الله عليه وسلم: رضى الرب فى رضى الوالد، وسخط الرب في سخط الوالد. (ترمذى)

Abdullah bin Amr reported that the Messenger of Allah said, "The pleasure of Lord is in the pleasure of the father, and the displeasure of the Lord is in tne displeasure of the father." (Tirmizi)

عن إبن عمر، أن رجلا اتى النبى صلى الله عليه وسلم، فقال: يا رسول الله! إنى أصبت ذنباً عظيماً، فهل لى من توبة؟ قال: هل لك من ام؟ قال: لا، قال: وهل لك من خالة؟ قال نعم، قال فبرها.

(ترمذي)

Ibn Omar reported that a man came to the Holy Prophet and enquired, "O Apostle of Allah ! I have certainiy committed a great sin. Is there any r pentance for me?" He enquired, "Have you got mother?" "No", replied he. He asked, "Have you got mother's sister?" "Yes", said he. He said, "Then accord her good treatment." (Tirmizi).

عن أبى امامة، أن رجلا قال: يا رسول الله! ما حق الوالدين على ولد هما؟ قال: هما جنتك ونارك. (إبن ماجه)

Abu Oman.ah reported that a man asked the Messenger of Allah, "What are the rights of the parents over the son?" He replied, "They are your Paradise and Hell." (Ibn Majah).

عن ابى بكره، قال: قال رسول الله صلى الله عليه و سلم: كل الذنوب يغفر الله تعالى منها ماشاء إلا عقوق الوالدين فانه يعجل لصاحبه فى الحيواة قبل المات. (البيهقى)

Abu Bakrah reported that the Messenger of Allah said, "The Almighty Allah may pardon all sins He pleases except disobedience to parents, and verily. He hastens (punishment) in life before death for one who commitis it."
(Baihaqi).

عن ابن عباس، قال: قال رسول الله صلى الله عليه وسلم: ما من ولد بار ينظر الى والديه نظرة رحمة إلا كتب الله له بكل نظرة حجة مبرورة، قالوا: وان نظر كل يوم مائة مرة، ؟ قال: نعم، الله اكبر واطيب. (البيهقي)

Ibn Abbas reported that the Messenger of Allah said, "No obedient son looks toward his parents with kindness but Allah writes for him one accepted pilgrimage for every such look." They enquired, "And if he looks hundred times every day?" "Yes", said he, "Allah is Greatest and most Benificient. (Baihaqi).

عن ابن عباس، قال: قال رسول الله صلي الله عليه وسلم: من كانت له انثي فلم يئدها ولم يهنها، ولم يؤثر ولده عليها—يعنى الذكور— ادخله الله الجنة. (ابو داؤد)

Ibn Abbas reported that the Messenger of Allah said, "Whoever has got a female child and then does neither bury her alive, nor treats her unjustly, nor perfers his son to her, meaning male children, Allah will admit him in Paradise." (Abu Daud).

عن عائشة، قالت: جاء اعرابى الى النبى صلى الله عليه وسلم، فقال: اتقبلون الصبيان؟ فما نقبلهم، فقال النبى صلى الله عليه وسلم: او املك لك ان نزع الله من قلبك الرحمة؟ (متفق عليه)

Ayesha reported that an Arab came to the Holy Prophet and said, "What! do you kiss the children? But we don't kiss them." Then the Messenger of Allah said, "Have I power for thee (to bestow kindness) while Allah has taken kindness out of thy heart?" (Bukhari, Muslims).

عن ابى هريرة، قال: قال رسول الله صلى الله عليه وسلم: ما من مولود الا يولد على الفطرة، فابواه يهودانه أوينصرانه ويمجسانه، كما تنتج البهيمة بهيمة جمعاء، هل تحسون فيها من جدعاء؟ ثم يقول: فطرة

الله التى فطر الناس عليها لاتبديل لخلق الله ذلك الدين القيم .

(متفق عليه)

Abu Hurairah reported that the Messenger of Allah said, "There is no child but is born up on nature (Islam), then his parents make him a Jew or a Chiristian or a Magian, as a beast is born entire in all its limbs (without defect). Do you see one among them (born) mutilated?" Then he said, the nature of Allah is in which he made man. There is no Changing in Allah's creation. This is the right religion." (30 : 30 Q).

(Bukhari, Muslim).

عن عمرو بن شعيب، عن ابيه، عن جده . ان رجلا اتى النبى صلى الله عليه وسلم فقال : ان لى مالا، وان والدى يحتاج الى مالى، قال انت ومالك لوالدك، ان اولادكم من اطيب كسبكم، كلوا من كسب اولادكم.

(ابو داؤد، ابن ماجه)

Amr bin Shuaib from his father, from his grandfather reported that a man came to the Prophet and said, "Verily I have got wealth and my father is in want of my wealth." He said, "Both you and your wealth belong to your father. Verily your children are the best of your earning. So eat of the earnings of your children."

(Abu Daud, Ibn Majah)

عن انس، قال: شهدنا بنت رسول الله عليه وسلم تدفن، ورسول الله صلى الله عليه وسلم جالس على القبر، فرايت عينيه تدمعان، فقال: هل فيكم من احد لم يقارف الليلة؟ فقال ابو طلحة : انا، قال فانزل في قبرها فنزل فى قبرها.

(بخاري)

Anas reported, "We were present at the burial of a daughter of the Messenger of Allah, and the Holy Prophet was seated near the grave. I saw his two eyes were shedding tears. He said, "Is there anybody amongst you who had no intercourse with his wife last night?" "I", replied Abu Talha. He said, "Then get down into her grave." He then got down into her grave. (Bukhari).

(3) FAMILY MEMBERS AND RELATIVES

Quran:

وَإِذْ أَخَذْنَا مِيثَاقَ بَنِي إِسْرَاءِيلَ لَا تَعْبُدُونَ إِلَّا اللَّهَ وَبِالْوَالِدَيْنِ إِحْسَانًا وَذِي الْقُرْبَىٰ

And remember we took a covenant from the chidren of Israel (to this effect) that you shall serve none but God; and treat with kindness your parents and kindred. (2 : 83)

وَآتَى الْمَالَ عَلَىٰ حُبِّهِ ذَوِي الْقُرْبَىٰ

2. (It is righteousness to) spend your substance, out of love for Him, for your kin. (2 : 177)

يَسْأَلُونَكَ مَاذَا يُنْفِقُونَ ۖ قُلْ مَا أَنْفَقْتُمْ مِنْ خَيْرٍ فَلِلْوَالِدَيْنِ وَالْأَقْرَبِينَ

3. They ask thee what they should spend (in charity). Say whatever you spend that is good, is for parents and kindred (2 : 215)

وَإِذَا حَضَرَ الْقِسْمَةَ أُولُو الْقُرْبَىٰ وَالْيَتَامَىٰ وَالْمَسَاكِينُ فَارْزُقُوهُمْ مِنْهُ وَقُولُوا لَهُمْ قَوْلًا مَعْرُوفًا ۝

4. And if at the time of division other relatives, or orphans, or poor, are present, feed them (out of the property) and speak to them words of kindness and justice. (4 : 8)

الَّذِينَ يُوفُونَ بِعَهْدِ اللَّهِ وَلَا يَنْقُضُونَ الْمِيثَاقَ ۝ وَالَّذِينَ يَصِلُونَ مَا أَمَرَ اللَّهُ بِهِ أَنْ يُوصَلَ

5. (Only men of understanding mind—) those who fulfil the pact of Allah, and break not the covenant, and those who join that which Allah has bidden to be joined. (13 : 20, 21)

إِنَّ اللَّهَ يَأْمُرُ بِالْعَدْلِ وَالْإِحْسَانِ وَإِيتَاءِ ذِي الْقُرْبَىٰ (النحل ٩٠)

6. Surely Allah enjoins justice and kindness (to others) and the giving to the kindred. (16 : 90)

وَآتِ ذَا الْقُرْبَىٰ حَقَّهُ

7. And give to the near of kin his due. (17 : 26)

وَلَا يَأْتَلِ أُولُو الْفَضْلِ مِنْكُمْ وَالسَّعَةِ أَنْ يُؤْتُوا أُولِي الْقُرْبَىٰ

8. And let not possessors of grace and abundance among you swear not to give to the near of kin. (24 : 22)

ذَٰلِكَ الَّذِي يُبَشِّرُ اللَّهُ عِبَادَهُ الَّذِينَ آمَنُوا وَعَمِلُوا الصَّالِحَاتِ ۗ قُلْ لَا أَسْأَلُكُمْ عَلَيْهِ أَجْرًا إِلَّا الْمَوَدَّةَ فِي الْقُرْبَىٰ

9. This it is of which Allah gives the good news to his servants who believe and do good. Say I ask of you naught in return for it but love for relatives. (42 : 23)

Hadis :

عن إبي هريرة، قال : قال رسول الله صلى الله عليه وسلم: خلق الله الخلق، فلما فرغ منه قامت الرحم فاخذت بحقوى الرحمن ، فقال: مه! قالت: هذا مقام العائذ بك من القطعية ، قال: الأ ترضين ان اصل من وصلك و اقطع من قطعك؟ قالت بلى يا رب! قال: فذاك.

(متفق عليه)

Abu Hurairah reported that the Messenger of Allah said, "Allah created creation. When He finished it the blood-tie got up and caught hold of the loin of the Merciful. So He said, "Stop." It said, "This is the place of one who seeks refuge to thee from the severer of blood-tie". He said, "Don't you like I should join the one who joins you and that I should sever connection with one who cuts off connection with you?" It replied, "Yes, O Lord!" He said; "Then let it be so." (Bukhari)

عن جبير بن مطعم، قال: قال رسول الله صلى الله عليه وسلم:
لايدخل الجنة قاطع. (متفق عليه)

Jubair bin Mut'em reported that the Messenger of Allah said, "One who cuts (blood-tie) shall not enter Paradise." (Bukhari; Muslim).

عن أبي هريرة، ان رجلاً، قال: يا رسول الله! ان لى قرابة،
اصلهم ويقطعونى، واحسن اليهم ويسيئون الى، واحلم عنهم ويجهلون
على، فقال: لئن كنت كما قلت فكانما تسفهم الملّ ولايزال معك من الله
ظهير عليهم مادمت على ذلك. (مسلم)

Abu Hurairah reported that a man asked, O Messenger of Allah! (Verily) I have got kindred with whom I live in unity while they treat me badly; I do them good while they do me evil; I am lenient to them, while they are brutal to me." He said "If you are as you say, It is as though you give them pills of hot ashes, and a helper from Allah against them will always be with you, so long as you remain upon that." (Muslim)

عن ابي بكرة، قال: قال رسول الله صلى الله عليه وسلم: ما من
ذنب احري أن يعجل الله لصاحبه العقوبة فى الدنيا، مع ما يدخر له في
الأخرة، من البغى وقطيعة الرحم. (ترمذى ـ ابوداؤد)

Abu Bakrah reported that the Messenger of Allah said, "There is no other sin for the doer of which Allah hastens punishment in the world alongwith what is in store for him in the next world than rebellion and severance of blood-connection." (Tirmizi, Abu Daud)

عن أبي هريرة، قال: قال رسول الله صلى الله عليه وسلم: تعلموا
من أنسابكم ما تصلون به ارحامكم، فأن صلة الرحم محبة فى الاهل،
مشراة فى المال، منسأة فى الأثر. (ترمذي)

Abu Hurairah reported that the Messenger of Allah said, "Learn from your ancestors with what thing to befriend your relations because joining of blood-tie is a cause of love within the household, a means of increase in wealth and a means of delaying death. (Tirmizi)

عن بهز بن حكيم، عن أبيه، عن جده، قال: قلت: يا رسول الله!
من ابر؟ قال امك، قلت ثم من؟ قال: امك، قلت: ثم من؟ قال امك،
قلت: ثم من؟ قال: أباك، ثم الأقرب فالأقرب. (ترمذى - أبوداؤد)

Bahaz-b-Hakeem from his father from his grand-father reported: I asked, "O Messenger of Allah! who is to be most obeyed?" He said, "Your mother." I asked, "Who is next?" He said, "Your mother." I asked, "Wuo is next? He said, "Your mother." I asked, "Who is next?" He said, "Your father and then your near relation. (Tirmizi, Abu Daud)

عن سلمان بن عامر، قال: قال رسول الله صلى الله عليه وسلم:
الصدقة على المسكين صدقة، و هى على ذي الرحم ثنتان صدقة وصلة.
(احمد، ترمذى، نسائي، ابن ماجه)

Salman bin Amer reported that the Holy Prophet said, "Alms to a poor man has one (merit)—Charity, and to a kinsman two (merits)—charity and connection."

(Ahmad, Tirmizi, Nasai, Ibn Majah)

عن أبي هريرة، قال: جاء رجل إلى النبى صلى الله عليه وسلم،
فقال: عندى دينار، قال، انفقه على نفسك، قال: عندى آخر، قال:
انفقه على ولدك، قال: عندي آخر، قال: انفقه على اهلك، قال: عندى
آخر، قال انفقه على خادمك، قال: عندى آخر، قال: انت اعلم.
(ابو داؤد، نسائى)

Abu Hurairah reported that a man came to the Messenger of Allah and said, "I have got a dinar" He said, "Spend it on your self." He said, "I have got another" He said, "Spend it on your child. He said, "I have got another." He said, "Spend it on your wife." He said, "I have got another." He replied, "Spend it on your servent."

He said, "I have got another." He replied, "you know better."
(Abu Daud Nasai)

عن جابر بن سمرة، قال: قال رسول الله صلى الله عليه وسلم: اذا اعطى الله أحدكم خيراً فليبدأ بنفسه واهل بيته. (مسلم)

Jaber bin Samorah reported that the Messenger of Allah said, "When Allah gives wealth to any of you, let him begin with himself and members of his house-hold." (Muslim)

(4) SERVANTS AND SLAVES

Quran:

يٰأَيُّهَا النَّاسُ إِنَّا خَلَقْنٰكُمْ مِّنْ ذَكَرٍ وَّأُنْثٰى وَجَعَلْنٰكُمْ شُعُوبًا وَّقَبَآئِلَ لِتَعَارَفُوا إِنَّ أَكْرَمَكُمْ عِنْدَ اللّٰهِ أَتْقٰكُمْ
إِنَّ اللّٰهَ عَلِيمٌ خَبِيرٌ ۝

1. O mankind, surely We have created you from a male and a female, and made you tribes and families that you may know each other. Surely the noblest of you with Allah is the most dutiful of you. Surely Allah is Knowing, Aware. (49 : 13)

وَأَنْكِحُوا الْأَيٰمٰى مِنْكُمْ وَالصّٰلِحِينَ مِنْ عِبَادِكُمْ وَإِمَآئِكُمْ إِنْ يَّكُونُوا فُقَرَآءَ يُغْنِهِمُ اللّٰهُ مِنْ فَضْلِهِ وَاللّٰهُ وَاسِعٌ عَلِيمٌ ۝
وَلْيَسْتَعْفِفِ الَّذِينَ لَا يَجِدُونَ نِكَاحًا حَتّٰى يُغْنِيَهُمُ اللّٰهُ مِنْ فَضْلِهِ وَالَّذِينَ يَبْتَغُونَ الْكِتٰبَ مِمَّا مَلَكَتْ أَيْمَانُكُمْ فَكَاتِبُوهُمْ
إِنْ عَلِمْتُمْ فِيهِمْ خَيْرًا وَّآتُوهُمْ مِّنْ مَّالِ اللّٰهِ الَّذِيٓ آتٰكُمْ

2. And marry those among you who are single, and those who are fit among your male slaves and your female slaves. If they are needy. Allah will make them free from want out of His grace. And Allah is Ample-giving, Knowing. And let those who cannot find a match keep chaste, until Allah makes them free from want out of His grace. And those of your slaves who ask for a writing (of freedom) give them give them the writing if you know any good in them and give them of the wealth of Allah which He has given you, (29 : 32 , 33)

وَمَنْ لَّمْ يَسْتَطِعْ مِنْكُمْ طَوْلًا أَنْ يَّنْكِحَ الْمُحْصَنٰتِ الْمُؤْمِنٰتِ فَمِنْ مَّا مَلَكَتْ أَيْمَانُكُمْ مِّنْ فَتَيٰتِكُمُ الْمُؤْمِنٰتِ

3. And those of you who have not the means wherewith to wed free believing women, they may wed believing girls from among those whom your right hands possess. (4 : 25)

وَالَّذِينَ هُمْ لِفُرُوجِهِمْ حٰفِظُونَ ۝ إِلَّا عَلٰىٓ أَزْوَاجِهِمْ أَوْ مَا مَلَكَتْ أَيْمَانُهُمْ فَإِنَّهُمْ غَيْرُ مَلُومِينَ ۝

4. (Successful indeed are the believers) who restrain their sexual passions—except in the presence of their mates or those whom their right hands possess, for such surely are not blamable. (23 : 5, 6)

وَمَآ أَدْرٰىكَ مَا الْعَقَبَةُ ۝ فَكُّ رَقَبَةٍ ۝

5. And what will make thee comprehend what the uphill road is? (It is) to free a slave. (90 : 12, 13)

Hadis:

عن عبدالله بن عمر، قال: جاء رجل إلى النبى صلى الله عليه وسلم، فقال: يا رسول الله! كم نعفوا عن الخادم؟ فسكت، ثم أعاد عليه الكلام، فصمت، فلما كانت الثالثة، قال اعفوا عنه كل يوم سبعين مرة.

(أبو داؤد)

Abdullah bin Omer reported that a man came to the Holy Prophet and said, "O Messenger of Allah! How many times shall we pardon a servent?" He remained silent. Then he repeated the question but he remained silent. When it was asked for the third time, he replied, "Pardon him 70 times every day." (Abu Daud)

عن أبى هريرة، قال: قال رسول الله صلى الله عليه وسلم، إذا صنع لاحدكم خادمه طعامه، ثم جاءه به وقد ولى حره ودخانه فليقعده معه فلياكل، وإن كان الطعام مشفوهاً قليلاً فليضع فى يده منه اكلة أو آكلين. (مسلم)

Abu Hurairah reported that the Messenger of Allah said, "When the servant of some one of you prepares his meal and then comes to him therewith, while its heat and vapour rise up, let him make him sit with him and take food. If the food consists of only a few morsels, let him take a morsel or two with his hand therefrom." (Muslim)

عن أبى هريرة، قال: قال رسول الله صلى الله عليه وسلم: للمملوك طعامه وكسوته ولا يكلف من العمل الا ما يطيق. (مسلم)

Abu Hurairah reported that the Messenger of Allah said, "Covenated slane shall get his food and clothing and shall not be troubled with work but what he is capable of." (Muslim)

عن علی، عن النبی صلی الله علیه وسلم انه کان یقول فی مرضه:
الصلاة وما ملكت ايمانكم. (احمد۔ أبو داؤد)

Ali reported from the Messenger of Allah that he was saying in his (last) illness, "Prayer and what your right hands have possessed. (Ahmad, Abu Dauad)

عن أبی بکر الصدیق، عن النبی صلی الله علیه وسلم قال: لا یدخل
الجنة سیٔ الملکة. (ترمذي ۔ ابن ماجه)

Abu Bakr Siddiq reported from the Messenger of Allah who said, "The doer of evil to the slaves shall not enter Paradise."
(Tirmizi—Ibn Majah)

عن أبي أمامة أن رسول الله صلى الله عليه وسلم وهب لعلى غلاماً،
فقال: لا تضربه فانی نهیت عن ضرب اهل الصلاة، وقد رایته یصلی.
(مشکاة)

Abu Omamah reported that the Messenger of Allah presented a slave to Ali and said, "Don't beat him, as I have been prohibited from beating those who pray, and I have indeed seen him praying." (Mishkat)

عن أبي ذر، قال: قال رسول الله صلى الله عليه وسلم: من لائمكم
من مملوكيكم فاطعموه مما تاكلون، واكسوه مما تكسون، ومن لايلائمكم
منهم فبيعوه ولاتعذبوا خلق الله. (احمد۔ ابو داؤد)

Abu Zar reported that the Messenger of Allah said, "whose from your slaves obeys you, give him food out of what you yourself eat, clothe him out of what you yourself wear. And whoso among them does not obey you, sell him and do not inflict punishment on the creation of Allah." (Ahmad, Abu Daud)

عن أنس، قال: خدمت النبى صلى الله عليه وسلم عشر سنين، فما
قال لى: اف ولا: لما صنعت؟ ولا: الا صنعت؟ (متفق عليه)

Anas reported served the Messenger of Allah for 10 years, but he did neither tell me (even) *uff* nor why have you done (this)? nor—why have you not done (this)? (Bukhari, Muslim)

عن أم العصين، قالت: قال رسول الله صلى الله عليه وسلم: إن
امر عليكم عبد مجدع يقودكم بكتاب الله، فاسمعوا له واطيعوا. (مسلم)

Ommul Hussain rcported that the Messenger of Allah said, "If a slave with limbs cut off be put in command over you to guide you by the Book of Allah, listen to him and obey." (Muslim)

(5) THE ORPHANS

QURAN :

وَبِالْوَالِدَيْنِ إِحْسَانًا وَبِذِي الْقُرْبَىٰ وَالْيَتَامَىٰ

1. And kindness to parents, kinsfolk and orphans. (4:36)

وَلْيَخْشَ الَّذِينَ لَوْ تَرَكُوا مِنْ خَلْفِهِمْ ذُرِّيَّةً ضِعَافًا خَافُوا عَلَيْهِمْ فَلْيَتَّقُوا اللَّهَ وَلْيَقُولُوا قَوْلًا سَدِيدًا

2. Let those (disposing of an estate) have the same fear in their minds as they would have for their own if they had left a helpless family behind: Let them fear God, and speak words of appropriate (comfort). (4 : 9)

فَأَمَّا الْيَتِيمَ فَلَا تَقْهَرْ

3. Therefore the orphans, oppress not. (93 : 9)

قُلْ مَا أَنْفَقْتُمْ مِنْ خَيْرٍ فَلِلْوَالِدَيْنِ وَالْأَقْرَبِينَ وَالْيَتَامَىٰ

4. Say: Whatever you spend that is good, is for parents and kindred and orphans. (4: 215)

وَلَا تَقْرَبُوا مَالَ الْيَتِيمِ إِلَّا بِالَّتِي هِيَ أَحْسَنُ حَتَّىٰ يَبْلُغَ أَشُدَّهُ

5. And come not nigh to the orphan's property, except to improve it until he attains the age of full strength. (6 : 152)

إِنَّ الَّذِينَ يَأْكُلُونَ أَمْوَالَ الْيَتَامَىٰ ظُلْمًا إِنَّمَا يَأْكُلُونَ فِي بُطُونِهِمْ نَارًا ۖ وَسَيَصْلَوْنَ سَعِيرًا

6. Those who unjustly eat up the property of orphans, eat up a fire into their own bodies; they will soon be joining a blazing Fire. (4 : 10)

وَآتُوا الْيَتَامَىٰ أَمْوَالَهُمْ ۖ وَلَا تَتَبَدَّلُوا الْخَبِيثَ بِالطَّيِّبِ ۖ وَلَا تَأْكُلُوا أَمْوَالَهُمْ إِلَىٰ أَمْوَالِكُمْ ۚ إِنَّهُ كَانَ حُوبًا كَبِيرًا

7. To orphans restore their property (when they reach their age), nor substitute (your) worthless things for (their) good ones, and devour not their substance (by mixing it up) with your own. For this is indeed a great sin. (4 : 2)

وَابْتَلُوا الْيَتَامَىٰ حَتَّىٰ إِذَا بَلَغُوا النِّكَاحَ فَإِنْ آنَسْتُمْ مِنْهُمْ رُشْدًا فَادْفَعُوا إِلَيْهِمْ أَمْوَالَهُمْ ۖ وَلَا تَأْكُلُوهَا إِسْرَافًا وَبِدَارًا
أَنْ يَكْبَرُوا ۚ وَمَنْ كَانَ غَنِيًّا فَلْيَسْتَعْفِفْ ۖ وَمَنْ كَانَ فَقِيرًا فَلْيَأْكُلْ بِالْمَعْرُوفِ ۚ فَإِذَا دَفَعْتُمْ إِلَيْهِمْ أَمْوَالَهُمْ
فَأَشْهِدُوا عَلَيْهِمْ ۚ وَكَفَىٰ بِاللَّهِ حَسِيبًا

8. Make trial of orphans until they reach the age of marriage; if then you find sound judgement in them, release their property to them, but consume it not wastefully, nor in haste against their growing up. If the guardian is well off, let him claim no remuneration, but if he is poor, let him have for himself what is just and reasonable. (4 : 6)

وَأَنْ تَقُومُوا لِلْيَتَامَىٰ بِالْقِسْطِ ۚ وَمَا تَفْعَلُوا مِنْ خَيْرٍ فَإِنَّ اللَّهَ كَانَ بِهِ عَلِيمًا

9. That you stand firm for justice to orphans. There is not a good deed which you do but God is well acquainted therewith. (4 : 127)

وَيَسْأَلُونَكَ عَنِ الْيَتَامَىٰ ۖ قُلْ إِصْلَاحٌ لَهُمْ خَيْرٌ

10. They ask thee concerning orphans. Say: the best thing to do is what is for their good. (2 : 220)

وَيُطْعِمُونَ الطَّعَامَ عَلٰى حُبِّهٖ مِسْكِيْنًا وَّيَتِيْمًا وَّاَسِيْرًا

11. And they give food, out of love for Him, to the poor and the orphan and the captive. (76 : 9)

اَرَءَيْتَ الَّذِيْ يُكَذِّبُ بِالدِّيْنِ ۞ فَذٰلِكَ الَّذِيْ يَدُعُّ الْيَتِيْمَ ۞ وَلَا يَحُضُّ عَلٰى طَعَامِ الْمِسْكِيْنِ ۞

12. Hast thou seen him who belies religion? That is the one who repulses the orphan, and encousages not the feeding of the indigent. (107 : 1—3)

HADIS :

عن ابی هريرة، قال: قال رسول الله صلى الله عليه وسلم: خير بيت فی المسلمين بيت فيه يتيم يحسن اليه ، وشر بيت فی المسلمين بيت فيه يتيم يساء اليه (ابن ماجه)

Abu Hurairah reported that the Messenger of Allah said, "The best home of Muslims is a home wherein there is an orphan who is treated well; and the worst home of Muslims is a home wherein there is an orphan who is treated badly. (Ibn Majah)

عن عمرو بن شعيب، عن ابيه، عن جده : أن رجلاً اتى النبی صلى الله عليه وسلم فقال: إنی فقير ليس لی شیء، و لی يتيم - فقال : كل من مال يتيمك غير مسرف ولا مبادر ولا متاثل .

(ابو داؤد، نسائی، ابن ماجه)

Amr bin Shuaib from his father, from his grandfather reported that a man came to the Holy Prophet and said, "I am a poor man and I have got nothing; but I have got an orphan." He said, "Eat of the properties of your orphan neither extravagantly, nor with haste, nor by hoarding." (Abu Daud, Nasai. Ibn Majah)

عن سهل بن سعد، قال: قال رسول الله صلى الله عليه وسلم. انا وكافل اليتيم له، ولغيره فى الجنة هكذا، واشار بالسبابة والوسطى وفرج بينهما شيئاً.

Sahal bin Sa'ad reported that the Messenger of Allah said, "I and he who takes charge of an orphan, whether his or of others, shall be in Paradise like this." He hinted with his fore-finger and middle finger leaving nothing between the two. (Bukhari)

عن ابن عباس، قال: قال رسول الله صلى الله عليه وسلم: من آوى يتيماً الى طعامه وشرابه اوجب الله له الجنة البتة، الا أن يعمل ذنباً لا يغفر - ومن عال ثلاث بنات أو مثلهن من الاخوات فادبهن ورحمهن حتى يغنيهن الله اوجب الله له الجنة. فقال رجل: يا رسول الله! أو اثنتين؟ قال أو اثنتين - حتى و قالوا: أو واحدة؟ لقال: واحدة. (بيهقى)

Ibn Abbas reported that the Messenger of Allah said, "Whoso gives shelter to an orphan with his food and drink, Allah will certainly grant for him Paradise unless he has committed a sin which can not be pardoned; and whosoever maintains three girls or sisters similar to them, and gives them training of good manners and is kind to them till Allah makes them free from wants Allah will make Paradise sure for him." A man asked, "O Messenger of Allah! if (they are) two?" He said, "(even) if two." If they had said: "And one," he would have replied, "And one." (Baihaqi)

عن عمرو بن شعيب، عن ابيه، عن جده. ان النبي صلى الله عليه وسلم خطب الناس فقال: الا من ولى يتيماً له مال فليتجر فيه، ولا يتركه حتي تا كله الصدقة. (ترمذى)

Amr bin Shuaib from his father, from his grandfather who reported that the Messenger of Allah addressed the people and said, "Beware whosoever is entrusted with an orphan having property, let him make merchandise therewith, and let him not leave it till zakat eats it up. (Tirmizi)

(6) THE NEIGHBOUR

QURAN :

وَالْجَارِ ذِى الْقُرْبٰى وَالْجَارِ الْجُنُبِ وَالصَّاحِبِ بِالْجَنْۢبِ وَابْنِ السَّبِيْلِ ۙ وَمَا مَلَكَتْ اَيْمَانُكُمْ

1. (And do good to) neighbours who are near, neighbours who are strangers, the companion by your side, the way-farer (you meet), and what your right hands posses. (4 : 36)

HADIS :

عن انس ، قال : قال رسول الله صلى الله عليه وسلم : لايدخل الجنة من لا يامن جاره بوائقه . (مسلم)

Anas reported that the Messenger of Allah said, "One whose neighbour is not safe from his mischiefs shall not enter Paradise." (Muslim)

عن عائشة و ابن عمر عن النبى صلى الله عليه وسلم ، قال : ما زال جبرائيل يوصينى بالجار حتى ظننت انه سيورثه . (متفق عليه)

2. Ayesha and Ibn Omer reported from the Messenger of Allah, who said, "Gabriel did not stop to advise me about neighbour till I thought he would soon make him an heir." (Bukhari, Muslim)

عن ابن مسعود، قال: قال رجل للنبى صلى الله عليه وسلم : يا رسول الله! كيف لى ان أعلم إذا احسنت أو إذا اسأت ؟ فقال النبى صلى الله عليه وسلم : إذا سمعت جيرانك يقولون : قد احسنت ، فقد احسنت و إذا سمعتهم يقولون : قد اسأت ، فقد اسأت. (ابن ماجه)

3. Ibn Masud reported that a man asked the Holy Prophet, "O Messenger of Allah ! How am I to know whether I did good and whether I did bad?" The Holy Prophet said, "When you hear your neighbours say you have indeed done good, you have certainly done

good; and when you hear them say you have indeed done bad, you have certainly done bad." (Ibn Majah)

عن ابى هريرة ، قال : قال رسول الله صلى الله عليه وسلم: يا نساء المسلمات! لاتحقرن جارة لجارتها ولو فر من شاة . (متفق عليه)

4. Abu Hurairah reported that the Messenger of Allah said, "O Muslim women! No female neighbour must hold in contempt her neighbour for even a hoof of goat." (Bukhari, Muslim)

عن ابى ذر، قال : قال رسول الله صلى الله عليه وسلم : إذا طبخت مرقة فاكثر ماءها، وتعاهد جيرانك . (مسلم)

5. Abu Zar reported that the Messenger of Allah said, "When you cook broth, increase its water and give it to your neighbours." (Muslim)

عن عائشة، قالت: يا رسول الله! ان لى جارين فإلى ايهما اهدى؟ قال : الى اقربهما منك باباً . (بخارى)

6. Ayesha asked, "O Messeeger of Allah! Verily I have got two neighbours. To whom among these two shall I send a present?" He said, "To one who is nearer of the two in respect of door." (Bukhari)

عن عقبه بن عامر، قال: قال رسول الله صلى الله عليه وسلم : اول خصمين يوم القيامة جاران . (احمد)

7. Oqbah bin A'mer reported that the Messenger of Allah said, "The first two disputants on the Resurrection Day will be two neighbours." (Ahmad)

عن عبدالله بن عمرو، قال : قال رسول الله صلى الله عليه وسلم: خير الأصحاب عند الله خيرهم لصاحبه، وخير الجيران عند الله خيرهم لجاره. (ترمذى)

Abdullah bin Amr reported shat the Messenger of Allah said, "The best of companions in the sight of Allah is one who is the best of them to his companions, and the best of neighbours near Allah is one who is the best of them to his neighbour." (Tirmizi)

(7) THE POOR AND THE DISTRESSED

QURAN :

وَبِالْوَالِدَيْنِ إِحْسَانًا وَبِذِي الْقُرْبَىٰ وَالْيَتَامَىٰ وَالْمَسَاكِينِ

1. **And kindness to parents, kinsfolk, orphans, and those in need.** **(4 : 46)**

وَفِي أَمْوَالِهِمْ حَقٌّ لِّلسَّائِلِ وَالْمَحْرُومِ ۝

2. **And in their wealth there was the right of the beggar and the have not.** **(51 : 19)**

وَأَمَّا السَّائِلَ فَلَا تَنْهَرْ ۝

3. **And him who asks, chide not. (93 : 10)**

خُذُوهُ فَغُلُّوهُ ۝ ثُمَّ الْجَحِيمَ صَلُّوهُ ۝ ثُمَّ فِي سِلْسِلَةٍ ذَرْعُهَا سَبْعُونَ ذِرَاعًا فَاسْلُكُوهُ ۝ إِنَّهُ كَانَ لَا يُؤْمِنُ بِاللَّهِ الْعَظِيمِ ۝
وَلَا يَحُضُّ عَلَىٰ طَعَامِ الْمِسْكِينِ ۝ فَلَيْسَ لَهُ الْيَوْمَ هَاهُنَا حَمِيمٌ ۝ وَلَا طَعَامٌ إِلَّا مِنْ غِسْلِينٍ ۝ لَّا يَأْكُلُهُ إِلَّا الْخَاطِئُونَ ۝

4. **Seize bind, then fetter him, then cast him into the burning Fire; then find him in a chain the length of which is several cubits. Surely he believed not in Allah, the Great ; nor did he urge the feeding of the poor. Therefore he has not here this day a true friend, nor any food except refuse, which none but the wrongdoers eat.** **(69 : 30-37)**

أَرَأَيْتَ الَّذِي يُكَذِّبُ بِالدِّينِ ۝ فَذَٰلِكَ الَّذِي يَدُعُّ الْيَتِيمَ ۝

5. **Hast thou seen him who belies The Day of Judgement? That is the one who repuless the orphan.** **(107 : 12)**

وَمَآ اَدْرٰىكَ مَا الْعَقَبَةُ ۝ فَكُّ رَقَبَةٍ ۝ اَوْ اِطْعٰمٌ فِیْ یَوْمٍ ذِیْ مَسْغَبَةٍ ۝ یَّتِیْمًا ذَا مَقْرَبَةٍ ۝ اَوْ مِسْكِیْنًا ذَا مَتْرَبَةٍ ۝

6. And what will make thee comprehend what the uphill road is? (It is) to free a slave, or to feed in a day of hunger and orphan nearly related, or the poor man lying in the dust. (90 : 12-16)

عَبَسَ وَتَوَلّٰٓى ۝ اَنْ جَآءَهُ الْاَعْمٰى ۝

7. He frowned and turned away, because the blind man came to him. (80 : 1,2)

وَ اِذَا حَضَرَ الْقِسْمَةَ اُولُوا الْقُرْبٰى وَ الْیَتٰمٰى وَ الْمَسٰكِیْنُ فَارْزُقُوْهُمْ مِّنْهُ وَقُوْلُوْا لَهُمْ قَوْلًا مَّعْرُوْفًا ۝

8. And if at the time of division other relativs, or orphans, or poor, are present, feed them out of the (property) and speak to them words of kindness and justice. (4 : 8)

HADIS :

عن ابی هریرة، قال: قال رسول الله صلی الله علیه و سلم: الساعی علی الارملة و المسکین کالساعی فی سبیل الله، واحسبه قال: کالقائم لایفتر و کالصائم لا یفطر. (متفق علیه)

Abu Hurairah reported that the Messenger of Allah said, "One who strives for the widow and the poor is like one who fights in the way of Allah." And I think he said, "I shall regard him as one who keeps up praying without break, and fasts without break" (Bukhari, Muslim).

عن مصعب بن سعد قال: رأی سعد ان له فضلا علی من دونه، فقال رسول الله صلی الله علیه وسلم هل تنصرون و ترزقون الا بضعفائکم. (البخاری)

Musa'ab bin Saad reported that Saad thought that he had got more than the others. The Messenger of Allah said, "Will you be helped and supported with provision except for the sake of the weak among you?" (Bukhari)

عن ابن عباس، قال: قال رسول الله صلى الله عليه وسلم: اطلعت فى الجنة، فرايت اكثر اهلها الفقراء، و اطلعت فى النار فرايت اكثر اهلها النسآء. (متفق عليه)

Ibn Abbas reported that the Messenger of Allah said, "I peeped into Paradise and found that the majority of its inmates were the poor and I peeped into the Fire and found that the majority of its inmates were women." (Bukhari, Muslim)

عن عبدالله بن عمرو، قال: قال رسول الله صلى الله عليه وسلم: ان فقراء المهاجرين يسبقون الأغنياء يوم القيامة الى الجنة باربعين خريفاً. (مسلم)

Abdullah bin Amr reported that the Messenger of Allah said, "Verily the poor refugee will go to Paradise forty springs before the rich on the Resurrection Day." (Muslim)

عن عائشة، قالت: ما شبع آل محمد من خبز الشعير يومين متتابعين حتى قبض رسول الله صلى الله عليه وسلم. (متفق عليه)

Ayesha reported: The family of Muhammad had never their fill of the bread of wheat for two consecutive days till the Messenger of Allah died. (Bukhari, Muslim)

عن ابى هريرة، قال: قال رسول الله صلى الله عليه وسلم: اذا نظر احدكم الى من فضّل عليه فى المال و الخلق، فلينظر الى من هو اسفل منه. (متفق عليه)

Abu Harairah reported that the Messenger of Allah said, "Whenever any of you turns his eyes towards one who has been given more of wealth and progessy let him look towards one who is inferior to himself." (Bukhari, Muslim)

عن عمران بن حصين، قال: قال رسول الله صلى الله عليه وسلم: ان الله يحب عبده المؤمن الفقير المتعفف ابا العيال. (ابن ماجه)

Imran bin Hussain reported that the Messenger of Allah said "Surely Allah loves His servant, believing, poor, abstaining from begging and father of a big family." (Ibn Majah)

عن محمود بن لبيد ان النبي صلى الله عليه وسلم. قال. اثنتان يكرههما ابن آدم: يكره الموت، والموت خير للمومن من الفتنة، ويكره قلة المال، وقلة المال اقل للحساب. (احمد)

Mahmud bin Labeed reported that the Messenger of Allah said, "There are two things which the son of Adam dislikes: hc dislikes death which is better than persecution for the believer; and he dislikes scarcity of means, while the scarcity of means is lighter for rendering account." (Ahmad)

عن انس، قال: قال رسول الله صلى الله عليه وسلم: افضل الصدقة ان تشبع كبداً جائعاً. (البيهقى)

Anas reported that the Messenger of Allah said, "The best charity is to satisfy a hungry belly." (Baihaqi)

عن ابن عمر، قال: قال رسول الله صلى الله عليه وسلم: ان لكل شئ مفتاحاً و مفتاح الجنة حب المساكين. (الدار قطنى)

Ibn Omer reported that the Messenger of Allah said, "Verily there is a key for every thing and the key to Paradise is love for the poor." (Darqutni)

(8) MUSLIMS AND THEIR MUTUAL RIGHTS AND DUTIES

QURAN:

إِنَّمَا الْمُؤْمِنُونَ إِخْوَةٌ فَأَصْلِحُوا بَيْنَ أَخَوَيْكُمْ وَاتَّقُوا اللّٰهَ لَعَلَّكُمْ تُرْحَمُونَ ۝ يٰٓأَيُّهَا الَّذِينَ اٰمَنُوا لَا يَسْخَرْ قَوْمٌ مِّنْ قَوْمٍ
عَسٰٓى أَنْ يَّكُونُوا خَيْرًا مِّنْهُمْ وَلَا نِسَآءٌ مِّنْ نِّسَآءٍ عَسٰٓى أَنْ يَّكُنَّ خَيْرًا مِّنْهُنَّ ۚ وَلَا تَلْمِزُوٓا أَنْفُسَكُمْ وَلَا تَنَابَزُوا بِالْأَلْقَابِ ۚ
بِئْسَ الِاسْمُ الْفُسُوقُ بَعْدَ الْإِيمَانِ ۚ وَمَنْ لَّمْ يَتُبْ فَأُولٰٓئِكَ هُمُ الظّٰلِمُونَ ۝ يٰٓأَيُّهَا الَّذِينَ اٰمَنُوا اجْتَنِبُوا كَثِيرًا مِّنَ الظَّنِّ
إِنَّ بَعْضَ الظَّنِّ إِثْمٌ وَّلَا تَجَسَّسُوا وَلَا يَغْتَبْ بَّعْضُكُمْ بَعْضًا ۚ أَيُحِبُّ أَحَدُكُمْ أَنْ يَّأْكُلَ لَحْمَ أَخِيهِ مَيْتًا فَكَرِهْتُمُوهُ ۚ
وَاتَّقُوا اللّٰهَ ۚ إِنَّ اللّٰهَ تَوَّابٌ رَّحِيمٌ ۝ يٰٓأَيُّهَا النَّاسُ إِنَّا خَلَقْنٰكُمْ مِّنْ ذَكَرٍ وَّأُنْثٰى وَجَعَلْنٰكُمْ شُعُوبًا
وَّقَبَآئِلَ لِتَعَارَفُوا ۚ إِنَّ أَكْرَمَكُمْ عِنْدَ اللّٰهِ أَتْقٰكُمْ ۚ إِنَّ اللّٰهَ عَلِيمٌ خَبِيرٌ ۝

1. **The believers are naught else than brothers. Therefore make peace between your brethren and observe your duty to Allah that haply ye obtain mercy. O ye who believe! Let not a folk deride a folk who may be better than they (are), nor let women (deride) women who may be better than they are; neither defame one another, nor insult one another by nicknames. Bad is the name of lewdness after faith. And whoso turneth not in repentance, such are evil doers. O ye who believe! Shun much suspicion; for lo! some suspicion is a crime. And spy not, neither backbite one another. Would one of you love to eat the flesh of his dead brother? Ye abhor that (so abhor the other)! And keep your duty (to Allah). Lo! Allah is Relenting, Merciful. O Mankind! Lo! We have created your male and female, and have made you nations and tribes that ye may know one another. Lo! the noblest of you, in the sight of Allah, is the best in conduct. Lo! Allah is Knower, Aware.**

(49: 10—13)

وَإِنْ طَآئِفَتٰنِ مِنَ الْمُؤْمِنِينَ اقْتَتَلُوا فَأَصْلِحُوا بَيْنَهُمَا ۚ فَإِنْ بَغَتْ إِحْدٰىهُمَا عَلَى الْأُخْرٰى فَقَاتِلُوا الَّتِي تَبْغِي حَتّٰى تَفِيٓءَ إِلٰٓى
أَمْرِ اللّٰهِ ۚ فَإِنْ فَآءَتْ فَأَصْلِحُوا بَيْنَهُمَا بِالْعَدْلِ وَأَقْسِطُوا ۚ إِنَّ اللّٰهَ يُحِبُّ الْمُقْسِطِينَ ۝

2. **And if two parties of the believers fall to fighting, make peace between them. Then if one of them does wrong to the other, fight**

ye that which does wrong, till it return unto the ordinance of Allah. Then if it returns, make peace between them with justice and act equitably. Surely Allah loves the equitable. (49 : 9)

وَمَا كَانَ لِمُؤْمِنٍ أَنْ يَقْتُلَ مُؤْمِنًا إِلَّا خَطَـًٔا

3. Never should a believer kill a believer; but (if it so happen) by mistake (4 : 92)

وَمَنْ يَقْتُلْ مُؤْمِنًا مُتَعَمِّدًا فَجَزَاؤُهُ جَهَنَّمُ خَالِدًا فِيهَا وَغَضِبَ اللَّهُ عَلَيْهِ وَلَعَنَهُ وَأَعَدَّ لَهُ عَذَابًا عَظِيمًا

If a man kills a believer intentionally, his recompense is Hell, to abide therein (for ever); and the wrath and the curse of Allah are upon him, and a dreadful penalty is prepared for him. (4 : 93)

HADIS :

عن النعمان بن بشير، قال : قال رسول الله صلى الله عليه وسلم: ترى المومنين فى تراحمهم و توادهم وتعاطفهم كمثل الجسد اذا اشتكى عضواً تداعى له سائر الجسد بالسهر والحمى. (متفق عليه)

Nu'man bin Bashir reported that the Messenger of Allah said, "You will see the believers in their mutual kindness, love and sympathy just like one body. When a limb complains, the whole body responds to it with sleeplessness and fever." (Bukhari, Muslim)

عن انس، قال : قال رسول الله صلى الله عليه وسلم، انصر اخاك ظالماً او مظلوماً. فقال رجل : يا رسول الله ! انصره مظلوماً، فكيف انصر ظالماً؟ قال : تمنعه عن الظلم فذالك نصرك اياه. (متفق عليه)

Anas reported that the Messenger of Allah said, "Help your brother, be he an oppressor or oppressed." A man enquired, ' O Messenger of Allah! I may help him when he is oppressed, but how can I help him when he is an oppressor?" He said, "You should prevent him from oppression. That will be your help to him." (Bukhari, Muslim)

عن ابى هريرة، قال: قال رسول الله صلى الله عليه وسلم: حق المسلم على المسلم ست. قيل: ما هن يا رسول الله؟ قال: اذا لقيته فسلم عليه، و اذا دعاك فاجبه، و اذا استنصحك فانصح له، واذا عطس فحمد الله فشمته، واذا مرض فعده، و اذا مات فاتبعه. (مسلم)

Abu Hurairah reported that the Messenger of Allah said, "The rights of a Muslim upon a Muslim are six." It was asked "O Messenger of Allah! What are those?" He said, "When you meet him, greet him, and when he calls you, respond to him; and when he seeks advice, give him advice, and when he sneezes and praises Allah, respond to him, and when he falls ill, visit him; and when he dies, follow him." (Muslim)

عن ابى هريرة، عنه قال: قال رسول الله صلى الله عليه وسلم: لا تدخلون الجنة حتى تؤمنوا، ولا تؤمنوا حتى تحابوا، اولا ادلكم على شئ اذا فعلتموه تحاببتم؟ افشوا السلام بينكم. (مسلم)

Abu Hurairah reported that the Messenger of Allah said, "You shall not enter paradise until you believe, and you will not believe, until you love one another. Shall I not guide you to a thing, when you wil do it, you will love one another? Spread greetings among you." (Muslim)

عن ابى خراش السلمي أنه سمع رسول الله صلى الله عليه وسلم يقول: من هجر اخاه سنة فهو كسفك دمه. (ابو داؤد)

Abu Kherash as-Solami reported that he heard the Messenger of Allah say, "Whoever forsakes his brother for a year is like one who sheds his blood." (Abu Daud)

عن ابن عمر، قال: صعد رسول الله صلى الله عليه وسلم المنبر، فنادى بصوت رفيع فقال: يا معشر من اسلم بلسانه ولم يفض الايمان الى قبله! لاتؤذوا المسلمين ولا تعيروهم، ولا تتبعوا عوراتهم، فانه من يتبع عورة اخيه المسلم يتبع الله عورته، ومن يتبع الله عورته يفضحه ولو فى جوف رحله. (ترمذی)

Ibn Omar reported that the Messenger of Allah ascended the pulpil and proclaimed with loud voice, and said, "O congregation! whose who accepted Islam with his tongue while faith is not firmly routed in his heart! Oppress not the believers, nor back-bite them, nor follow their secrets; for verily whose followed secrets of his Muslim brother, Allah will follow his secrets; and whosoever's secrets are followed by Allah, he is put by Him in disgrace even though he is in the midst of his habitation." (Tirmizi)

عن سعيد بن زيد، عن النبى صلى الله عليه وسلم، قال: ان من اربى الربوا الاستطالة فى عرض المسلم بغير حق. (ابو داؤد)

Sayeed bin Zaid reported from the Holy Prophet who said, "Verily the most compound of usury is prolonging (tongue of evil) unjustly in respect of the honour of a Muslim." (Abu Daud)

عن ابن عمر، ان رسول الله صلى الله عليه وسلم قال: المسلم اخ المسلم لايظلمه، ولايسلمه ومن كان فى حاجة اخيه كان الله فى حاجته، ومن فرج عن مسلم كربه فرج الله عنه كربة من كربات يوم القيامة، ومن ستر مسلماً ستره الله يوم القيامة. (متفق عليه)

Ibn Omar reported that the Messenger of Allah said, "A Muslim is brother to a Muslim. Neither he oppresses him, nor hands him over (to another). And whose comes in need of his brother, Allah comes in his need; whoso removes a calamity of a Muslim, Allah will remove one of his calamities from the calamities on the Resurrection Day, and whoso covers the fault of a Muslim, Allah will cover his sins on the Resurrection Day. (Bukhari, Muslim).

عن ابى هريرة، قال: قال رسول الله صلى الله عليه وسلم: مر رجل بغصن شجرة على ظهر طريق، فقال لأنحين هذا عن طريق المسلمين لا يؤذيهم، فأدخل الجنة. (متفق عليه)

Abu Hurairah reported that the Messenger of Allah said, "A man passed by a branch of a tree (lying) on the surface of the road. So he said: I must remove it from the way of the muslims that it may not injure them: so he was admitted in Paradise." (Bukhari, Muslim).

عن ابى هريرة، قال: قال رسول الله صلى الله عليه وسلم: حق المسلم على المسلم خمس: ردّ للسلام، وعيادة المريض، واتباع الجنائز، و اجابة الدعوة وتشميت العاطس. (متفق عليه)

Abu Hurairah reported that the Messenger of Allah said, "The rights of a Muslim over a Muslim are five: to return greeting to visit the sick, to follow the bier of a dead man, to accept invitatiou, and to respond to the sneezer," (Bukhari, Mualim).

عن جابر، قال: قال رسول الله صلى الله عليه وسلم: كل معروف صدقه، وإن من المعروف أن تلقى اخاك بوجه طلق، وان تفرغ من دلوك فى اناء اخيك. (احمد، ترمذى)

Jaber reported that the Messenger of Allah said, "Every good deed is charity, and it is of good deeds that you meet your brotner (Muslim) with a cheerful countenance, and that you pour down from your bubket into thc bucket of your brother." (Ahmad, Tirmizi).

عن اسامه بن شريك، قال: قال رسول الله صلى الله عليه وسلم: ايّما رجل خرج يفرّق بين امتى فاضربوا عنقه. (النسائى)

Osama bin Shuraik reported that the Messenger of Allah said, "Whoso comes out to make division among my fellowers, smite his neck. (Nasai).

Remarks :

1. The foundation of the social system of Islam rest on the conception that all the human beings are equal and belong to one universal brotherhood, Ii announces that all men in the world have sprung from the same parents (Adam and Eve), and therefore are brothers and are equal in their status as human beings. Islam rejects all distinctions of birth, class, race, colour and language etc. It seeks to build a principled and ideological society as against the racial, national and parochial societies existing in thc world. Anyone who believes in One God as his Master and Lord, hnd accepts the guidance of thc prophets as the law of his life, can be a member of the Muslim society.

2. The first and foremost institution of human society is the unit of family. A family is established by the coming together of a man and a woman. This contact brings up a new generation, and then produces ties of kinship and community, which gradually develop into a large society. Moreover, it may be mentioned here that Islam holds every form of extra-marital sex relationship as sinful and forbidden and makes it a crime in law.

3. Islam lays down in express and definite terms the rights and duties which spring from marriage. Before Islam, specially among the Arabs, the wife had no locus standi either in law or in society. The Quran and the Holy Prophet effected a complete revolution in the status and position of woman. Now, instead of "the gate of evil", "the road to inequity", "the poison of the asp", she became a safeguard for her husband against sin, a bulwark against inroads of the devil, a lighthouse of virtue that saves man from destruction, and a great force with potential to transform male rudeness into angelic nobility.

4. The mutual relations of husband and wife and their respective duties, as described by Quran and Hadith, may be summarised as under :—

(a Duties of husband towards wife :-

(i) She is a trust in his hand. He shall treat her kindly.
(ii) He shall not hate her.
(iii) He shall not be too strict to her in order to make her conform to his wishes.
(iv) A mild beating (with tooth-stick etc., not with whip or stick), admonition, or separation from bed, is allowed only in some extreme cases.
(v) He shall give enough time to keep company with his wife in amusing pursuits.
(vi) He shall allow none to interfere in their conjugal matters and pry into the secrets of their sexual life.
(vii) Besides providing food and clothing, he should spend something for his wife.
(viii) In case of several wives, distribution of companionship with each wife shall be made equally.
(ix) He shall provide food, clothing, and abode to his wife.

(x) In case of death, the wife gets a share in husband's property, and the husband in wife's property.

(xi) He shall give her education (especially about the fundamentals of Islam).

(b) Duties of wives towards husbands :-

(i) The wife is bound to live with her husband unless she is unfit for conjugal relations and shall not, deny him pleasures of flesh.

(ii) She shall be obedient in all respects and administer his comforts even by shortening religious duties.

(iii) She shall not spend out of the property of her husband without his permission.

(iv) She shall guard her chastity.

(v) She shall look after his possessions in his absence and shall protect herself against sin.

In short, both husband and wife are equal partners in life, having quite distinct functions, which are suited to his or her nature. The husband is mainly required to earn for the maintenance of the family and the wife is responsible for the management of the house-hold and the bringing up of the children.

5. In Islam, next to the duty to Allah, comes the duty towards parents. Parents are the immediate cause of our birth and without them, we could not have seen the light of the day. Therefore great stress has been laid by Quran and Hadith regarding obedience to parents. Among parents, mother's place in respect of obedience has been placed much above father. Earning children are bound to maintain their poor parents. Anyhow, duty towards the Almighty is greater than that towards parents. So when there arises a conflict between the two duties, the latter must be sacrificed in preference to the former. Even in this case, parents are to be treated with kindness, dignity and respect.

6. Just as obedience towards parents has been strictly enjoined upon the children, the parents also have got some duties towards their children. For example, a father must provide for the maintenance of his infant children, and in absence of nurse the mother is bound to suckle her infant at breast. Parents are bound to give good education and training to their young children beginning from the study of the

Holy Quran. Parents should greet their children when entering the house and show affection and kindness in their dealings. It is enjoined upon the parents to lead their offspring towards proper religion i. e., Islam and they are responsible for the children's character and good conduct. Parents should give good names to their children on the 7th day of their brith and perform *aqiqah* (birth) ceremony by sacrificing two goats for a male child, and one goat for a female child. Immediately on birth, proclamation of Allah's name (i. e., Azan and Aqamat) should be infused into them through ear, and honey or other sweet things should be given to them for suckling. When children reach six years, education should be imparted to them and when they reach thirteen years of age, they should be forced to offer prayers.

7. Beyond the limited circle of family the next social sphere which is sufficiently wide is that of kinship and blood relationship. The duty towards relatives has been placed next to the duty towards parents. Islam laid stress regarding duties towards family members and other near relatives. Islam wants them all to be affectionate, co-operative and helpful toward each other.

8. Islam created a revolution in the status and position of slaves. No distinction of honour was held between a slave and a free man in all matters except piety. The Islamic reforms in this respect were disected toward gradual abolition of the institution of slavery .It forbade enslavement of Muslim men and women, and repeatedly adviced human treatment of slaves regarding food, clothing, and abode etc. Islam encourages that slaves and servents shall be forgiven for minor faults, however numerous they may be, and they shall not be scourged and beaten. They shall not be engaged in works which they are incapable of doing, and should always be assisted in their labour by the master in a spirit of brotherhood and fellow-feeling. Their maintenance is incumbent upon the master as the latter takes their entire services without allowing them to work for themselves. The Holy Prophet speaks of servants and slaves as brethren since all are discended from the same father, Adam. Allah has placed one under another for convenient management of wordly business. The slaves in Islam enjoyed ranks and position unparalled in the history of the world.

9. The Prophet was a great benefactor to the cause of helpless orphans. The Holy Quran also laid special stress upon feeding and

clothing of the poor and the helpless orphans Greatest care should be taken in handling the property of an orphan as it is nothing but a sacred trust, any infringement of which would amount to playing with fire.

10. Duty to neighbours has been placed next to duty toward parents, children and relatives. The supreme importance given to this duty towards neighbours by the Holy Prophet was not witnessed before in any system of law or religion. The Holy Prophet has said that the rights of the neighbours were so overwhelmingly emphasised to him by the angel Gabriel that he aprehended that neighbours might be made to partake of one's inheritance.

11. There are three kinds of neighbours :-

(i) one who is a Muslim as well as a relative,

(ii) one who is a Muslim;

(iii) and the one who is a non-Muslim.

The first has got three rights, second two, and the third one, in consideration of the first being a Muslim, a relative, and a neighbour.

A neighbour may also be casual or temporary with whom one has occasion to live or travel for some time.

12. Allah and His Apostle love the poor. We should also love them in order to ensure divine love. Every true follower of Islam must love them not only in words but also in deeds. The Holy Prophet himself declared in ecstacy that he liked to live as a poor man, die as a poor man, and to have resurrection with the poor. Greater duties have been imposed upon the rich as *zakat, sadaqah* and spending wealth in charity for the needy, while the poor men have been exempted from them.

13. The distressed and the needy include all helpless sufferers either in normal circumstances such as want of food, clothing, abode, or sickness etc. or in abnormal circumstances such as flood, earthquake, famine or other calamities of nature. Great reward has been promised by the Quran for helping the needy and delivering them from the clutches of the enemies. In the public treasury of Islam there was a fixed portion for the poor, neady and the distressed. No poor had to beg from door to door. They were maintained by the state.

14. Islam lays the foundation of the grand susperstructure of one brotherhood in which all men and women whatever may be their rank,

colour, creed, country, or status in society have got equal rights and duties. Piety and duty are the regulating principles for organising this brotherhood.

15. There are certain general rights and duties of members of this brotherhood which have been mentioned in the Quran and Hadith and may be summed up as follows :—

(a) Life, blood and property of Muslims are unlawful to another Muslim.

(b) In case of dispute between two members of the brotherhood, other members shall try to bring a compromise among about them, failing which they shall meet out punishment to the aggressor by joining with the oppressed. (Quran 49:9).

(c) No Muslim is allowed to let a misunderstanding remain between himself and another Muslim for more then there days.

(d) Every Muslim is duty bound to visit another Muslim in his sickness, be present when he dies, follow the bier of his dead body, accept his invitation, make Salaam to him when he meets him, respond to him when he sneezes and seek his betterment always in his presence and absence.

(e) He shall remove the harmful things and nuisances from the path of a Muslim.

(f) He shall give food, clothing and accommodation to other Muslims who are in need of them.

(g) He shall not backbite or follow the secret of other members of the society.

(h) He shall give his brother Muslim good advice and prohibit him from wrong-doing.

(i) He shall be attached to Jama'at or consensus of opinion and keep united to the general body of the Muslims like limbs of one body or bricks of one building.

(j) He shall share the sorrows and happiness of his brother.

(k) Unjust repression of Muslim is disallowed.

(l) He shall meet a Muslim with a smiling countenance, and will always be ready to help him in his needs.

STATE AND GOVERNMENT

(1) Sovereignty :

Al-Quran

قُلِ اللّٰهُ خَالِقُ كُلِّ شَيْءٍ وَّهُوَ الْوَاحِدُ الْقَهَّارُ ۝ (رعد ١٦)

1. Say :Allah is the Creator of all things, and He is the One, the Almighty. (13:16)

لَهٗ مَا فِي السَّمٰوٰتِ وَمَا فِي الْاَرْضِ وَمَا بَيْنَهُمَا وَمَا تَحْتَ الثَّرٰى ۝ (طٰہٰ ٦)

2. Unto Him belongeth whatsoever is in the heavens and whatsoever is in the earth, and whatsoever is between them, and whatsoever is beneath the sod. (20:6)

يُدَبِّرُ الْاَمْرَ مِنَ السَّمَآءِ اِلَى الْاَرْضِ (السجدہ ٥)

3. He rules (all) affairs from the heavens to the earth. (38:5)

اَلَمْ تَعْلَمْ اَنَّ اللّٰهَ لَهٗ مُلْكُ السَّمٰوٰتِ وَالْاَرْضِ (بقرہ ١٠٧)

4. Knowest thou not that to God belongeth the dominion of the heavens and the earth? (2:107)

اِنِ الْحُكْمُ اِلَّا لِلّٰهِ (انعام ٥٧)

5. The Command rests with none but God. (6:57)

مَا لَهُمْ مِّنْ دُوْنِهٖ مِنْ وَّلِيٍّ وَّلَا يُشْرِكُ فِيْ حُكْمِهٖ اَحَدًا ۝ (کہف ٢٦)

6. They have no protector other than He; nor does He share His Command with any person whatsoever. (18:26)

يَقُولُونَ هَل لَّنَا مِنَ الْأَمْرِ مِن شَيْءٍ ۗ قُلْ إِنَّ الْأَمْرَ كُلَّهُ لِلَّهِ
(آل عمران ١٥٤)

7. They said : Have we any hand in the affair ? Say : The affair is wholly (in the hands) of Allah. (3:154)

وَهُوَ الْقَاهِرُ فَوْقَ عِبَادِهِ ۚ وَهُوَ الْحَكِيمُ الْخَبِيرُ (انعام ١٨)

8. He is Omnipotent over His slaves, and He is the Wise, the Knower. (6:18)

عَالِمُ الْغَيْبِ وَالشَّهَادَةِ الْكَبِيرُ الْمُتَعَالِ (رعد ٩)

9. He is Knower of the invisible and the visible, the Great, the High, Exalted. (13:9)

الْمَلِكُ الْقُدُّوسُ السَّلَامُ الْمُؤْمِنُ الْمُهَيْمِنُ الْعَزِيزُ الْجَبَّارُ الْمُتَكَبِّرُ (حشر ٢٣)

10. (He is Allah, than whom there is no other God)—The Sovereign Lord, the Holy one, Peace, the Keeper of Faith, the Guardian, the Majestic, the Compeller, the Superb. (59:23)

الْحَيُّ الْقَيُّومُ ۚ لَا تَأْخُذُهُ سِنَةٌ وَلَا نَوْمٌ ۚ لَّهُ مَا فِي السَّمَاوَاتِ وَمَا فِي الْأَرْضِ (بقره ٢٥٥)

11. (God ! there is no God but He)—the Living, the Self-subsisting, Eternal. No slumber can seize Him nor sleep. His are all things in the heavens and on earth. (2:255)

بِيَدِهِ مَلَكُوتُ كُلِّ شَيْءٍ وَإِلَيْهِ تُرْجَعُونَ (يٰس ٨٣)

12. (Therefore glory be to Him) in whose hand is the dominion over all things ! Unto Him you will be brought back. (36:83)

وَهُوَ يُجِيرُ وَلَا يُجَارُ عَلَيْهِ
(مؤمنون ٨٨)

13. (In whose hand is the dominion over all things and) He protecteth, while against Him there is no protection. (23:88)

وَاللّٰهُ يَحْكُمُ لَا مُعَقِّبَ لِحُكْمِهٖ (رعد ۴۱)

14. And Allah pronounces a doom—there is no repeller of His decree. (13:41)

لَا يُسْـَٔلُ عَمَّا يَفْعَلُ وَهُمْ يُسْـَٔلُوْنَ (انبیاء ۲۳)

15. He will not be questioned as to that which He doeth, but they will be questioned. (21:23)

لَا مُبَدِّلَ لِكَلِمٰتِهٖ وَلَنْ تَجِدَ مِنْ دُوْنِهٖ مُلْتَحَدًا (کہف ۲۷)

16. There is none who can alter His words. And thou wilt find no refuge beside Him. (18:27)

اَلَيْسَ اللّٰهُ بِاَحْكَمِ الْحٰكِمِيْنَ (التین ۸)

17. Is not Allah the most conclusive of all judges? (95:8)

قُلِ اللّٰهُمَّ مٰلِكَ الْمُلْكِ تُؤْتِى الْمُلْكَ مَنْ تَشَآءُ وَتَنْزِعُ الْمُلْكَ مِمَّنْ تَشَآءُ وَتُعِزُّ مَنْ تَشَآءُ وَتُذِلُّ مَنْ تَشَآءُ
بِيَدِكَ الْخَيْرُ اِنَّكَ عَلٰى كُلِّ شَىْءٍ قَدِيْرٌ (آل عمران ۲۶)

18. Say : O God ! Lord of Power (and Rule), thou givest power to whom thou pleasest, and thou strippest off power from whom thou pleasest ; thou endowest with honour whom thou pleasest, and thou bringest low whom thou pleasest : in Thy hand is all Good. Verily over all things thou hast power. (3:26)

قُلْ اَعُوْذُ بِرَبِّ النَّاسِ مَلِكِ النَّاسِ اِلٰهِ النَّاسِ (الناس ۱-۳)

19. Say : I seek refuge in the Lord of men, the King of men, the God of men. (114:1-3)

وَمَنْ لَّمْ يَحْكُمْ بِمَآ اَنْزَلَ اللّٰهُ فَاُولٰٓئِكَ هُمُ الْكٰفِرُوْنَ (مائدہ ۴۴)

20. If any do fail to judge by (the light of) what God hath revealed, they are (no better than) unbelievers. (5:47)

حديث شريف

HADITH.

١ــ. عن ابى الدرداء قال قال رسول الله صلى الله عليه وسلم ان الله تعالى يقول انالله لااله الآ انا مالك الملوك و ملك الملوك قلوب الملوك فى يدى و ان العباد اذا اطاعونى حولت قلوب ملوكهم عليهم بالرحمة و الرافة و ان العباد اذا عصونى حولت قلوبهم باسخطة و النقمة فسا مدهم سوءَ العذاب ۰۰۰۰ (ابونعيم)

1. Abu Darda'a reported, that the Messenger of Allah said: Verily the Almighty Allah says I am Allah, there is no deity except Myself. I am Master of Kings and King of Kings; Hearts of Kings are in My hand. Verily as for the servants when they obey Me, I change the hearts of kings towards them with mercy and rewards; and verily as for the servants, when they disobey Me, I change their hearts with displeasure and punishment. So they inflict grievous punishment upon them. (Abu Nayeem)

٢ــ. عن النواس بن سمعان قال قال رسول الله صلى الله عليه وسلم لاطاعة المخلوق فى معصية الخالق (شرح السنة)

2. Nawas b Sama'an reported that the Holy Prophet said there is no obedience to the created in disobedience to the Creator (Sharh-us-Sunnah).

REMARKS.

(1) The word sovereignty is derived from the Latin word Superamus which means supreme. The Definitions of the term are varied but it always signifies the biggest governmental and legal authority of some sort (Encyclopaedia of social sciences).

(2) In the terminolgy of political science, this word is used in the sense of absolute overlordship or complete suzerainty. If a person or group of persons or an institution is to be sovereign, it would mean that the word of that person, group or institution is law. A sovereign has the undisputed right to impose his orders on all subjects of the state and the subjects are under an absolute obligation to obey him, be it willingly or unwillingly. No outside agency, excepting his own will, imposes any limitations or restriction on his power to rule. Laws come into existence by dint of the will of the sovereign and place all subjects of the state under an obligation to obey them, but no law binds the sovereign himself. Whatever he does, is just and nobody can question his conduct or his orders and enforcement. It is thus inescapable that the sovereign should be accepted as being absolutely above all aberrations and errors, even though he may not actually be so.

(3) In Islam (all political, legal and popular) sovereignty belongs to Allah alone. It is binding on every Muslim that he must acknowledge Him as the sovereign in his moral, social, cultural, economic and political spheres of life.

(4) Islam altogether repudiates the philosophy of the western democracy in which the sovereignty of the people is accepted, and the absolute powers of legislation rest in the hands of the people. Law-making is their prerogative and legislation must correspond to the mood and temper of their opinion.

(5) As belief in the unity and sovereignty of Allah is the foundation of the social and moral systems of Islam, it is also the very starting point of the Islamic political philosophy.

(6) God is the real law-giver, and authority of absolute legislation rests in Him. No person, class or group, not even the entire population of the state as a whole, can lay claim to sovereignty. The believers can not resor to totally independent legislation nor can they modify any law which God has laid down. It is to be noted here that God has retained the right of legislation in His own hand not in order to deprive man of his natural freedom but to safeguard that very freedom.

(7) An Islamic state must, in all respects, be founded upon the law laid down by God through His Prophet. The government which runs such a state will be entitled to obedience in its capacity as a political agency set up to enforce the laws of God and the practices of His Prophet (P.H.).

All administrative matters and all questions about which no explicit injunction is to be found in the Shariah are settled by the consensus of opinion among the Muslims by way of Ijtihad.

These remarks have been compiled with the help of "Islamic law and constitution" by Maulana Syed Abul Ala. Lahore-1960.

(2) Government And Administration :

أَنَّ الْأَرْضَ يَرِثُهَا عِبَادِيَ الصَّالِحُونَ (الانبیاء - ۱۰۵)

My righteous servants will inherit the land. (21 : 105)

إِنَّ الْأَرْضَ لِلَّهِ يُورِثُهَا مَن يَشَاءُ مِنْ عِبَادِهِ
(اعراف - ۱۲۸)

Surely the land is Allah's. He gives it for an inheritance to such of His servants as He pleases. (7 : 128)

هُوَ الَّذِي جَعَلَكُمْ خَلَائِفَ فِي الْأَرْضِ
(فاطر - ۳۹)

He it is that has made you successors in the earth. (35 : 39)

وَاذْكُرُوا إِذْ جَعَلَكُمْ خُلَفَاءَ مِن بَعْدِ قَوْمِ نُوحٍ وَزَادَكُمْ فِي الْخَلْقِ
بَسْطَةً فَاذْكُرُوا آلَاءَ اللَّهِ لَعَلَّكُمْ تُفْلِحُونَ (اعراف - ۶۹)

And remember when He made you successors after Noah's people and increased you in excellence of make. So remember the bounties of Allah, that you may be successful. (7 : 69)

وَاذْكُرُوا إِذْ جَعَلَكُمْ خُلَفَاءَ مِن بَعْدِ عَادٍ وَبَوَّأَكُمْ فِي الْأَرْضِ تَتَّخِذُونَ مِن سُهُولِهَا
قُصُورًا وَتَنْحِتُونَ الْجِبَالَ بُيُوتًا فَاذْكُرُوا آلَاءَ اللَّهِ وَلَا تَعْثَوْا فِي الْأَرْضِ مُفْسِدِينَ (اعراف - ۷۴)

And remember when He made you successors after 'Ad and settled you in this land, you make mansions on its plains and hew out homes in the mountains. So remember Allah's bounties and act not corruptly in the land, making mischief. (7 : 74)

قَالَ عَسٰى رَبُّكُمْ اَنْ يُّهْلِكَ عَدُوَّكُمْ وَيَسْتَخْلِفَكُمْ فِى الْاَرْضِ فَيَنْظُرَ كَيْفَ تَعْمَلُوْنَ ۞ (اعراف-۱۲۹)

He said : It may be that your Lord will destroy your enemy and make you rulers in the land, that He will see how you act. (7 : 129)

وَعَدَ اللّٰهُ الَّذِيْنَ اٰمَنُوْا مِنْكُمْ وَعَمِلُوا الصّٰلِحٰتِ لَيَسْتَخْلِفَنَّهُمْ فِى الْاَرْضِ كَمَا اسْتَخْلَفَ الَّذِيْنَ مِنْ قَبْلِهِمْ
وَلَيُمَكِّنَنَّ لَهُمْ دِيْنَهُمُ الَّذِى ارْتَضٰى لَهُمْ وَلَيُبَدِّلَنَّهُمْ مِّنْ بَعْدِ خَوْفِهِمْ اَمْنًا يَعْبُدُوْنَنِىْ لَا يُشْرِكُوْنَ بِىْ شَيْئًا
(نور-۵۵)

God has promised to those among you who believe and work righteous deeds, that He will, of a surety, grant them in the land inheritance (of power), as He granted it to those before them, that He will establish in authority their religion—the one which He has chosen for them ; and that He will change (their state), after the fear in which they (lived), to one of security and peace : They will worship Me (above) and not associate aught with Me. (24 : 55)

لَقَدْ اَرْسَلْنَا رُسُلَنَا بِالْبَيِّنٰتِ وَاَنْزَلْنَا مَعَهُمُ الْكِتٰبَ وَالْمِيْزَانَ لِيَقُوْمَ النَّاسُ بِالْقِسْطِ (حديد-۲۵)

Certainly We sent Our messengers with clear arguments, and sent down with them the Book and the measure, that men may conduct themselves with equity. (57 : 25)

اَلَّذِيْنَ اِنْ مَّكَّنّٰهُمْ فِى الْاَرْضِ اَقَامُوا الصَّلٰوةَ وَاٰتَوُا الزَّكٰوةَ وَاَمَرُوْا
بِالْمَعْرُوْفِ وَنَهَوْا عَنِ الْمُنْكَرِ وَلِلّٰهِ عَاقِبَةُ الْاُمُوْرِ ۞ (حج-۴۱)

Those who, if We establish them in the land, will keep up prayer and pay *Zakat* and enjoin good and forbid evil. And Allah's is the end of affairs. (22 : 41)

وَتَعَاوَنُوْا عَلَى الْبِرِّ وَالتَّقْوٰى وَلَا تَعَاوَنُوْا عَلَى الْاِثْمِ وَالْعُدْوَانِ وَاتَّقُوا اللّٰهَ (مائده-۲)

And help one another in righteousness and piety, and help not one another in sin and aggression, and keep your duty to Allah. (5 : 2)

وامرهم شوری بینهم
(شوری-۳۸)

And whose affairs are (decided) by counsel among themselves. (42 : 38)

ان اکرمکم عند الله اتقکم (حجرات-۱۳)

Surely the noblest of you with Allah is the most dutiful of you. (49 : 13)

یایها الذین امنوا اطیعوا الله واطیعوا الرسول واولی الامر منکم فان تنازعتم فی شیء فردوه الی الله
والرسول ان کنتم تؤمنون بالله والیوم الاخر (نساء-۵۹)

O You who believe, obey Allah and obey the Messenger and those in authority from among you, then if you quarrel about any thing, refer it to Allah and Messenger, if you believe in Allah and the Last Day. (4 : 59)

یداود انا جعلنک خلیفة فی الارض فاحکم بین الناس بالحق ولا تتبع الهوی فیضلک عن سبیل الله ان
الذین یضلون عن سبیل الله لهم عذاب شدید بما نسوا یوم الحساب (ص-۲۶)

O David (Daud), surely We have made thee a ruler in the Land : So judge between men justly and follow not desire, lest it lead thee astray from the path of Allah. Those who go astray from the path of Allah, for them is surely a severe chastisement because they forgot the day of Reckoning. (38 : 26)

ولا تطیعوا امر المسرفین الذین یفسدون فی الارض ولا یصلحون (شعراء ۱۵۱-۱۵۲)

And follow not the bidding of those who are extravagant, who make mischief in the land, and mend not (their ways).

AHADITH.

عن عبدالله بن عمر قال قال رسول الله صلى الله عليه وسلم الا كلكم راع و كلكم مسئول عن رعيته فالامام الذي على الناس راع و هو مسئول عن رعيته والرجل راع على اهل بيته و هو مسئول عن رعيته و المراة راعية على اهل بيت زوجها و ولده و هي مسئوية عنهم و عبد الرجل راع على مال سيده و هو مسئول عنه الا فكلكم راع وكلكم مسئول عن رعيته . (متفق عليه)

Abdullah-b-Omar reported that the Messenger of Allah said : Behold ! each one of you is a king, and each one of you will be asked about his subjects. A leader is a king over the people and he will be asked about his subjects, a man is a king over the members of his household and he will be asked about his subjects, a woman is a queen over the members of the household of her husband and of his children, and she will be asked about them, a servant is a king over the property of his master, and he will be asked about it. Behold! each one of you is a king, and each one of you will be asked about his subjects. (Agreed)

عن عبدالله بن عمر قال سمعت رسول الله صلى الله عليه وسلم يقول ما من عبداً يسترعيه الله رعيته فلم يحطها بنصيحة الا لم يجد رائحة الجنة (متفق عليه)

Abdullah-b-Omar reported : I heard the Messenger of Allah say : There is no man who is appointed by Allah to work after his subjects and who afterwards does not come down to them with admonition except that he will not find fragrance of Paradise. (Agreed)

عن ابي سعيد قال رسول الله صلى الله عليه وسلم ما بعث الله من بنى الا استخلط من خليفة الا كانت له بطانتان بطانة تامره بالمعروف وتحضه عليه و بطانة تامره بالشر و تحضه عليه والمعصوم من عصمه الله (البخارى)

Abu Sayeed reported that the Messenger of Allah said: Allah did not send any prophet, nor did he invest any with ruling power but for whom there were two ministers—one minister who enjoins good and gives injunctions to carry it out and another who enjoins evil and goods thereto, and one innocent is he whom Allah protects. (Bukhari).

عن عائشة قالت قال رسول الله صلي الله عليه وسلم اللهم من ولى من امر امتى شيئاً فشق عليهم فاشفق عليه و من ولى من امر امتى شيئاً فرفق بهم فارفق به (مسلم)

Ayesha reported that the Prophet said: O Allah! whoso is given power over any of the affairs of my people and then he gives trouble to them, give trouble to him; and whoso is given power over any of the affairs of my people and then he shows mercy to them, show mercy to him. (Muslim)

عن عبدالرحمان بن سمرة قال قال لى رسول الله صلى الله عليه وسلم لا تسال الامارة فانك ان اعطيتها عن مسئلة و كلت اليها و ان اعطيتها عن غير مسئلة اعنت عليها (متفق عليه)

Abdur Rahman b-Samorah reported that the Messenger of Allah said: Don't seek to rule because if it is given to you for asking, you will be entrusted to it; and if it is given to you without asking, you will be aided therein. (Agreed)

عن ابى امامة عن النبى صلى الله عليه وسلم ان الامير اذا

ابتغ الريبة في الناس افسدهم (ابو داؤد)

Abu Omamah reported from the Prophet who said : when a ruler seeks to have doubt in men, he makes them revolt. (Abu-Daud)

عن ابي هريرة قال قال رسول الله صلى الله عليه وسلم من

اطاعنى فقد اطاع الله و من عصاني فقد عصى الله و من يطع الامير

فقد اطاعنى و من يعصى الامير فقد عصاني و انما الامام جنة يقاتل

من ورائه و يتقى به فان امر بتقوى الله و عدل فان له بذلك اجراً

و ان قال بغيره فان عليه منه (متفق عليه)

Abu Hurairah reported that the Messenger of Allah said : Whoso obeys me, obeys Allah ; and whoso disobeys me, disobeys Allah ; and who obeys a ruler, obeys me and whoso disobeys a ruler, disobeys me. Verily an Imam is a shield who fights in his absence and protects in. If he enjoins to fear Allah and does justice, there is reward for him for that, and if he enjoin otherwise, there is against him therefrom. (Agreed)

عن ابن عمر قال قال رسول الله صلى الله عليه وسلم السمع

و الطاعة على المرء المسلم فيما احب و كره ما لم يومر بمعصية فاذا

امر بمعصية فلا سمع ولا طاعة (متفق عليه)

Ibn-Omar reported that the Holy Prophet said : There is hearing and obeying on a Muslim in what is pleasing and displeasing to him so long as he is not ordered with a sinful act. When he is ordered a sinful act, there is no hearing and obeying. (Agreed)

عن انس عن النبي صلى الله عليه وسلم قال اسمعوا و اطيعوا و ان استعمل حبشي كان راسه زبيبة (بخاری)

Anas reported that the Prophet of Allah said: "Hear and obey though a Negro whose head is like a raisin is appointed (to rule over you").

Remarks :-

(1) According to Islam, Sovereignty belongs to God alone, and anyone who holds power and rule in accordance with the laws of God would undoubtedly be vicegerent of the Supreme Ruler and will not be authorised to exercise any powers other than those delegated to him.

(2) The Caliphate granted by God to the faithful is the popular vicegerency and not limited to any family, clan, class or race etc.

(3) The mission of the prophets is to create conditions in which the mass of the people will be assured of social justice in accordance with the standards enunciated by God in His Books.

(4) The purpose of the state visualised by the Holy Quran is not negative but positive. The aims and objects of a state should be ;

(i) to prevent people from exploiting each other,

(ii) to safeguard their liberty,

(iii) to protect its subjects from foreign invasion,

(iv) to evolve and develop a well balanced system of social justice,

(v) to eradicate all forms of evils and to encourage all types of virtue and excellence mentioned by God.

(5) In an Islamic State, the Government should be constituted and run in mutual consultation with people. Hazrat Umar is

said to have said that there is no Caliphate (خلافة) without consultation. The head of the state shall function not in an autocratic but in a consultative (Shura) manner. He will discharge his duties in consultation with persons holding responsible position in the Government and with the elected representatives of the people.

(6) The head of the state is called Imam, Amir or Khalifa. His election depends entirely on the will of the general public and nobody has the right to impose himself forcibly as their Amir. The Amir will carry on the administrative work with the help of a *Majlis-e-Shura* (Consultative body).

(7) Just as a servant is entrusted with certain property for which he is responsible to the master, the king or the ruler is entrusted with the care of the people and guarding their rights; for the proper discharge of his duties, he is responsible in the first place to God who is the real Master, and then to people in relation to whom he occupies the position of a servant.

(8) It is a government mixed with religion. The temporal and spiritual head is centered in the same person.*

——: o :——

* For detailed discussion, see Islamic Law and constitution by Abul Ala Maududi. (N. A.)

(3) The ruler and the ruled :

وَإِذِ ابْتَلَىٰ إِبْرَٰهِـۧمَ رَبُّهُۥ بِكَلِمَـٰتٍ فَأَتَمَّهُنَّ ۖ قَالَ إِنِّى جَاعِلُكَ لِلنَّاسِ إِمَامًا ۖ قَالَ وَمِن ذُرِّيَّتِى ۖ قَالَ لَا يَنَالُ عَهْدِى ٱلظَّـٰلِمِينَ ﴿١٢٤﴾

(بقرہ ۱۲۴)

And (remember) when his Lord tried Abraham with (His) Commands, and he fulfilled them, He said, Surely I will make thee a Leader of men. (Abraham) said : And of my offspring. My Covenant does not include the wrong-doers, said He. (2 : 124)

وَقَالَ لَهُمْ نَبِيُّهُمْ إِنَّ ٱللَّهَ قَدْ بَعَثَ لَكُمْ طَالُوتَ مَلِكًا ۚ قَالُوٓا۟ أَنَّىٰ يَكُونُ لَهُ ٱلْمُلْكُ عَلَيْنَا وَنَحْنُ أَحَقُّ بِٱلْمُلْكِ مِنْهُ
وَلَمْ يُؤْتَ سَعَةً مِّنَ ٱلْمَالِ ۚ قَالَ إِنَّ ٱللَّهَ ٱصْطَفَىٰهُ عَلَيْكُمْ وَزَادَهُۥ بَسْطَةً فِى ٱلْعِلْمِ وَٱلْجِسْمِ ۖ وَٱللَّهُ يُؤْتِى مُلْكَهُۥ مَن يَشَآءُ ۚ
وَٱللَّهُ وَٰسِعٌ عَلِيمٌ ﴿٢٤٧﴾ (بقرہ ۲۴۷)

And their prophet said to them : Surely Allah has raised Saul to be a King over you. They said : How can he have kingdom over us while we have a greater right to kingdom than he, and he has not been granted abundance of wealth ? He said : Surely Allah has chosen him above you, and has increased him abundantly in knowledge and physique. And Allah grants His Kingdom to whom He pleases. Ann Allah is Amplegiving, Knowing. (2 : 247)

إِنَّ ٱللَّهَ يَأْمُرُكُمْ أَن تُؤَدُّوا۟ ٱلْأَمَـٰنَـٰتِ إِلَىٰٓ أَهْلِهَا وَإِذَا حَكَمْتُم بَيْنَ ٱلنَّاسِ أَن تَحْكُمُوا۟ بِٱلْعَدْلِ ۚ إِنَّ ٱللَّهَ نِعِمَّا يَعِظُكُم بِهِۦٓ ۗ
إِنَّ ٱللَّهَ كَانَ سَمِيعًۢا بَصِيرًا ﴿٥٨﴾ يَـٰٓأَيُّهَا ٱلَّذِينَ ءَامَنُوٓا۟ أَطِيعُوا۟ ٱللَّهَ وَأَطِيعُوا۟ ٱلرَّسُولَ وَأُو۟لِى ٱلْأَمْرِ مِنكُمْ ۖ (نساء ۵۸-۵۹)

Surely Allah commands you to make over trusts to those worthy of them, and that when you judge between people, you judge with justice. Surely Allah admonishes you with what is excellent. Surely Allah is ever Hearing, Seeing. O you who believe, obey Allah and obey the Messenger and those in authority from among you. (4 : 58, 59)

قَالَ اجْعَلْنِي عَلَىٰ خَزَائِنِ الْأَرْضِ ۖ إِنِّي حَفِيظٌ عَلِيمٌ
(يوسف ٥٥)

He said Place me (in authority) over the treasures of the land ; surely I am a good keeper, knowing well. (12 : 55)

وَلَا تُطِعْ مَنْ أَغْفَلْنَا قَلْبَهُ عَن ذِكْرِنَا وَاتَّبَعَ هَوَاهُ وَكَانَ أَمْرُهُ فُرُطًا (كهف ٢٨)

And follow not him whose heart we have made unmindful of our remembrance, and he follows his low desires and his case exceeds due bounds. (18 : 28)

وَشَدَدْنَا مُلْكَهُ وَآتَيْنَاهُ الْحِكْمَةَ وَفَصْلَ الْخِطَابِ
(ص ٢٠)

And we strengthened his kingdom and we gave him wisdom and a clear judgement. (38 : 20)

وَلَا تُطِيعُوا أَمْرَ الْمُسْرِفِينَ ۝ الَّذِينَ يُفْسِدُونَ فِي الْأَرْضِ وَلَا يُصْلِحُونَ ۝ (شعراء ١٥١-١٥٢)

And obey not the biddings of the extravagant who make mischief in the land and act not aright. (26 : 151,151)

وَتَعَاوَنُوا عَلَى الْبِرِّ وَالتَّقْوَىٰ ۖ وَلَا تَعَاوَنُوا عَلَى الْإِثْمِ وَالْعُدْوَانِ ۚ وَاتَّقُوا اللَّهَ ۖ إِنَّ اللَّهَ شَدِيدُ الْعِقَابِ ۝ (مائده ٢)

And help one another in righteousness and piety, and help not one another in sin and aggression, and keep your duty to Allah. Surely Allah is severe in requiting (evil). (5 : 2)

إِنَّمَا جَزَاءُ الَّذِينَ يُحَارِبُونَ اللَّهَ وَرَسُولَهُ وَيَسْعَوْنَ فِي الْأَرْضِ فَسَادًا أَن يُقَتَّلُوا أَوْ يُصَلَّبُوا أَوْ تُقَطَّعَ أَيْدِيهِمْ وَأَرْجُلُهُم
مِّنْ خِلَافٍ أَوْ يُنفَوْا مِنَ الْأَرْضِ ۚ ذَٰلِكَ لَهُمْ خِزْيٌ فِي الدُّنْيَا ۖ وَلَهُمْ فِي الْآخِرَةِ عَذَابٌ عَظِيمٌ ۝ إِلَّا الَّذِينَ تَابُوا مِن قَبْلِ
أَن تَقْدِرُوا عَلَيْهِمْ (مائده ٣٣-٣٤)

The only punishment of those who wage war against Allah and His Messenger and strive to make mischief in the land is that they

should be murdered or crucified, or their hands and their feet should be cut off on opposite sides, or they should be imprisoned. This shall be a disgrace for them in this world, and in the Hereafter they shall have a grievous chastisement. Except those who repent before you overpower than. (5 : 38, 34)

إِنَّ أَكْرَمَكُمْ عِنْدَ اللّٰهِ أَتْقٰكُمْ (حجرات ١٣)

Surely the noblest of you with Allah is the most dutiful of you. (49 : 13)

HADITH :

عن عمر بن الخطاب قال قال رسول الله صلى الله عليه وسلم ان افضل عباد الله عند الله منزلة يوم القيمة امام عادل رفيق و ان شر الناس عند الله منزلة يوم القيامة امام جائرٌ خرق (البيهقي)

Omar-b-al-Khattab reported that the Messenger of Allah said: Verily the best of the servants of Allah in rank in the sight of Allah on the Resurrection Day will be a ruler, just and kind; and verily the worst of men in rank in the sight of Allah on the Resurrection Day will be a ruler, tyrannical and hard-hearted. (Baihaqi).

عن عبدالله بن عمرو قال قال رسول الله صلى الله عليه وسلم ان المقسطين عند الله على منابر من نور عن يمين الرحمن و كلتا يديه يمين الذين يعدلون فى حكمهم و اهليهم و ما ولوا (مسلم)

Abdullah-b-Amr reported that the Messenger of Allah said: Verily the just persons near Allah will be upon pulpits of light on

the right side of the Merciful, and both His hands are just in their orders and in their family, and what they are given to rule. (Muslim)

عن ابى سعيد قال قال رسول الله صلى الله عليه وسلم ان

احب الناس الي الله يوم القيامة و اقربهم منه مجلساً امام عادل و ان

ابغض الناس الى الله يوم القيامة و اشدهم عذاباً و فى رواية و

ابعدهم منه مجلساً امام جائر (مشكواة)

Abu Sayeed reported that the Prophet said: Verily the dearest of men near Allah on the Resurrectin Day and the nearest before Him for company will be a just ruler, and verily the most disagreeable of the people near Allah on the Resurrection Day and one deserving of the most severe punishment among them (in a narration : the most distant of them in company to Him) will be a tyrannical ruler. (Mishkat)

عن ابى امامة عن النبى صلى الله عليه وسلم انه قال ما من

رجل يلى امر عشرة فما فوق ذلك الا اتاه الله عزوجل مغلولا يوم

القيامة يده الى عنقه فكه بره او اوبقه اثمه اولها علامة و اوسطها

ندامة و آخرها خزي يوم القيامة (احمد - بيهقى)

Abu Omamah reported from the Messenger of Allah who said: There is no man who rules the affairs of ten men or more than that, but the Almighty and Glorious Allah will resurrect him as a treacherous man on the Resurrection Day with his hands upon his neck. His piety will either set him free, or his sin will destroy him. Its beginning will be blasphemy, its middle repentance and its end disgrace on the Resurrection Day. (Ahmed-Baihaqi)

عن ابن عمر ان النبي صلى الله عليه وسلم قال ان السلطان ظل الله في الأرض ياوي اليه كل مظلوم من عباده فاذا عدل كان له الاجر و علي الرعية الشكر و اذا جار كان عليه الامر و على الرعية الصبر

(بيهقي)

Ibn Omar reported that the Messenger of Allah said: Verily the Sultan is a shade of Allah on earth. Every oppressed man out of His servants takes shelter with him. When he administers justice, there is gratitude on the part of the subjects and when he oppresses, there is sin on him, and there is then patience upon the subjects. (Baihaqi)

عن انس قال قال رسول الله صلى الله عليه وسلم يسروا و لا تعسروا و سكنوا و لا تنفروا

(متفق عليه)

Anas reported that the Messenger of Allah said: Give ease and not trouble, give tranquillity and not oppression. (Agreed)

عن يحى بن هاشم قال قال رسول الله صلى الله عليه وسلم كما تكونون كذلك يومر عليكم

(احمد - بيهقي)

Yahya-b-Hashem reported that the Messenger of Allah said: As you are, so a commander will be appointed over you.

(Ahmed-Baihaqi)

عن عوف بن مالك الاشجعى عن رسول الله صلى الله عليه وسلم قال خيار ائمتكم الذين تحبونهم و تحبونكم و تصلون عليهم و يصلون عليكم و شرار ائمتكم الذين تبغضونهم و يبغضونكم و

تلعنونهم و يلعنونكم قال قلنا يا رسول الله افلا ننابذهم عند ذلك

قال لا ما اقاموا فيكم الصلواة لا ما اقاموا فيكم الصلواة الا من

ولى عليه و آل فراه ياتى شيئاً من معصية الله فليكره ما ياتى من

معصية الله ولا ينزعن يداً من طاعة (مسلم)

Auf-b-Malek al Ashjayi reported from the Messenger of Allah who said : The best of your Imams are those whom you send blessings and those who send blessings to you. The worst of your Imams are those whom you hate and those whom you curse and those who curse you. We asked: O Messenger of Allah, shall we not then overthrow them at that time? "No" said he, "till they establish prayer among you; no, till they establish prayer among you except one over whom a governor is appointed." He will then see whether he does anything in transgression of God's law. Let him dislike what he does regarding transgressing of Allah's law, he must not take off (his) hand out of allegiance. (Muslim)

عن ام سلمة قالت قال رسول الله صلى الله عليه وسلم يكون

عليكم امراء تعرفون و تنكرون فمن انكر فقد برئ و من كره فقد

سلم و لكن من رضى و تابع قال افلا نقاتلهم قال لا ما صلوا

لا ما صلوا اى من كره بقلبه و انكر بقلبه (مسلم)

Omme-Salmah reported that the Messenger of Allah said : There will be over you rulers (some of) whom you will like and (some) you will dislike. Whoso will deny will become free, and whoso will dislike will be safe; and there will be those who become pleased and follow. He asked: shall we not fight with them? "No", said he, "so long as they pray; no, so long as they pray"; that is, one who dislikes with his heart and rejects with his heart. (Muslim)

عن وائل بن حجر قال سال سلمة بن يزيد رسول الله صلى الله عليه وسلم قال يا نبی الله ارايت ان قامت علينا امراء يسئلونا حقهم و يمنعونا حقنا فما تامرنا قال اسمعوا و اطيعوا فانما عليهم ما حملوا و عليكم ما حملتم (مسلم)

Wael-b-Hugr reported : Salamah-b-Yazid asked the Messenger of Allah : O Prophet of Allah, inform me in case the rulers stand demanding their rights and denying our rights—what then do you enjoin on us ? He said: Hear and obey, because there is against them what has been given to them to bear, and there is against you what you what you have been given to bear (of responsibilities). (Muslim)

عن ابي سعيد قال قال رسول الله صلى الله عليه وسلم افضل الجهاد من قال كلمة حق عند سلطان جائر

(ترمذی، ابو داؤد، ابن ماجه)

Abu Sayeed reported that the Prophet said: The best Jihad is (that of) one who says a true word to a tyrannical King. (Ibn Majah, Tirmizi, Abu Daud)

(4) Fundamental Rights.

Quran.

وَلَا تَقْتُلُوا النَّفْسَ الَّتِي حَرَّمَ اللّٰهُ إِلَّا بِالْحَقِّ ۗ وَمَنْ قُتِلَ مَظْلُومًا فَقَدْ جَعَلْنَا لِوَلِيِّهٖ سُلْطٰنًا فَلَا يُسْرِفْ فِّي الْقَتْلِ ۖ
إِنَّهٗ كَانَ مَنْصُورًا ۝ (بنی اسرائیل - ۳۳)

And slay not the life which Allah hath forbidden save with right. Whoso is slain wrongfully, We have given power unto his heir, but let him not commit excess in slaying. Lo ! he will be helped. (17:33)

وَمَنْ يَّقْتُلْ مُؤْمِنًا مُّتَعَمِّدًا فَجَزَآؤُهٗ جَهَنَّمُ خٰلِدًا فِيْهَا وَغَضِبَ اللّٰهُ عَلَيْهِ وَلَعَنَهٗ وَأَعَدَّ لَهٗ عَذَابًا عَظِيْمًا ۝ (نساء - ۹۳)

Whoso slayeth a belie-ver of set purpose, his reward is hell for ever. Allah is wrath against him and He hath cursed him and prepared for him an awful doom. (4:93)

وَلَا تَأْكُلُوْٓا أَمْوَالَكُمْ بَيْنَكُمْ بِالْبَاطِلِ وَتُدْلُوْا بِهَآ إِلَى الْحُكَّامِ لِتَأْكُلُوْا فَرِيْقًا مِّنْ أَمْوَالِ النَّاسِ بِالْإِثْمِ وَأَنْتُمْ تَعْلَمُوْنَ ۝
(بقرہ - ۱۸۸)

And eat not up your property among yourselves in vanity, nor seek by it to gain the hearing of the judges that ye may knowingly devour a portion of the property of other wrongfully. (2:188)

يٰٓأَيُّهَا الَّذِيْنَ اٰمَنُوْا لَا تَأْكُلُوْٓا أَمْوَالَكُمْ بَيْنَكُمْ بِالْبَاطِلِ إِلَّآ أَنْ تَكُوْنَ تِجَارَةً عَنْ تَرَاضٍ مِّنْكُمْ ۚ وَلَا تَقْتُلُوْٓا
أَنْفُسَكُمْ ۚ إِنَّ اللّٰهَ كَانَ بِكُمْ رَحِيْمًا ۝ (نساء - ۲۹)

O ye who believe ! Squander not your wealth among yourselves in vanity, except it be a trade by mutual consent, and kill not one another. Lo ! Allah is ever Merciful unto you. (4 : 29)

يٰٓاَيُّهَا الَّذِيْنَ اٰمَنُوْا لَا يَسْخَرْ قَوْمٌ مِّنْ قَوْمٍ عَسٰٓى اَنْ يَّكُوْنُوْا خَيْرًا مِّنْهُمْ وَلَا نِسَآءٌ مِّنْ نِّسَآءٍ عَسٰٓى اَنْ يَّكُنَّ خَيْرًا مِّنْهُنَّ ۚ وَلَا
تَلْمِزُوْٓا اَنْفُسَكُمْ وَلَا تَنَابَزُوْا بِالْاَلْقَابِ ۭ بِئْسَ الِاسْمُ الْفُسُوْقُ بَعْدَ الْاِيْمَانِ ۚ وَمَنْ لَّمْ يَتُبْ فَاُولٰٓئِكَ هُمُ الظّٰلِمُوْنَ ۝ يٰٓاَيُّهَا
الَّذِيْنَ اٰمَنُوا اجْتَنِبُوْا كَثِيْرًا مِّنَ الظَّنِّ ۡ اِنَّ بَعْضَ الظَّنِّ اِثْمٌ وَّلَا تَجَسَّسُوْا وَلَا يَغْتَبْ بَّعْضُكُمْ بَعْضًا ۭ اَيُحِبُّ اَحَدُكُمْ اَنْ
يَّاْكُلَ لَحْمَ اَخِيْهِ مَيْتًا فَكَرِهْتُمُوْهُ ۭ وَاتَّقُوا اللّٰهَ ۭ اِنَّ اللّٰهَ تَوَّابٌ رَّحِيْمٌ ۝ (حجرات - ۱۱،۱۲)

O ye who believe ! Let not a folk deride a folk who may be better than they (are), nor let women (deride) women who may be better than they are; neither defame one another, nor insult one another by nicknames. Bad is the name of lewdness after faith. And whoso turneth not in repentance, such are evil-doers. (49 : 11,12)

اِنَّ الَّذِيْنَ يَرْمُوْنَ الْمُحْصَنٰتِ الْغٰفِلٰتِ الْمُؤْمِنٰتِ لُعِنُوْا فِى الدُّنْيَا وَالْاٰخِرَةِ ۠ وَلَهُمْ عَذَابٌ عَظِيْمٌ ۝ (نور - ۲۳)

Lo ! as for those who traduce virtuous, believing women (who are) careless, cursed are they in the world and the hereafter. Theirs will be an awful doom. (24 : 23)

وَلَا تُصَعِّرْ خَدَّكَ لِلنَّاسِ (لقمان - ۱۸)

Turn not thy cheek in scorn towards folk. (31 : 18)

يٰٓاَيُّهَا الَّذِيْنَ اٰمَنُوْا لَا تَدْخُلُوْا بُيُوْتًا غَيْرَ بُيُوْتِكُمْ حَتّٰى تَسْتَاْنِسُوْا وَتُسَلِّمُوْا عَلٰٓى اَهْلِهَا ۭ (نور - ۲۷)

O ye who believe ! Enter not houses other than your own without first announcing your presence and invoking peace upon the folk thereof. (24 : 27)

لَا يُحِبُّ اللّٰهُ الْجَهْرَ بِالسُّوْٓءِ مِنَ الْقَوْلِ اِلَّا مَنْ ظُلِمَ ۭ وَكَانَ اللّٰهُ سَمِيْعًا عَلِيْمًا ۝ (نساء - ۱۴۸)

Allah loveth not the utterance of harsh speech save by one who hath been wronged. Allah is ever Hearer, Knower. (4 : 148)

لُعِنَ الَّذِينَ كَفَرُوا مِن بَنِي إِسْرَائِيلَ عَلَىٰ لِسَانِ دَاوُودَ وَعِيسَى ابْنِ مَرْيَمَ ۚ ذَٰلِكَ بِمَا عَصَوا وَّكَانُوا يَعْتَدُونَ
كَانُوا لَا يَتَنَاهَوْنَ عَن مُّنكَرٍ فَعَلُوهُ ۚ لَبِئْسَ مَا كَانُوا يَفْعَلُونَ (مائده - ۷۸، ۷۹)

Those of the children of Israel who went astray were cursed by the tongue of David, and of Jesus, son of Mary. That was because they rebelled and used to transgress. They restrained not one another from the wickedess they did. Verily evil was that they used to do. (5 : 78 : 79)

كُنتُمْ خَيْرَ أُمَّةٍ أُخْرِجَتْ لِلنَّاسِ تَأْمُرُونَ بِالْمَعْرُوفِ وَتَنْهَوْنَ عَنِ الْمُنكَرِ وَتُؤْمِنُونَ بِاللَّهِ (آل عمران - ۱۱۰)

Ye are the best community that hath been raised up for mankind. Ye enjoin right conduct and forbid in decency ; and ye believe in Allah. (3 : 110)

وَلْتَكُن مِّنكُمْ أُمَّةٌ يَدْعُونَ إِلَى الْخَيْرِ وَيَأْمُرُونَ بِالْمَعْرُوفِ وَيَنْهَوْنَ عَنِ الْمُنكَرِ ۚ وَأُولَٰئِكَ هُمُ الْمُفْلِحُونَ
وَلَا تَكُونُوا كَالَّذِينَ تَفَرَّقُوا وَاخْتَلَفُوا مِن بَعْدِ مَا جَاءَهُمُ الْبَيِّنَاتُ ۚ وَأُولَٰئِكَ لَهُمْ عَذَابٌ عَظِيمٌ
(آل عمران - ۱۰۴، ۱۰۵)

And there may spring from you a nation who invite to goodness, and enjoin right conduct and forbid indecency. Such are they who are successful. And be ye not as those who separated and disputed after the clear proofs had come unto them. For such there is an awful doom. (3 : 104-105)

لَا إِكْرَاهَ فِي الدِّينِ (بقرة - ۲۵۶)

There is no compulsion in religion. (2 : 256)

وَالْفِتْنَةُ أَشَدُّ مِنَ الْقَتْلِ (بقرة - ۱۹۱)

Persecution is worse than slaughter. (2 : 191)

وَلَا تَسُبُّوا الَّذِينَ يَدْعُونَ مِنْ دُونِ اللَّهِ فَيَسُبُّوا اللَّهَ عَدْوًا بِغَيْرِ عِلْمٍ (انعام-۱۰۹)

And a buse not those whom they call upon beside Allah, lest exceeding the limits, they abuse Allah through ignorance. (6 : 109)

وَلَا تَكْسِبُ كُلُّ نَفْسٍ إِلَّا عَلَيْهَا ۚ
وَلَا تَزِرُ وَازِرَةٌ وِزْرَ أُخْرَىٰ ۚ
(انعام-۱۶۵)

And no soul earns (evil) but against itself. Nor does a bearer of burden bear the burden of another. (6 : 165)

يَا أَيُّهَا الَّذِينَ آمَنُوا إِنْ جَاءَكُمْ فَاسِقٌ بِنَبَإٍ فَتَبَيَّنُوا أَنْ تُصِيبُوا قَوْمًا بِجَهَالَةٍ فَتُصْبِحُوا عَلَىٰ مَا فَعَلْتُمْ نَادِمِينَ (حجرات-۶)

O you who believe, if an unrighteous man brings you news look carefully into it, lest you harm a people in ignorance, then be sorry for what you did. (49 : 6)

إِنَّ فِرْعَوْنَ عَلَا فِي الْأَرْضِ وَجَعَلَ أَهْلَهَا شِيَعًا يَسْتَضْعِفُ طَائِفَةً مِنْهُمْ (قصص-۴)

Surely Pharaoh exalted himself in the land and made its people into parties, weakening one party from among them. (28 : 4)

Ahadith.

١ــ عن عمر بن الاحوص قال سمعت رسول الله صلى الله عليه وسلم يقول فى حجته الوداع اى يوم هذا قالو يوم الحج الاكبر قال فان دمائكم واموالكم واعراضكم بينكم حرام كحرمة يومكم هذا فى بلدكم هذا الا ! يجنى جانٍ الا على نفسه الا لا يجنى جان على ولده ولا مولود على والده .... (ابن ماجه ترمذى)

Amr-b-al-Ahwas reported : I heard the Apostle of Allah ask at the Farewell pilgrimage: : What day is this? They replied: The day of the greatest pilgrimage. He said : Your lives and your poperties and your honours are sacred to one another like the sacredness of this day of yours in this city of yours. Behold ! no oppress or oppresses but against his own soul. Behold ! no oppressor oppresses against his son, nor son against his father............ (Ibn Majah, Tirmizi).

٢ــ عن ابى بكرة ال خطبنا النبى صلى الله عليه وسلم يوم النحر قل .... فان دماءكم و اموالكم و اعراضكم حرام كحرمة يومكم هذا فى بلدكم هذا فى شهركم هذا وستلقون ربكم فيسأ لكم عن اعمالكم الا فلا ترجعوا بعدى ضلالا يضرب بعضكم رقاب بعض (متفق عليه)

Abu Bakrah reported: The prophet gave sermon to us on the day of sacrifice. He said : Verily your lives and your properties and your honour are sacred to you like the sacredness of this day of yours in this City of yours, in this month of yours. You will soon meet your lord and He will ask you of your action. Behold! do not return to misguidence after me, some of you striking the neck of others...(Agreed).

٣— عن حذيفة قال قال رسول الله صلى الله عليه وسلم والذى نفسى بيده لتامرن بالمعروف و تنهون عن المنكر او ليو شكن الله ان يبعث عليكم عذاباً من عنده ثم لتد عنه ولا يستجاب لكم (ترمذى)

Huzaifah reported that the Messenger of Allah said: By Him in Whose hand I reporse! You must enjoin right and forbid wrong, or else God will certainly send down chastisement upon you; then you will call to Him, but He will not respond to you. (Tirmizi)

٤— عن جابر بن عبدالله قال قال رسول الله صلى الله عليه وسلم كل المسلم على المسلم حرام دمه و ماله وعرضه (مسلم)

Jaber-b-Abdullah reported that the Apostle of Allah said: "The blood, property, and honour of a Muslim must be sacred (inviolable) to every (other) Muslim. (Muslim)

٥— عن عبدالله بن عمر قال قال النبى صلى الله عليه وسلم اياكم والظن فان الظن اكذب الحديث ولا تجسسوا ولا تحسسوا لا توذوا المسلمين ولا تغيروا ولا تتبعوا عوراتهم فانه من يتبع عورة اخيه المسلم يتبع الله عورته (ترمذى)

Abdullah-b-Omer reported that the Prophet said: Beware of suspicion, for suspicion (may be based on) a most untrue information, and do not spy upon one another, and do not try to bare each other's hidden failings. Do not hurt other Muslims; do not impute evil to them, and do not try to uncover their nakedness: for, behold, if anyone tries to uncover the nakedness of his brother Muslim, God will uncover his own nakedness. (Tirmizi)

٦ــ عن ابو سعيد قال قال رسول الله صلي الله عليه وسلم ايما مسلم كسا مسلم ثوباً على عرى كساه الله من خضر الجنة وايما مسلم اطعم مسلماً علي جوع اطغمه الله من ثمار الجنة وايما مسلم سقى مسلماً على ضماء سقاه الله من الرحيق المختوم

(ترمذى - ابوداؤد)

Abu Said reported that Messenger of Allah said: If a Muslim clothes another Muslim in his nudity God, will clothe him with the green freshness of Paradise; and if ā Muslim feeds a Muslim who is hungry, God will give him to eat of the fruits of Paradise; and if a Muslim gives a drink to a thirsty Muslim, God will let him drink from the fountain of Paradise. (Tirmizi, Abu Daud).

Remarks.

(1) Rights are those conditions of social life without which man cannot be at his best, or give of his best what is needful for the adequate development and expression of his personality. All doctrines of freedom, therefore, assume the existence of rights. As Laski has aptly said, "Every state is known by the rights that it maintains."

(2) The fundamental rights granted by Islam fourteen hundred years ago, may be summed up as follows:-

(a) the right of life and security of person, the most fundamental of all rights. This includes also the right to defend one self against attack. It demands punishment of those who attempt to commit suicide.

(b) The right to liberty and free movement. "Mere life without movement would be meaningless and with out the exercise of the human faculties it could not rise above the level of animals." It implies that no one may be wrongly arrested, detained or coerced in any manner, not justified by law. In Muwatta of Imam Malik, we find that لا يوسر رجل فى الاسلام يغير عدل "no man may be imprisioned, in Islam, without justice). In *Kitabul Khiraj*, Imam Abu

Yousuf says that ليس للامام ان يخرج شيأ من احدالابحق ثابت معروف (And it is not for an Imam (ruler) to seize anything from a person without a patently established right.)

(c) the right of property.

(d) the right of contract. A contract is a transaction in which two or more persons, or bodies of persons, freely impose certain obligations upon each other to act in a certain way with regard to some definite object.

(e) the right of free speech, press, reputation, discussion, and public meetings to express opinion and exchange views without restraint and to protest against the tyranny and injustice of others. In means that every individual is free to think and express his opinion in public without any interference.

(f) the right of assembly and association.

(g) the right of worship, religion and conscience.

(h) the right to family life.

(i) the right of equality. This means the absence of legal discrimination against any individual, group, class or race—the equality of all persons before law.

(j) the right to education i.e., the state should make adequate provision for educating its citizens.

(k) the right to work in order to provide a man with facilities to perform his function and earn living in order to maintain his life.

(3) There are some political rights also, which consist of :-

(i) the right to vote.

(ii) the right to be elected.

(iii) the right to hold public offices.

(iv) the right to petition for grievances, and

(v) the right of criticizing the government.*

---

*The above remarks have been compiled with the help of books written by Dr. Kapoor and Gilchrist. (N.A.)

(5) The Administration of Justice

Quran :

إِنَّ اللَّهَ يَأْمُرُكُمْ أَنْ تُؤَدُّوا الْأَمٰنٰتِ إِلٰى أَهْلِهَا وَإِذَا حَكَمْتُمْ بَيْنَ النَّاسِ أَنْ تَحْكُمُوا بِالْعَدْلِ إِنَّ اللَّهَ نِعِمَّا يَعِظُكُمْ بِهٖ
إِنَّ اللَّهَ كَانَ سَمِيعًا بَصِيرًا ۝ (نساء - ٥٨)

Lo ! Allah Commendeth you that ye restore deposits to their owners, and if ye judge between mankind, that ye judge justly. Lo ! comely is this which Allah admonisheth you. Lo ! Allah is ever Hearer, Seer. (4 : 58)

يٰأَيُّهَا الَّذِينَ اٰمَنُوا كُونُوا قَوّٰمِينَ بِالْقِسْطِ شُهَدَاءَ لِلّٰهِ وَلَوْ عَلٰى أَنْفُسِكُمْ أَوِ الْوَالِدَيْنِ وَالْأَقْرَبِينَ إِنْ يَكُنْ غَنِيًّا
أَوْ فَقِيرًا فَاللَّهُ أَوْلٰى بِهِمَا فَلَا تَتَّبِعُوا الْهَوٰى أَنْ تَعْدِلُوا وَإِنْ تَلْوُوا أَوْ تُعْرِضُوا فَإِنَّ اللَّهَ كَانَ بِمَا تَعْمَلُونَ خَبِيرًا ۝
(نساء - ١٣٥)

O ye who believe ! Be ye staunch in justice, witnesses for Allah even though it be against yourselves or (your) parents or (your) kindred, whether (the case be of) a rich man or a poor man, for Allah is nearer unto both (than ye are). So follow not passion lest ye lapse (from truth) and if ye laspe or fall away, than lo ! Allah is ever informed of what ye do. (4 : 135)

يٰأَيُّهَا الَّذِينَ اٰمَنُوا كُونُوا قَوّٰمِينَ لِلّٰهِ شُهَدَاءَ بِالْقِسْطِ وَلَا يَجْرِمَنَّكُمْ شَنَاٰنُ قَوْمٍ عَلٰى أَلَّا تَعْدِلُوا اعْدِلُوا
هُوَ أَقْرَبُ لِلتَّقْوٰى وَاتَّقُوا اللَّهَ إِنَّ اللَّهَ خَبِيرٌ بِمَا تَعْمَلُونَ ۝ (مائده - ٨)

O ye who believe ! Be steadfast witnesses for Allah in equity, and let not hatred of any people seduce you that ye deal not justly. Deal justly ; that is nearer to your duty. Observe your duty to Allah. Lo ! Allah is informed of what ye do. (5 : 8)

إن الله يأمر بالعدل والإحسان وإيتاي ذي القربى وينهى عن الفحشاء والمنكر والبغي يعظكم لعلكم تذكرون (نحل - ٩٠)

Lo ! Allah enjoineth justice and kindness and giving to kinsfolk, and forbiddeth lewdness and abomination and wickedness. He exhorteth you in order that ye may take heed. (16 : 90)

ولا تتبع أهواءهم وقل آمنت بما أنزل الله من كتب وأمرت لأعدل بينكم (شوریٰ - ١٥)

And follow not their low desires and say : I believe in what Allah has revealed of the Book, and I am commanded to do justice between you. (42 : 15)

وإذا قلتم فاعدلوا ولو كان ذا قربى (انعام - ١٥٣)

And when you speak be just, though it be (against) a relative. (6 : 153)

وإن حكمت فاحكم بينهم بالقسط إن الله يحب المقسطين (مائدہ - ٤٢)

And if thou judge, judge between them with equity. Surely Allah loves the equitable. (5 : 42)

قل أمر ربي بالقسط (اعراف - ٢٩)

Say My Lord enjoins justice. (7 : 29)

لقد أرسلنا رسلنا بالبينت وأنزلنا معهم الكتب والميزان ليقوم الناس بالقسط (حدید - ٢٥)

Certainly We sent our messengers with clear arguments, and sent down with them the Book and the measure, that men may conduct themselves with equity. (57 : 25)

اَلزَّانِيَةُ وَالزَّانِيْ فَاجْلِدُوْا كُلَّ وَاحِدٍ مِّنْهُمَا مِائَةَ جَلْدَةٍ ۖ وَّلَا تَاْخُذْكُمْ بِهِمَا رَاْفَةٌ فِيْ دِيْنِ اللّٰهِ اِنْ كُنْتُمْ
تُؤْمِنُوْنَ بِاللّٰهِ وَالْيَوْمِ الْاٰخِرِ ۚ وَلْيَشْهَدْ عَذَابَهُمَا طَآئِفَةٌ مِّنَ الْمُؤْمِنِيْنَ ۝ (نور-٢)

Tha adulterer and adulteress, scourge ye each one of them (with) a hundred stripes. And let not pity for the twain withhold you from obedience to Allah, if ye believe in Allah and the Last Day. And let a party of believers witness their punishment. (24 : 2)

—— : o : ——

HADITH

عن ابى بكرة قال سمعت رسول الله صلى الله عليه وسلم
يقول لا يقضين حاكم بين اثنين و هو غضبان (متفق عليه)

Abu Bakrah reported : I heard the Messenger of Allah say : No judge shall pass a decree between two men while he is angry. (Agreed)

عن عبدالله بن عمرو و ابى هريرة قال قال رسول الله
صلى الله عليه وسلم اذا حكم الحاكم فاجتهدوا خطأ فاله اجر واحد
(متفق عليه)

Abdullah-b-'Ámr and Abu Hurairah reported that the Messenger of Allah said : When a judge wishes to pass a decree, and then strives hard and decides justly, there are two rewards for him : but when he wishes to pass a decree, and then strives hard but commits a mistake, there is one reward for him. (Agreed)

عن بريدة قال قال رسول الله صلى الله عليه وسلم القضاة
ثلثة واحدة فى الجنة و اثنان فى النار فاما الذى فى الجنة فرجل
عرف الحق فقضي به و رجل عرف الحق فجار فى الحكم فهو فى
النار و رجل قضى للناس على جهل فهو فى النار
(ابو داؤد - ابن ماجه)

Boraidah reported that the Prophet said : judges are of three kinds : One kind will be in Paradise and the two in Hell. As for one who will be in Paradise, he is a man who recognises truth and gives a decree accordingly, and a man who recognises truth but is unjust in decree is in Hell, and a man who passes as decree for the people out of ignorance is in Hell. (Abu Daud, Ibn Majah)

عن عبدالله بن ابی اوفی قال قال رسول الله صلی الله علیه وسلم ان الله مع القاضی ما لم یجر فاذا جار تخلی عنه و لزمه الشیطان (ترمذي ، ابن ماجه)

Abdullah-b-Abi Aufa reported that the Messenger of Allah said : Verily, Allah is with a judge so long as he is not unjust. When he is unjust (willingly), He goes off from him, and the devil keeps attached to him. (Tirmizi, Ibn Majah).

عن علي قال بعثنی رسول الله صلي الله عليه وسلم الى اليمن قاضياً فقلت يا رسول الله ترسلنی و انا حدبث السن ولا اعلم لی بالقضاء قال ان الله سيهدي قلبك و يثبت لسانك اذا تقاضىنا اليك رجلان فلا تقض للاول حتى تسمع كلام الآخر فانه احري ان يتبين لك القضاء قال فما شككت فی قضاء بعد

(ترمذی ، ابوداؤد ، ابن ماجه)

Ali reported : The Messenger of Allah sent me to Yemen as a judge. I said : O Messenger of Allah ! you are sending me while I am young in years and I have no knowledge of judgeship., He said : Verily Allah will soon give guidance to your heart and make your tongue firm. When two persons come to you for decision, don't give a decree in favour of the first till you hear the argument of the other, because that is more necessary that may become clear to you. He said : I had afterwards never entertained any doubt in decision. (Tirmizi, Abu Daud, Ibn Majah)

Remarks :

(i) Administration of justice is a Divine ordinance and a practice of the Holy Prophet which ought to be followed.

(ii) In the administration of justice there shall be no distinction between the strangers and relatives, between the Muslim and non-Muslims, and between the high and low. All stand equal in the eye of Islamic law of justice.

(iii) There is no such reservation as "The king can do no wrong" or "The king is above all party politics". The king is as much subject to law as a commoner and must appear before the judge for trial.

Although, in the life-time of the Holy Prophet, judges were appointed by the prophet himself taking into consideration their knowledge in Shariat law, character and piety, yet they were quite independent in delivering their judgement. The very fact that a judge (Qazi) could accept a suit even against the very person of the Prophet and could try him in an open court, is an index of the independence of the Judiciary in an Islamic State.

(iv) As for the qualification of a judge, we understand that no person can be appointed a judge unless he is found to be well versed in Divine Law (Shariat) i.e., he possesses sound knowledge of Quranic Principles, Traditions of the Prophet and the precedents of his companions. He should be an adult male in full possession of his mental faculties, a free citizens, Muslim by faith, irreproachable in character, and sound of sight and hearing; sober, calm, cool, free from any kind of outside pressure or temptation, and should be independent of official interference. He must not feel kindness in awarding the ordained sentences for the prescribed crimes. He must not accept any present or bribery from the parties to a case.

(v) The judges are required to apply the Quranic law in the first instance, and secondly the traditions of the Prophet; and in the absence of any injunctions in both these sources, they are required to exercise the right of their own judgement. These were the clear instructions given to Muaz-b-Jabal when he was appointed the Qazi of Yemen by the Prophet himself. Thus the Prophet had allowed his companion *ijtihad* during his own life-time.

On the appointment of Qazi Shurayh, one of the most just and efficient judges of the time, Hazrat Umar is said to have issued him the following instruction: "If thou knowest nothing on the subject in the whole of the Book of God, then decide according to what thou findest in the precedent decisions of the Prophet of God.

If thou knowest nothing on the subject in the decisions of the Prophet, then decide according to what thou findest in the decision of the rightly guided Caliphs. If thou knowest nothing on the subject in the whole corpus of the decisions of the rightly guided Caliphs, then exercise thy personal opinion and consult men of learning and piety."

(vi) The following are the duties of a judge :—

(a) He must administer justice without making any distinction between the high and the low, the rich and then poor, the ruler and a commoner.

(b) He must decide disputes and cases with as much speed and promptness as possible; to delay justice is a part of injustice.

(c) Settlement of disputes, restoration, of rights, execution of wills, execution of the prescribed punishments, protection of the weak against the strong and enforcement of the Divine law.

(vi) In order to help the judges and also the public, who needed clarification on some point of Islamic law, Hazrat Umar systematized the institution of jurisconsults (افتاء). He authorised only a few famous, capable and trustworthy scholars to give legal opinion on application without charging any fee. The important institution justified the state in assuming that every citizen knows the law. It is very surprising that although the modern states assert the legal manion : 'Ignorance of law is no excuse' they have not yet provided for any such free institution.

(vii) The chief feature of judiciary in Islam has been its separation from the executive. Upto the time of Hazrat Abu Bakr, the Caliph himself and his administrative officers also acted as judges. But as soon as administration became well established, the Caliph Umar completely separated the judiciary from other departments, established courts of justice, appointed judges and laid down rules in regard to judicial procedure. In order to maintain justice, the Caliph appointed judges in consultation with the members of his Advisory Council (مجلس شوریٰ) throughout the state.*

*These remarks have been compiled with the help of following books :—

(i) Translation of Mishkat by Maulana Fazlul Karim.

(ii) Islamic state, a Historical Survey by Dr. A.H. Siddiqi.

(iii) Theory and Practice of Modern Government by Finer.

(iv) Principles of Political Science by Gilchrist. (N.A.)

THE ECONOMIC SYSTEM

(1) General Principles

Al-Quran

يَا أَيُّهَا النَّاسُ اعْبُدُوا رَبَّكُمُ الَّذِي خَلَقَكُمْ وَالَّذِينَ مِن قَبْلِكُمْ لَعَلَّكُمْ تَتَّقُونَ ۝ الَّذِي جَعَلَ لَكُمُ الْأَرْضَ فِرَاشًا
وَالسَّمَاءَ بِنَاءً وَأَنزَلَ مِنَ السَّمَاءِ مَاءً فَأَخْرَجَ بِهِ مِنَ الثَّمَرَاتِ رِزْقًا لَّكُمْ (بقرہ ۲۱-۲۲)

O mankind ! Serve your Lord who created you and those before you, so that you may ward off (evil). Who made the earth a resting place for you and heaven a structure, and sends down rain from the clouds, then brings forth with it fruits for your sustenance. (2 : 22)

اللَّهُ الَّذِي خَلَقَ السَّمَاوَاتِ وَالْأَرْضَ وَأَنزَلَ مِنَ السَّمَاءِ مَاءً فَأَخْرَجَ بِهِ مِنَ الثَّمَرَاتِ رِزْقًا لَّكُمْ وَسَخَّرَ لَكُمُ الْفُلْكَ لِتَجْرِيَ فِي الْبَحْرِ بِأَمْرِهِ
وَسَخَّرَ لَكُمُ الْأَنْهَارَ ۝ وَسَخَّرَ لَكُمُ الشَّمْسَ وَالْقَمَرَ دَائِبَيْنِ وَسَخَّرَ لَكُمُ اللَّيْلَ وَالنَّهَارَ ۝ وَآتَاكُم مِّن كُلِّ مَا سَأَلْتُمُوهُ وَإِن تَعُدُّوا
نِعْمَتَ اللَّهِ لَا تُحْصُوهَا (ابراهیم ۳۲ تا ۳۴)

Allah is He Who created the heavens and the earth and sent down water from the clouds, then brought forth with it fruits as a sustenance for you, and He has made the ships subservient to you to run their course in the sea by His command, and He has made the rivers subservient to you. And He has made subservient to you the night and the day. And He gives you of all you ask of Him. And if you count Allah's favours, you will not be able to number them. (14 : 32-34)

وَلَقَدْ مَكَّنّٰكُمْ فِی الْاَرْضِ وَجَعَلْنَا لَكُمْ فِيهَا مَعَايِشَ (اعراف-١٠)

And certainly we established you in the earth, and made therein means of livelihood for you. (7 : 10)

كُلُوا مِنْ رِّزْقِ رَبِّكُمْ وَاشْكُرُوا لَهٗ (سبا-١٥)

Eat of the sustenance of your Lord and give thanks to Him. (34 : 15).

وَهُوَ الَّذِی جَعَلَكُمْ خَلٰٓئِفَ الْاَرْضِ وَرَفَعَ بَعْضَكُمْ فَوْقَ بَعْضٍ دَرَجٰتٍ لِّيَبْلُوَكُمْ فِی مَآ اٰتٰكُمْ (انعام-١٦٦)

And He is Who has made you successors in the land and exalted some of you in rank above others, that He may try you by what He has given you. (6: 166)

نَحْنُ قَسَمْنَا بَيْنَهُمْ مَّعِيشَتَهُمْ فِی الْحَيٰوةِ الدُّنْيَا وَرَفَعْنَا بَعْضَهُمْ فَوْقَ بَعْضٍ دَرَجٰتٍ لِّيَتَّخِذَ بَعْضُهُمْ بَعْضًا سُخْرِيًّا وَرَحْمَتُ رَبِّكَ خَيْرٌ مِّمَّا يَجْمَعُوْنَ ۝ (زخرف-٣٢)

We portion out among them their livelihood in the life of this world, and we exalt some of them above others in rank, that some of them may take others in Service. And the mercy of thy Lord is better than that which they amass. (43 : 32)

وَلَا تَتَمَنَّوْا مَا فَضَّلَ اللّٰهُ بِهٖ بَعْضَكُمْ عَلٰى بَعْضٍ لِلرِّجَالِ نَصِيبٌ مِّمَّا اكْتَسَبُوْا وَلِلنِّسَآءِ نَصِيبٌ مِّمَّا اكْتَسَبْنَ وَسْئَلُوا اللّٰهَ مِنْ فَضْلِهٖ اِنَّ اللّٰهَ كَانَ بِكُلِّ شَیْءٍ عَلِيمًا ۝ (نساء-٣٢)

And covet not that by which Allah has made some of you excel others. For men is the benefit of what they earn. And for woman is the benefit of what they earn. And ask Allah of His grace. Surely Allah is ever Knower of all things. (4 : 32)

وَاللّٰهُ فَضَّلَ بَعْضَكُمْ عَلٰى بَعْضٍ فِى الرِّزْقِ (نحل-٧١)

And Allah has made some of you excel others in the means of subsistence. (16 : 71)

قُلْ مَنْ حَرَّمَ زِيْنَةَ اللّٰهِ الَّتِىْٓ اَخْرَجَ لِعِبَادِهٖ وَالطَّيِّبٰتِ مِنَ الرِّزْقِ (اعراف-٣٢)

Say : Who has forbidden the adornment of Allah, which He has brought forth for His servants, and the good provisions. (7 : 32)

وَكُلُوْا مِمَّا رَزَقَكُمُ اللّٰهُ حَلٰلًا طَيِّبًا وَّاتَّقُوا اللّٰهَ الَّذِىْٓ اَنْتُمْ بِهٖ مُؤْمِنُوْنَ (مائدہ-٨٨)

And eat of the lawful and good things that Allah has given you, and keep your duty to Allah, in whom you believe. (5 : 88)

كُلُوْا وَاشْرَبُوْا وَلَا تُسْرِفُوْا اِنَّهٗ لَا يُحِبُّ الْمُسْرِفِيْنَ (اعراف-٣١)

Eat and drink and be not prodigal. Surely He noves not the prodigals. (7 : 31)

لَا تَاْكُلُوْٓا اَمْوَالَكُمْ بَيْنَكُمْ بِالْبَاطِلِ اِلَّآ اَنْ تَكُوْنَ تِجَارَةً عَنْ تَرَاضٍ مِّنْكُمْ (نساء-٢٩)

(O you who believe), devour not your property among yourselves by illegal methods except that it be trading by your mutual consent. (4 : 29)

وَاَحَلَّ اللّٰهُ الْبَيْعَ وَحَرَّمَ الرِّبٰوا (بقرہ-٢٧٥)

And Allah has allowed trading and forbidden usury. (2 : 275)

وَاِنْ تُبْتُمْ فَلَكُمْ رُءُوْسُ اَمْوَالِكُمْ (بقرہ-٢٧٩)

And if you repent, then you shall have your capital. (2 : 279)

إِذَا تَدَايَنتُم بِدَيْنٍ إِلَىٰ أَجَلٍ مُّسَمًّى فَاكْتُبُوهُ (بقرہ-۲۸۲)

(O you who believe), when you contract a debt for a fixed time, write it down. (2 : 282)

خُذْ مِنْ أَمْوَالِهِمْ صَدَقَةً (توبہ-۱۰۳)

Take alms out of their property. (9 : 103)

وَفِي أَمْوَالِهِمْ حَقٌّ لِّلسَّائِلِ وَالْمَحْرُومِ (ذاریات-۱۹)

And in their wealth there was a due share for the beggar and for one who is denied (good). (51 : 19)

يَا أَيُّهَا الَّذِينَ آمَنُوا إِنَّمَا الْخَمْرُ وَالْمَيْسِرُ وَالْأَنصَابُ وَالْأَزْلَامُ رِجْسٌ مِّنْ عَمَلِ الشَّيْطَانِ فَاجْتَنِبُوهُ (مائدہ-۹۰)

O you who believe, intoxicants and games of chance and (sacrificing to) stones set up and dividing by arrows are only an uncleanness, the devil's work, so shun it (that you may succeed) (5 : 90)

وَابْتَغِ فِيمَا آتَاكَ اللَّهُ الدَّارَ الْآخِرَةَ وَلَا تَنسَ نَصِيبَكَ مِنَ الدُّنْيَا وَأَحْسِن كَمَا أَحْسَنَ اللَّهُ إِلَيْكَ وَلَا تَبْغِ الْفَسَادَ
فِي الْأَرْضِ (قصص-۷۷)

And seek the abode of the hereafter by means of what Allah has given thee, and neglect not thy portion of the world, and do good (to others) as Allah has done good to thee, and seek not to make mischief in the land. (28: 77)

إِنَّمَا الصَّدَقَاتُ لِلْفُقَرَاءِ وَالْمَسَاكِينِ وَالْعَامِلِينَ عَلَيْهَا وَالْمُؤَلَّفَةِ قُلُوبُهُمْ وَفِي الرِّقَابِ وَالْغَارِمِينَ وَفِي سَبِيلِ اللَّهِ
وَابْنِ السَّبِيلِ فَرِيضَةً مِّنَ اللَّهِ (توبہ-۶۰)

(Zakat) Charity is only for the poor and needy, and those employed to administer it, and those whose hearts are made to incline (to truth), and (to free) the captives, and those in debt, and in the way of Allah and for the way-farer an ordinance from Allah. (9 : 60)

AHADITH :

عن ابى هريرة قال قال رسول الله صلى الله عليه وسلم قال

الله تعالى انفق يا ابن آدم انفق عليك . (متفق عليه)

Abu Hurairah reported that the Messenger of Allah said : The Almighty Allah says : O son of Adam ! spend, you will then be spent for. (Agreed)

عن ابى امامة قال قال رسول الله صلى الله عليه وسلم يا ابن

آدم ان تبذل الفضل خير لك و ان تمسكه شر لك ولا تلام على

كفاف و ابدء بمن تعول . (مسلم)

Abu Omamah reported that the Messenger of Allah said : O son of Adam! that you spend wealth is good for you and that you withhold it is bad for you, and you should not be backbited for miserliness. Begin with those who are in your family. (Muslim)

عن عائشة قالت سمعت رسول الله صلى الله عليه وسلم يقول

ما خالطت الزكواة مالا قط الا اهلكته . (الشافعى - بخارى)

Ayesha reported : I heard the Messenger of Allah say : Zakat never mixes with a property but to destroy it. (Shafeyi, Bukhari)

عن جابر قال لعن رسول الله صلى الله عليه وسلم اكل الربوا

و موكله و كاتبه و شاهديه و قال هم سواء . (مسلم)

Jaber reported that the Messenger of Allah cursed the devourer of usury, its payer, its seribe, and its two witness. And he said that they are equal (in sin). (Muslim)

عن معمر قال قال رسول الله صلى الله عليه وسلم من احتكر فهو خاطئ . (مسلم)

Memar reported that the Messenger of Allah said : Whoever monopolises is a sinner. (Muslim)

عن ابن عباس قال قال رسول الله صلى الله عليه وسلم الحقوا الفرائض باهلها . (متفق عليه)

Ibn Abbas report that the Messenger of Allah said : Pay the fixed shares of inheritance to the persons entitled to them. (Agreed)

REMARKS :

(1) Islam can not approve of an economic policy which destroys the rights conferred by the Shariat, however attractive its name may be and whatever pretensions of welfare it may make. What Islam aims at is that whatever be the form or mechanism of economic activity, the principles prescribed by it should find a permanent place in such activities under all circumstances and in all ages.

(2) All that is found on earth, in the heavens, the oceans, the stars, and others have been made subservient to man by Allah. God has created all these resources for the benefit of mankind. It is therefore :-

(a) The birth-right of every human being to try and secure his share out of the world. All men enjoy this right equally and none can be deprived of it, nor should one man get precedence over another. There can be no compulsion on any individual, race, or class, for taking to certain means of livelihood or adopting certain professions. All are entitled to equal opportunities in the economic realm.

(b) Similarly no distinction is valid in Islam which would result in creating a monopoly of a particular means of livelihood for a particular person, class, race, or group of people.

(c) Resources which are provided by nature free of cost, and which can be used directly by man may be utilized freely and every one is entitled to benefit from them to the extent of his needs.

(d) It is not fair that things created by God for the benefit of mankind should be taken possession of by anyone and kept in an idle and unused state.

(2) Islam recognizes private ownership. The right of ownership which one may acquire by permisible legal means is to be honoured under all circumstances.

(3) Human nature has been so ordained that divergence, variety and inequality among men in their modes and standard of living seems to be the most natural thing.

(4) The equality in which Islam believes is equality in respect of the opportunities of struggle for securing livelihood and climbing the upper-most rung of the ladder of well-being and prosperity. Islam does not agree with those who desire to enforce complete (and artificial) equality in respect of the means of production and the fruits of economic endeavour.

(5) Islam has forbidden all forms of activity which tend to damage or harm the rightful interest of the individual or society. The hoarding of goods in order to artificially raise their prices, speculation, profiteering and monopoly of the essential means of production by an individual or groups which lead to the deprivation of the majority, are all forbidden. Exploitation of all kinds is absolutely disallowed. The institution of interest or usury has been declared unlawful in Islam. All games of chance including lotteries and horse racing have been prohibited.

(6) Islam demands that in all contractual participations, the profit as well as the risk should be shared by both the contracting parties.

(7) "So that this (wealth) may not circulate solely among the rich from among you". (59 : 7). It is on the busis of this fundamental principle that Islam has constructed its economic system. It makes, on the one hand, a distinction between the necessary minimum and the desirable plenitude, and on the other hand, between those orders and iujunctions which are accompanied by material sanctions and those which are not so, but for which Islam contents itself with persuasion and education only.

(8) In matters of inheritance both the individual right of disposing of one's wealth, and the collective right in as much as one is a member of society must be simultaneously satisfied. In this direction Islam has taken two steps. Firstly, the obligatory distribution of the goods of a deceased person among his close relatives, and secondly, a restriction on the freedom of bequest through wills and testaments.

(9) While the Quran claims that wealth is the grace and good bestowed by God Almighty, it also stresses the fact that it is to be considered a mere means to certain ends, not an end itself. When one is convinced of this conception of wealth as a means to an end, it is the real cause of the acceptance of cooperation and not competition as the prevailing principle of economic life.

(10) Taxes in Islam come under two different categories; one is chargeable from Muslims and the other from non-Muslims. The taxes chargeable from Muslims are generally known as *sadaqat* and considered a religious obligation, the non-observance of which deprive a Muslim of all his rights to be located as member of the brotherhood of the faith.

Note :—The above remarks have been compiled from the following books : Introduction to Islam, Islamic way of Islam, Studies in Islamic History etc. (N. A.)

(ii) Trade & Commerce:

يسئلونك ماذا احل لهم قل احل لكم الطيبت (مائدہ-۴)

They ask thee as to what is made lawful for them. Say : (all) good things are made lawful for you. (5 : 4)

يايها الذين امنوا لا تاكلوا اموالكم بينكم بالباطل الا ان تكون تجارة عن تراض منكم
و لا تقتلوا انفسكم (النساء-۲۹)

O you who believe, devour not your wealth among yourselves by illegal methods except that it be trading by your mutual consent. And kill not one another. (4 : 29)

واحل الله البيع وحرم الربوا (بقرہ-۲۷۵)

And Allah has allowed trading and forbidden usury. (2 : 275)

يايها الذين امنوا اذا تداينتم بدين الى اجل مسمى فاكتبوه وليكتب بينكم كاتب بالعدل (بقرہ-۲۸۲)

O you who believe, when you contract a debt for a fixed time, write it down. And let a scribe write it down between you with fairness. (2 : 282)

ولا تسئموا ان تكتبوه صغيرا او كبيرا الى اجله ذلكم اقسط عند الله واقوم للشهادة وادنى الا ترتابوا الا
ان تكون تجارة حاضرة تديرونها بينكم فليس عليكم جناح الا تكتبوها واشهدوا اذا تبايعتم (بقرہ-۲۸۲)

And be not averse to writing it whether it is small or large along with the time of its falling due. This is more equitable in the sight of Allah and makes testimony surer and the best way to keep away from doubts. But when it is ready merchandise which you give and take among yourselves from hand to hand, there is no blame on you in not writing it down. And have witnesses when you sell one to another. (2 : 282)

وَلَا تَتَمَنَّوْا مَا فَضَّلَ اللّٰهُ بِهٖ بَعْضَكُمْ عَلٰى بَعْضٍ ؕ لِلرِّجَالِ نَصِيْبٌ مِّمَّا اكْتَسَبُوْا ؕ وَلِلنِّسَآءِ نَصِيْبٌ مِّمَّا اكْتَسَبْنَ ؕ
وَسْـَٔلُوا اللّٰهَ مِنْ فَضْلِهٖ ؕ (النساء - ۳۲)

And covet not that by which Allah has made some of you excel others. For men is the benefit of what they earn. And for women is the benefit of what they earn. And ask Allah of His grace. (4 : 32)

وَاَوْفُوا الْكَيْلَ اِذَا كِلْتُمْ وَزِنُوْا بِالْقِسْطَاسِ الْمُسْتَقِيْمِ ؕ (بنی اسرائیل - ۳۵)

And give full measure when you measure out, and weigh with a true balance. (17 : 35)

رِجَالٌ ۙ لَّا تُلْهِيْهِمْ تِجَارَةٌ وَّلَا بَيْعٌ عَنْ ذِكْرِ اللّٰهِ وَاِقَامِ الصَّلٰوةِ وَاِيْتَآءِ الزَّكٰوةِ ۙ يَخَافُوْنَ يَوْمًا تَتَقَلَّبُ
فِيْهِ الْقُلُوْبُ وَالْاَبْصَارُ ۙ (نور - ۳۷)

Men whom neither merchandise nor selling diverts from remembrance of Allah and the keeping up of prayers and the paying of the poor rate—they fear a day in which the hearts and the eyes will turn about. (24 : 37)

فَاِذَا قُضِيَتِ الصَّلٰوةُ فَانْتَشِرُوْا فِى الْاَرْضِ وَابْتَغُوْا مِنْ فَضْلِ اللّٰهِ وَاذْكُرُوا اللّٰهَ كَثِيْرًا لَّعَلَّكُمْ تُفْلِحُوْنَ ۝
(جمعه - ۱۰)

But when the prayer is ended, disperse abroad in the land and seek of Allah's bounty, and remember Allah much that you may be successful. (62 : 10)

وَّجَعَلْنَا النَّهَارَ مَعَاشًا ۝
(النبأ - ۱۱)

And made the day for seeking livelihood. (78 : 11)

وَيْلٌ لِّلْمُطَفِّفِيْنَ ۝ الَّذِيْنَ اِذَا اكْتَالُوْا عَلَى النَّاسِ يَسْتَوْفُوْنَ ۝ وَاِذَا كَالُوْهُمْ اَوْ وَّزَنُوْهُمْ يُخْسِرُوْنَ ۝ (التطفیف - ۱ تا ۳)

Woe to the cheaters! who, when they take the measure (of their dues) from men, take it fully, and when they measure out to others or weigh out for them, they give less than is due. (83 : 1—3)

AHADITH

عن جابر قال قال رسول الله صلى الله عليه وسلم رحم الله رجلاسمحاً اذا باع و اذا اشتري و اذا اقتضى . (بخارى)

Jaber reported that the Messenger of Allah said : May Allah be kind to a man of gentle dealings when he purchases and when he gives decision. (Bukhari)

عن ابى قتادة قال قال رسول الله صلى الله عليه وسلم اياكم و كثرة الحلف فى البيع فانه ينفق ثم يمق . (مسلم)

Abu Qatada reported that the Messenger of Allah said : Be careful of excessive swearing in sale, because it finds market but then reduces (blessings). (Muslim)

عن ابي سعيد قال قال رسول الله صلى الله عليه وسلم التاجر الصدوق الامين مع النبيين و الصديقين و الشهداء .

(ترمذى ، ابن ماجه ، غريب)

Abu Sayeed reported that the Messenger of Allah said : The truthful, trustworthy merchant will be with the prophets, the truthful and martyrs. (Tirmizi, Ibn Majah, Rare)

عن عبيد بن رفاعة عن ابيه عن النبى صلى الله عليه وسلم قال التجار يحشرون يوم القيامة فجاراً الا من اتقي و بر و صدق .

(ابن ماجه ، ترمذي)

Obaid-b-Rafa'a from his father reported that the Holy Prophet said : The merchants will be gathered on the Resurrection Day as transgressors except those who were fearful of Allah, pious and truthful. (Ibn Majah, Tirmizi)

عن ابى هريرة قال عن سمعت رسول الله صلي الله عليه وسلم يقول الحلف منفعة للسلعة ملقة للبركة . (متفق عليه)

Abu Hurairah reported that the Messenger of Allah said : Oath is a means of bargain for the commodities but a cause of deterioration in blessing. (Agreed)

عن ابى هريرة عن النبى صلي الله عليه وسلم قال لا يتفرقن اثنان الا عن تراض . (ابو داؤد)

Abu Hurairah reported from the Messenger of Allah who said : The two (seller & buyer) must not part away except by mutual consent. (Abu Daud)

عن ابن عمر قال رجل رسول الله صلى الله عليه وسلم انى اخدع فى البيوع فقال اذا بايعت فقل لا خلابة فكان الرجل يقوله .

(متفق عليه)

Ibn Omar reported that a man said to the Holy Prophet : Verily I am cheated in sale. He said : when sale is held, say—There's no cheating. The man used to utter it. (Agreed)

عن ابن عمر قال قال رسول الله صلى الله عايه وسلم المتبايعان كل واحد منهما بالخيار على صاحبه ما لم يتفرقا الا بيع الخيار .

(متفق عليه)

Ibn Omar reported that the Messenger of Allah said : the buyer & seller each of them has got option on his partner so long as they have not separated themselves except the option of buying. (Agreed)

عن عبدالله بن مسعود قال قال رسول الله صلى الله عليه وسلم اذا ختلف البيعان فالقول قول البائع و المتباع با لخيار رواه الترمذى و فى رواية بن ماجة قال البيعان اذاختلفا و المبيع قائم بعينه وليس بينهما بينة فالقول ما قال البائع او يتراد ان البيع . (ترمذى، ابن ماجه)

Abdullah-b-Mas'ud reported that the Messenger of Allah said : Where the seller & buyer differ, swearing is the swearing of the seller, and the purchaser has got the right of option. Tirmizi narrated it. In a narration of Ibn-Majah, he said, "when the seller and the buye diagree, and the seller is standing on his ownposition while there is no prof between them, then the other is what the seller takes or both should rescind the sale". (Tirmizi-Ibn Majah).

عن جابر قال نهى رسول الله صلى الله عليه وسلم عن المغابرة و المحاقلة و المزانبة و المحاقلة ان يبيع الرجل الزرع بمائة فرق حنطة و المزانبة ان يبيع التمر في رؤس النخل بمائة فرق و المغابرة كراء الارض بالثلث و الربع. (مسلم)

Jaber reported that the Messenger of Allah forbade Mukhabarah, Mubaqalah and Muzabanah. Mubaqalah is a man's selling corn for one hundred Farq (a weight of nearly eight seers) of wheat, and Muzabanah is to sell dry dates upon the heads of date trees for one hundred Farq. And Mukhabarah is to let out land for one-third or one-fourth (of produce). (Muslim)

عن ابن عمر قال قال رسول الله صلى الله عليه وسلم لا تلقوا السلع حتى يهبط بها الى السوق. (متفق عليه)

Ibn Omar reported that the Messenger of Allah said: Don't meet merchandise beforehand till it is taken down in market. (Ageed)

عن ابی هریرة قال نهی رسول الله صلی الله علیه وسلم عن
بیع الحصاة و عن بیع الغرر. (مسلم)

Abu Hurairah reported that the Holy Prophet forbade sale by stone-throwing and the sale of unpossessed things. (Muslim)

عن واثلة بن الاسقع قال سمعت رسول الله صلی الله علیه وسلم
یقول من باع عیباً لم ینبه لم یزل فی مقت الله او لم تزل الملائکة تلعنة.
(ابن ماجه)

Wasclah-b-Asqa'a reported: I heard the Messenger of Allah say: Whoso sells a defective thing without disclosing it continues to be in the wrath of Allah or angels continue to curse him. (Ibn Majah)

عن ابن عمر ان النبی صلی الله علیه وسلم نهی عن بیع الکالی
بالکالی. (دارقطنی)

Ibn Omar reported that the Holy Prophet forbade sale on credit. (Darqutni)

عن ابی سعید الخدری قال قال رسول الله صلی الله علیه وسلم
من اسلف فی شيءٍ فلا یصرفه الی غیزه قبل ان یقبضه.
(ابو داؤد ، ابن ماجه)

Abu Sayeed al Khodri reported that the Messenger of Allah said: Whoever advances a thing for something, let him not transfer it to another before he possesses it. (Abu Daud, Ibn Majah)

عن ابن عباس قال قال رسول الله صلی الله علیه وسلم لاصحاب
الکیل و المیزان انکم قد ولیتم امرین هلکت فیهما الامام السابقة فیلکم
(ترمذی)

Ibn Abbas reported that the Messenger of Allah said to the owners of measurement and weight: You have been certainly entrusted with two affairs about which the former natives before you were destroyed. (Tırmizi)

عن معمر قال قال رسول الله صلی الله عليه وسلم من احتكر فهو خاط . (مسلم)

Memar reported that the Messengers of Allah said : Whoever monopolises is a sinner. (Muslim)

Remarks.

— The Arabic word far trading is bai (بيع) which means both buying & selling.

— Trade & commerce play a very important part in the acquisition of wealth. The Muslims also spread far and wide through commercial enterprises and for propagating the religion of Islam. According to the Quran & Hadith, it is next to Jihad. The Quran pays a great deal of attention to commerce. It gives us encouragement to take up business. Seeking wealth has been sanctioned & encouraged There is, there fore no sin in seeking addition of wealth after wealth. The Holy Prophet said: Take to trade, because there are nine portions in trade out of ten portions of possession.

— The companions of the Holy Prophet carried on maritime and land trade throughout the then known world and the Arab merchants carried the torch of the new light to the darkest corners of the world. The Prophet himself carried on trade as an agent of Hazrat Khadija. Hazrat Abu Bakr had cloth business. Hazrat Umar carried on corn-trade. Hazrat Usman had cloth business. Imam Abu Hanifa had cloth business.

— Honesty is the secret of success in every thing. "Good will" is a valuable asset to a tradesman. It cannot be attained unless there are honest and kind dealings with customers.

— The Holy Prophet classed an honest merchant with a Prophet on account of the merchant's following Shariat rules in trade, classed him with the truthful on account of his being steadfast to truth, and classed him with martyrs on account of his fighting with heavy odds in treading the path of virtue and honesty in his profession.

— Tradesmen should be strict and impartial with regard to weights and measures.

Sale is contracted by declaration and acceptance expressed uniquivocally in words or in expressions conveying the same meaning. The acceptance may be deferred until the breaking up of the meeting whether the declaration be made personally or by letter or message.

— There are four kinds of sale :-

(a) Muqaezah (مقائضه) i. e sale of kind for kind.

(b) Sirfi (صرف)i e. sale of cash for cash as sale of gold for silver.

(c) Silm (سلم) sale of a credit for kind in cash as crops are taken for payment in future., and

(d) Mutlaq (مطلق) i. e. free sale as sale of a thing in cash for price in cash.

— The power to withhold or accept in trade is called option. It occurs before the sale is complete and there are due proposals and acceptance. A purchaser has got the right of option and may reject an article upon inspection of the article if he has not seen it at the time of purchase. A seller has no option of inspection after sale.

— There are two kinds of sale which are illegal. One kind is simply invaild.(فاسد). It can be validacted by subsequent remark of the condition witch marks it invalid. Another kind is void (باطل). It is illegal *abinitio* and nothing can legalise it. In the former the purchaser can become owner, while in the latter he can not.

— The following things have been declared unlawful in trade.—

(1) Muzabanah (مزابنه) i.e. sale of a known quantity for unknown quantity of price.

(2) Sunnayah (ثنيه) i.e. Sale of fruits upon trees after leaving some fruits from the subject matter of sale.

(3) Mukhabarah (مخابره) i.e. Transfer of a limited and not absolute interest in a land.

(4) Muhaqalah (محاقله) i e. sale of corn in exchange of a like quantity of wheat by conjecture.

(5) Muawamah (معاومه) i.e. sale of fruits while upon trees for one year, two years or more whether the fruits appear or not.

(6) Mulamasah (ملامسه) i.e. Sale by touch.

(7) Munabazah (منابذه) i.e. Sale by throwing stone at the commodity of sale.

(8) Hablul-Habalah (حبل الحباله) i.e. Sale of foetus in womb.

(iii) Generalities :

(a) Land & Labour :

وَهُوَ الَّذِي أَنشَأَ جَنَّاتٍ مَّعْرُوشَاتٍ وَغَيْرَ مَعْرُوشَاتٍ وَالنَّخْلَ وَالزَّرْعَ مُخْتَلِفًا أُكُلُهُ وَالزَّيْتُونَ وَالرُّمَّانَ مُتَشَابِهًا وَغَيْرَ مُتَشَابِهٍ كُلُوا مِن ثَمَرِهِ إِذَا أَثْمَرَ وَآتُوا حَقَّهُ يَوْمَ حَصَادِهِ وَلَا تُسْرِفُوا إِنَّهُ لَا يُحِبُّ الْمُسْرِفِينَ ۝ (انعام-١٤٢)

And He is who produces gardens, trellised and intrellised, and palms and seed-produce of which the fruits are of various sorts, and pomegranates-like and unlike. Eat of its fruits when it bears fruit, and pay the due of it on the day of its reaping, and be not prodigal. Surely He loves not the prodigals. (6: 142)

أَوَلَمْ يَرَوْا أَنَّا نَسُوقُ الْمَاءَ إِلَى الْأَرْضِ الْجُرُزِ فَنُخْرِجُ بِهِ زَرْعًا تَأْكُلُ مِنْهُ أَنْعَامُهُمْ وَأَنفُسُهُمْ أَفَلَا يُبْصِرُونَ ۝ (السجدة ٢٧)

See they not that we drive the water to a land having no herbage, then we bring forth there by seed produce, of which their cattle and they themselves eat. Will they not then see? (32 : 27)

قَالَتْ إِحْدَاهُمَا يَا أَبَتِ اسْتَأْجِرْهُ إِنَّ خَيْرَ مَنِ اسْتَأْجَرْتَ الْقَوِيُّ الْأَمِينُ ۝

One of them said : Only father, employ him ; surely the best of those they there cannot employ is the strong, the faithful one. (28 : 26)

قَالَ اجْعَلْنِي عَلَىٰ خَزَائِنِ الْأَرْضِ إِنِّي حَفِيظٌ عَلِيمٌ ۝ (يوسف ٥٥)

He said : Place me (in authority) over the treasures of the land : Surely I am a good keeper, knowing well. (12 : 55)

وَمَنْ يَّغْلُلْ يَاْتِ بِمَا غَلَّ يَوْمَ الْقِيٰمَةِ (آل عمران-١٦٠)

And whoever acts dishonestly will bring his dishonesty on the day of Resurrection. (3 : 160)

اِنَّ اللّٰهَ يَاْمُرُكُمْ اَنْ تُؤَدُّوا الْاَمٰنٰتِ اِلٰٓى اَهْلِهَا (نساء-٥٨)

Surely Allah commands you to make over trust to those worthy of them. (4 : 58)

وَّاٰتُوْهُمْ مِّنْ مَّالِ اللّٰهِ الَّذِيْٓ اٰتٰىكُمْ (نور-٣٣)

And give them of the wealth of Allah which He has given you. (24 : 35)

(b) State Expenditure:

اِنَّمَا الصَّدَقٰتُ لِلْفُقَرَآءِ وَالْمَسٰكِيْنِ وَالْعٰمِلِيْنَ عَلَيْهَا وَالْمُؤَلَّفَةِ قُلُوْبُهُمْ وَفِي الرِّقَابِ وَالْغٰرِمِيْنَ وَفِيْ سَبِيْلِ اللّٰهِ
وَابْنِ السَّبِيْلِ فَرِيْضَةً مِّنَ اللّٰهِ وَاللّٰهُ عَلِيْمٌ حَكِيْمٌ (توبه-٦٠)

(Zakat) Charity is only for the poor and the needy, and those employed to administer it, and those whose hearts are made to incline (to bruk), and (to free) the captives, and those in debt, and in the way of Allah and for the way farer an ordinance from Allah. And Allah is Knowing, Wise. (9 : 60)

(c) Debt & Mortgage :

وَاِنْ كُنْتُمْ عَلٰى سَفَرٍ وَّلَمْ تَجِدُوْا كَاتِبًا فَرِهٰنٌ مَّقْبُوْضَةٌ (بقره-٢٨٣)

And if you are on a journey and you cannot find a scribe, a security may be taken into possession. (2 : 213)

يٰۤاَيُّهَا الَّذِيْنَ اٰمَنُوْۤا اِذَا تَدَايَنْتُمْ بِدَيْنٍ اِلٰۤى اَجَلٍ مُّسَمًّى فَاكْتُبُوْهُ ؕ (بقرہ - ۲۸۲)

O you who believe, when you contract a debt for a fixed time write it down. (2 : 282)

وَاِنْ كَانَ ذُوْ عُسْرَةٍ فَنَظِرَةٌ اِلٰى مَيْسَرَةٍ ؕ وَاَنْ تَصَدَّقُوْا خَيْرٌ لَّكُمْ اِنْ كُنْتُمْ تَعْلَمُوْنَ ۝ (بقرہ - ۲۸۰)

And if (the debtor) is in straitness, let there be postponement till (the time of) ease. And that you remit (it) as alms is better for you, if you did but know. (2 : 280)

يٰۤاَيُّهَا الَّذِيْنَ اٰمَنُوا اتَّقُوا اللّٰهَ وَذَرُوْا مَا بَقِيَ مِنَ الرِّبٰوۤا اِنْ كُنْتُمْ مُّؤْمِنِيْنَ ۝ (بقرہ - ۲۷۸)

O you who believe, keep your duty to Allah and relinquish what remains (due) from usury, if you are believers. (2 : 278)

يَمْحَقُ اللّٰهُ الرِّبٰوا وَيُرْبِى الصَّدَقٰتِ ؕ (بقرہ - ۲۷۶)

Allah will blot out usury, and He causes charity to prospe (2:276)

AHADITH

عن جابر قال قال رسول الله صلى الله عليه وسلم من كانت له ارض فليزرعها او ليمنحها اخاه فان ابى فليمسك ارضة (متفق عليه)

Jaber reported that the Holy Prophet said : Whoso has got land, let him cultivate it or let it out to his brother. If he denies, let him keep his land to himself. (Agreed)

عن قيس ابن مسلم عن ابى جعفر قال ما بالمدينة اهل بيت هجرة الا يزرعون على الثلث والربع وزارع على وسعد بن مالك وعبدالله ابن مسعود وعمر بن عبدالعزيز والقاسم وعروة وآل ابى بكر وآل عمرو وآل على وابن سيرين وقال عبدالرحمن ابن الاسود كنت اشارك عبدالرحمن بن يزيد فى الزرع وعامل عمر الناس على ان جاء عمر بالبذر من عنده فله الشطر وان جاوا بالبذر فلهم كذا (بخارى)

Qais-b-Muslim reported from Abu Jaber : There were no inmates of any refuging house at Medina who did not cultivate (land) on condition of 3rd or 4th (of produce). Ali, Sa'ad-b-Malek, Abdullah-b-Mas'ud, Omar-b-Abdul Aziz, Qasim, Urwah, the family members of Abu Bakr, the family members of Omar, the family members of Ali and Ibn Sirin had cultivation. Abdur Rahman-b-Aswad said I was a partner with Abdur Rahman-b-Yezid in cultivation. And Omar engaged the people and labour on condition that if Omar gave seeds from himself, there was half for him, and if they supplied the seeds, they should have such a portion. (Bukhari)

عن ابن عمران رسول الله صلى الله عليه وسلم اعطى خيبر اليهود على ان

يعملوها ويزرعوها ولهم شطر ما خرج منها (بخاري)

Ibn 'Umran reported that the Messenger of Allah granted (the lands of) Khaibar to the Jews on condition that they would labour thereon (with their wealth) and cultivated them and for them there would be half of what yield there from. (Bukhari)

عن عبدالله بن مغفل قال زعم ثابت بن الضحاك ان رسول الله صلى الله نهى عن المزارعة و امر بالمواجرة قال لا بأس بها (مسلم)

Abdullah-bin Mugaffal reported that Sabet-e-Zuhhak held that the Messenger of Allah prohibited agricultural leases and enjoined mutual labour. The said : There's no have in it. (Muslim)

عن ابن عمر قال قال النبي صلى الله عليه وسلم من اخذ من الارض شيئاً بغير حقه خسف به يوم القمة الى سبع ارضين (بخارى)

Ibn Omar reported that the Holy Prophet said : "Whoever takes any part of land without having a right to it, he shall be, as a punishment for it, sunk down into earth on the day of Resurrection to the depth of seven earths." (Bukhari)

عن ابى ابن عباس ان النبي صلى الله عليه وسلم احتجم فاعطى الحجام اجره واستعط (متفق عليه)

Ibn Abbas reported that the Messenger of Allah took cupping and paid the cupper his wages. (Agreed).

عن ابي هريرة عن النبي صلى الله عليه وسلم قال ما بعث الله نبياً الا رعى الغنم فقال اصحابه وانت قال نعم كنت ارعى علي قراريط لاهل مكة (بخارى)

Ibn Hurairah reported from the Holy Prophet who said : Allah did not raise up any Prophet who did not graze goats. His companions asked : You to ? "Yes" said he, "I used to tend goats for the inhabitants of Mecca for some Qirats". (Bukhari)

عنه قال قال رسول الله صلى الله عليه وسلم قال الله تعالى ثلثة انا
انا خصمهم يوم القامة رجل اعطى غدي ورجل باع حرا فاكل ثمنه
ورجل استاجره اجيره اجيراً فاستوفى منه ولم يعطه اجره (بخارى)

Same reported that the Messenger of Allah said : The Almighty Allah said—there will be three persons whose apponent I shall become on the Resurrection Day : A man who gave in My name and then broke trust, and a man who sold a free man and enjoyed his price, and a man who engaged a labourer and enjoyed full labour from him but did not pay him his wages. (Bukhari)

عن عبد الله بن عمر قال قال رسول الله صلى الله عليه وسلم اعطوا
الاجير اجرة قبل ان يجف عرقه (ابن ماجه)

Abdullah reported that the Messenger of Allah said : Pay the labourer his wages before his sweat dries up. (Ibn Majah)

عن ابى موسى قال قال النبى صلى الله عليه وسلم الخازن الامين الذى
يودى ما امر به طيبة نفسه احد المتصدقين (بخارى)

Ibn Musa reported that the Holy Prophet said : The faithful treasurer who pay what he is ordered with a willing heart is one of those who give charity. (Bukhari)

عن خباب قال كنت قيناً فى الجاهلية وكان لى على العاص ابن وائل
دين فاتيته اتقا ضاه قال لا اعطيك حتي تكفر بمحمد صلى الله عليه وسلم
فقلت لا اكفر حتي يميتك الله ثم تبعث (بخارى)

Khabbab said : I was a blacksmith in the days of ignorance, and I had a debt due from 'As ibn Wail. So I came to him demanding it. He said, I will not give it to thee until thou deniest Muhammad. I said, I will not deny even if Allah cause thee to die and thou art then raised to life. (Bukhari)

عن سلمة ان النبي صلى الله عليه وسلم اتى بجنازة ليصلي عليها فقال هل عليه من دين قالوا لا فصلي عليه ثم اتى بجنازة اخرا فقال هل عليه من دين قالوا نعم قال صلوا على صاحبكم قال ابو قتادة على دينه يا رسول الله فصلى عليه (بخارى)

Salmah reported, A bier was brought to the Holy Prophet, that he may say funeral prayers over it. He said : Was he in debt ? "They said, No. So he said prayers over it. Another bier was brought to his and he said : "Was he in debt?" They said yes. He said : Say prayer over your companion." Abu Qatadah said I will pay his debt, O Messenger of Allah ! So he said funeral prayers over it. (Bukhari)

Remarks :

1. The Arabic word for the tilling of land and cultivation is Harth (حرث) and Muzara'h (مزارعه). Muzara'ah also caries the meaning of making a contract with another for labour on land to sow and till it for a share of its produce. There is another word Mosaqat (مساقاة) which means watering.

2. Cultivation and gardening are most important factors of production with which people and other animals sustain themselves. Really speaking, the whole civilized world is always greatly indebted to the tillers of the soil.

3. The Holy Quran draws attention to the necessity of turning waste-lands into gardens by making arrangements for watering it, and growing good useful crops. Hadith speaks of it as an art of great merit. Impetus is given to the cultivation of waste-land. Any how it is warned at the same time that a people who give themselves up entirely to agriculture neglecting other lines of their development, are not capable of great and gloreous deeds.

4. The Arabic word for labour is Ijarah (اجارة). It signifies compensation for work done, or wages paid by one man to another for the service rendered.

5. The two basic rules, laid down in connection with labour, in Quran and Hadith, are that:—

(a) The servant shall do his work faithfully and to the best of his ability and

(b) That the master shall pay him fully for the service rendered. Unfaithfulness is severely condemned.

6. Labour has been always dignified. Even the prophets who were the chosen one of Allah engaged themselves in manual labour. The Holy Prophet also even tended flocks sheeps for wages of nearly a two pice per day in Mecca (Bukh. 37 : 2)

7. [1]The Quran has prescribed the principles regulating the budget of state expenditure of Islam in the following terms:

"Verily the Sadaqat (i. e. taxes on Muslims) are only for the poor, and the needy, and those who work for these (taxes), and those whose hearts are to be reconciled and to free the necks (i. e. slaves and prisoners of war), and the heavily indebted, and in the path of God, and for the way farer...a duty imposed by God ; God is known Wise." (9: 60)

8. Lending and borrowing are a necessary condition in human, economic and commercial transactions, and the rules relating to them are laid down in the Holy Quran. Every such transaction should be written down, and the writing should be dictated by the person who owes the debt.

Mortgaging of property is also allowed but the apparent condition of being on a journey or there being no scribe is simply a statement of the difficulties under which it becomes a necessity. A debtor in straitened circumstances must be dealt with leniently, and if he is unable to pay, the debt should be remitted. Contracting a debt when a man did not intend to pay, it is denounced and the Holy Prophets' anxiety to pay his debt is shown in Ahadith. Deferring payment by one who has the means is condemned as unjust and may even be punished. The Muslim state is required to pay the debts of those who contract debt due to need ; it must even maintain uncared...for families. Mortgaging of property as security for payment of debt is allowed, and the mortgage is allowed to derive benefit from it. Usary, even interest, any how is forbiden.[2]

1. Introduction to Islam—Dr. Hamidullah p.144.

2. See "Manual of Hadith" pp.316, 317.

(d) Food & Drinks—Lawful & unlawful :—

يٰٓاَيُّهَا النَّاسُ كُلُوْا مِمَّا فِي الْاَرْضِ حَلٰلًا طَيِّبًا ۡ وَّلَا تَتَّبِعُوْا خُطُوٰتِ الشَّيْطٰنِ (بقرہ-۱۶۸)

O mankind ! Eat of that which is lawful and wholesome in the earth, and follow not the footsteps of the devil. (2 : 168)

كُلُوْا مِنْ طَيِّبٰتِ مَا رَزَقْنٰكُمْ (بقرہ-۵۷)

Eat of the good things wherewith we have provided you. (2 : 57)

يٰٓاَيُّهَا الَّذِيْنَ اٰمَنُوْا لَا تُحَرِّمُوْا طَيِّبٰتِ مَآ اَحَلَّ اللّٰهُ لَكُمْ وَلَا تَعْتَدُوْا
اِنَّ اللّٰهَ لَا يُحِبُّ الْمُعْتَدِيْنَ ۝ وَكُلُوْا مِمَّا رَزَقَكُمُ اللّٰهُ حَلٰلًا طَيِّبًا
(مائدہ-۸۷-۸۸)

O you who believe ! Forbid not the good things which Allah hath made lawful for you, and transgress not. Lo ! Allah loveth not transgressors. Eat of that which Allah hath bestowed on you as food lawful and good. (5 : 87,88)

يٰبَنِيْٓ اٰدَمَ خُذُوْا زِيْنَتَكُمْ عِنْدَ كُلِّ مَسْجِدٍ وَّكُلُوْا وَاشْرَبُوْا وَلَا تُسْرِفُوْا ۚ اِنَّهٗ لَا يُحِبُّ الْمُسْرِفِيْنَ ۝ قُلْ مَنْ حَرَّمَ زِيْنَةَ اللّٰهِ
الَّتِيْٓ اَخْرَجَ لِعِبَادِهٖ وَالطَّيِّبٰتِ مِنَ الرِّزْقِ (اعراف-۳۱،۳۲)

O children of Adam ! Look to your adornment at every place of worship, and eat and drink, but be not prodigal. Lo ! He loveth not the prodigals. Say, who hath forbidden the adornment of Allah which He hath brought forth for his bondmen, and the good things of His providing ? (7 : 31,32)

وَإِنَّ لَكُمْ فِي الْأَنْعَامِ لَعِبْرَةً نُّسْقِيكُم مِّمَّا فِي بُطُونِهِ مِن بَيْنِ فَرْثٍ وَدَمٍ لَّبَنًا خَالِصًا سَائِغًا لِّلشَّارِبِينَ ۝ وَمِن ثَمَرَاتِ النَّخِيلِ وَالْأَعْنَابِ تَتَّخِذُونَ مِنْهُ سَكَرًا وَرِزْقًا حَسَنًا (نحل-٦٦،٦٧)

And lo ! in the cattle there is a lesson for you. We give you to drink of that which is in their bellies, from betwixt the refuse and the blood, pure milk palatable to the drinkers and of the fruits of the date-palm, and grapes, whenever you devise strong drink and (also) good nourishment. (16 : 66,67)

يَا أَيُّهَا الَّذِينَ آمَنُوا إِنَّمَا الْخَمْرُ وَالْمَيْسِرُ وَالْأَنصَابُ وَالْأَزْلَامُ رِجْسٌ مِّنْ عَمَلِ الشَّيْطَانِ فَاجْتَنِبُوهُ لَعَلَّكُمْ تُفْلِحُونَ ۝ (مائده-٩٠)

O ye who believe! Strong drink and games of chance and idols and divining arrows are only an infamy of Satan's handiwork. Leave it aside in order that ye may succeed. (5 : 90)

حُرِّمَتْ عَلَيْكُمُ الْمَيْتَةُ وَالدَّمُ وَلَحْمُ الْخِنزِيرِ وَمَا أُهِلَّ لِغَيْرِ اللَّهِ بِهِ وَالْمُنْخَنِقَةُ وَالْمَوْقُوذَةُ وَالْمُتَرَدِّيَةُ وَالنَّطِيحَةُ وَمَا أَكَلَ السَّبُعُ إِلَّا مَا ذَكَّيْتُمْ وَمَا ذُبِحَ عَلَى النُّصُبِ وَأَن تَسْتَقْسِمُوا بِالْأَزْلَامِ ذَٰلِكُمْ فِسْقٌ (مائده-٣)

Forbidden unto you (for food) are carrion and blood and swine-flesh, and that which hath been dedicated unto any other than Allah, and the strangled, and the dead through beating and the dead through falling from a height, and that which hath been killed by (the goring of) horns, and the devoured of wild beasts, saving that which ye make lawful (by the death stroke), and that which hath been immolated unto idols. And (forbidden is it) that ye swear by the divining arrows. This is abomination. (5 : 3)

إِنَّمَا حَرَّمَ عَلَيْكُمُ الْمَيْتَةَ وَالدَّمَ وَلَحْمَ الْخِنزِيرِ وَمَا أُهِلَّ بِهِ لِغَيْرِ اللَّهِ فَمَنِ اضْطُرَّ غَيْرَ بَاغٍ وَلَا عَادٍ فَلَا إِثْمَ عَلَيْهِ (بقره-١٧٣)

He hath forbidden you only carrion, and blood, and swineflesh, and that which hath been immolated to (the name of) any other than Allah. But he who is driven by necessity, neither craving nor transgressing, it is no sin for him. (2 : 173)

فَكُلُوا مِمَّا رَزَقَكُمُ اللّٰهُ حَلٰلًا طَيِّبًا وَّاشْكُرُوا نِعْمَتَ اللّٰهِ (نحل-١١٤)

So eat of the lawful and good food which Allah hath provided for you, and thank the bounty of your Lord. (16 : 114)

فَكُلُوا مِمَّا غَنِمْتُمْ حَلٰلًا طَيِّبًا وَّاتَّقُوا اللّٰهَ (انفال ٦٩)

Now enjoy what ye have won, as lawful and good, and keep your duty to Allah. (9 : 69)

اَلَّذِيْنَ يَتَّبِعُوْنَ الرَّسُوْلَ النَّبِيَّ الْاُمِّيَّ الَّذِيْ يَجِدُوْنَهٗ مَكْتُوْبًا عِنْدَهُمْ فِي التَّوْرٰىةِ وَالْاِنْجِيْلِ يَاْمُرُهُمْ بِالْمَعْرُوْفِ
وَيَنْهٰىهُمْ عَنِ الْمُنْكَرِ وَيُحِلُّ لَهُمُ الطَّيِّبٰتِ وَيُحَرِّمُ عَلَيْهِمُ الْخَبٰٓئِثَ وَيَضَعُ عَنْهُمْ اِصْرَهُمْ وَالْاَغْلٰلَ الَّتِيْ كَانَتْ
عَلَيْهِمْ (اعراف-١٥٧)

Those who follow the Apostle, the unlettered Prophet, whom they find mentioned in their own (scriptures) in the Law and the Gospel; for he commands them what is just and forbids them what is evil; he allows them as lawful what is good (and pure) and prohibits them from what is bad (and impure); he releases them from their heavy burdens and from the yokes that are upon them. (7 : 157)

كُلُوْا وَاشْرَبُوْا مِنْ رِّزْقِ اللّٰهِ (بقره-٦٠)

Eat and drink of that which Allah hath provided. (2 : 60)

(e) **Begging.** :

لِلْفُقَرَآءِ الَّذِيْنَ اُحْصِرُوْا فِيْ سَبِيْلِ اللّٰهِ لَا يَسْتَطِيْعُوْنَ ضَرْبًا فِي الْاَرْضِ يَحْسَبُهُمُ الْجَاهِلُ اَغْنِيَآءَ مِنَ التَّعَفُّفِ
(بقره-٢٧٣)

(Charity is) for those in need, who, in God's cause, are restricted (from travel), and cannot move about in the land, seeking (for trade or work). The ignorant man thinks, because of their modesty, that they are free from want. (2 : 273)

الشَّيْطٰنُ يَعِدُكُمُ الْفَقْرَ وَيَأْمُرُكُمْ بِالْفَحْشَآءِ (بقرہ-۲۶۸)

The devil promiseth you destitution and enjoineth on you leudness. (2 : 268)

فَكُلُوْا مِنْهَا وَاَطْعِمُوا الْبَآئِسَ الْفَقِيْرَ (حج-۲۸)

Then eat thereof and feed therewith the poor unfortunate. (17 : 28)

وَاِنْ تُخْفُوْهَا وَتُؤْتُوْهَا الْفُقَرَآءَ فَهُوَ خَيْرٌ لَّكُمْ (بقرہ-۲۷۱)

If ye publish your almsgiving, it is well, but if ye hide it and give it to the poor, it will be better for you. (2 : 271)

اِنَّمَا الصَّدَقٰتُ لِلْفُقَرَآءِ وَالْمَسٰكِيْنِ (توبہ-۶۰)

The alms are only for the poor and the needy. (9 : 60)

وَالَّذِيْنَ فِيْٓ اَمْوَالِهِمْ حَقٌّ مَّعْلُوْمٌ لِّلسَّآئِلِ وَالْمَحْرُوْمِ (معارج ۲۴،۲۵)

And in whose wealth there is a right acknowleged for the beggar and the destitute. (70 : 24, 25)

وَاَمَّا السَّآئِلَ فَلَا تَنْهَرْ (ضحیٰ-۱۰)

Therefore the beggar drive not away. (93 : 10)

AHADITH :

عن ابی هریرة قال قال رسول الله صلی الله علیه وسلم من طلب الدنیا حلالاً استعفافاً عن المسئلة وسعیاً علی اهله و تعطفاً علی جاره لقی الله تعالی فی یوم القیامه و وجهه مثل القمر لیلة البدر ومن طلب الدنیا حلالاً مکاثراً مفاخراً امرائیاً لقی الله تعالی و هو علیه غضبان (بیهقی ـ ابونعیم)

Abu Hurairah reported that the Messenger of Allah said : whoso seeks the world in a lawful manner abstaining from begging, and striving for his family and being sympathetic to his neighbour, he will meet the Almighty Allah on the Resurection Day while his face will be like the moon in full moon-night, and whoso seeks the world in a lawful manner, seeking wealth boastfully out of show, he will meet the Almighty Allah while he would be wrathful to him. (Baihaqi, Abu Nayeem)

عن ابی هریرة قال قال رسول الله صلی الله علیه وسلم ان الله طیب . لا یقبل الا طیباً وان الله امر المومنین بما امر به المرسلین فقال یا ایها الرسل کلوا من الطیبات و اعملوا صالحاً وقال یا ایها الذین آمنوا کلوا من طیبات ما رزقنکم ثم ذکر الرجل یطیل السفر اشعث اغبر یمد یدیه الی السماء یا رب یارب ومطعمه حرام، و بمبلسه حرام وغذی بالحرام فانی یستجاب لذلك (مسلم)

Abu Hurairah reported that the Messenger of Allah said : Verily Allah is pure. He does not accept but what is pure. And verily Allah ordered the believers with which He ordered the prophets. He said : O prophets ! eat of the pure things and do good deeds. And He said : Eat of the pure things which we provided you. Then he mentioned about a man dishevelled in hair and laden with dust, making his journey long and extending his hand towards heaven : O Lord ! O Lord ! while his food was unlawful, his drink unlawful, his dress unlawful and he was nourished with unlawful things. He can be responded to for that. (Muslim)

عن النعمان بن بشير قال قال رسول الله صلى الله عليه وسلم الحلال بين والحرام بين وبينهما مشتبهات ، لا يعلمهن كثير من الناس فمن اتقى الشبهات استبرا لدينه وعرضه ومن وقع في الشبهات وقع في الحرام كالراعى يرعى حول الحمى يوشك ان يوقع فيه الا و ان لكل ملك حمى الا و ان حمى الله محارمه الا وان فى الجسد مضغة اذا صلحت صلح الجسد كله واذا فسدت فسد الجسد كله الا وهى القلب (متفق عليه)

Nu'man-b-Bashir reported that the Messenger of Allah said : Lawful things are manifest and unlawful things are also manifest, and between the two are the doubtful things which many people do not know. Whoso guards against the doubtful things, he makes his religion and honour pure ; and whoso falls in the doubtful things, falls in unlawful things like a shepherd who grazes his flock round a reserved pasture ground and doubts grazing therein. Behold! there is a reserved meadow of Allah in His forbidden things. Behold ! there is a piece of flesh in the body. When it is sound, the whole body is sound, and when it is unsound, the whole body becomes unsound. Behold ! it is the heart, (Agreed).

عن العرباض بن سارية ان رسول الله صلى الله عليه وسلم نهى يوم خيبر عن كل ذى ناب من السباع و عن كل ذى مخلب من الطير و عن لحوم الحمر الاهلية و عن المجثمه و عن الخليسة و ان توطأ الحبالى حتى يضعن ما فى بطونهن قال محمد بن يحيى سئل عن ابو عاصم عن المجثمة فقال ان ينصب الطير اوالشئ فيرمى و سئل عن الخليسة فقال الذئب او السبع يدركه الرجل فياخذ منه فتموت فى يده قبل ان يزكيها (ترمذى)

Irbad-b-Sariyah reported that the Messenger of Allah forbade on the day of Khaiber the eating of every beast having attacking teeth and every bird having attacking claws, and the meat of domestic asses, and of animals which die before slaughter, and sexual intercourse with pregnant woman till they put down what is in the their bellies. Muhammad-b-Yahya said that Abu A'sem was asked about Mujassamah. He said : It is to aim a bird or any thing and then to throw at it. And he was asked about Khalisah. He said : Wolf or ferocious beast which a man attacks and from which something is taken and then it dies in his hand before it is sacrificed. (Tirmizi)

عن عبدالرحمن بن شبل ان النبي صلى الله عليه وسلم نهي عن اكل لحم الضب (ابوداؤد)

Abdur Rahman-b-Shibl reported that the Prosphet prohibited the eating of meat of lizards. (Abu Daud)

عن جابر ان النبي صلى الله عليه وسلم نهى عن اكل الهرة و اكل ثمنها

(ابوداؤد - ترمذي)

Jaber reported that the Prophet prohibited the eating of cats and taking its price. (Abu Daud, Tirmizi)

عن ابن عمر قال قال رسول الله صلى الله عليه وسلم احلت لنا ميتتان و دمان الميتتان الحوت و الجراد و الدمان الكبد و الطحال

(احمد - ابن ماجه - دارقطنى)

Ibn Omer reported that the Messenger of Allah said : Two dead things and two bloods have been made lawful for us : the dead things are fishes and locusts, and the bloods are liver and spleen. (Ahmed, Ibn Majah, Darqutni)

عن ابن عباس قال كان اهل الجاهلية ياكلون اشياء ويتركون اشياء تقذراً فبعث الله نبيه و انزل كتابه واحل حلاله و حرم حرامه فما احل فهو حلال و ما حرم فهو حرام و ما سكت عنه فهو عفو و تلاقل لا اجد فيما اوحى الى محرماً على طاعم يطعمه الا ان يكون ميتة او دما - الآية - (ابو داؤد)

Ibn Abbas reported that the Pre-Islamic Arabs used to eat some things and leave other things out of hatred. Then Allah sent this Prophet and sent down this book and made lawful His lawful things and made unlawful His unlawful things. So whatever He made lawful is lawful, and whatever He made unlawful is unlawful, and whatever he remained silent from is pardonable. He recited—Say : I don't find anything prohibited in what was revealed to me for eater to eat except what dies of itself, the verse. (6 : 146 Q)—(Abu Daud)

عن حذيفة قال سمعت رسول الله صلى الله عليه وسلم يقول لا تلبسوا الحرير و لا الديباج و لا تشربوا فى آنيه الذهب و الفضة و لا تاكلوا فى صحافها فإنها لهم فى الدنيا و هى لكم فى الآخرة

(متفق عليه)

Hazaifah reported : I heard the Messenger of Allah say : Don't put on silk and embroidered silk, and drink not in cups of gold and take no food in plates made thereof, because they are for them (unbelievers) in this world and they are for you in the next world. (Agreed)

عن الزبير بن العوام قال قال رسول الله صلى الله عليه وسلم لان ياخذ احدكم حبله فياتى بخرمة حطب على ظهره فيبعها خير له من ان يسئال الناس اعطوه او منعوه (بخارى)

Zubair-b-Awam reported that the Messenger of Allah said : That one of you takes his rope and then comes with a load of wood upon his back and sells it is better than to beg of men whether they give or reject. (Bukhari)

عن ابن عمر ان رسول الله صلى الله عليه وسلم و هو على المنبر و هو يذكر الصدقة و التعفف عن المسئله اليد العايا خير من اليد السفلى و اليد العليا هى المنفقة و السفلى هى السائلة (متقق عليه)

Ibn Omer reported that the Holy Prophet said while he was on the pulpit speaking about charity and refraining from begging : the upper hand is better than the lower, and the upper hand is that which gives and the lower that which begs. (Agreed).

REMARKS :

Defferent things have go different properties for different used and they have naturally got different effects on the body. The Almighty Allah knows out constitution perfectly well and He knows how to keep it best in health. As soundness of mind depends on soundness of body, therefore food and drink may be said to be one of the principal causes which lead a man to vice and virtue. Tae control of food and drink is the control of the vices and promotion of virtues.

In respect of food and drink it is worth mentioning, that what the Quran & Hadith prohibited is unlawful and what is besides that is lawful. There are certain things which have not been expressly permitted or prohibited. These are doubtful things.

The following food & things have been expressly prohibited by the Quran & Hadith.

1. Food on which Allah's name is not taken or meat of a lawful animal or bird which is not slaughtered in the name of Allah.

2. Every thing which is offered to idols.

3. All enimals which die of themselves without slaughter in the name of Allah.

4. All bloods flowing.

5. All beasts and birds of prey.

6. All unclean things rapugnant to health & morality.

There is a reservation in case of extreme necessity, such as possibility of death for want of food. In that circumstance, a small quantity of unlawful things which can barely save life becomes lawful.

Every thing is lawful which has not been prohibited.

Any thing distasteful or repugnant to nature should not be eaten, as may injure health although the thing to be eaten is lawful.

There is no better food than what is acquired from lawful earnings. Allah will not repond to a man who eats unlawful food.

The Holy prophet of Islam did not leave the poor from scathing condemnation & threatening with eternal Hell. He left instructions to the rich not to return a beggar. At the same time the mutual duties and obligations of the beggars and those begged have been laid down for peaceful progress of society. The Prophet not only delivered the oretical advice but also definite rules, so that there might be no poverty in Islam and no poor man to beg from door to door. There are the rules of charity: Zakat, Sadaqah, Fitrah, and the duties towards the neighbours and needy relatives.

Begging is unlawful in Islam because :—

(a) by begging, a man loses reliance upon Allah,

(b) the beggar lowers himself before his fellow creatures,

(c) the beggar gives uneasy trouble to one begged.

Begging is however lawful for one who is compelled by necessity to beg or whose every thing has been accidentally destroyed. A man who is in dire necessity of food, abode and clothing can also beg.

THE LEGAL SYSTEM

(i) Sources of Law :

(a) Al-Quran (الكتاب)

تنزيل الكتب لا ريب فيه من رب العلمين (سجدہ-۲)

The revelation of the Book, there is no doubt in it, is from the Lord of the worlds. (32 : 2)

كتب انزلنه اليك مبرك ليدبروا (ص-۳۰)

(This is) a Scripture that we have revealed unto thee, full of blessing, that they may ponder over its revelation. (38 : 30)

قل انما اتبع ما يوحى الي من ربي هذا بصائر من ربكم وهدى ورحمة لقوم يؤمنون (اعراف-۲۰۳)

Say : I follow only that which is inspired in me from my Lord. This (Quran) is insight from your Lord, and a guidance and a mercy for a people that believe. (7 : 203)

انا انزلنا اليك الكتب بالحق لتحكم بين الناس بما ارىك الله (نساء-۱۰۵)

Lo ; We reveal unto thee the Scripture with the truth, that thou mayest judge between mankind by that which Allah showeth thee. (4 : 105)

ولقد جئنهم بكتب فصلنه على علم هدى ورحمة لقوم يؤمنون (اعراف-۵۲)

Verily we have brought them a Scripture which we expound with knowledge, a guidance and a mercy for a people who believe. (7 : 52)

وَمَآ أَنزَلْنَا عَلَيْكَ الْكِتٰبَ إِلَّا لِتُبَيِّنَ لَهُمُ الَّذِى اخْتَلَفُوا فِيهِ (نحل-۶۴)

And we have not revealed to thee the Book except that thou mayest make clear to them that wherein they differ. (16 : 64)

إِنَّ هٰذَا الْقُرْاٰنَ يَهْدِى لِلَّتِى هِىَ أَقْوَمُ
(الاسراء-۹)

Surely this Quran guides to that which is most upright. (17 : 9)

لَا يَأْتِيهِ الْبَاطِلُ مِنْ بَيْنِ يَدَيْهِ وَلَا مِنْ خَلْفِهِ (حم سجدہ-۴۲)

Falsehood cannot come at it from before it or behind it. (41 : 42)

نَزَّلَ عَلَيْكَ الْكِتٰبَ بِالْحَقِّ مُصَدِّقًا لِّمَا بَيْنَ يَدَيْهِ وَأَنزَلَ التَّوْرٰىةَ وَالْإِنجِيلَ (آل عمران-۳)

He has revealed to thee the Book with truth, verifying that which is before it, and He revealed the Torah and the Gospel. (3 : 3)

أَفَغَيْرَ اللّٰهِ أَبْتَغِى حَكَمًا وَهُوَ الَّذِىٓ أَنزَلَ إِلَيْكُمُ الْكِتٰبَ مُفَصَّلًا (انعام-۱۱۵)

Shall I then seek a judge other than Allah, when He it is who has sent down to you the Book fully explained ? (6 : 115)

وَهٰذَا كِتٰبٌ أَنزَلْنٰهُ مُبٰرَكٌ فَاتَّبِعُوهُ وَاتَّقُوا لَعَلَّكُمْ تُرْحَمُونَ (انعام-۱۵۶)

And this is a Book we have revealed, full of blessings ; so follow it and keep your duty that mercy may be shown to you. (6 : 156)

وَنَزَّلْنَا عَلَيْكَ الْكِتٰبَ تِبْيَانًا لِّكُلِّ شَىْءٍ
وَهُدًى وَرَحْمَةً وَبُشْرٰى لِلْمُسْلِمِينَ
(نحل-۸۹)

And we have revealed the Book to thee explaining all things and a guidanee and mercy and good news for those who submit. (16 : 89)

(b) The Sunnah

لقد من الله على المؤمنين إذ بعث فيهم رسولا من أنفسهم يتلوا عليهم آيته ويزكيهم ويعلمهم الكتب والحكمة
وإن كانوا من قبل لفي ضلل مبين (آل عمران-۱۶۴)

Certainly Allah conferred a favour on the believers when He raised among them a Messenger from among themselves, reciting to them His revelations and purifying them, and teaching them the Book and the wisdom, although before that they were surely in manifest error. (3:164)

وأنزلنا إليك الذكر لتبين للناس ما نزل إليهم
(نحل-۴۴)

And We have revealed to thee the Reminder that thou mayest make clear to men that which has been revealed to them. (16 : 44)

وكيف تكفرون وأنتم تتلى عليكم آيت الله وفيكم رسوله (آل عمران)

And how can you disbelieve while to you are recited the revelations of Allah, and among you is His Messenger. (3 : 101)

وما أرسلنا من رسول إلا ليطاع بإذن الله (نساء-۶۴)

And We sent no messenger but that he should be obeyed by Allah's command. (4 : 64)

وما كان لمؤمن ولا مؤمنة إذا قضى الله ورسوله أمرا أن يكون لهم الخيرة
من أمرهم ومن يعص الله ورسوله فقد ضل ضللا مبينا (احزاب-۳۶)

And it behoves not a believing man or a believing woman, when Allah and His Messenger have decided an affair, to exercise a choice in their matter. And whoever disobeys Allah and His Messenger, he surely strays off to manifest error. (33 : 56)

لقد كان لكم في رسول الله أسوة حسنة (احزاب-۲۱)

Certainly you have in the Messenger of Allah an excellent exemplar. (33 : 21)

فَآمِنُوا بِاللَّهِ وَرَسُولِهِ النَّبِيِّ الْأُمِّيِّ الَّذِي يُؤْمِنُ بِاللَّهِ وَكَلِمَاتِهِ وَاتَّبِعُوهُ لَعَلَّكُمْ تَهْتَدُونَ (اعراف ١٥٨)

So believe in Allah and His Messenger, the Ummi Prophet who believes in Allah and His words, and follow him so that you may be guided aright. (7 : 158)

(c) Ijtihad (اجتهاد) i.e. Ijma & Qiyas :

فَاعْتَبِرُوا يَا أُولِي الْأَبْصَارِ (حشر ٢)

So take a lesson, O you who have eyes. (59 : 2)

وَشَاوِرْهُمْ فِي الْأَمْرِ (آل عمران ١٥٩)

And consult them in (important) matters. (3 : 139)

وَمَن يُشَاقِقِ الرَّسُولَ مِن بَعْدِ مَا تَبَيَّنَ لَهُ الْهُدَىٰ وَيَتَّبِعْ غَيْرَ سَبِيلِ الْمُؤْمِنِينَ نُوَلِّهِ
مَا تَوَلَّىٰ وَنُصْلِهِ جَهَنَّمَ وَسَاءَتْ مَصِيرًا (نساء ١١٥)

And whoso opposeth the Messenger after the guidance (of Allah) has been manifested unto him, and follows other than the way of the believers, We turn him to that to which he (himself) turns and expose him unto hell—a hapless journey's end ! (4 : 115)

AHADITH :

عن معاذ بن جبل : ان رسول الله صلى الله عليه وسلم لما بعثه الى اليمن قال : كيف تقضى اذا عرض لك قضاء ؟ قال اقضي بكتاب الله . قال فان لم تجد فى كتاب الله ؟ قال: فبسنة رسول الله قال: فان لم تجد فى سنة رسول الله ؟ قال : اجتهد برأى ولا آلو . قال فضرب رسول الله صلى الله عليه وسلم على صدره و قال: الحمد لله الذي وفق رسول رسول الله لما يرضى به رسول الله ! (ترمذى - ابوداؤد)

Mūādh bin Jabal reported that when he was being sent (as governor or Qadi) to Yemen, the Prophet asked him : "How will you decide the cases that will be brought before you?" Mūādh replied : " I shall decide them according to the Book of God."—"And if you find nothing concerning (a particular matter) in the Book of God ?"— "Then I shall decide it according to the Sunnah of God's Apostle."— "And if you find nothing about it in the Sunnah of God's Apostle ?" —"Then", replied Mūādh, "I shall exercise my own judgement without the least hesitation." Thereupon the Prophet slapped him upon the chest and said: "Praised be God, who has caused the messages of God's Messenger to please the latter !" (Tirmizi and Abu Daud)

عن ابو برده قال قال رسول الله صلى الله عليه وسلم اصحابى امانة لامتى (مسلم) .

Abu Burdah reported that the Apostle of Allah said : "My Campanions are a trust committed to my community. (Muslim)

عن عبدالله ابن عمر قال قال رسول الله صلى الله عليه وسلم ان الله لايجمع امتى على ضلالة (ترمذى)

Abdullah-bin-Umar reported that the Apostle of Allah said: "Never will God make my community agree on a wrong course." (Tirmizi)

وعنه قال قال رسول الله صلى الله عليه وسلم اتبعوا السواد الأعظم (ابن ماجه)

Same reported that the Apostle of Allah said: "Follow the largest group." (Ibn Majah)

عن معاذ بن جبل قال قال رسول الله صلى الله عليه وسلم عليكم بالجماعة والعامة (احمد)

Muādh-bin-Jabal reported that the Holy Prophet said: "It is your duty to stand by the united community and the majority." (Ahmad)

Remarks.

1. Law is the essential foundation of civil society.

2. Islam is a religion that takes care of the whole individual. It makes use of both moral and legal sanctions, because it realises that both morality and law are necessary for the smooth working of political and social life. Law without morality cannot make righteous, and morality without law cannot prevent evil-doing.

3. The sphere of law in Islam is very wide. There is no field of life which is not ruled by law. There can be no life without law and there has to be some authority to enforce law. Islam is a religion which demands respect for law because it stands for orderly, disciplined, and regular habits of life and dislikes indisciplines, lawlessness, and care-free methods of work,

4. The Islamic law is supreme over political authority. The ruler or leader does not create the law. The Divine Law is the real sovereign and the highest authority is an Islamic state. Even the ruler is subject to this law.

5. Islam has a definite and clear-cut system of law. As far as the Islamic conception of law is concerned, the entire "Shariah" stands as synonymous with law. Because the entire code of life has been decreed by Allah. Anyhow, we can apply (narrowly) the term "Islamic law" to those portions only which demand the sanction of state power for their enforcement.

6. The main objective of the *shariah* is to construct human life on the basis of Marufat (معروفات—virtues) and to cleanse it of the Munkarat (منكرات vices). It lays down the entire scheme of life in such a manner that virtues may flourish and vices may not venom human life. The Shariah is a complete scheme of life and an all-embracing social order—nothing superfluous, nothing lacking.

7. Islamic law came into existence when Adam started his life on earth. After having passed through a long process of purging and pruning, Islamic law (or Islamic Shariah) was revealed to the Holy Prophet in its comprehensive and final shape.

8. Islamic law was finalized during the life-time of the Holy Prophet; its movement has nevertheless not ceased. Finalization does not imply complete immobility.

9. In Islam complete legal sovereignty belongs to Allah, in the sense in which the term is understood in jurisprudence and political science.

10. Generally the main sources of Islamic law are said to be four: the Quran (قرآن) and the Sunnah (سنة or Hadith) being called (الدولته القطعيه or) absolutely sure arguments, while Ijma (اجماع) or Unanimous agreement of the Muslim Jurists, and Qiyas (قياس) or reasoning or analogy are called arguments obtained by exertion (or الدولته الاجتهاديه).

11. Thus the original source from which all principles, laws & ordinances of Islam are drawn is the Holy Book called Al-Quran (or الكتاب). Sunnah or Hadith is the second source from which the laws of Islam are drawn. Sunnah, in conjunction with the Quran, formulates and completes the Supreme Law of the real Sovereign.

12. However, Islam does not totally exclude human legislation. But this, according to Islam, is and should be subject to the supremacy of Divine Law and within the limits prescribed by it. This type of legislation & the first means of effecting movement and evolution in Islamic law is Ijtihad (اجتهاد)

13. The word "Ijtihad" literally means to put in the maximum of effort in performing a job, but technically it signifies "maximum effort to ascertain, in a given problem or issue, the injunction of Islam & its real intent.

14. The basic idea of Ijtihad is that man should try to bring under the governance of the Shariah even those matters regarding which the Quran & Sunnah have not laid down any clear-cut injunctions. Thus as regards Ijtihad or original legislation, it requires the jurist to have not only a deep knowledge of Islamic law but also a developed sense of interpreting matters in the true Islamic spirit. A Mujtahid should possess the following qualifications :—

(i) Faith in the Shairah & conviction of its truthfulness; with the intention to follow it.

(ii) Proper knowledge of the Arabic language and literature.

(iii) Such knowledge of & insigh in the teachings of the Quran & Sunnah as would enable one not only to be conversant with the details of Islamic injunctions and their application in actual practice but fully to appreciate the basic principles of Shariah and its objectives.

(iv) Acquaintance with the contributions of the earlier jurists and thinkers (مجتہدین) of Islam.

(v) Acquaintance with the problems & conditions of our times—the new problems of life to which an answer is sought.

(vi) Commendable character & conduct according to the Islamic ethical standards.

15 The purpose of Ijtihad is not to replace "Divine Law" by man-made law. Its real object is to properly understand that Supreme Law and to impart dynamism to the legal system of Islam by keeping it in conformity with the fundamentals of the Shariah and abreast of the changing conditions of the world. That is why we can say that Islamic law has been so constituted as to combine successfully two contradictory characteristics. From one angle, Islamic law is rigid & immutable and no changes in the social environment of man can alter it (Quran and Sunnah). From another angle, Islamic law is sufficiently flexible and broad to remain capable in all circumtances of fashioning human life according to its eternal norms.

The contribution that Ijtihad has made in the enrichment of Islamic law is testified by the vast treasure of Islamic Fiqh that we possess to day.*

*For details see: Islamic law & constitution (Abul Ala)
قانون تدوین اسلامی (Islahi) and monthly magazine 'The Voice of Islam' (N.A.)

(ii) Administration of Justice :

Al-Quran

يٰاَيُّهَا الَّذِيْنَ اٰمَنُوْا كُوْنُوْا قَوّٰمِيْنَ بِالْقِسْطِ شُهَدَاۤءَ لِلّٰهِ وَلَوْ عَلٰى اَنْفُسِكُمْ اَوِ الْوَالِدَيْنِ وَالْاَقْرَبِيْنَ اِنْ يَّكُنْ غَنِيًّا
اَوْ فَقِيْرًا فَاللّٰهُ اَوْلٰى بِهِمَا فَلَا تَتَّبِعُوا الْهَوٰى اَنْ تَعْدِلُوْا وَاِنْ تَلْوٗا اَوْ تُعْرِضُوْا فَاِنَّ اللّٰهَ كَانَ بِمَا تَعْمَلُوْنَ خَبِيْرًا
(نساء-١٣٥)

O you who believe, be maintainers of justice, bearers of witness for Allah, even though it be against your own selves or (your) parents or near relations—whether he be rich or poor, Allah has a better right over them both. So follow not (your) low desires, lest you deviate. And if you distort or turn away from (truth), surely Allah is ever Aware of what you do. (4 : 135)

يٰاَيُّهَا الَّذِيْنَ اٰمَنُوْا كُوْنُوْا قَوّٰمِيْنَ لِلّٰهِ شُهَدَاۤءَ بِالْقِسْطِ وَلَا يَجْرِمَنَّكُمْ شَنَاٰنُ قَوْمٍ عَلٰى اَلَّا تَعْدِلُوْا اِعْدِلُوْا
(مائدہ-٨)

O you who believe ! be steadfast witnesses for Allah in equity, and let not hatred of any people seduce you that you deal not justly. Deal justly. (5 : 8)

اِنَّ اللّٰهَ يَاْمُرُ بِالْعَدْلِ وَالْاِحْسَانِ وَاِيْتَاۤئِ ذِى الْقُرْبٰى وَيَنْهٰى عَنِ الْفَحْشَاۤءِ وَالْمُنْكَرِ وَالْبَغْيِ (نحل-٩٠)

Surely, Allah enjoins justice and the doing of good (to others) and the giving to the kindred, and he forbids indecency and evil and rebellion. (16 : 90)

اِنَّ اللّٰهَ يَاْمُرُكُمْ اَنْ تُؤَدُّوا الْاَمٰنٰتِ اِلٰى اَهْلِهَا وَاِذَا حَكَمْتُمْ بَيْنَ النَّاسِ اَنْ تَحْكُمُوْا بِالْعَدْلِ اِنَّ اللّٰهَ نِعِمَّا يَعِظُكُمْ بِهٖ
(نساء-٥٨)

Surely Allah commands you to make over trusts to those worthy of them, and that when you judge between people, you judge with justice. Surely Allah admonishes you with what is excellent. (4 : 58)

فَلَا وَرَبِّكَ لَا يُؤْمِنُوْنَ حَتّٰى يُحَكِّمُوْكَ فِيْمَا شَجَرَ بَيْنَهُمْ ثُمَّ لَا يَجِدُوْا فِيْٓ اَنْفُسِهِمْ حَرَجًا مِّمَّا قَضَيْتَ
وَيُسَلِّمُوْا تَسْلِيْمًا (نساء-٦٥)

But no, by thy Lord ! they believe not until they make thee a judge of what is in dispute between them, then find not any straitness in their hearts as to that which thou decidest and submit with full submission. (4 : 65)

وَاِذَا قُلْتُمْ فَاعْدِلُوْا وَلَوْ كَانَ ذَا قُرْبٰى (انعام-١٥٣)

And when you speak, be just, though it be (against) a relative. (6 : 152)

وَقُلْ اٰمَنْتُ بِمَآ اَنْزَلَ اللّٰهُ مِنْ كِتٰبٍ وَاُمِرْتُ لِاَعْدِلَ بَيْنَكُمْ
(شوریٰ-١٥)

And say : I believe in what Allah has revealed of the Book, and I am commanded to do justice between you. (42 : 15)

وَاسْتَشْهِدُوْا شَهِيْدَيْنِ مِنْ رِّجَالِكُمْ فَاِنْ لَّمْ يَكُوْنَا رَجُلَيْنِ فَرَجُلٌ وَّامْرَاَتٰنِ مِمَّنْ تَرْضَوْنَ مِنَ
الشُّهَدَآءِ اَنْ تَضِلَّ اِحْدٰىهُمَا فَتُذَكِّرَ اِحْدٰىهُمَا الْاُخْرٰى وَلَا يَاْبَ الشُّهَدَآءُ اِذَا مَا دُعُوْا (بقرة-٢٨٢)

And call to witness from among you men two witnesses ; but if there are not two men, then one man and two women from among those whom you choose to be witnesses, so that if one of the two errs, the one may remind the other. And the witnesses must not refuse when they are summoned. (2 : 282)

وَلَا تَكْتُمُوا الشَّهَادَةَ وَمَنْ يَّكْتُمْهَا فَاِنَّهٗٓ اٰثِمٌ قَلْبُهٗ (بقرة-٢٨٣)

And conceal not testimony. And whoever conceals it, his heart is surely sinful. (2 : 283)

وَالَّذِيْنَ يَرْمُوْنَ الْمُحْصَنٰتِ ثُمَّ لَمْ يَاْتُوْا بِاَرْبَعَةِ شُهَدَآءَ فَاجْلِدُوْهُمْ ثَمٰنِيْنَ جَلْدَةً وَّلَا تَقْبَلُوْا لَهُمْ شَهَادَةً اَبَدًا
(نور-٤)

And those who accuse free women and bring not four witnesses, flog them (with) eighty stripes and never accept their evidence. (24 : 4)

AHADITH :

عن بريده قال قال رسول الله صلى الله عليه وسلم القضاة ثلثة واحده في الجنة و اثنان في النار فاما الذى فى الجنة فرجل عرف الحق فقضى به و رجل عرف الحق فجار فى الحكم فهو فى النار و رجل قضى للناس على جهل فهو فى النار . (ابو داؤد ابن ماجه)

Boraidah reported that the Prophet said : Judges are of three kinds : One kind will be in Paradise and the two in Hell. As for one who will be in Paradise, he is a man who recognises truth and gives a decree accordingly, and a man who recognises truth but is unjust in decree is in Hell, and a man who passes decree for the people but out of ignorance is in Hell. (Abu Daud, Ibn-e-Majah)

عن عبدالله بن ابى اوفى قال قال رسول الله صلى الله عليه وسلم ان الله مع القاضى مالم يجر فاذا جار تخلى عنه و لزمه الشيطان

(ترمذى - ابن ماجه)

Abdullah-b-Abi Aufa reported that the Messenger of Allah said : Verily Allah is with a judge so long as he is not unjust. When he is unjust (intentionally), He goes off from him, and the devil keeps attached to him. (Tirmizi, Ibn-e-Majah)

عن ابى بكرة قال سمعت قال رسول الله صلى الله عليه وسلم يقول لايقضين حاكم بين اثنين وهو غضبان (متفق عليه)

Abu Bakrah reported : I heard the Messenger of Allah say : No judge shall pass a decree between two men while he is angry. (Agreed)

عن علي قال بعثني رسول الله صلي الله عليه وسلم الى اليمن قاضياً فقلت يا رسول الله ترسلني وانا حدیث السن ولا اعلم لی بالقضاء قال ان الله يهدى قلبك و يثبت لسانك اذا تقاضا اليك رجلان فلا تقض للاول حتی تسمع كلام الآخر فانه اخرى ان يتبين لك القضاء قال فما شككت فی قضا بعد . (ترمذي - ابو داؤد - ابن ماجه)

Ali reported : The Messenger of Allah sent me to Yemen as a judge. I said : O Messenger of Allah! you are sending me while I am young in years and I have no knowledge of judgeship. He said : Verily Allah will soon give guidance to your heart and make your tongue firm. When two persons come to you for decision, don't give decree in favour of the first till you hear the argument of the other, because that is more necessary that decision may become clear to you. He said : I had afterwards never entertained any doubt in decisions. (Tirmizi, Abu Daud, Ibn-e-Majah)

عن سعيد بن المسيب ان مسلما ويهوديا اختصما الى عمر فراي الحق لليهودى فقضى له عمر به فقال له اليهودى والله لقد قضيت بالحق فقر به، عمر بالدرة وقال ما يدريك فقال اليهودي والقد انا نجد فی التوراة انه ليس قاض يقضى بالحق الا كان عن يمينه ملك وعن شماله ملك ليسدد انه ويرفقانه للحق مادام مع الحق فاذا ترك الحق عرجاه و ترکاه

(مالك)

Sayeed-b-al-Musayyeb reported that a Muslim and a Jew quarreled with each other before Umar. He saw justice in favour of the Jew. So Umar gave him a decree thereof Then the Jew said : By Allah, you have decided with truth. Then Umar beat him with a stick and said : What has informed you? Then the Jew said : By Allah! we find in the Torah that there is no judge who judges with truth but an angel is by his right hand and an angel by his left-hand side, helping him and giving means of help for truth so long as he remains on truth; but when he gives up truth, they give him up and leave him. (Malek)

عن عمرو بن شعيب عن ابيه عن جده ان النبي صلي الله عليه وسلم قال البنية على المدعى واليمين على المدعىٰ عليه (ترمذی)

Amr-b-Shuaib reported from his father from his grandfather that the Messenger of Allah said : Proof is up on the plaintiff and oath is up on the defendant. (Tirmizi)

عن ابن عباس ان النبی صلی الله عليه وسلم قال لرجل حلفه احلف بالله الذي لا اله الا هو وماله عندك شيء يعنى للمدعى (ابو داؤد)

Ibn Abbas reported that the Messenger of Allah said to a man who took oath before him: Take oath before him. Take oath in the name of Allah except whom there is no god. There is nothing to you for him, that is for the claimant, in your possession. (Abu Daud)

عن ابی امامه قال قال رسول لله صلی الله عليه وسلم من اقتطع حق امرى مسلم بيمينه فقد اوجب الله له النار و حرم عليه الجنة فقال له رجل و ان كان شيئاً يسيراً يا رسول الله؟ قال وان كان قضيباً من اراك (مسلم)

Abu Omamah reported that the Prophet said : Whoso takes the right of a Muslim with his oath, Allah makes Hell sure for him and Paradise unlawful. A man asked him: O Prophet of Allah, even though it be a small thing? He said : Even if it is a rod of Arak. (Muslim)

عن زيد بن خالد قال قال رسول الله صلى الله عليه وسلم الا اخبركم بخير الشهداء الذی یاتي بشهادته قبل ان يسامها (مسلم)

Zaid-e-Khalid reported that the Messenger of Allah said : Shall I not inform you about the best of witnesses?—He who comes with his deposition before he is asked for it. (Muslim)

عن عمر بن شعيب عن ابيه عن جده عن النبي صلى الله عليه وسلم قال لا تجوز شهادة خائن ولا خائنة زان ولا زانيه ولا ذی عمر على اخيه و رد شهادة القانع لاهل البيت (ابو داؤد)

Amr-b-Shuaib reported from his father from his grandfather that the Messenger of Allah said : Deposition of a treacherous man or woman is not lawful, nor of a fornicator or fornicatress, nor of a man having enmity with his brother. He also rejected the deposition of a man who is pleased with the members of his family. (Abu Daud)

Remarks :

1. The conception of justice in Islam is that it should be impartial and that there should be no discrimination between high and low, prince and peasant, white and black, Muslim and non-Muslim, and between the strangers and the relatives. It becomes incumbent upon the Head of the state to provide free impartial justice to all, irrespective of caste, creed, colour, nationality, race, status or sex. All are equal in the eye of law, and justice should be done to all people where justice is due. For the dispensation of justice, the Head of the state should appoint highly qualified, competent and responsible persons as judges.

2. Al-Mawardi, the celebrated Muslim jurist during Abbasids, prescribed the following qualifications for judges :-

(i) They should be in possession of sound knowledge of Islam and Shariah;

(ii) Should possess irreproachable character;

(iii) Should possess full mental faculties, and be sound of sight and hearing;

(iv) Should be Muslims;

(v) Should be adults;

(vi) Should be free citizens.

3. The judges were required to perform the following duties :-

(i) Settlement of disputes and restoration of rights.

(ii) Administration of the properties of minors and the insane.

(iii) Supervision of endowments and execution of wills.

(iv) Encouraging and arranging the marriages of widows and enforcing the period of their waiting.

(v) Control over subordinates and watching their conduct.

4. In order to facilitate the work of judges, a new institution of Mufti (مفتی) was systematised by Umar the Great. A few famous and trustworthy scholars were authorised to give legal opinion, on applica-

tion, without charging any fee. This important institution justified the state in assuring that every citizen knew the law, for it gave a free opportunity to every person to know such legal details which he or she did not already know.

5. The judiciary was fully developed during the Abbasid Caliphate. The caliph or his representatives in the provinces used to appoint judges but from the time of caliph Haroon-ur-Rashid, the office of "Chief Justice" was also instituted and the entire judicial function was entrusted to him.

6. In order to assist the judges in the administration of justice another class of officers was established which was like the notaries public of modern times; they were called Aadils (عادل).

7. There is no such reservation as "The king can do no wrong" or "The king is above all party politics, or "The king is above law". In Islam, the king or the ruler is as much subject to law as a commoner and must appear before the judge (قاضی) for trial. There are recorded cases of this kind not only regarding Hazrat Umar and Hazrat Ali but even the Ummayyad and Abbasid caliphs.

8. Some important points in connection with the procedure may be summed up as follows :—

(a) A judge should treat all the parties equally;

(b) the burden of proof lies on the plaintiff or the parties equally.

(c) the defendent or accused should swear in the absence of evidence;

(d) the judge could review his own judgement;

(e) the date of hearing should be fixed in advance;

(f) in the absence of the defendant, the case should be decided *exparte*, and

(g) every Muslim is qualified to give evidence provided he has not undergone any punishment previously and provided his false testimony has not been already proved;

(h) there should be at least two male witnesses or one man and two women.

9. The system of examination-in-chief followed by cross examination in such a way that one witness might not hear the account given by another was first adopted by Hazrat Ali.

10. Perhaps the most characteristic feature of Islam is its attitude regarding the non-Muslims in the award of social and judicial autonomy,

(iii) Crimes & Punishment

Al-Quran

يَٰٓأَيُّهَا ٱلَّذِينَ ءَامَنُوا كُتِبَ عَلَيْكُمُ ٱلْقِصَاصُ فِى ٱلْقَتْلَى ٱلْحُرُّ بِٱلْحُرِّ وَٱلْعَبْدُ بِٱلْعَبْدِ وَٱلْأُنثَىٰ بِٱلْأُنثَىٰ فَمَنْ عُفِىَ لَهُۥ
مِنْ أَخِيهِ شَىْءٌ فَٱتِّبَاعٌۢ بِٱلْمَعْرُوفِ وَأَدَآءٌ إِلَيْهِ بِإِحْسَٰنٍ ذَٰلِكَ تَخْفِيفٌ مِّن رَّبِّكُمْ وَرَحْمَةٌ فَمَنِ ٱعْتَدَىٰ
بَعْدَ ذَٰلِكَ فَلَهُۥ عَذَابٌ أَلِيمٌ ۝ وَلَكُمْ فِى ٱلْقِصَاصِ حَيَوٰةٌ يَٰٓأُولِى ٱلْأَلْبَٰبِ لَعَلَّكُمْ تَتَّقُونَ ۝ (بقرہ ـ ۱۷۸، ۱۷۹)

O ye who believe! Retaliation is prescribed for you in the matter of the murdered; the freeman for the freeman, and the slave for the slave, and the female for the female. And for him who is forgiven somewhat by his (injured) brother, presentation according to usage and payment unto him in kindness. This is an alleviation and a mercy from your Lord. He who transgresseth after this will have a painful doom. And there is life for you in retaliation, O men of understanding, that Ye may ward off (evil). [2 : 178, 179]

وَٱلْفِتْنَةُ أَكْبَرُ مِنَ ٱلْقَتْلِ وَلَا يَزَالُونَ يُقَٰتِلُونَكُمْ حَتَّىٰ يَرُدُّوكُمْ عَن دِينِكُمْ إِنِ ٱسْتَطَٰعُوا وَمَن يَرْتَدِدْ مِنكُمْ عَن
دِينِهِۦ فَيَمُتْ وَهُوَ كَافِرٌ فَأُولَٰٓئِكَ حَبِطَتْ أَعْمَٰلُهُمْ فِى ٱلدُّنْيَا وَٱلْآخِرَةِ (بقرہ ـ ۲۱۷)

And persecution is worse than killing. And they will not cease from fighting against you till they have made you renegades from your religion, if they can. And whoso becometh a renegade and dieth in his disbelief, such are they whose works have fallen both in the world and the Hereafter. [2 : 217]

وَمَا كَانَ لِمُؤْمِنٍ اَنْ يَّقْتُلَ مُؤْمِنًا اِلَّا خَطَـًٔا ۚ وَمَنْ قَتَلَ مُؤْمِنًا خَطَـًٔا فَتَحْرِيْرُ رَقَبَةٍ مُّؤْمِنَةٍ وَّدِيَةٌ مُّسَلَّمَةٌ اِلٰۤى اَهْلِهٖۤ
اِلَّاۤ اَنْ يَّصَّدَّقُوْا ۚ فَاِنْ كَانَ مِنْ قَوْمٍ عَدُوٍّ لَّكُمْ وَهُوَ مُؤْمِنٌ فَتَحْرِيْرُ رَقَبَةٍ مُّؤْمِنَةٍ ۚ وَاِنْ كَانَ مِنْ قَوْمٍ بَيْنَكُمْ وَبَيْنَهُمْ
مِّيْثَاقٌ فَدِيَةٌ مُّسَلَّمَةٌ اِلٰۤى اَهْلِهٖ وَتَحْرِيْرُ رَقَبَةٍ مُّؤْمِنَةٍ ۚ فَمَنْ لَّمْ يَجِدْ فَصِيَامُ شَهْرَيْنِ مُتَتَابِعَيْنِ ۫ تَوْبَةً مِّنَ اللّٰهِ ؕ
وَكَانَ اللّٰهُ عَلِيْمًا حَكِيْمًا ۝ وَمَنْ يَّقْتُلْ مُؤْمِنًا مُّتَعَمِّدًا فَجَزَآؤُهٗ جَهَنَّمُ خَالِدًا فِيْهَا وَغَضِبَ اللّٰهُ عَلَيْهِ وَلَعَنَهٗ وَاَعَدَّ
لَهٗ عَذَابًا عَظِيْمًا ۝ (نسآء-۹۲،۹۳)

It is not for a believer to kill a believer unless (it be) by mistake. He who hath killed a believer by mistake must set free a believing slave, and pay the blood-money to the family of the slain, unless they remit it as a charity. If he (the victim) be of a people hostile unto you, and he is a believer, then (the penance is) to set free a believing slave. And if he cometh of a folk between whom and you there is covenant, then the blood-money must be paid unto his folk and (also) a believing slave must be set free. And whoso hath not the therewithal must fast two consecutive months. A penance from Allah. Allah is Knower, Wise. Whoso slayeth a believer of set purpose, his reward is wrath against him, and he hath cursed him and prepared for him an awful doom. [4:92,93].

كَتَبْنَا عَلٰى بَنِيْۤ اِسْرَآءِيْلَ اَنَّهٗ مَنْ قَتَلَ نَفْسًا بِغَيْرِ نَفْسٍ اَوْ فَسَادٍ فِى الْاَرْضِ
فَكَاَنَّمَا قَتَلَ النَّاسَ جَمِيْعًا ؕ وَمَنْ اَحْيَاهَا فَكَاَنَّمَاۤ اَحْيَا النَّاسَ جَمِيْعًا ؕ وَلَقَدْ جَآءَتْهُمْ رُسُلُنَا بِالْبَيِّنٰتِ ثُمَّ اِنَّ كَثِيْرًا مِّنْهُمْ
بَعْدَ ذٰلِكَ فِى الْاَرْضِ لَمُسْرِفُوْنَ ۝ اِنَّمَا جَزٰٓؤُا الَّذِيْنَ يُحَارِبُوْنَ اللّٰهَ وَرَسُوْلَهٗ وَيَسْعَوْنَ فِى الْاَرْضِ فَسَادًا اَنْ يُّقَتَّلُوْۤا
اَوْ يُصَلَّبُوْۤا اَوْ تُقَطَّعَ اَيْدِيْهِمْ وَاَرْجُلُهُمْ مِّنْ خِلَافٍ اَوْ يُنْفَوْا مِنَ الْاَرْضِ ؕ ذٰلِكَ لَهُمْ خِزْىٌ فِى الدُّنْيَا وَلَهُمْ فِى الْاٰخِرَةِ
عَذَابٌ عَظِيْمٌ ۝ اِلَّا الَّذِيْنَ تَابُوْا مِنْ قَبْلِ اَنْ تَقْدِرُوْا عَلَيْهِمْ ۚ (مائدہ-۳۲،۳۳،۳۴)

We decreed for the children of Israel that whosoever killeth a human being for other than manslaughter or corruption in the earth, it shall be as if he had killed all mankind and whoso, saveth the life of one, it shall be as if he had saved the life of all mankind. Our messengers came unto then of old with clear proofs (of Allah's Sovereignty) but afterwards, lo many of them became prodigals in the earth. The only reward of those who make war upon Allah and His Messenger and strive after corruption in the land will be that they will be killed or crucified, or have their hands and feet on alternative sides cut off, or will be expelled out of the land. Such will be their degradation in the world, and in the hereafter their will be an awful doom. Save those who repent before you overpower them. [5 : 32,33,34]

وَالسَّارِقُ وَالسَّارِقَةُ فَاقْطَعُوٓا أَيْدِيَهُمَا جَزَآءًۢ بِمَا كَسَبَا نَكَالًا مِّنَ اللّٰهِ (مائده-٣٨)

As for the thief, both male and female, cut off their hands. It is the reward of their own deeds: an exemplary punishment from Allah. [5 : 38]

وَلَا تَقْتُلُوا النَّفْسَ الَّتِي حَرَّمَ اللّٰهُ إِلَّا بِالْحَقِّ (انعام-١٥١)

And that ye slay not the life which Allah hath made sacred, save in the course of justice. [6 : 151]

وَلَا تَقْرَبُوا الزِّنٰىٓ إِنَّهُ كَانَ فَاحِشَةً وَسَآءَ سَبِيلًا
وَلَا تَقْتُلُوا النَّفْسَ الَّتِي حَرَّمَ اللّٰهُ إِلَّا بِالْحَقِّ وَمَنْ قُتِلَ مَظْلُومًا فَقَدْ جَعَلْنَا لِوَلِيِّهِ سُلْطَانًا فَلَا يُسْرِفْ فِّي الْقَتْلِ
إِنَّهُ كَانَ مَنْصُورًا (بني اسرائيل-٣٢-٣٣)

Nor come nigh to adultery, for it is a shameful (deed) and an evil, opening the road (to other evils). Nor take life—which Allah has made sacred—except for just cause. And if anyone is slain wrongly, we have given his heir authority (to demand Qisas or to forgive) : but let him not exceed bounds in the matter of taking life; for he is helped (by the law). [17 : 32, 33]

اَلزَّانِيَةُ وَالزَّانِي فَاجْلِدُوا كُلَّ وَاحِدٍ مِّنْهُمَا مِائَةَ جَلْدَةٍ وَّلَا تَأْخُذْكُمْ بِهِمَا رَأْفَةٌ
فِي دِينِ اللّٰهِ إِنْ كُنْتُمْ تُؤْمِنُونَ بِاللّٰهِ وَالْيَوْمِ الْآخِرِ وَلْيَشْهَدْ عَذَابَهُمَا طَآئِفَةٌ مِّنَ الْمُؤْمِنِينَ (نور-٢)

The woman and the man guilty of adultery or fornication—flog each of them with a hundred stripes ; let not compassion move you in their case, in a matter prescribed by Allah, if ye believe in Allah and the Last Day : and let a p[illegible]y of the Believers witness their punishment.

وَالَّذِيْنَ يَرْمُوْنَ الْمُحْصَنٰتِ ثُمَّ لَمْ يَاْتُوْا بِاَرْبَعَةِ شُهَدَآءَ فَاجْلِدُوْهُمْ ثَمٰنِيْنَ جَلْدَةً وَّلَا تَقْبَلُوْا لَهُمْ شَهَادَةً اَبَدًا ۚ وَاُولٰٓئِكَ هُمُ الْفٰسِقُوْنَ ۙ اِلَّا الَّذِيْنَ تَابُوْا مِنْۢ بَعْدِ ذٰلِكَ وَ اَصْلَحُوْا (نور-۴ و ۵)

And those who launch a charge against chaste women, and produce not four witnesses (to support their allegation),—flog them with eighty stripes ; and reject their evidence even after ; for such men are wicked transgressors ; unless they repent thereafter and mend (their conduct). [24 : 4, 5]

وَجَزٰٓؤُا سَيِّئَةٍ سَيِّئَةٌ مِّثْلُهَا
(شوریٰ - ۴۰)

The guerdon of an ill deed is an ill the like thereof. [42 : 40]

AHADITH :

عن على عن النبى صلى الله عليه وسلم قال من اصاب حداً فجعل عقوبتـه في الدنيا فالله اعدل من ان يثنى على عبده العقوبة في الآخرة و من اصاب حداً فسره الله عليه وعفى عنـــه فالله اكرم من ان يعود فى شىء قد عفا عنه . (ترمذى، ابن ماجه)

Ali reported from the Holy Prophet who said: Whoso commits an ordained crime, his sentence is hastened in this world. Then Allah is much more just than that He should make the punishment double on His servant in the next world. Whoso commits an ordained crime and then Allah conceals it from him and pardons him, Allah is more honourable than that He should return to a thing which He has pardoned. (Tirmizi, Ibn Majah).

عن عائشة ان قريشاً اهمهم شان المرأة المخزوميته التى سرقت فقالوا من يكلم فيها رسول الله صلى الله عليه وسلم فقالوا ومن يجترى عليه الا اسامة بن زيد حِب رسول الله صلى الله عليه وسلم فكلمه اسامه فقال رسول الله صلى الله عليه وسلم تشفع فى حد من حدود الله ثم قام فاختطب ثم قال انما اهلك الذين قبلكم انهم كانوا اذا سرق فيهم الشريف تركوه واذا سرق فيهم الضعيف اقاموا عليه الحد و ايم الله لو ان فاطمة بنت محمد سرقت لقطعت يدها. (متفق عليه)

Ayesha reported that verily as for the Quraish—the affair of a woman of Makhzoom tribe who had stolen gave them much anxiety. They said: who will plead for her to the Messenger of Allah? They said: Who will dare it than Osamah, son of Zaid, who is favourite of the Messenger of Allah? Then Osamah pleaded to him. The Messenger of Allah said: You plead for a crime out of the ordained crimes of Allah! Then he got up and delivered Sermon. Afterward he said: Verily those who were before you were destroyed, because when a noble man from them committed theft, they let him off, and when a workman committed theft from among them, they exempted sentence on him. By Allah, had Fatimah, daughter of Muhammad, committed theft, I would have cut off her hand. (Agreed).

عن عبدالله ابن مسعود قال قال رسول الله صلى الله عليه وسلم اول ما يقضى بين الناس يوم القيامة فى الدماء (متفق عليه)

Abdullah-Masud reported that the Messenger of Allah said: The first of what will be decided on the Resurrection Day among the people will be about (murder).

عن عبدالله بن عمرو قال قال رسول الله صلى عليه وسلم من قتل معاهداً لم يرح رائحة الجنة وان ريحها توجد من سيرة اربعين خريفاً. (بخارى)

Abdullah-b-Amr reported that the Messenger of Allah said: Whoso kills a covenanted man shall not perceive the odour of Paradise, and verily its odour will be felt from a distance of 40 years' (journey), (Bukhari).

عن ابن عباس قال قال رسول الله صلى الله عليه وسلم لاتقام الحدود
في المساجد ولا يقاد بالولد الوالد . (ترمذی ، دارمی)

Ibn Abbas reported that the Messenger of Allah said: No sentences shall be executed within the mosque, and no blood-wit shall be realised from a father in exchange of (his) child. (Tirmizi, Darimi).

عن عمرو بن شعيب عن ابيه عن جده ان رسول الله صلي الله عليه وسلم قال
من قتل متعمداً اوفع الي اولياء المقتول فان شأوا قتلوا و ان شآء وا اخذوا الدية
وهى ثلثون حقة وثلثون جذعة واربعون خلفة وما صالحوا عليه فهو لهم .
(ترمذی)

Amr-b-Shuib from his father from his grand-father reported that the Messenger of Allah said: Whoso kills intentionally shall be handed over to the relations of the killed. If they like, they may kill, and if they like, they may take blood-wit; and that is 30 she-camels of 4 years old, 30 she-camels of 5 years old, 40 pregnant she-camels; and there is for them what they compromise upon. (Tirmizi)

عن عمرو بن شعيب عن ابيه عن جده قال قضى رسول الله صلى الله
عليه وسلم فى المواضح خمساً خمساً من لابل وفى الاسنان خمساً خمساً من لابل
(ابو داؤد ـ نسائی ـ دارمی)

Amr-b-Shuib reported from his father from his grand-father that the Messenger of Allah gave decision for wound—five camels for each, and for teeth—5 camels for each. (Abu Daud, Nisai, Darimi)

عن ابن عباس عن النبي صلى الله عليه وسلم انه جعل الدية
اثنى عشر الفاً . (ترمذی ـ ابو داؤد ـ نسائی)

Abu Abbas reported from the Prophet that the fixed blood-price at 12000 *dirhams*. (Tirmizi, Abu Daud, Nisai)

عن ابى الدرداء قال قال رسول الله صلى الله عليه وسلم كل ذنب عسى الله ان يغفره الا من مات مشركاً او من يقتل مومناً متعمداً.

(ابو داؤد)

Abu-Darda'a reported that the Messenger of Allah said: Perchance Allah will forgive every man except (the sin of) one who dies a polytheist, or one who kills a believer deliberately. (Abu Daud)

عن ابى هريرة قال قال رسول الله صلى الله عليه وسلم يخنق نفسه يخنقها فى النار و الذي يطعنها يطعنها فى النار. (بخارى)

Abu Hurairah reported that the Messenger of Allah said: whoso strangles himself to death, will strangle it in Hell ; and whoso shoots it, will shoot it in Hell. (Bukhari)

عن جابر ان رجلاً زنى بامراة فامر به النبى صلي الله عليه وسلم فجلد الحد ثم اخبر انه محصن فامر به فرجم. (ابو داؤد)

Jaber reported that a man committed fornication with a woman. The Holy Prophet passed order about him, and he was inflicted with the ordained stripes. Afterwards he was informed that he was a married man. So he passed order about him and he was stoned to death. (Abu Daud)

عن عائشة قالت اتى رسول الله صلى الله عليه وسلم بسارق فقطعه فقالوا ما كنا نراك تبلغ به هذا قال لو كانت فاطمة لقطعتها.

(نسائى)

Ayesha reported that a thief was brought to the Messenger of Allah. He cut off (his hand). They said: We did not consider that you would take this measure about him. He said: Had she been Fatimah, I would have certainly cut off her (hand). (Nisai)

عن ابی سلمة عن ابی هریرة ان رسول الله صلی الله علیه وسلم قال فی السارق ان سرق فاقطعوا یدہ ثم ان سرق فاقطعوا رجله ثم ان سرق فاقطعوا یده ثم ان سرق فاقطعوا رجله . (مشکواة)

Abu Salmah reported from Abu Hurairah that the Messenger of Allah said about a thief : If he steals, cut off his hand. If he steals again, cut off his leg. If he steals again, cut off his (other) hand. If he steals again, cut off his (other) leg. (Mishkat)

عن السائب بن یزید قال کان یوتیٰ بالشارب علیٰ عهد رسول الله صلی الله علیه وسلم و امرة ابی بکر وصدراً من خلافة عمر فاقوم علیه بایدینا ونعالنا و اودیتنا حتی کان آخر امرة عمرة فجلد اربعین حتی اذا عتوا وفسقوا جلد ثمانین (بخاری)

Sayeb-b-Yazid reported: A drunkard was to be arrested during the time of the Messenger of Allah, during the rule of Abu Bakr and at the beginning of the Caliphate of Omar, and we used to beat him with our hands, shoes & sheets, till at the end of the rule of Omar, he inflicted 40 stripes, till when they rebelled & transgressed, he inflicted 80 stripes. (Bukhari)

Remarks :

If we study the policy adopted by Islam in prescribing punishment, we shall realise that Islam tries in the first place to purify society from circumstances that may lead to crime. After taking such precaution, Islam prescribes a preventive and just punishment which may be inflicted upon persons who have no reasonable justification for their crimes.

Islam never prescribes punishments haphazardly nor does it execute them without due consideration. Islam holds the balance of justice in the right manner and insists on examining all conditions & circumstances connected with the offence. On studying a crime, Islam takes into account two considerations at the same time: the view-point of the criminal and that of the community against which aggression took place

In the light of such consideration, Islam prescribes the fair punishment which is in accordance with the dictates of sound logic & wise reasoning and which must not be affected by delinquent theories and national or individual whim[1].

The penal laws of Islam are called HUDUD (حدود). This word means prevention, restraint, prohibition and hence a restrictive ordinance or statute of God, repecting things lawful & things unlawful.

In Fiqh, the word *hudud* is limited to punishments for crimes mentioned by the Quran or the Hadith, while other punishments left to the discretion of the Imam (or Khalifah) or the ruler, are spoken of as TAZIR (تعزیر) which means chastisement. The general word for punishment is *uquba* (عقوبہ).

The Holy Quran lays down a general law for the punishment of offence in the following words : "And the recompense of evil (سیئہ) is punishment (سیئہ) proportionate thereto, but whoever forgives and amends, he shall have his reward from Allah : (42 : 40)

This may be noted here that the Holy Quran generally adopts the same word for punishment as for the crime. The adoption of the same word evil for the crime and its punishment indicates that punishment itself, though justified by the circumstances, is a necessary evil[2].

All Crimes may be divided into three categories:

(1) Crimes against God demanding al-Hadd e.g. Adultery (by a married person) punishable with being stoned; fornication (by an unmarried person) punishable with one hundred stripes; false occusation (of a married person) of adutery punishable with eighty stripes; apostasy punishable with death; drinking wine punishable with eighty lashes; theft punishable with the amputation of the right hand, at first; and highway robbery punishable with the loss of hands and feet come under al-Hadd. The caliph or the judge would not pardon offences coming under al-Hadd, as they are crimes against God which can be pardoned by Him alone.

(2) Crimes against man demanding retribution (القصاص) & blood-money (دیت). Most of the crimes against man, such as murder, injury, insult, etc. could be compounded for by agreement among the parties.

1. Islam the misunderstood Religion, pp. 245-247.
2. The Religion of Islam, p. 745.

(3) Certain crimes like rebelleon, and embezzlement of public money were considered against the state. Such crimes could be forgiven bv the Head of the State.[1]

Everybody, Muslim or non-Muslim, is equal in that eye of the criminal law. The Prophet said that their bloods are equal. Hazrat Ali said: The blood of the protected non-Muslim (ذمی) is like the blood of the Muslims & his goods and chattles are like those of the Muslims. The only distinction that can be made is with the execution of the sentences for minor crimes which have been left to the discretion of the judges & magistrates.

The major crimes for which punishments have been ordained are the following:—

(1) Murder (2) Dacoity & rebellion (3) Whoredom
(4) Theft (5) Accusation of whoredom.

Undoubtedly, the greatest crime known to society is murder (قتل) or the taking away of the life of another man. Hence the extreme penalty of law has been prescribed for murder. Murder of a Muslim is unlawful except for three reasons :—

(i) For the murder of a man unjustly & without right.
(ii) For commission of adultery in marriage wedlock.
(iii) For retrogression from the religion of Islam. Abu-Hanifa holds that a woman rebel cannot be lawfully murdered.

Besides the sentence of death or the payment of the blood-money, there is still a great punishment reserved for a murderer to be meted out on the Resurrection Day.

Suicide is not less than murder. Such a person will permanently reside in Hell, as he killed a soul which remembered Allah, or which, if alive, would have remembered Him.[2]

Some European & others who have not studied the reality of the Islamic concept of crime & punishment consider the punishments prescribed by Islam as barbarous and degrading to human dignity. They wrongly imagine that such punishments—like the European civil punishments—will be inflicted every day. They also fancy that the Islamic society indulges in daily executions of flogging, hand-cutting, and stoning. But the fact is that such deterrant punishments have been executed very rarely. The fact that the punishment for theft has been executed only six times throughout a period of four hundred years is a clear evidence that such punishment was primarily meant to prevent crime.[3]

(1) Islamic State, a historical survey. pp. 41-42.

(2) English translation of Mishkat. 'Maulana Fazlul Karim.

(3) Islam the misunderstood Religion, p. 252.

THE ETHICAL SYSTEM

(i) The Ethical View-Point :

قَوْلٌ مَّعْرُوْفٌ وَّمَغْفِرَةٌ خَيْرٌ مِّنْ صَدَقَةٍ (البقرہ - ۲۶۳)

A kind word and forgiveness is better than charity. (2 : 263)

وَاِنَّكَ لَعَلٰى خُلُقٍ عَظِيْمٍ (القلم - ۴)

Ad surely thou hast sublime morals.

وَلْتَكُنْ مِّنْكُمْ اُمَّةٌ يَّدْعُوْنَ اِلَى الْخَيْرِ وَيَاْمُرُوْنَ بِالْمَعْرُوْفِ وَيَنْهَوْنَ عَنِ الْمُنْكَرِ وَاُولٰٓئِكَ هُمُ الْمُفْلِحُوْنَ
(آل عمران - ۱۰۳)

And there may spring from you a nation who invite to goodness, and enjoin right conduct and forbid indecency. Such are they who are successful. (3 : 103)

كُنْتُمْ خَيْرَ اُمَّةٍ اُخْرِجَتْ لِلنَّاسِ تَاْمُرُوْنَ بِالْمَعْرُوْفِ وَتَنْهَوْنَ عَنِ الْمُنْكَرِ وَتُؤْمِنُوْنَ بِاللّٰهِ (آل عمران - ۱۰۹)

You are the best nation raised up for men : you enjoin good and forbid evil and you believe in Allah. (3 : 109)

قُلْ اِنَّ صَلَاتِيْ وَنُسُكِيْ وَمَحْيَايَ وَمَمَاتِيْ لِلّٰهِ رَبِّ الْعٰلَمِيْنَ
(الانعام - ۱۶۳)

Say : My prayer and my sacrifice, and my life and my death are surely for Allah, the Lord of the worlds. (6 : 163)

اَلَّذِيْنَ اِنْ مَّكَّنّٰهُمْ فِى الْاَرْضِ اَقَامُوا الصَّلٰوةَ وَاٰتَوُا الزَّكٰوةَ وَاَمَرُوْا بِالْمَعْرُوْفِ وَنَهَوْا عَنِ الْمُنْكَرِ ؕ
وَلِلّٰهِ عَاقِبَةُ الْاُمُوْرِ ۝ (حج - ۴۱)

Those who, if we establish them in the land, will keep up praye and pay the poor-rate and enjoin good and forbid evil. And Allah's is the end of affairs. (22 : 41)

وَالَّذِيْنَ يَجْتَنِبُوْنَ كَبٰٓئِرَ الْاِثْمِ وَالْفَوَاحِشَ وَاِذَا مَا غَضِبُوْا هُمْ يَغْفِرُوْنَ ۝ (شوریٰ - ۳۷)

And those who shun the great sins and indecencies, and whenever they are angry they forgive. (42 : 37)

اِنَّ اَكْرَمَكُمْ عِنْدَ اللّٰهِ اَتْقٰكُمْ ؕ اِنَّ اللّٰهَ عَلِيْمٌ خَبِيْرٌ ۝ (حجرات - ۱۳)

Surely the noblest of you with Allah is the most dutiful of you. Surely Allah is Knowing, Aware. (49 : 13)

فَاَلْهَمَهَا فُجُوْرَهَا وَتَقْوٰىهَا ۝ (الشمس - ۸)

And inspired it (with consciousne:s of) what is wrong for it and (what is) right for it. (91 : 8)

لَقَدْ كَانَ لَكُمْ فِىْ رَسُوْلِ اللّٰهِ اُسْوَةٌ حَسَنَةٌ لِّمَنْ كَانَ يَرْجُوا اللّٰهَ وَالْيَوْمَ الْاٰخِرَ وَذَكَرَ اللّٰهَ كَثِيْرًا ۝ (احزاب - ۲۱)

Certainly you have in the Messenger of Allah an excellent exemplar for him who hopes in Allah and the Day Hereafter and remembers Allah much. (33 : 21)

AHADITH :

عن عبدالله بن عمرو قال قال رسول الله صلي الله عليه وسلم ان من احبكم الى احسنكم اخلاقا (بخارى)

Abdullah-b-Amr reported that the Messenger of Allah said : Verily the dearest to me among you is he who is the best of you in conduct. (Bukhari)

عن عبدالله بن عمرو قال قال رسول الله صلى الله عليه وسلم ان من خيارکم احسنکم اخلاقا . (متفق عليه)

Abdullah-b-Amr reported that the Messenger of Allah said : The best of you is he who is the best of you in conduct. (Agreed)

عن حارثة بن وهب قال قال رسول الله صلى الله عليه وسلم لايدخل الجنة الجواظ ولا الجعظرى . (ابو داؤد)

Haresah-b-Wahab reported that the Messenger of Allah said : He whose conduct is bad and harsh shall not enter Paradise. (Abu Daud)

عن ابى الدرداء عن النبي صلى الله عليه وسلم قال ان اثقل شئ يوضع فى ميزان المومن يوم القيامة خلق حسن و ان الله يغبض الفاحش البذى . (ترمذى)

Abu-Darda reported from the Messenger of Allah who said: Verily the heaviest thing which will be placed in the measuring scale of a believer on the Resurrection day will be good conducts, and verily Allah will be enraged on the indecent, the extravagent. (Tirmizi)

عن معاذ قال كان آخر ما وصانى به رسول الله صلى الله عليه وسلم حين وضعت رجلى فى الغرز ان قال يا معاذ احسن خلقك للناس . (مالك)

Muaz reported : The last of what the Messenger of Allah advised me with when I put my feet in the stirrup was O Muaz ! make your treatment with the people good. (Malek)

عن مالك بلغه ان رسول الله صلى الله عليه وسلم قال بعثت لاتمم حسن الاخلاق . (موطا و احمد عن ابى هريرة)

Malek reported that the Messenger of Allah said : Verily I have been sent to complete good manners. (Muatta, Ahmad from Abu Hurairah).

عن رجل من مزينة قال قالوا يا رسول الله ما خير ما اعطى الانسان قال الخلق الحسن . (بيهقى)

A man of Muzaina tribe reported that they asked : O Messenger of Allah! what is the best of what man has been given? "Good conduct" replied he. (Baihaqi)

عن عبدالله بن عمرو قال كان رسول الله صلى الله عليه وسلم يقول اللهم انى اسئلك الصحة و العفة و الامانة و حسن الخلق و الرضا بالقدر . (بيهقي)

Abdullah-b-Amr reported that the Messenger of Allah used to pray : O Allah ! verily I seek from thee health, peace of mind, truth, good conduct and satisfaction with lot. (Baihaqi)

عن ابى ثعلبة ان رسول الله صلى الله عليه وسلم ان احبكم الى و اقربكم منى يوم القيامة احسنكم اخلاقاً و ان ابغضكم وابعدكم منى مساويكم اخلاقاً الثرثارون المتشدقون المتفيهقون . (بيهق)

Abu Sa'labah reported that the Messenger of Allah said : Verily the dearest to me among you and the nearest to me among you on the Resurrection Day will be one who is best of you in conduct, and verily the most disliked by me among you and the farthest from me on the Resurrection Day will be those who are the worst of you in conduct—the talkative, the unjust, the proud. (Baihaqi)

Remarks :

1. Moral sense is inborn in man and through the ages it has served as the common man's standard of moral behaviour, approving certain qualities and disapproving others. Thus the sense of good and evil is inherent in the very nature of man.

2. The greatest problem that has confronted man from time immemorial is the moral problem. Islam gives this problem the importance it deserves.

3. There is only one correct basis for morality and that is presented by Islam. There we get an answer to all the basic ethical questions (i.e. the life-purpose of man, the goal of all his endeavours, ethical standard, distinction of good & evil, the sanction behind the moral law, the motive force) free from the weaknesses and fallacies from which the viewpoints expressed by secular & religious philosophers alike suffer.

4. Islam gives a comprehensive code of behaviour for the individual and shows him the highest possible moral excellence. It also gives ethical principles on which the edifice of truly righteous society can be raised and which, if accepted as the basis of individual and collective conduct, can save human life from the chaos & anarchy that have overtaken it to-day.

5. It would be meaningless to build up any ethical system without first deciding the real position of man in the universe. Islam tells us clearly that the status of man in this world is that of an *abd* (عبد) who is also *Khalifatullah* (خليفة الله) i.e. the deputy & vicegerent of God. All things in the world belong to God. Even man's own body & the capacities with which he is endowed are not in fact his own, but are a trust from the God.

6. If the position assigned to man by Islam is accepted by him, then it is automatically settled that :-

   (a) to emerge successfully from the test prescribed by God & to attain His pleasure constitute the supreme good & the ultimate objective of human life.

(b) the criterion of right & wrong for human conduct lies in determining how far it helps or hinders man in the attainment of this supreme good,

(c) the real source of man's knowledge of good & evil is found in the guidance furnished by God through His prophets—other sources of knowledge can be employed only as auxiliaris and aids to it, but none of them deserves to be treated as its substitute.

(d) the real sanction for morality lies in the love for & the fear of Allah—the real motive force which would compel us to observe the canons of morality and to abstain from immoral conduct.

(e) Allah's law, because of its Divine origin, is self-enforcing. Its sanction exists in the mind of the believer who finds happiness in seeking God's pleasure & is desirous of attaining the standard of perfection.

7. Islam very clearly states its concept of *tawhid*, which, in fact, constitutes the real source of all its moral thinking. The idea that the test set by God is not confined to any one aspect of life or to any particular branch of human activity but extends to all aspects of life and all spheres of action, enlarges the field of morality and makes it co-extensive with life. This is the moral domain of human life. The concept of life hereafter produces two important effects which are not obtainable from any other source :-

   (i) it lends to morality a basis which is strong and unshakable;

   (ii) it imparts stability and firmness to human character & provides firm foundation for human society.

8. Good conduct is the crown of the prophets, the truthful & the pious. The Holy Prophet was the most perfect man in all branches of virtues which go to make up good conduct. He is, therefore, termed as perfect example for a believer.

Note: These remarks have been compiled & taken from the book "The Ethical View-Point of Islam."

(N.A.)

(2) Motive & action in the way of Allah:

وَمِنَ النَّاسِ مَنْ يَّتَّخِذُ مِنْ دُوْنِ اللّٰهِ اَنْدَادًا يُّحِبُّوْنَهُمْ كَحُبِّ اللّٰهِ ۭ وَالَّذِيْنَ اٰمَنُوْٓا اَشَدُّ حُبًّا لِّلّٰهِ ۭ (بقرہ-۱۶۵)

Yet of mankind are some who take into themselves (objects of worship which they set as) rivals to Allah, loving them with a love like that of Allah that is due to Him (only). Those who believe are stauncher in their love for Allah. (2 : 165)

وَمِنَ النَّاسِ مَنْ يَّشْرِيْ نَفْسَهُ ابْتِغَاۗءَ مَرْضَاتِ اللّٰهِ ۭ وَاللّٰهُ رَءُوْفٌۢ بِالْعِبَادِ ۝ (بقرہ-۲۰۷)

And of mankind is he who would sell himself, seeking the pleasure of Allah : and Allah hath Compassion on (His) bondmen. (2 : 207)

قُلْ اِنَّ صَلَاتِيْ وَنُسُكِيْ وَمَحْيَايَ وَمَمَاتِيْ لِلّٰهِ رَبِّ الْعٰلَمِيْنَ ۝ (انعام-۱۶۳)

Say : My prayer and my sacrifice and my life and my death are surely for Allah, the Lord of the worlds (6 :163)

مَنْ كَانَ يُرِيْدُ الْعَاجِلَةَ عَجَّلْنَا لَهٗ فِيْهَا مَا نَشَاۗءُ لِمَنْ نُّرِيْدُ ثُمَّ جَعَلْنَا لَهٗ جَهَنَّمَ ۚ يَصْلٰىهَا مَذْمُوْمًا
مَّدْحُوْرًا ۝ وَمَنْ اَرَادَ الْاٰخِرَةَ وَسَعٰى لَهَا سَعْيَهَا وَهُوَ مُؤْمِنٌ فَاُولٰۗىِٕكَ كَانَ سَعْيُهُمْ مَّشْكُوْرًا ۝ (بنی اسرائیل ۱۹)

Whoso desires this transitory life, We hasten to him therein what We please for whomsoever we desire ; then we assign to him the hell : he will enter it despised, driven away. And whoso desiresthe Hereafter and strives for it with the effort necessary, being a believer, for such, their effort findeth favour (with their Lord). (17 : 18, 19)

مَنْ كَانَ يُرِيدُ حَرْثَ الْآخِرَةِ نَزِدْ لَهُ فِي حَرْثِهِ ۖ وَمَنْ كَانَ يُرِيدُ حَرْثَ الدُّنْيَا نُؤْتِهِ مِنْهَا وَمَا لَهُ فِي الْآخِرَةِ مِنْ نَصِيبٍ
(شوریٰ - ۲۰)

Whoso desires the tilth of the Hereafter, we give him increase in his tilth; and whoso desires the tilth of this world, we give him thereof; and he has no portion in the Hereafter (42: 20)

وَمَا خَلَقْتُ الْجِنَّ وَالْإِنْسَ إِلَّا لِيَعْبُدُونِ (الذاریٰت - ۵۶)

And I created the jinn and human kind only that they might worship Me. (51 : 56)

يَا أَيُّهَا الَّذِينَ آمَنُوا لَا تَتَّخِذُوا عَدُوِّي وَعَدُوَّكُمْ أَوْلِيَاءَ تُلْقُونَ إِلَيْهِمْ بِالْمَوَدَّةِ وَقَدْ كَفَرُوا بِمَا جَاءَكُمْ مِنَ الْحَقِّ
يُخْرِجُونَ الرَّسُولَ وَإِيَّاكُمْ أَنْ تُؤْمِنُوا بِاللَّهِ رَبِّكُمْ إِنْ كُنْتُمْ خَرَجْتُمْ جِهَادًا فِي سَبِيلِي وَابْتِغَاءَ مَرْضَاتِي
تُسِرُّونَ إِلَيْهِمْ بِالْمَوَدَّةِ وَأَنَا أَعْلَمُ بِمَا أَخْفَيْتُمْ وَمَا أَعْلَنْتُمْ ۚ وَمَنْ يَفْعَلْهُ مِنْكُمْ فَقَدْ ضَلَّ سَوَاءَ السَّبِيلِ
(ممتحنہ - ۱)

O you who believe ! Choose not My enemy and your enemy for friends. Do you give them friendship when they disbelive in that truth which has come unto you, driving out the messenger and you because you believe in Allah, your Lord ? If you have come forth to strive in My way and seeking My good pleasure, (show them not friendship). Do you show friendship unto them in secret, when I am best Aware of what you hide and what you proclaim ? And whoever does it among you, he verily has strayed from the right way. (60 :1)

وَمَا لِأَحَدٍ عِنْدَهُ مِنْ نِعْمَةٍ تُجْزَىٰ إِلَّا ابْتِغَاءَ وَجْهِ رَبِّهِ الْأَعْلَىٰ (اللیل - ۱۹، ۲۰)

And none has with him any favour for reward, except as seeking (to fulfil) the purpose of his Lord Most High. (92 : 19, 20)

مَنْ كَانَ يُرِيدُ الْحَيَاةَ الدُّنْيَا وَزِينَتَهَا نُوَفِّ إِلَيْهِمْ أَعْمَالَهُمْ فِيهَا وَهُمْ فِيهَا لَا يُبْخَسُونَ أُولَٰئِكَ الَّذِينَ لَيْسَ لَهُمْ فِي
الْآخِرَةِ إِلَّا النَّارُ ۖ وَحَبِطَ مَا صَنَعُوا فِيهَا وَبَاطِلٌ مَا كَانُوا يَعْمَلُونَ (ھود - ۱۵، ۱۶)

Whoever desires this world's life and its finery, we repay them their deeds therein, and they are not made to suffer loss in it. These are they for whom there is nothing but Fire in the Hereafter. And what they work therein is fruitless and their deeds are vain.

(11 : 15,16)

وَالَّذِيْنَ صَبَرُوا ابْتِغَآءَ وَجْهِ رَبِّهِمْ وَاَقَامُوا الصَّلٰوةَ وَاَنْفَقُوْا مِمَّا رَزَقْنٰهُمْ سِرًّا وَّعَلَانِيَةً وَّيَدْرَءُوْنَ بِالْحَسَنَةِ السَّيِّئَةَ اُولٰٓئِكَ لَهُمْ عُقْبَى الدَّارِ (رعد - ٢٢)

And those who are steadfast seeking the pleasure of their Lord, and keep up prayer and spend of that which We have given them, secretly and openly, and repel evil with good ; for such is the (happy) issue of the abode. (13 : 22)

AHADITH:

١ - عن عمر بن الخطاب قال قال رسول الله صلى الله عليه وسلم انما الاعمال بالنيات و إنما لامرىء ما نوى فمن كان هجرته الى الله و رسوله فهجرته الى الله و رسوله و من كان هجرته الى الدنيا يصيبه اوامراة يتزوجها فهجرته الى ما هاجراليه۔ (متفق عليه)

'Umar-b-al-Khattab reported that the Messenger of Allah said : Actions are judged by motives. There is surely for man what he intends. So whosoever's hijrat is towards Allah and His Apostle, his hijrat is for Allah and His Apostle ; and whoso ever's hijrat is towards the world which he seeks or towards a woman whom he intends to marry, his hijrat is towards that for which he makes hijrat (emigration). (Agreed)

٢ - عن ابى هريرة قال قال رسول الله صلى الله عليه وسلم ان الله لاينظر الى صوركم و اموالكم ولكن ينظر الى قلوبكم واعمالكم۔ (مسلم)

Abu Hurairah reported that the Messenger of Allah said : Verily Allah looks not to your figures, not to your wealth, but He looks to your hearts and deeds. (Muslim)

٣ - عن عبد الله بن عمرو قال قال رسول الله صلى الله عليه و سلم من كانت الدنيا نية جعل ا فقره بين عينيه۔ (ابن ماجه)

Abdullah-b. Amr reported that the Holy Prophet said : Whoever has got the world as his object, Allah keeps up his poverty before his eyes. (Ibn Majah)

٤ - عن ابی ہریرۃ قال قال رسول اللہ صلی اللہ علیہ وسلم انما یبعث الناس
علی نیاتھم (ابن ماجہ)

Abu Hurairah reported that the Messenger of Allah said : Verily people will be raised up according to their intentions. (Ibn Majah)

٥ - عن معاویہ انہ کتب الی عائشہ رضہ ان اکتبی الی کتاباً توصینی
فیہ و لا تکثری فکتبت سلام علیک اما بعد فانی سمعت رسول اللہ
صلی علیہ وسلم یقول من التمس رضی اللہ بسخط الناس کفاہ اللہ
مؤنۃ الناس و من التمس رضی الناس بسخط اللہ و کلہ اللہ الی الناس
والسلام علیک۔ (ترمذی)

Muawiyah reported that he wrote to Ayesha : Write to me a letter advising me therein, and do not make excess. So she wrote : Peace be on you ; as for next, I have certainly heard the Messenger of Allah say : Whoso seeks pleasure of Allah with pleasure of men, Allah will be sufficient for him as a Protector from men, and whoso seeks pleasure of men with displeasure of Allah, Allah hands him over to men—And peace be on you. (Tirmizi)

٦ - عن ابی ہریرۃ قال قال رسول اللہ صلی اللہ علیہ وسلم ان اول الناس
یقضی علیہ یوم القیامۃ رجل استشہد فاتی بہ فعرفہ نعمتہ فعرفھا فقال
فما علمت فیھا قال قاتلت فیک حتی استشہدت قال کذبت ولکنک
قاتلت لان یقال جری فقد قیل ثم امر بہ فسحب علی وجہہ حتی
القی فی النار ورجل تعلم العلم و علمہ و قرء القرآن فاتی بہ فعرفہ
نعمہ فعرفھا قال فما علمت فیھا قال تعلمت العلم و علمتہ و قرات
فیک القرآن قال کذبت ولکنک تعلمت العلم لیقال انک عالم وقرأت
القرآن لیقال ھو قاری فقد قیل ثم امر بہ فسحب علی وجہہ حتی القی
فی النار و رجل وسع اللہ علیہ واعطہ من اصناف المال کلہ فاتی
بہ فعرفہ نعمہ فعرفھا قال فما علمت فیھا قال ما ترکت من سبیل

تحب ان ينفق فيها الا انفقت فيها لك قال كذبت و لكنك فعلت
يقال هو جواد فقــد قيل ثم امر به فسحب على وجـــهه ثم القى
فى النار۔ (مسلم)

Abu Hurairah reported that the Messenger of Allah said : Surely the first man who will be brought for judgment on the Resurrection Day will be one who was (well-known as) a martyr. He will be brought and be reminded of the favours on him which he will recognise, Then He will ask : what did you do therein ? He will reply : I fought for thee till I was a martyr. He will retort : You have spoken falsehood ; nay, you have fought for being called a hero, and surely you have been so called. Then the order (of judgement) will be passed against him and consequently he will be dragged down upon his face till he will be thrown into the fire. Another will be the man who acquired knowledge and taught it (to men) and read the Quran. He will be brought for judgment and be reminded of the favours on him which he will recognise. Allah will ask him : what did you do therein ? He will reply : I acquired learning and taught it and read the Quran for thee. He will say : You have spoken falsehood, and you have acquired learning that you might be called a reader, and you were so called. Then order will be passed against him and so he will be dragged down upon his face till he will be thrown into the fire. Another man whom Allah gave ample wealth and whom. He gave wealth of every description will be brought and will be reminded of the favours on him which he will recognise. He will ask : What did you do therein? He will reply : I left not a single way wherein thou desired to be spent but that I did not spend it therein for thy sake. He will retort : Surely you have spoken falsehood ; nay, you spent it that you might be called a philanthropic man and you were so called. Then order will be passed against him and so he will be dragged down upon his face and will be thrown into the fire. (Muslim)

۷ ـ عن ابى هريرة قال قال رسول الله صلى الله عليه وسلم ان الله تعالى يقول يوم القيامة اين المتحابون بجلالى اليوم اظلهم في ظلى يوم لاظل الا ظلى (مسلم)

Abu Hurairah reported that the Messenger of Allah said : Verily the Almighty Allah will proclaim on the Resurrection Day : Where are on today the mutual lovres of My Magnificence? I shall give them shade under My shade on the day when there will be no shade except My shade. (Muslim)

۸ ـ عن ابى ذر قال خرج علينا رسول الله صلى الله عليه وسلم قال اتدرون اى الاعمال احب الى الله تعالي قال قائل الصلوة و الزكواة و قال قائل الجهاد قال النبى صلى الله عليه وسلم ان احب الاعمل الى الله تعالى الحب فى الله و البغض فى الله (احمد ـ ابو داؤد)

Abu Zarr reported that the Messenger of Allah came to us and asked : Do you know which of the actions is dearest to the Glorious Allah ? Someone replied : Prayer and Zakat. Another said : Holy war. Then the Holy Prophet said : Of the actions dearest to the Almighty Allah, verily there is love for Allah and hate for Allah.

(Ahmad--Abu Daud)

Remarks :

(1) Motive or intention or نيت forms the basis of all human actions. It is the criterion by which actions of men are judged. Actions are held to be good or bad, just or unjust, criminal or innocent according as the motives are good or bad just or unjust, Where there is a will, there is a way and, action. No will, no action. As is the will, so is the action. As there is life and body of a man, so there is life and body of an action. Will is the life and its outward manifestation is the body.

(2) Niyyet or motive for the sake of Allah is a touch-stone for bearing fruits in all our wordly action, religious or temporal. Sleep, food, walking, talking etc. if done with the intention of ultimate good to soul or to relations or other men, or towards progress of Islam, carry religious merit. The more numerous are the motives for an action, the greater are the rewards with this exception that nothing can bring more reward than the action done with the sole motive of seeking the pleasure of Allah.

(3) The motive of our struggles and actions in life must be to please Allah just as the object of an obedient and dutiful servant is to please his master. Such an idea in mind creates a wonderful mental force which nobody in the world can check. Such a man is born for Allah, lives for Allah, thinks for Allah, acts for Allah, utters words for Allah and dies for Allah. Such a man is therefore said to be on the way of Allah.

(4) All actions done to seek pleasure of Allah and to obey Him and His Prophet are action on the way of Allah—to fight for Islam, to carry on missionary activities for propagation of Islam, to start for pilgrimage, to give food to the hungry and drink to the thirsty, to walk in the paths of acquiring theological and religious knowledge, and to work for earnings to provide food and clothing to family members and to oneself etc.

(5) To reach the object of love (Allah) is the goal of human beings. Islam is the way of Allah which is the most straight and shortest. The sojourners in this path are all friends towards one another, and must help one another to reach the goal. The motto of the sojourners in the way of Allah must have sympathy and fellow-feeling for the sake of Allah, and not for any personal consideration.

(6) Every action of a Muslim is actuated by divine love, as everything besides Allah is void and perishable. A Muslim must begin everything in the name of Allah saying: بسم الله الرحمان الرحيم

(In the name of Allah, the Most Merciful, the Compassionate.) Thus the remembrance of Allah perveates the whole atmosphere of the life of a Muslim.

(7) Actions for show or ریا in any sense or form with the intention of show are unlawful and have been greatly condemned by the Almighty Allah & His Apostle. The Quran condemns this evil of show in more than one place, because everything on the earth must be done for the sake of Allah, and nothing which is done for other than Allah will bear fruit in the Next World.

(8) Love and hate are two contradictory terms. If a Muslim loves the teachings of Islam and their great teacher, he cannot but love those who follow those teachings and also love for Allah and His Apostle. On the other hand, it is natural with him to hate those who reject the teachings of Islam and do not obey the commandments of Allah and His Apostle. The two things, love and hate, can not occur together in a human heart. This signifies how the true Muslim should deal with the unbelievers, and the people of the Book like the Jews and the Christians and the Muslim innovators and the sinners.

(9) The great difference between the former and the present Muslims is that the former Muslims did every thing for the sake of Allah and the Next World, while the majority of the present Muslims are totally bankrupt in this niyyat and work for name and fame which bear no fruit either in this world or in the Next. *

* Remarks heve been compiled and taken from the Tr: of Mishkat (Eng) by F. Kasim (N.A.).

(3) Moderation and stead fastness.

وَكَذٰلِكَ جَعَلْنٰكُمْ اُمَّةً وَّسَطًا لِّتَكُوْنُوْا شُهَدَآءَ عَلَى النَّاسِ وَيَكُوْنَ الرَّسُوْلُ عَلَيْكُمْ شَهِيْدًا (بقرہ-۱۴۳)

And thus We have appointed you a middle nation, that you may be witness against mankind, and (that) the Messenger may be a witness against you.

كُنْتُمْ خَيْرَ اُمَّةٍ اُخْرِجَتْ لِلنَّاسِ تَاْمُرُوْنَ بِالْمَعْرُوْفِ وَتَنْهَوْنَ عَنِ الْمُنْكَرِ وَتُؤْمِنُوْنَ بِاللّٰهِ (آل عمران-۱۰۹)

You are the best nation raised up for men: you enjoin good and forbid evil and you believe in Allah. (3 : 109)

وَلَا تَعْتَدُوْا اِنَّ اللّٰهَ لَا يُحِبُّ الْمُعْتَدِيْنَ (مائدہ-۸۷)

And exceed not the limits. Surely Allah loves not those who exceed the limits. (5 :87)

وَلَا تَجْهَرْ بِصَلَاتِكَ وَلَا تُخَافِتْ بِهَا وَابْتَغِ بَيْنَ ذٰلِكَ سَبِيْلًا (بنی اسرائیل ۱۱۰)

And utter not thy prayer loudly nor be silent in it, and seek a way betweeen these. (17:110)

وَلَا تَجْعَلْ يَدَكَ مَغْلُوْلَةً اِلٰى عُنُقِكَ وَلَا تَبْسُطْهَا كُلَّ الْبَسْطِ فَتَقْعُدَ مَلُوْمًا مَّحْسُوْرًا (بنی اسرائیل-۲۹)

And make not thy hand to be shackled to thy neck, nor stretch it forth to the utmost (limit) of its stretching forth, lest thou sit down blamed, stripped off. (17:29)

وَاقْصِدْ فِي مَشْيِكَ وَاغْضُضْ مِن صَوْتِكَ (لقمٰن-١٩)

And pursue the right cousre in thy going about and lower thy voice. (31: 19)

إِنَّ الَّذِينَ قَالُوا رَبُّنَا اللَّهُ ثُمَّ اسْتَقَامُوا تَتَنَزَّلُ عَلَيْهِمُ الْمَلَٰئِكَةُ أَلَّا تَخَافُوا وَلَا تَحْزَنُوا وَأَبْشِرُوا بِالْجَنَّةِ الَّتِي كُنتُمْ تُوعَدُونَ ۝ (حٰم السجدة-٣٠)

Lo ! those who say : Our Lord is Allah, and afterward are upright, the angels descend upon them, saying : Fear not nor grieve, but hear good tidings of the Paradise which you are promised. (41:30)

وَأْمُرْ أَهْلَكَ بِالصَّلَوٰةِ وَاصْطَبِرْ عَلَيْهَا
(طٰه-١٣٢)

And enjoin upon thy people worship, and be constant therein. (20:132)

يَٰبَنِيٓ ءَادَمَ خُذُوا زِينَتَكُمْ عِندَ كُلِّ مَسْجِدٍ وَكُلُوا وَاشْرَبُوا وَلَا تُسْرِفُوٓا إِنَّهُ لَا يُحِبُّ الْمُسْرِفِينَ ۝ (اعراف-٣١)

O children of Adam ! Look to your adornment at every place of worship, and eat and drink and be not prodigal; surely He loves not the prodigals. (7:31)

وَالَّذِينَ إِذَآ أَنفَقُوا لَمْ يُسْرِفُوا وَلَمْ يَقْتُرُوا وَكَانَ بَيْنَ ذَٰلِكَ قَوَامًا ۝ (فرقان-٦٧)

And they (are the servants of the Beneficent) who, when they spend are neither extravagant nor parsimonious, and the just mean is ever between these. (25:67)

AHADITH :

عن طلحة بن عبيدالله قال جآء رجل الى رسول الله صلى الله عليه وسلم من اهل نجد ثائر الراس نسمع دوى صوته و لا نفقه ما يقول حتى دنى من رسول الله صلى الله عليه وسلم فاذا هو يسئال عن الإسلام فقال رسول الله صلي الله عليه وسلم خمس صلوات فى اليوم و الليلة فقال هل على غيرهن فقالا الا ان تطوع قال رسول الله صلى الله عليه وسلم و صيام شهر رمضان فقال هل على غيره قال لا الا ان تطوع قال و ذكر له رسول الله صلى الله عليه وسلم الزكواة فقال هل على غيرها فقال لا الا ان تطوع فا دبر الرجل و هو يقول والله لا ازيد على هـذا ولا انقص منه فقال رسول الله صلى الله عليه وسلم افلح الرجل ان صدق. (متفق عليه)

Talha-b-Obaidullah reported that a man of the inhabitants of Najd came to the Messenger of Allah with dishevelled hair. We heard the confusion of his voice and could not understand what he said till he came near the Messenger of Allah when lo ! he was asking about Islam. The Messenger of Allah said : Prayer for five times in a day and a night. He enquired : Have I not got to do besides these? "No" said he "except what you voluntarily do". The Messenger of Allah mentioned about fasting of Ramzan. He enquired: Have I not got to fast besides this? "No" replied the Prophet, "except what you do willingly." He said that the Holy Prophet then told him about Zakat. He enquired : Have I got to pay besides this? "No" said he "except what you voluntarily pay." The man then went away saying : By Allah, I shall do neither more nor less than this. Then the Messenger of Allah remarked : The man has got salvation if he has spoken the truth. (Agreed)

عن انس قال جآء ثلثة رهط الى ازواج النبى صلى الله عليه وسلم يسئلون عن عبادة النبي صلي الله عليه وسلم فلما اخبروا بها كانهم

تقالوها فقالوا اين نحن من النبى صلى الله عليه وسلم وقد غفر الله ما تقدم من ذنبه وما تاخر فقال احدهم اما انا فاصلى الليل ابداً وقال الآخر انا اصوم النهار ابداً ولا افطر وقال الآخر انا اعتزل النساء فلا اتزوج ابداً فجاء النبى صلى الله عليه وسلم اليهم فقال انتم الذين قلتم كذا و كذا اما و الله انى لا خشكم لله و اتقكم له لكنى اصوم و افطرو اصلى و ارقد و اتزوج النساء فمن رغب عن سنتي فليس منى . (متفق عليه)

Anas reported that three persons came to the wives of the Holy Prophet to enquire about acts of piety of the Prophet. When they were informed of them, they considered them little as it were and said: Where are we in comparison with the Holy Prophet while Allah has forgiven what is past of his sins and what will be in future. One of them said: As for me, I pray all night long. And another man said: I fast the day all along and do not break. And another said: I keep aloof from women and shall never marry. Then the Holy Prophet came to them and said: Are you the persons saying such and such thing? Behold! By Allah, I fear Allah more than yourselves and I am most dutiful among you for Him, but still I keep fast and break it, and keep up prayer and keep awake at night and take wives. So whoever turns away from my way is not of me. (Agreed).

عن مطرف بن عبدالله قال قال رسول الله صلي الله عليه وسلم خير الامور اوسطها . (بيهقى)

Matref-e-Abdullah reported that the Messenger of Allah said: The best of affairs is their mean. (Baihaqi)

عن انس ان رسول الله صلى الله عليه وسلم كان يقول لا تشددوا علي انفسكم فيشدد الله عليكم فان قوماً من بنى اسرائيل شددوا على

انفسهم فشدد الله عليهم فتلك بقايا هم فى الصوامع و الديار و رهبانية ن ابتدعوها ما كتبنا عليهم . (ابو داؤد)

Anas reported that the Messenger of Allah used to say : Don't subject yourselves to excessive hardship lest Allah inflict hardship on you. Surely there was a people out of the children of Israil who put rigours on themselves, and consequently Allah also was severe on them. Those are their reminiscences in the synagogues and churches. And monkery they invented it. We did not ordain it for them, (5 : 87 Quran). (Abu Daud).

عن عائشة قالت قال رسول الله صلى الله عليه وسلم خذوا من الاعمال ما تطيقون فان الله لا يمل حتى تملوا . (متفق عليه)

Ayesha reported that the Messenger of Allah said: Take of action what you can, because Allah inflicts no trouble till you inflict. (Agreed)

عن عائشة قالت قال رسول الله صلى الله عليه وسلم احب الاعمال الى الله ادومها و ان قل . (متفق عليه)

Aysha reported that the Messenger of Allah said: The most pleasing of actions to Allah is that which is done continuously though it be little. (Agreed)

عن عبدالله بن عمرو بن العاص قال قال لى رسول الله صلى الله عليه وسلم يا عبدالله الم اخبر انك تصوم النهار و تقوم الليل فقلت بلى يا رسول الله صلى الله عليه وسلم قال فلا تفعل صم و افطر و قم و نم فان لجسدك عليك حقاً و ان لعينك عليك حقاً و ان لزوجك عليك حقاً و ان لزورك عليك حقا . (متفق عليه)

Abdullah-b-Amr-b-As reported : The Messenger of Allah asked me : O Abdullah ! did I not inform that you should keep fast the day and stand up the night (praying)? "Yes", replied I, "O Messenger of Allah". He said : Don't do (it); fast and break, stand up (for prayer) and sleep, because there is surely a duty on you for your body, a duty on you for your eyes, a duty on you for your wife, and a duty on you for your neighbour. (Agreed)

عن سفيان بن عبدالله الثقفي قال قلت يا رسول الله صلى الله عليه وسلم قل لى فى الاسلام قولا لا اسأل عنه احدا بعدك (و في رواية غيرك) قال قل آمنت بالله ثم استقم . (مسلم)

Sufyan-b-Abdullah-al-Saqafi reported : I enquired : O Messegger of Allah ! tell me a word about Islam which I shall not ask anybody after you. (And in a narration—besides you). He replied : Say : I believed in Allah; then be steadfast. (Muslim)

Remarks

— In the onward march and advancement of human soul, nothing is more valuable than moderation and steadiness on a fixed principle. A rolling stone gathers no moss. The two extremes of every action are bad, and the mean between the two extremes is best according to Islam.

— Neither monkery nor inactivity has been prescribed by Islam, because it knows that "hasty climbest, soonest fall".

— A man can be morally and religiously beautiful if he has got within him all the attributes of a human being on the scale of moderation and proportion.

— The virtue of moderation is a condition precedent to steadfastness because after the greatest enthusiasm, there comes a period of rest and langour due to over-exhaustion. At that time, there is complete cessation of work. The steadyman goes on and on with his work till he is crowned with success. The virtue of steadiness can be kept, therefore, in the mean between the two extremes.

— The life of the Holy Prophet affords a striking example how a steadfast man clinging firm to his resolve can succeed in the long run. His unswerving steadfastness under the most trying calamities when the bravest of hearts may sinc drew admiration from foes and friends alike. The most furious storms of persecutions, temptations and calamities could not make his move an inch from his noble mission. This was because he had an iron faith in Allah and in the truth of his mission. When the Quraish offered him a kingdom and put before him temptation, he replied : I want neither pelf, nor power. I have been commission by Allah as a warner to mankind. I deliver His massage to you. He said to his uncle Abu Taleb on this occasion: O uncle ! should they place the sun in my right hand, and the moon in my left in order to make me renounce my mission, it shall not be done. It shall never be given up until it should please Allah to make it a triumph or I perish in the attempt.[1]

1. These remarks have been taken and compiled from the Eng. tr. Mishkat by Maulana F. Karim. (N.A.)

MORAL VALUES

(i) Truth and False-hood :

يَاأَيُّهَا الَّذِينَ آمَنُوا اتَّقُوا اللَّهَ وَكُونُوا مَعَ الصَّادِقِينَ ﴿١١٩﴾ (توبة-١١٩)

O you who believe, keep your duty to Allah and be with the truthful. (9:119).

وَاذْكُرْ فِي الْكِتَابِ إِبْرَاهِيمَ إِنَّهُ كَانَ صِدِّيقًا نَبِيًّا ﴿٤١﴾
(مريم-٤١)

And mention Abraham in the Book. Surely he was a truthful man, a prophet. (19:41).

وَوَهَبْنَا لَهُمْ مِنْ رَحْمَتِنَا وَجَعَلْنَا لَهُمْ لِسَانَ صِدْقٍ عَلِيًّا ﴿٥٠﴾ (مريم-٥٠)

And We gave them of Our mercy, and We granted them a truthful mention of eminence. (19:50).

وَاذْكُرْ فِي الْكِتَابِ إِدْرِيسَ إِنَّهُ كَانَ صِدِّيقًا نَبِيًّا ﴿٥٦﴾ وَرَفَعْنَاهُ مَكَانًا عَلِيًّا ﴿٥٧﴾ (مريم-٥٦،٥٧)

And mention Idris in the Book. Surely he was a truthful man, a prophet, and We raised him to an elevated state. (19:56,57).

وَلَمَّا رَأَى الْمُؤْمِنُونَ الْأَحْزَابَ قَالُوا هَٰذَا مَا وَعَدَنَا اللَّهُ وَرَسُولُهُ وَصَدَقَ اللَّهُ وَرَسُولُهُ وَمَا زَادَهُمْ إِلَّا إِيمَانًا
وَتَسْلِيمًا ۝ مِنَ الْمُؤْمِنِينَ رِجَالٌ صَدَقُوا مَا عَاهَدُوا اللَّهَ عَلَيْهِ فَمِنْهُمْ مَنْ قَضَىٰ نَحْبَهُ وَمِنْهُمْ مَنْ يَنْتَظِرُ
وَمَا بَدَّلُوا تَبْدِيلًا ۝ لِيَجْزِيَ اللَّهُ الصَّادِقِينَ بِصِدْقِهِمْ وَيُعَذِّبَ الْمُنَافِقِينَ إِنْ شَاءَ أَوْ يَتُوبَ عَلَيْهِمْ إِنَّ اللَّهَ كَانَ
غَفُورًا رَحِيمًا ۝ (احزاب - ۲۲، ۲۳، ۲۴)

And when the believers saw the allies, they said: This is what Allah and His Messenger promised us, and Allah and His Messenger spoke the truth. And it only added to their faith and submission. Of the believers are men who are true to the (covenant) they made with Allah; so of them is he who has accomplished his vow, and of them is he who yet waits, and they have not changed in the least—that Allah may reward the truthful for their truth, and chastise the hypocrites, if He please, or turn to them (mercifully). Surely Allah is ever Forgiving, Merciful. (33:22,23,24).

إِنَّ الْمُسْلِمِينَ وَالْمُسْلِمَاتِ وَالْمُؤْمِنِينَ وَالْمُؤْمِنَاتِ وَالْقَانِتِينَ وَالْقَانِتَاتِ وَالصَّادِقِينَ وَالصَّادِقَاتِ ......
...... أَعَدَّ اللَّهُ لَهُمْ مَغْفِرَةً وَأَجْرًا عَظِيمًا ۝ (احزاب - ۳۵)

Surely the men who submit and the women who submit, and the believing men and the believing women, and the obeying men and the obeying women, and the truthful men and the truthful womene Allah has prepared for them forgiveness and a mighty reward. (33:35).

فَمَنْ أَظْلَمُ مِمَّنْ كَذَبَ عَلَى اللَّهِ وَكَذَّبَ بِالصِّدْقِ إِذْ جَاءَهُ أَلَيْسَ فِي جَهَنَّمَ مَثْوًى لِلْكَافِرِينَ ۝
وَالَّذِي جَاءَ بِالصِّدْقِ وَصَدَّقَ بِهِ أُولَٰئِكَ هُمُ الْمُتَّقُونَ ۝ لَهُمْ مَا يَشَاءُونَ عِنْدَ رَبِّهِمْ ذَٰلِكَ جَزَاءُ
الْمُحْسِنِينَ ۝ لِيُكَفِّرَ اللَّهُ عَنْهُمْ أَسْوَأَ الَّذِي عَمِلُوا وَيَجْزِيَهُمْ أَجْرَهُمْ بِأَحْسَنِ الَّذِي كَانُوا يَعْمَلُونَ ۝
(زمر - ۳۲ تا ۳۵)

Who is then more unjust than he who utters a lie against Allah and denies the truth, when it comes to him? IS THERE not in hell an abode for the disbelievers? And he who brings the truth and accepts the truth—such are the dutiful. They shall have from their Lord what they please. Such is the reward of the doers of good—That Allah may ward off from them the worst of what they did, and give them their reward for the best of what they did. (39:35).

إِنَّمَا الْمُؤْمِنُونَ الَّذِينَ آمَنُوا بِاللَّهِ وَرَسُولِهِ ثُمَّ لَمْ يَرْتَابُوا وَجَاهَدُوا بِأَمْوَالِهِمْ وَأَنْفُسِهِمْ فِي سَبِيلِ اللَّهِ أُولَٰئِكَ هُمُ
الصَّادِقُونَ ﴿١٥﴾ (حجرات-١٥)

The believers are those only who believe in Allah and His Messenger, then they doubt not, and struggle hard with their wealth and their lives in the way of Allah. Such are the truthful ones. (49:15).

فَأَمَّا مَنْ أَعْطَىٰ وَاتَّقَىٰ ﴿٥﴾
وَصَدَّقَ بِالْحُسْنَىٰ ﴿٦﴾ فَسَنُيَسِّرُهُ لِلْيُسْرَىٰ ﴿٧﴾ (الليل ٥،٦،٧)

Then as for him who gives and keeps his duty, and accepts what is good—We facilitate for him (the way to) ease. (92:5,6,7).

قَالَ اللَّهُ هَٰذَا يَوْمُ يَنْفَعُ الصَّادِقِينَ صِدْقُهُمْ لَهُمْ جَنَّاتٌ تَجْرِي مِنْ تَحْتِهَا الْأَنْهَارُ خَالِدِينَ فِيهَا أَبَدًا
رَضِيَ اللَّهُ عَنْهُمْ وَرَضُوا عَنْهُ ذَٰلِكَ الْفَوْزُ الْعَظِيمُ ﴿١١٩﴾ (مائدہ-١١٩)

Allah will say: This is a day when their truth will profit the truthful ONES. For them are gardens where in flow rivers abiding therein for ever. Allah is well pleased with them and they are well pleased with Allah. That is the mighty achievement. (5:119).

رَبِّ هَبْ لِي حُكْمًا وَأَلْحِقْنِي بِالصَّالِحِينَ ﴿٨٣﴾ وَاجْعَلْ لِي لِسَانَ صِدْقٍ فِي الْآخِرِينَ ﴿٨٤﴾ (شعراء-٨٣،٨٤)

My Lord, grant me wisdom, and join me with the righteous, and ordain for me a goodly mention in later generations. (26:83,84).

طَاعَةٌ وَقَوْلٌ مَعْرُوفٌ فَإِذَا عَزَمَ الْأَمْرُ فَلَوْ صَدَقُوا اللَّهَ لَكَانَ خَيْرًا لَهُمْ ﴿٢١﴾ (محمد-٢١)

Obedience and a gentle word (are proper). Then when the affair is settled, it is better for them if they remain true to Allah. (47.21).

وَقُلْ جَاءَ الْحَقُّ وَزَهَقَ الْبَاطِلُ إِنَّ الْبَاطِلَ كَانَ زَهُوقًا ﴿٨١﴾ (بنی اسرائیل)

Truth has appeared and falsehood has vanished; Surely falsehood is a thing to vanish. (17:81)

لَيْسَ الْبِرَّ أَنْ تُوَلُّوا وُجُوهَكُمْ قِبَلَ الْمَشْرِقِ وَالْمَغْرِبِ وَلَٰكِنَّ الْبِرَّ مَنْ آمَنَ بِاللَّهِ وَالْيَوْمِ الْآخِرِ وَالْمَلَائِكَةِ وَالْكِتَابِ وَالنَّبِيِّينَ وَآتَى الْمَالَ عَلَىٰ حُبِّهِ ذَوِي الْقُرْبَىٰ وَالْيَتَامَىٰ وَالْمَسَاكِينَ وَابْنَ السَّبِيلِ وَالسَّائِلِينَ وَفِي الرِّقَابِ وَأَقَامَ الصَّلَاةَ وَآتَى الزَّكَاةَ وَالْمُوفُونَ بِعَهْدِهِمْ إِذَا عَاهَدُوا وَالصَّابِرِينَ فِي الْبَأْسَاءِ وَالضَّرَّاءِ وَحِينَ الْبَأْسِ أُولَٰئِكَ الَّذِينَ صَدَقُوا وَأُولَٰئِكَ هُمُ الْمُتَّقُونَ (بقرہ - ۱۷۷)

Righteousness is this that one should believe in Allah, and the Last Day, and the angels, and the book, and the prophets, and give away wealth out of love for Him to the near of kin and the orphans, and the needy, and the wayfarers and the beggars, and for the captives, and keep prayer, and pay the poor-rate, and those who keep their treaty when they make ONE and the patient in tribulation and adversity and time of stress. Such are they who are sincere. Such are the God-fearing. (2:177).

وَالَّذِينَ لَا يَشْهَدُونَ الزُّورَ وَإِذَا مَرُّوا بِاللَّغْوِ مَرُّوا كِرَامًا (فرقان - ۷۲)

(The faithful slaves of the Beneficent are they) who will not witness vanity, but when they pass near senseless play, pass by with dignity (25:72).

AHADITH:

۱- عن ابی بکرة قال قال رسول الله صلی الله علیه وسلم الا انبئکم باکبر الکبائر الا ! شرك بالله و عقوق الو الدین الا ! و قول الزور (متفق علیه)

Abu Bakarah reported that the Messenger of Allah said : Shall I not inform you about the greatest of great sins (گناہ کبیرہ)? Behold! setting up a partner with Allah, disobedience to parents, and be hold false talk. (Agreed).

۲- عن عبدالله بن مسعود قال قال رسول الله صل الله علیه وسلم علیکم بالصدق فان الصدق یهدی الی البر و ان البر یهدی الی الجنة وما یزال الرجل یصدق و یتحری الصدق حتی یکتب عند الله صدیقاً وایاکم و

الكذب فان الكذب يهدى الى الفجور و ان الفجور يهدى الى النار وما يزال الرجل يكذب ويتحرى الكذب حتى يكتب عند الله كذاباً (متفق عليه)

Abdullah-b-Mas'ud reported that the Messenger of Allah said: You shall speak the truth for truth leads to piety and piety leads to Paradise. A man continues to speak the truth and to adhere to truth till he is enrolled near Allah as a great truthful man. Beware of falsehood and verily faslehood leads to transgression and trangression leads to the fire. A man continues to speak falsehood and to adhere to falsehood till he is enrolled as a great liar in the sight of Allah. (Agreed).

٣- عن ابن مسعود قال ان الشيطان ليتمثل فى صورة الرجل فياتى القوم فيحدثهم بالحديث من الكذب فيتفرقون فيقول الرجل منهم سمعت رجلاً أعرف وجهه ولا ادرى ما اسمه يحدث (مسلم)

Ibn-e-Mas'ud reported that the Messenger of Allah said: Verily the devil takes the form of a man and then comes to a people and communicates false traditions to them that they may differ. One of them says: I heard a man whose face I know but whose name I do not know speaking (so). (Muslim).

٤- عن عبادة بن الصامت ان النبى صل الله عليه وسلم قال اضمنو الى ستاً من انفسكم اضمن لكم الجنة اصدقوا اذا حدثتم و اوفوا اذا وعدتم و ادوا اذا ئتمنتم و احفظوا فروجكم و غضوا البصاركم وكفوا ايديكم (بيهقى)

Abdah-b-Swamet reported that the Holy Prophet said: Assure me six things from your selves; I shall then assure Paradise for you. Speak the truth when you talk, fulfil when you promise, fulfil trust when you are entrusted, guard your private parts, shut up your eye-sights and withhold your hands. (Baihaqi)

۵۔ عن انس قال قال رسول اللہ صلی علیہ وسلم اذا مدح الفاسق غضب الرب تعالیٰ واھتزلہ العرش (بیہقی)

Anas reported that the Messenger of Allah said : Whenever a transgressor is praised, the Almighty Allah becomes angry and the throne shakes for him (Bachaqi)

۶۔ عن الحسن بن علی قال حفظت من رسول اللہ صلی اللہ علیہ وسلم دع مایریبك الی مالا یریبک فان الصدق طمانیة وان الکذب ریبة

(احمد۔ ترمذی۔ نسائی)

Hasan-b-Ali reported, I remembered from the Messenger of Allah: Give up what appears doubtful to thee for what does not appear doubtful to thee; and verily truth is peace of mind, falsehood is doubt. (Ahmad, Tirmizi, Nisai).

۷۔ عن بهز بن حکیم عن ابیه عن جده قال قال رسول‌اللہ صلی‌اللہ علیه وسلم ویل لمن یحدث فیکذب لیضحك به القوم ویل له

(احمد۔ ترمذی۔ ابوداؤد۔ دارمی)

Bahaz-b-Hakim reported from h's father and his father from his grand-father that the Messenger ofAllah said : Woe to him who holds talk, and talks falsehood to make people laugh thereby. Woe to him. (Ahmad, Tirmizi, Abu Daud, Darimi).

۸۔ عن ابی هریرة قال قال رسول اللہ صلی اللہ علیه وسلم من لم یدع قول الزور والعمل به فلیس للہ حاجة فی ان یدع طعامه وشرابه

(بخاری)

Abu Hurairah reported that the Messenger of Allah said : Who so does not give up false talk and action according to it, there is no need for Allah that he gives up his food and his drink. (Bukhari).

Remarks :

1) Falsehood in talk and promise is a great sin, while truthfulness is a great virtue. Truth is light, while falsehood is a darkness

2) The Quran itself laid down the virtues of the truthful as is evident from the extracts.

(2) Promise and Trust :

وَبِعَهْدِ اللّٰهِ اَوْفُوْا (انعام-۱۵۳)

And fulfil the covenant of Allah (6 : 153)

يٰۤاَيُّهَا الَّذِيْنَ اٰمَنُوْۤا اَوْفُوْا بِالْعُقُوْدِ (مائدہ-۱)

O ye who believe ! Fulfil your undertakings (5 : 1)

وَاَوْفُوْا بِالْعَهْدِ اِنَّ الْعَهْدَ كَانَ مَسْئُوْلًا (بنی اسرائیل)

And keep the covenant. Lo ! of the covenant it will be asked. (17 : 34)

بَلٰى مَنْ اَوْفٰى بِعَهْدِهٖ وَاتَّقٰى فَاِنَّ اللّٰهَ يُحِبُّ الْمُتَّقِيْنَ (آل عمران-۷۶)

Nay, but (the chosen of Allah is) he who fulfilleth his pledge and wardeth off (evil) ; for Allah loveth those who ward off (evil) : (3 : 76)

فَمَنْ نَّكَثَ فَاِنَّمَا يَنْكُثُ عَلٰى نَفْسِهٖ وَمَنْ اَوْفٰى بِمَا عٰهَدَ عَلَيْهُ اللّٰهَ فَسَيُؤْتِيْهِ اَجْرًا عَظِيْمًا (فتح-۱۰)

So whosoever breaketh his oath, breaketh it only to his soul's hurt; while whosoever keepeth his covenant with Allah, on him will He bestow innense reward. (48 : 10)

إِلَّا الَّذِينَ عَاهَدتُّم مِّنَ الْمُشْرِكِينَ ثُمَّ لَمْ يَنقُصُوكُمْ شَيْئًا وَلَمْ يُظَاهِرُوا عَلَيْكُمْ أَحَدًا فَأَتِمُّوا إِلَيْهِمْ عَهْدَهُمْ
إِلَىٰ مُدَّتِهِمْ (توبہ-۴)

Excepting those of the idolaters with whom ye (Muslims) have a treaty, and who have since abated nothing of your right nor have supported anyone against you. (As for these), fulfil their treaty to them till their term. (9 : 4)

وَالْمُوفُونَ بِعَهْدِهِمْ إِذَا عَاهَدُوا ۖ وَالصَّابِرِينَ فِي الْبَأْسَاءِ وَالضَّرَّاءِ وَحِينَ الْبَأْسِ ۗ
أُولَٰئِكَ الَّذِينَ صَدَقُوا ۖ وَأُولَٰئِكَ هُمُ الْمُتَّقُونَ (بقرہ-۱۷۷)

And those who keep their treaty when they make one and the patient in tribulation and adversity and time of stress. Such are they who are sincere. Such are the God-fearing. (2 : 177)

فَبِمَا نَقْضِهِم مِّيثَاقَهُمْ لَعَنَّاهُمْ وَجَعَلْنَا قُلُوبَهُمْ قَاسِيَةً (مائدہ-۱۳)

And because of their breaking their covenant, we have cursed them and made hard their hearts. (5 : 13)

وَالَّذِينَ هُمْ لِأَمَانَاتِهِمْ وَعَهْدِهِمْ رَاعُونَ وَالَّذِينَ هُمْ عَلَىٰ صَلَوَاتِهِمْ يُحَافِظُونَ أُولَٰئِكَ هُمُ الْوَارِثُونَ الَّذِينَ يَرِثُونَ
الْفِرْدَوْسَ هُمْ فِيهَا خَالِدُونَ (مؤمنون-۸تا۱۱)

And who are shepherds of their pledge and their covenant, and who pay heed to their prayers. These are the heirs who will inherit Paradise. There they will abide. (23 : 8—11)

وَمِنْهُم مَّنْ عَاهَدَ اللَّهَ لَئِنْ آتَانَا مِن فَضْلِهِ لَنَصَّدَّقَنَّ وَلَنَكُونَنَّ مِنَ الصَّالِحِينَ فَلَمَّا آتَاهُم مِّن
فَضْلِهِ بَخِلُوا بِهِ وَتَوَلَّوا وَّهُم مُّعْرِضُونَ (توبہ-۷۵،۷۶)

And of them is he who made a covenant with Allah (saying) : If He give us of His bounty we will give alms and become of the righteous. Yet when He gave them of His bounty, they hoarded it and turned away, averse. (9 : 75,76)

وَالَّذِينَ يَنقُضُونَ عَهْدَ اللَّهِ مِن بَعْدِ مِيثَاقِهِ وَيَقْطَعُونَ مَا أَمَرَ اللَّهُ بِهِ أَن يُوصَلَ وَيُفْسِدُونَ فِي
الْأَرْضِ ۙ أُولَٰئِكَ لَهُمُ اللَّعْنَةُ وَلَهُمْ سُوءُ الدَّارِ ۝ (رعد - ٢٥)

And those who break the covenant of Allah after ratifying it, and sever that which Allah hath Commanded should be joined, and make mischief in the earth ; theirs is the curse and theirs the ill abode. (13 : 25)

وَاذْكُرْ فِي الْكِتَابِ إِسْمَاعِيلَ ۚ إِنَّهُ كَانَ صَادِقَ الْوَعْدِ وَكَانَ رَسُولًا نَّبِيًّا ۝ (مریم - ٥٤)

And make mention in the Scripture of Ismael. Lo! he was a keeper of his promise, and he was a messenger (of Allah), a Prophet. (19 : 54)

لَا يُؤَاخِذُكُمُ اللَّهُ بِاللَّغْوِ فِي أَيْمَانِكُمْ وَلَٰكِن يُؤَاخِذُكُم بِمَا عَقَّدتُّمُ الْأَيْمَانَ ۖ فَكَفَّارَتُهُ إِطْعَامُ عَشَرَةِ مَسَاكِينَ
مِنْ أَوْسَطِ مَا تُطْعِمُونَ أَهْلِيكُمْ أَوْ كِسْوَتُهُمْ أَوْ تَحْرِيرُ رَقَبَةٍ ۖ فَمَن لَّمْ يَجِدْ فَصِيَامُ ثَلَاثَةِ أَيَّامٍ ۚ ذَٰلِكَ كَفَّارَةُ
أَيْمَانِكُمْ إِذَا حَلَفْتُمْ ۚ وَاحْفَظُوا أَيْمَانَكُمْ ۚ (مائدہ - ٨٩)

Allah will not take you to task for that which is unintentinal in your oaths, but He will take you to task for the oaths which ye swear in earnest. The expiation thereof is the feeding of ten of the needy with the average of that wherewith ye feed your own folk, or the clothing of them, or the liberation of a slave, and for him who findeth not (the wherewithal to do so) then a three days' fast. This is the expiation of your oaths. (5 : 89)

إِنَّا عَرَضْنَا الْأَمَانَةَ عَلَى السَّمَاوَاتِ وَالْأَرْضِ وَالْجِبَالِ فَأَبَيْنَ أَن يَحْمِلْنَهَا وَأَشْفَقْنَ مِنْهَا وَحَمَلَهَا الْإِنسَانُ ۖ إِنَّهُ
كَانَ ظَلُومًا جَهُولًا ۝ (احزاب - ٧٢)

Lo, we offered the trust unto the heavens and the earth and hills but they shrank from bearing it and were afraid of it. And man assumed it. Lo, he hath proved a tyrant and a fool. (33 : 72)

وَمَا كَانَ لِنَبِيٍّ أَن يَغُلَّ ۚ وَمَن يَغْلُلْ يَأْتِ بِمَا غَلَّ يَوْمَ الْقِيَامَةِ ۚ ثُمَّ تُوَفَّىٰ كُلُّ نَفْسٍ مَّا كَسَبَتْ وَهُمْ لَا يُظْلَمُونَ ۝
(آل عمران - ١٦١)

It is not for any Prophet to deceive (mankind). Whoso deceiveth will bring his deceit with him on the Day of Resurrection. Then every one will be paid in full what he hath earned ; and they will not be wronged. (3 : 161)

وَإِذْ أَخَذَ رَبُّكَ مِنْ بَنِيٓ ءَادَمَ مِنْ ظُهُورِهِمْ ذُرِّيَّتَهُمْ وَأَشْهَدَهُمْ عَلَىٰٓ أَنْفُسِهِمْ أَلَسْتُ بِرَبِّكُمْ قَالُوا بَلَىٰ شَهِدْنَا
أَنْ تَقُولُوا يَوْمَ الْقِيَٰمَةِ إِنَّا كُنَّا عَنْ هَٰذَا غَٰفِلِينَ ۝ أَوْ تَقُولُوٓا إِنَّمَآ أَشْرَكَ ءَابَآؤُنَا مِنْ قَبْلُ وَكُنَّا ذُرِّيَّةً
مِّنْ بَعْدِهِمْ أَفَتُهْلِكُنَا بِمَا فَعَلَ الْمُبْطِلُونَ ۝ (اعراف-۱۷۲، ۱۷۳)

And (remember) when thy Lord brought forth from the Children of Adam from their veins, their seed, and made them testify of themselves, (saying) : Am I not your Lord ? They said : yes, verily. We testify. (That was) lest ye should say at the Day of Resurrection: Lo! of this we were unaware ; or lest ye should say : (It is) only (that our fathers ascribed partners to Allah of old and we were (their) seed after them. Wilt thou destroy us on account of that which those who follow falsehood died ? (7 : 172, 173)

إِنَّ اللَّهَ يَأْمُرُكُمْ أَنْ تُؤَدُّوا الْأَمَٰنَٰتِ إِلَىٰٓ أَهْلِهَا وَإِذَا حَكَمْتُمْ بَيْنَ النَّاسِ أَنْ تَحْكُمُوا بِالْعَدْلِ (نساء-۵۸)

Lo ! Allah Commandeth you that you restore deposits to their owners, and if you judge between mankind, that you judge justly. (4 : 58)

AHADITH :

عبدالله بن ابی الحسماء قال بايعت النبی صلی الله عليه وسلم قبل ان
يبعث و بقيت له بقية فوعدته ان آتيه بها فی مكانه فنسيت فذكرت بعدثلث
فاذا هو فی مكانه قال لقد شقت علی انا ههنا من ثلث انتظرك۔

(ابو داؤد)

Abdullnh-b-Abi-Hasma'a reported : I took fealty to the Holy Prophet before he was raised up (as a Prophet), and there was price due to him (from me). So I promised to come to him therewith at the (appointed) place. Then I forgot but I remembered after three days, when lo ! he was at the (appointed) place. He said : You have put trouble to myself. I am here since three days waiting for you. (Abu Daud)

عن ابی هریره رفعه قال ان الله عزوجل یقول انا ثالث الشریکین مالم یخن احدهما صاحبه فاذا خانه خرجت من بینهما. (ابو داؤد)

Abu Hurairah raised it (to Prophet) who said: Verily the Almighty and Glorious Allah says : I am the Third of the two cosharers so long as one of the two does not commit treachery with his friend. Then when he commits treachery with him, I go out from the midst of the two. (Abu Daud)

عنه عن النبی صلی الله علیه وسلم قال اد الامانة الی من ائتمنك ولا تخن من خانك. (ترمذی ۔ ابو داؤد)

Same reported from the Holy Prophet who said : Pay trust to one who has entrusted you; and be not treacherous to one who was treacherous to you. (Timmizi, Abu-Daud)

عن جابر بن عبدالله عن النبی صلی الله علیه وسلم قال اذا حدث الرجل الحدیث ثم التفت فهی امانة. (ترمذی — ابو داؤد)

Jaber-b-Abdullah reported from the Holy Prophet who said : when a man gives an information and then draws attention (for keeping it secret), it is a trust. (Timmizi-Abu-Daud)

عن جابر قال قال رسول الله صلی الله علیه وسلم المجالس بالامانة الاثلثة مجالس سفك دم حرام او فرج حرام او اقتطاع مال بغیر حق. (ابو داؤد)

Jaber reported that the Messenger of Allah said : All meetings are on trust except three—the meetings for shedding unlawful blood, or for unlawful private parts, or for taking away property without just cause. (Abu-Daud)

عن سفیان بن اسد الحضرمی قال سمعت رسول الله صلی الله علیه وسلم یقول کبرت خیانة ان تحدث اخاك حدیثاً هولك مصدق و انت به کاذب. (ابو داؤد)

Sufyan-b-Asad-al-Hazrami reported : I heard the Messenger of Allah say : It is the height of breach of trust that you communicate a news to your brother which he believes true for you while you (take) it for him as untrue. (Abu Daud)

عن انس قال خطبنا رسول الله صلى الله عليه وسلم قال لا ايمان لمن لا امانة له ولا دين لمن لاعهد له. (بيهق)

Anas reported : Hardly did the Messenger of Allah address us without saying : There is no faith in him who has got no trust, and no religion for him who has got no promise. (Baihaqi)

عن عبدالله بن عمر ان رسول الله صلي الله عليه وسلم قال اربع اذاكن فيك فلا عليك ما فاتك الدنيا حفظ امانة و صدق حديث و حسن خليقة و عفة فى طعمة. (احمد - بيهقى)

Abdullah-b-Aum reported that the Messenger of Allah said : When four things are in you, there is nothing against you in the world which may cause you loss : guarding of trust, truthfulness in speech, beauty of conduct, and moderation in good. (Ahmad, Baihaqi)

Remarks :

1. The performance of promise on the part of individuals as well as nations is one of the first essentials of the welfare of humanity; hence the stress laid upon it by the Holy Quran and Hadith. Faithlessness to treaties and pledges, on the part of nations, has wrought the greatest havoc on humanity. Just as no society can prosper until individual members are true to their mutual agreements and promises to each other, so humanity at large can never have place unless nations are true to their agreements. It is the very first necessity of social relations.

2. For promise, the Holy Quran has generally used these words : عهد and ميثاق which cover all sorts of ties, engagements, compacts, contracts, leagues, treaties and also all Divine ordinances and covenants imposed by God as well as the mutual agreements made by man.

3. The first and foremost covenant of Allah referred to in the Holy Quran (7 : 172) is the evidence of His Unity to which human nature bears witness. This covenant was impressed upon the heart and soul of man to acknowledge and obey the one God. The confirmation of this covenant is brought about by the prophets in general and by the Holy Prophet in particular. This covenant of Allah to obey Him and His messenger implicitly is an injunction as well as compact. The very first Kalimah of Islam also reminds us of the same.

4. Allah has enjoined upon the Muslims to fulfil their promises. The Holy Quran says that "O you who believe! Fulfil your undertakings (5 : 1) and it is said that "Blissful are the believers, those who fulfil all their obligations" (financial or otherwise) (23 : 8-11). The prophets are mentioned in the Quran as the foremost figures in keeping a promise (19 : 54). Our Holy Prophet Muhammad (Peace be upon him) never spoke a lie in his whole life, and whatever he promised, he kept to the last whether it was for or against him. For this reason he won the title of Al-Sadiq and Al-Amin before he reached the age of Prophethood, a title so rare in the then Arab society.

5. Secrecy and trust are the basis of the proceedings of all meetings and consultations. Trust is also a moral responsibility, which us aman sense of answerableness for all acts of thought and conduct.

6. Trust or promise may also mean duties. The Holy Prophet himself explained the word امانت as meaning government, affairs or state. The Holy Prophet said : When the Amanat (Trust) is wasted, wait for the قیامت i.e. the hour of the doom. It was asked, how will the trust be wasted, O Messenger of Allah? He said, when government is entrusted to those unworthy of it, then wait for the doom. (Bukhari)

7. According to the Quran, trust is a thing which distinguishes man from other animals and things. For this, man is called the noblest of creation. He is best who fulfils this trust according to its dictation, and he is worst who gives against its dictations and commits breach of trust or acts treacheroualsly against his own soul. Man shall have to stand up on the Resurrection Day to answer the use and misuse of this great trust in him in this world.

Similar is the trust of one man to trust in another. A trustworthy man is a great asset to society and the greater the number of such trusted men in society, the greater will be its prosperity. They are the most valuable treasures in the life of a brotherhood as they are repositors of the confidence of the public. It is a fact of Islamic History that when the Holy Prophet was about to leave for Madina, he left behind Hazrat Ali so that he might hand over the trusts to their respective owners which were deposited with the Holy Prophet by the Meccans in spite of their deadly opposition.

8. According to Hadith all the proceedings of any meeting and consultations are included in the meaning of trust. In three cases, however, the proceedings shall be disclosed under all circumstances irrespective of conditions :-

1. To murder a man unjustly.
2. To commit fornication with a strange woman by abduction or kidnapping, etc.
3. And to rob another's property by theft or dacoity. (1)

(1) These remarks have been written with the help of the English translation of Mishkat by M. F. Karim and commentaries on Quran by A. Majid Daryabadi, Mohammad Ali, Abdullah Y. Ali, etc., etc. (N. A.).

(3) Honour and Dishonour :

يَا أَيُّهَا النَّاسُ اتَّقُوا رَبَّكُمُ الَّذِي خَلَقَكُم مِّن نَّفْسٍ وَاحِدَةٍ وَخَلَقَ مِنْهَا زَوْجَهَا وَبَثَّ مِنْهُمَا رِجَالًا كَثِيرًا
وَنِسَاءً ۚ وَاتَّقُوا اللَّهَ الَّذِي تَسَاءَلُونَ بِهِ وَالْأَرْحَامَ ۚ إِنَّ اللَّهَ كَانَ عَلَيْكُمْ رَقِيبًا (نساء - ١)

O people, keep your duty to your Lord, who created you from a single being and created your mate of the same (kind), and spread from these two many men and women. And your duty to Allah, by whom you demand one of another (your rights), and (to) the ties of relationship. Surely Allah is ever a Watcher over you.

(4 : 1)

يَا أَيُّهَا النَّاسُ إِنَّا خَلَقْنَاكُم مِّن ذَكَرٍ وَأُنثَىٰ وَجَعَلْنَاكُمْ شُعُوبًا وَقَبَائِلَ لِتَعَارَفُوا ۚ إِنَّ
أَكْرَمَكُمْ عِندَ اللَّهِ أَتْقَاكُمْ ۚ إِنَّ اللَّهَ عَلِيمٌ خَبِيرٌ (حجرات - ١٣)

O mankind, surely We have created you from a male and a female and made you tribes and families that you may know each other. Surely the noblest of you with Allah is the most dutiful of you. Surely Allah is Knowing, Aware. (49 : 13)

وَاتَّقُوا اللَّهَ وَاعْلَمُوا أَنَّ اللَّهَ مَعَ الْمُتَّقِينَ (بقره - ١٩٤)

And keep your duty to Allah, and know that Allah is with those who keep their duty. (2 : 194)

وَتَزَوَّدُوا فَإِنَّ خَيْرَ الزَّادِ التَّقْوَىٰ ۚ وَاتَّقُونِ يَا أُولِي الْأَلْبَابِ (بقره - ١٩٧)

And make provision for yourselves, the best provision being to keep one's duty. And keep your duty to Me, O men of understanding.

(2 : 197)

وَإِنَّ هَٰذِهِ أُمَّتُكُمْ أُمَّةً وَاحِدَةً وَأَنَا رَبُّكُمْ فَاتَّقُونِ (مؤمنون - ٥٢)

And surely this your community is one community, and I am your Lord, so keep your duty to Me. (23 : 52)

AHADITH

عن ابى هريرة قال سئل رسول الله صلى الله عليه وسلم اى الناس
اكرم فقال اكرمهم عند الله اتقاهم قالوا ليس عن هذا نسئلك قال
فاكرم الناس يوسف نبى الله بن نبى الله بن نبى الله بن نبى الله بن
خليل الله قالوا ليس عن هذا نسئلك قال فعن معادن العرب تسالونى
قالوا نعم قال فخياركم فى الجاهلية خياركم فى الاسلام اذا فقهوا
(متفق عليه)

Abu Hurairah reported that the Messenger of Allah was asked: Who among men is the most honourable? He said: The most honourable of them to Allah is one who is the most pious of them. They said: We don't ask you about it. He said: then the most honourable of men was Joseph, Prophet of Allah, son of the Prophet of Allah, son of the Prophet of Allah, son of the Friend of Allah. They said: We don't ask you about it. He enquired: Are you then asking me about the best of the Arabs? "Yes", replied they. He said: The best of you in the dark ages are the best of you in Islam when they are learned in theology. (Agreed)

٢- عن ابى ذر ان رسول الله صلى الله عليه وسلم قال له انك لست
بخير من احمر و اسود الا ان تفضله بتقوىٰ (احمد)

Abu Zar reported that the Messenger of Allah said: You are in no way better than the Red and the Black except that you surpass them on account of piety. (Ahmed)

٣ عن ابى هريرة عن النبى صلى الله عليه وسلم قال لينتهين اقوام
يفتخرون بابائهم الذين ماتوا انما هم فحم من جهنم او ليكونن
اهون على الله من الجعل الذى يدهده الغزء بانفه ان الله قد اذهب

عنكم عصبية الجاهلية و فخرها بالاباء انما هو مومن تقى او فاجر
شقى الناس كلهم بنو آدم وآدم من تراب (ترمذى- ابو داؤد)

Abu Hurairah reported that the Messenger of Allah said : There will surely appear peoples who will boast of their forefathers who died. They will certainly be coals of the hell or they will certainly become more hateful to Allah than the filth which a man throws off after smelling by his nose. Surely Allah removed from you the evils of the age of ignorance and its boast of ancestors. He is certainly a pious believer or an unfortunate sinner. Men, everyone of them, are children of Adam, and Adam was from dust. (Tirmizi, Abu Daud)

٤ - عن عمر قال قال رسول الله صلى الله عليه وسلم لا تطروني كما
اطرت النصارى بن مريم فانما انا عبده فقولوا عبدالله و رسوله
(متفق عليه)

Omar reported that the Messenger of Allah said : Don't praise me too much just as the Christians praised the son of Allah and His Messenger. (Agreed)

٥ - عن انس قال جاء رجل الى النبى صلى الله عليه وسلم فقال يا
خيرالبرية فقال رسول الله صلى الله عليه وسلم ذاك ابراهيم
(مسلم)

Anas reported that a man came to the Holy Prophet and said : "O the best of creation !" Then the Holy Prophet said : He was Abraham. (Muslim)

٦ . عن جبير بن مطعم ان رسول الله صلى الله عليه وسلم قال ليس
منا من دعا الى عصبية و ليس منا من قاتل عصبية و ليس منا من
مات على عصبية . (ابو داؤد)

Jubair-b-Mutim reported that the Messenger of Allah said : He is not of us who calls for tribal cause, and he is not of us who fights for tribal cause, and he is not of us who dies for tribal cause. (Abu Daud)

Remarks :

1. Islam recognizes that by birth every man is equal in honour and respect as men and women are members of one family, being the children of Adam. As there is no boast of pedigree between brothers of the same family, there cannot be such boast among the members of the common brotherhood of men. Everybody is born sinless and pure, and not with a bundle of sins on his back. As years grow in the life of a man, he may increase his honour and respect or may go down towards dishonour according as his actions are good or bad.

2. Besides the origin of man was from earth and then of semen and as such man has got nothing to boast of origin and ancestry. If there should be any basis of honour among men, it is, according to the Quran, based on piety and duty (49 : 13). The highest honour is, therefore, reserved for one who is most pious. Such was the Prophet Mohammad (P. H.) who was the most pious of men and therefore the most honourable.

3. This basis of honour and respect sounds the death-knell of all superiority or inferiority in society on account of birth, geographical limitations, economic embarrassments, race and colour, etc. The grand Magna Charta of honour is piety, good works and good actions.

(4) Hypocrisy (انفاق)

وَمِنَ النَّاسِ مَنْ يَّقُوْلُ اٰمَنَّا بِاللّٰهِ وَبِالْيَوْمِ الْاٰخِرِ وَمَا هُمْ بِمُؤْمِنِيْنَ ۘ يُخٰدِعُوْنَ اللّٰهَ وَالَّذِيْنَ اٰمَنُوْا ۚ وَمَا يَخْدَعُوْنَ اِلَّآ
اَنْفُسَهُمْ وَمَا يَشْعُرُوْنَ ۭ فِيْ قُلُوْبِهِمْ مَّرَضٌ ۙ فَزَادَهُمُ اللّٰهُ مَرَضًا ۚ وَلَهُمْ عَذَابٌ اَلِيْمٌ ڏ بِمَا كَانُوْا يَكْذِبُوْنَ (البقرہ-۸-۱۰)

And there are some deople who say : We believe in Allah and the Last Day, and they are not believers. They seek to deceive Allah and those who believe, and they perceive not. In their hearts is a disease, so Allah increased their disease, and for them is a painful chsatisement because they lie (2 : 8-10).

بَشِّرِ الْمُنٰفِقِيْنَ بِاَنَّ لَهُمْ عَذَابًا اَلِيْمَا ۨ الَّذِيْنَ يَتَّخِذُوْنَ الْكٰفِرِيْنَ اَوْلِيَاۗءَ مِنْ دُوْنِ الْمُؤْمِنِيْنَ ۭ (النساء-۱۳۸)

Give news to the hypocrites that for them is a painful chastisement (4 : 138).

اِنَّ الْمُنٰفِقِيْنَ يُخٰدِعُوْنَ اللّٰهَ وَهُوَ خَادِعُهُمْ ۚ (نساء-۱۴۲)

The hypocrites seek to deceive Allah, and He will requite their deceit to them (4 : 142).

مُّذَبْذَبِيْنَ بَيْنَ ذٰلِكَ ڰ لَآ اِلٰى هٰٓؤُلَاۗءِ وَلَآ اِلٰى هٰٓؤُلَاۗءِ
(نساء-۱۴۳)

Wavering between that (and this) — (belonging) neither to these nor to those (4 : 143).

اِنَّ الْمُنٰفِقِيْنَ فِي الدَّرْكِ الْاَسْفَلِ مِنَ النَّارِ ۚ وَلَنْ تَجِدَ لَهُمْ نَصِيْرًا ۙ (نساء-۱۴۵)

The hypocrites are surely in the lowest depths of the Fire, and thou wilt find no helper for them (4 : 145).

يٰٓاَيُّهَا النَّبِيُّ جَاهِدِ الْكُفَّارَ وَالْمُنٰفِقِيْنَ وَاغْلُظْ عَلَيْهِمْ ۭ وَمَاْوٰىهُمْ جَهَنَّمُ ۭ وَبِئْسَ الْمَصِيْرُ (توبہ-۷۳)

O Prophet, strive hard against the dis-b li vers and the hyocrites and be firm against them. Be harsh with them. Their ultimate abode is hell, a hapless journey's end (9 : 73).

وَلَا تُصَلِّ عَلَىٰ أَحَدٍ مِّنْهُم مَّاتَ أَبَدًا وَلَا تَقُمْ عَلَىٰ قَبْرِهِ ۖ إِنَّهُمْ كَفَرُوا بِاللَّهِ وَرَسُولِهِ وَمَاتُوا وَهُمْ فَاسِقُونَ ۝
(توبہ-۸۴)

And never offer prayer for any one of them who dies, nor stand by his grave. Surely they disbelieved in Allah and His Messenger and they died in transgression.

لَّئِن لَّمْ يَنتَهِ الْمُنَافِقُونَ وَالَّذِينَ فِي قُلُوبِهِم مَّرَضٌ وَالْمُرْجِفُونَ فِي الْمَدِينَةِ لَنُغْرِيَنَّكَ بِهِمْ ثُمَّ لَا يُجَاوِرُونَكَ فِيهَا
إِلَّا قَلِيلًا ۝ مَّلْعُونِينَ ۖ أَيْنَمَا ثُقِفُوا أُخِذُوا وَقُتِّلُوا تَقْتِيلًا ۝ (احزاب-۶۰،۶۱)

If the hypocrites and those in whose hearts is a disease and the agitators in Madinah desist not We shall certainly urge thee on against them, then they shall not be thy neighbours in it but for a little while—accused; wherever they are found they will be seized and slain (33 : 60, 61).

إِذَا جَاءَكَ الْمُنَافِقُونَ قَالُوا نَشْهَدُ إِنَّكَ لَرَسُولُ اللَّهِ ۗ وَاللَّهُ يَعْلَمُ إِنَّكَ لَرَسُولُهُ وَاللَّهُ يَشْهَدُ إِنَّ الْمُنَافِقِينَ لَكَاذِبُونَ ۝
اتَّخَذُوا أَيْمَانَهُمْ جُنَّةً فَصَدُّوا عَن سَبِيلِ اللَّهِ ۚ إِنَّهُمْ سَاءَ مَا كَانُوا يَعْمَلُونَ ۝ ذَٰلِكَ بِأَنَّهُمْ آمَنُوا ثُمَّ كَفَرُوا فَطُبِعَ عَلَىٰ
قُلُوبِهِمْ فَهُمْ لَا يَفْقَهُونَ ۝ وَإِذَا رَأَيْتَهُمْ تُعْجِبُكَ أَجْسَامُهُمْ ۖ وَإِن يَقُولُوا تَسْمَعْ لِقَوْلِهِمْ ۖ كَأَنَّهُمْ خُشُبٌ مُّسَنَّدَةٌ ۖ
يَحْسَبُونَ كُلَّ صَيْحَةٍ عَلَيْهِمْ ۚ هُمُ الْعَدُوُّ فَاحْذَرْهُمْ ۚ قَاتَلَهُمُ اللَّهُ ۖ أَنَّىٰ يُؤْفَكُونَ ۝ (المنافقون-۱-۴)

When the hypocrites come to thee, they say : We bear witness that thou art indeed Allah's Messenger. And Allah knows thou art indeed His Messenger. And Allah bears witness that the hypocrites are surely liars. They take shelter under their oaths, thus turning (men) from Allah's way. Surely evil is that which they do. That is because they believed, then disbelieved; thus their hearts are sealed, so they understand not. And when thou seest them, their persons please thee; and if they speak, thou listenest to their speech. They are like pieces of wood, clad with garments. They think every cry to be against them. They are the enemy, so beware of them. May Allah destroy them. How they are turned back (63 : 1-4).

AHADITH

١ - عن ابى هريرة قال قال رسول الله صلى الله عليه وسلم آية المنافق ثلث اذا حدث كذب و اذا وعد اخلف و اذا تمن خان

(متفق عليه)

Abu Hurairah reported that the Messenger of Allah said : The signs of a hypocrite are three. When he talks, he speaks falsehood; and when he promises, he breaks, and when he is entrusted, commits treachery. (Agreed).

٢ - عن ابن عمر قال قال رسول الله صلى الله عليه وسلم مثل المنافق كالشاة العائرة بين الغنمين تعير الى هذه مرة و الى هذه مرة

(مسلم)

Ibn Omar reported that the Messenger of Allah said : The parable of a hypocrite is as a goat roaring between two goats, going once unto this and once unto that. (Muslim).

٣ - عن ابى هريرة قال قال رسول الله صلى الله عليه وسلم شر الناس يوم القيمة ذا الوجهين الذى يأتى هـٰو لاء بوجه وهـٰو لاء بوجه

(متفق عليه)

Abu Hurariah reported that the Messenger of Allah said : You will find the worst of men on the Resurrection Day, having two faces, who will come to these man with one face and to these with another. (Agreed).

٤ - عن عمار قال قال رسول الله صلى الله عليه وسلم من كان ذا وجهين فى الدنيا كان له يوم القيمة لسانان من نار (دارمى)

Ammar reported that the Messenger of Allah said : Whoever has got two faces in this world, there shall be two tongues of fire for him on the Resurrection Day. (Darimi).

٥ - عن حذيفة عن النبي صلى الله عليه وسلم قال لا تقولوا للمنافق سيد فانه ان يك سيداً فقد اسخطتم ربكم (ابو داؤد)

Huzaifah reported from the Holy Prophet who said: Don't address a hypocrite as "master", because if he becomes master, you will indeed incur displeasure of your Lord. (Abu Daud).

٦ - عن عبد الله بن عمرو قال قال رسول الله صلى الله عليه وسلم اربع من كن فيه كان منافقاً خالصاً و من كانت فيه خصلة منهن كانت فيه خصلة من النفاق حتى يدعها اذا ائتمن خان و اذا حدث كذب و اذا عاهد غدر و اذا خاصم فجر (متفق عليه)

Abdullah-Amr reported that Messenger of Allah said: Whoso has got four things in him is a true hypocrite, and whoso got a habit therefrom in him has got in him a habit of hypocrisy till he gives it up; when he is trusted, he is unfaithful; and when he speaks, he speaks falsehood; and when he makes a promise, he proves treacherous, and when he quarrels, he commits sin. (Agreed).

Remarks :

Hypocrisy is an evil and a spiritual and moral disease. Actually speaking, it is the weakness of heart, for having not the courage to deny anything openly. It arises out of a word uttered by the tongue or a motion shown by signs and gestures, but they do not correspond in heart or mind. Therefore, there is always a contradiction between the tongue and mind or in thought and action of a hypocrite. It means, his body and mind act differently. With reference to religion, it is obviously an insincerity which is the worst crime ever known to human nature. Thus insincerity in religion is the worst of all sins.

Hypocrisy is an evil which gives birth to other religious, social and moral evils, such as falsehood, deceit, treachery, unfaithfulness, and show, etc.

The hypocrites as a particular class, were the insincere people who accepted the message of Islam only with their lips, and faith did not go deep down into their hearts. They were a source of constant trouble to the Holy Prophet at Madinah. They left no stone unturned at the time of the Prophet in collusion with the neighbouring Jews and Christians to blot out the truth of Islam from the soil of Arabia. Before the arrival of the Holy Prophet at Madinah, Abdullah-b-Ubayy was a person of note there, and expected to become the leader and ruler of that city. But the Prophet's advent and his recognition by all the communities of Madinah as head of the state, robbed him of those dearly cherished hopes, and he (Abdullah-b-Ubayy) along with his followers, adopted an attitude of hypocrisy.

Hypocrites have been particularly included in the class of unbelievers by the Quran and Hadith, and a severe and strong condemnation has been made of them. Accordingly, they will receive punishment both in this world and the next. The sin of hypocrisy is so great in the eyes of Islam that the Holy Prophet was commanded and sanctioned to carry on Jihad against disbelievers and hypocrites. He and the Caliph succeeding him did not accept Zakat from the hypocrites. Hence, in the life hereafter, the hypocrites were spoken of as being in the lowest depths of the Fire.

(5) Kindness and Oppression :

قُلْ يٰعِبَادِيَ الَّذِيْنَ اَسْرَفُوْا عَلٰٓى اَنْفُسِهِمْ لَا تَقْنَطُوْا مِنْ رَّحْمَةِ اللّٰهِ اِنَّ اللّٰهَ يَغْفِرُ الذُّنُوْبَ جَمِيْعًا

اِنَّهٗ هُوَ الْغَفُوْرُ الرَّحِيْمُ (زمر-۵۳)

Say : O Thy servants who have been prodigal regarding their souls, despair not of the mercy of Allah; surely Allah forgives sins altogether. He is indeed the Forgiving, the Merciful. (39 : 53).

رَبَّنَا وَسِعْتَ كُلَّ شَيْءٍ رَّحْمَةً وَّعِلْمًا (مؤمن-۷)

Our Lord, Thou embraced all things in mercy and knowledge. (40 : 7).

هُوَ الرَّحْمٰنُ الرَّحِيْمُ (حشر-۲۲)

He is the Beneficent, the Merciful. (59 : 22).

رَبَّنَآ اٰمَنَّا فَاغْفِرْ لَنَا وَارْحَمْنَا وَاَنْتَ خَيْرُ الرّٰحِمِيْنَ (مومنون-۱۰۹)

Our Lord, we believe, so forgive us and have mercy on us, and Thou are the Best of those who show mercy. (23 : 109).

لَقَدْ جَاۗءَكُمْ رَسُوْلٌ مِّنْ اَنْفُسِكُمْ عَزِيْزٌ عَلَيْهِ مَا عَنِتُّمْ حَرِيْصٌ عَلَيْكُمْ بِالْمُؤْمِنِيْنَ رَءُوْفٌ رَّحِيْمٌ (توبہ-۱۲۸)

Certainly a Messenger has come to you from among yourselves; grievous to him is your falling into distress, most solicitous for you ; to the believers (he is) compassionate, merciful. (9 : 128).

وَالَّذِيْنَ مَعَهٗٓ اَشِدَّاۗءُ عَلَى الْكُفَّارِ رُحَمَاۗءُ بَيْنَهُمْ (فتح-۲۹)

And those with him are firm of heart against the disbelievers, compassionate among themselves. (48 : 29)

إِنَّ الشِّرْكَ لَظُلْمٌ عَظِيمٌ ۞ (لقمان-١٣)

Surely ascribing partners (to Him) is a grievous iniquity. (31 : 13).

إِنَّ اللَّهَ لَا يَظْلِمُ مِثْقَالَ ذَرَّةٍ (نساء-٤٠)

Surely Allah wrongs not the weight of an atom. (4 : 40).

لَا يُحِبُّ اللَّهُ الْجَهْرَ بِالسُّوءِ مِنَ الْقَوْلِ إِلَّا مَنْ ظُلِمَ (نساء-١٤٨)

Allah loves not the public utterance of hurtful speech, except by one who has been wronged. (4 : 148).

وَاللَّهُ لَا يُحِبُّ الظَّالِمِينَ ۞ (آل عمران-١٣٩)

And Allah loves not the wrongdoers. (3 : 139).

قَوْلٌ مَعْرُوفٌ وَمَغْفِرَةٌ خَيْرٌ مِنْ
صَدَقَةٍ يَتْبَعُهَا أَذًى (بقرة-٢٦٣)

A kind word with forgiveness is better than charity followed by injury. (2 :263).

قُلْ إِنَّمَا حَرَّمَ رَبِّيَ الْفَوَاحِشَ مَا ظَهَرَ مِنْهَا وَمَا بَطَنَ وَالْإِثْمَ وَالْبَغْيَ بِغَيْرِ الْحَقِّ وَأَنْ تُشْرِكُوا بِاللَّهِ مَا لَمْ يُنَزِّلْ بِهِ
سُلْطَانًا وَأَنْ تَقُولُوا عَلَى اللَّهِ مَا لَا تَعْلَمُونَ ۞ (اعراف-٣٣)

Say: My Lord forbids only indecencies, such of them as are apparent and such as are concealed, and sin and unjust rebellion, and that you associate with Allah that for which He has sent down no authority, and that you say of Allah what you know not. (7 : 33).

وَتَعَاوَنُوا عَلَى الْبِرِّ وَالتَّقْوَىٰ وَلَا تَعَاوَنُوا عَلَى الْإِثْمِ وَالْعُدْوَانِ (مائدہ-۲)

And help one another in right causes and piety, and help not one another in sin and aggression. (5 : 2)

إِنَّ اللَّهَ يَأْمُرُ بِالْعَدْلِ وَالْإِحْسَانِ وَإِيتَاءِ ذِي الْقُرْبَىٰ وَيَنْهَىٰ عَنِ الْفَحْشَاءِ وَالْمُنكَرِ وَالْبَغْيِ (نحل-۹۰)

Surely Allah enjoins justice and the doing of good (to others) and the giving to the kindred, and He forbids indecency and evil and rebellion. (16 : 90)

وَالَّذِينَ إِذَا أَصَابَهُمُ الْبَغْيُ هُمْ يَنتَصِرُونَ ۝ وَجَزَاءُ سَيِّئَةٍ سَيِّئَةٌ مِّثْلُهَا ۖ فَمَنْ عَفَا وَأَصْلَحَ فَأَجْرُهُ عَلَى اللَّهِ ۚ
إِنَّهُ لَا يُحِبُّ الظَّالِمِينَ ۝ وَلَمَنِ انتَصَرَ بَعْدَ ظُلْمِهِ فَأُولَٰئِكَ مَا عَلَيْهِم مِّن سَبِيلٍ ۝ إِنَّمَا السَّبِيلُ عَلَى الَّذِينَ
يَظْلِمُونَ النَّاسَ وَيَبْغُونَ فِي الْأَرْضِ بِغَيْرِ الْحَقِّ ۚ أُولَٰئِكَ لَهُمْ عَذَابٌ أَلِيمٌ ۝ (شوریٰ-۳۹تا۴۲)

And those, who when great wrong afflicts them, defend themselves. And the recompense of evil is punishment like it; but whoever forgives and amends, his reward is with Allah. Surely He loves not the wrongdoers. And those who defend themselves after being oppressed, these it is against whom there is no way (of blame). The way is (of blame) only against those who oppress men and revolt in the earth unjustly. For such there is a painful chastisement. (42 : 39-42).

AHADITH :

١- عن جرير النبي صلى الله عليه وسلم قال من يحرم الرفق يحرم الخير (مسلم)

Jarir reported that the Messenger of Allah said ; He who is devoid of kindness is devoid of (all) good. (Muslim).

٢- عن عائشة ان رسول الله صلى الله عليه وسلم قال أن الله رفيق يحب الرفق و يعطى على الرفق ما لا يعطى على العنف وما لا يعطى على ما سواه (مسلم)

Ayesha reported that the Messenger of Allah said : Verily Allah is kind; He loves kindness and He bestows on kindness what He bestows on severity and what is besides it. (Muslim).

٣- عن ابن عمران النبي صلى الله عليه وسلم قال الظلم ظلمات يوم القيمة (متفق عليه)

Ibn Omar reported that the Messenger of Allah said : Oppression will be intense darkness on the Resurrection Day. (Agreed).

٤- عن أبي هريرة قال قال رسول الله صلى الله عليه وسلم من كانت له مظلمة لاخيه من عرضه أو شئ فليتحلله ، منه اليوم قبل أن لا يكون دينار ولا درهم إن كان له عمل صالح اخذ منه بقدر مظلمته وإن لم تكن له حسنات أخذ من سيات صاحبه فحمل عليه - (بخارى)

Abu Hurairah reported : Whoso has got due to him a right of oppression or anything from his brother out of his honour, let him pardon him today (in the world) before there comes any silver or gold coin (as compensation). If he has got good deeds, something out of these in proportion to the right of oppression will be taken; and if he has got no good deeds, some of the bad deeds of the oppressed will be taken and will be put as a burden on him (oppressor). (Bukhari).

٥- عن حذيفة قال قال رسول الله عليه وسلم لاتكونوا امعة تقولون أن أحسن الناس أحسنا وإن ظلموا ظلمنا ولكن وطنوا أنفسكم إن أحسن الناس أن تحسنوا وإن اساؤا فلا تظلموا (ترمذي)

Huzaifah reported that the Messenger of Allah said: Don't be silly by saying. If people do good and if they oppress, we will oppress; but console yourselves that if the people do good, you will do good; and if they do evils, you will not oppress. (Tirmizi).

٦- عن ابن مسعود قال لما نزلت الذين آمنوا و لم يلبسوا ايمانهم بظلم شق ذلك على أصحاب رسول الله صلى الله عليه وسلم و قالوا يا رسول الله أينا لم يظلم نفسه فقال رسول الله صلى الله عليه وسلم ليس ذاك إنما هو الشرك الم تسمعوا قول لقمان لابنه لا تشرك بالله أن الشرك لظلم عظيم (متفق عليه)

Ibn Masud reported that when it was revealed—Those who believed and did not mix their faith with oppression—it proved hard to the companions of the Messenger of Allah, and they said: O Messenger of Allah! who is of us who has not oppressed himself?

The Messenger of Allah said: That is not so; it is simply polytheism. Have you not heard the sermon of Luqman to his son: Don't set up partner with Allah; verily polytheism is a great oppression. (Agreed).

٧- عن جابر قال قال رسول الله صلى الله عليه وسلم اتقوا الظلم فإن الظلم ظلمات يوم القيمة واتقوا الشح فان الشح اهلك من كان قبلكم حملهم على أن سفكوا وماءهم واستحلوا محارمهم (مسلم)

Jaber reported that the Messenger of Allah said: Fear oppression because oppression will be intense darkness on the Resurrection Day; and fear niggardliness because niggardliness destroyed those who were before you. It led them to such an extent that they shed their blood and knew unlawful things as lawful. (Muslim).

٨- عن على قال قال رسول الله صلى الله عليه وسلم اياك ودعوة المظلوم فانما يسال الله حقه و ان الله يمنع ذا حق حقه (بيهقى)

Ali reported that the Messenger of Allah said : Take care of the invocation of the oppressed person, because he will surely ask his right to Allah, and verily Allah does not deny the right of a man having right. (Baihaqi).

٩- عن اوس بن شرحبيل أنه سمع رسول الله صلى الله عليه وسلم يقول من مشى مع ظالم ليقويه وهو يعلم أنه ظالم ، فقد خرج من الاسلام (بيهقى)

Aus-b-Shurhabil reported that he heard the Messenger of Allah say : Whoever walks with a tyrant to empower him knowing that he is tyrant has indeed gone out of Islam. (Baihaqi).

١٠- عن عياض بن حمار قال قال رسول الله صلى الله عليه وسلم أهل الجنة ثلثة ذو سلطان مقسط متصدق موفق ورجل رحيم رقيق القلب لكل ذى قربى ومسلم وعفيف متعفف ذو عيال واهل النار خمسة الضعيف الذى لا زبر له الذين هم فيكم تبع لايبغون اهلاً ولا مالاً والخائن الذى لايخفى له طمع وان دق الا خانه ورجل لايصبح ولا يمسى الا وهو يخادعك عن اهلك ومالك وذكر البخل والكذب والشنظير الفحاش (مسلم)

Eyaz b. Himar reported that the Messenger of Allah said : The inmates of Paradise are (of) three (kinds) : A king, true and merciful; a kind man soft of heart for every kinsman and Muslim; and a contented beggar having a big family abstaining from begging. And the inmates of the Fire are five : The weak (in morals) who have got no self-control, who have got followers among you, who neither seek wives nor property; and the treacherous man whose avarice is not secret for him and who, if he promises, breaks it; and a man who does not get up at dawn and at dusk but to cheat you regarding your family and property; and he mentioned the misers and the liars and the indecent rogues.

(Muslim).

Remarks :

Kindness and oppression are two opposite terms. Kindness is an attribute, while oppression is an evil. Kindness is most liked by Allah but oppression is always disliked by Him.

As kindness is an attribute of Allah and in showing kindness the Almighty Allah does not distinguish between man and man, similarly, we are asked to follow this attribute of Allah whenever occasion demands it in every walk of life without any distinction. The tyrants and oppressors will get severe punishment both in this world and in the Hereafter.

In the annals of the world, the kindness of the Holy Prophet stands unique. The Meccans who all along subjected him and his companions to the bitterest persecution and barbarous tortures, were given general amnesty when the Holy Prophet conquered Mecca. He said : "This day I shall treat you as brothers. There is no blame upon you. You are free ! You can go."

Kindness adorns everything, while harshness disgraces everything. A soft heart is near Allah, while a hard heart is remote from Him.

Oppression is of two kinds—oppression on the soul and oppression on the creatures of Allah. Oppression on soul is a very grievous thing and the greatest oppression on the soul is polytheism or setting up equals with Allah (شرک). Oppression upon creatures may be of different kinds—on physique, on mind and on religious sentiments, etc.

(6) Control of Tongue :

يَا أَيُّهَا الَّذِينَ آمَنُوا لَا يَسْخَرْ قَوْمٌ مِّن قَوْمٍ عَسَىٰ أَن يَكُونُوا خَيْرًا مِّنْهُمْ وَلَا نِسَاءٌ مِّن نِّسَاءٍ عَسَىٰ أَن يَكُنَّ خَيْرًا مِّنْهُنَّ ۖ وَلَا
تَلْمِزُوا أَنفُسَكُمْ وَلَا تَنَابَزُوا بِالْأَلْقَابِ ۖ بِئْسَ الِاسْمُ الْفُسُوقُ بَعْدَ الْإِيمَانِ ۚ وَمَن لَّمْ يَتُبْ فَأُولَٰئِكَ هُمُ الظَّالِمُونَ ۞ يَا أَيُّهَا
الَّذِينَ آمَنُوا اجْتَنِبُوا كَثِيرًا مِّنَ الظَّنِّ إِنَّ بَعْضَ الظَّنِّ إِثْمٌ ۖ وَلَا تَجَسَّسُوا وَلَا يَغْتَب بَّعْضُكُم بَعْضًا ۚ أَيُحِبُّ أَحَدُكُمْ أَن
يَأْكُلَ لَحْمَ أَخِيهِ مَيْتًا فَكَرِهْتُمُوهُ ۚ وَاتَّقُوا اللَّهَ ۚ إِنَّ اللَّهَ تَوَّابٌ رَّحِيمٌ ۞ يَا أَيُّهَا النَّاسُ إِنَّا خَلَقْنَاكُم مِّن ذَكَرٍ وَأُنثَىٰ
وَجَعَلْنَاكُمْ شُعُوبًا وَقَبَائِلَ لِتَعَارَفُوا ۚ إِنَّ أَكْرَمَكُمْ عِندَ اللَّهِ أَتْقَاكُمْ ۚ إِنَّ اللَّهَ عَلِيمٌ خَبِيرٌ ۞
(حجرات ١١ تا ١٣)

O you who believe, let not people laugh at people, perchance they may be better than they ; nor let women laugh at women, perchance they may be better than they are ; neither defame one another, nor insult one another by nicknames. Bad is the name of lewdness, after faith. And whoso turneth not in repentance, such are evil-doers. O you who believe ! Shun much suspicion ; for lo ! some suspicion is a crime. And spy not, neither backbite one another. Would one of you love to eat the flesh of his dead brother? You abhor that (so abhor the other) ! And keep your duty (to Allah). Lo ! Allah is Relenting, Merciful. O mankind, Surely We have created you from a male and a female, and made you tribes and families that you may know each other. Surely the novelest of you, in the sight of Allah, is the best in conduct. Lo ! Allah is Knower, Aware. (49 : 11-13)

يَا أَيُّهَا الَّذِينَ آمَنُوا إِن جَاءَكُمْ فَاسِقٌ بِنَبَإٍ فَتَبَيَّنُوا أَن تُصِيبُوا قَوْمًا بِجَهَالَةٍ فَتُصْبِحُوا عَلَىٰ مَا فَعَلْتُمْ نَادِمِينَ ۞
(حجرات - ٦)

O you who believe, if an evil-liver brings you tidings, verify it, lest you harm a people in ignorance and afterward repent of what you did. (49 : 6)

فَاجْتَنِبُوا الرِّجْسَ مِنَ الْأَوْثَانِ وَاجْتَنِبُوا قَوْلَ الزُّورِ ۞ (حج - ٣٠)

So shun the filth of the idols and shun false words. (22 : 30)

وَلَا تَكُن لِّلْخَائِنِينَ خَصِيمًا ۞ وَاسْتَغْفِرِ اللَّهَ ۖ إِنَّ اللَّهَ كَانَ غَفُورًا رَّحِيمًا ۞ وَلَا تُجَادِلْ عَنِ الَّذِينَ يَخْتَانُونَ
أَنفُسَهُمْ ۚ إِنَّ اللَّهَ لَا يُحِبُّ مَن كَانَ خَوَّانًا أَثِيمًا ۞ (نساء - ١٠٥ تا ١٠٧)

And be not thou a pleader for the treacherous ; And seek forgiveness of Allah. Lo ! Allah is ever Forgiving, Merciful. And plead not on behalf of (people) who deceive themselves. Lo ! Allah loveth not one who is treacherous and sinful. (4 : 105-107)

وَالَّذِينَ يُؤْذُونَ الْمُؤْمِنِينَ وَالْمُؤْمِنٰتِ بِغَيْرِ مَا اكْتَسَبُوا فَقَدِ احْتَمَلُوا بُهْتَانًا وَإِثْمًا مُّبِينًا (احزاب - ۵۸)

And those who annoy believing men and believing women undeservedly, they bear the guilt of slander and manifest sin. (33 : 58)

فَلَا تُطِعِ الْمُكَذِّبِينَ ۝ وَدُّوا لَوْ تُدْهِنُ فَيُدْهِنُونَ ۝ وَلَا تُطِعْ كُلَّ حَلَّافٍ مَّهِينٍ ۝ هَمَّازٍ مَّشَّاءٍۭ بِنَمِيمٍ ۝ مَّنَّاعٍ لِّلْخَيْرِ مُعْتَدٍ أَثِيمٍ ۝ عُتُلٍّۭ بَعْدَ ذٰلِكَ زَنِيمٍ ۝ أَن كَانَ ذَا مَالٍ وَبَنِينَ ۝ (القلم - ۸ تا ۱۴)

So obey not those who are rejectors. They wish that thou shouldst be pliant, so they (too) would be pliant. And obey not any mean swearer, defamer, spreader abroad of slanders, hinderer of the good, transgressor, malfactor, greedy therewithal, intrusive. It is because he is possessed of wealth and children. (68 : 8-14)

وَيْلٌ لِّكُلِّ هُمَزَةٍ لُّمَزَةٍ ۝ (همزہ - ۱)

Woe unto every slanderer, defamer! (104:1)

وَلَا تَسُبُّوا الَّذِينَ يَدْعُونَ مِن دُونِ اللَّهِ فَيَسُبُّوا اللَّهَ عَدْوًا بِغَيْرِ عِلْمٍ (انعام - ۱۰۹)

And abuse not those whom they call upon besides Allah, lest, exceeding the limits, they abuse Allah through ignorance. (6 : 109)

فَلَا رَفَثَ وَلَا فُسُوقَ وَلَا جِدَالَ فِي الْحَجِّ (بقرہ - ۱۹۷)

There shall be no immodest speech nor abusing nor alteration in the pilgrimmage. (2 :197)

AHADITH :

١- عن ابى هريرة قال قال رسول الله صلى الله عليه وسلم ان العبد ليتكلم بالكلمة من رضوان الله لا يلقى لها بالا يرفع الله بها درجات وإن العبد ليتكلم بالكلمة من سخط الله لا يلقى لها بالا يهوى بها فى جهنم (بخارى)

Abu Hurairah reported that the Messenger of Allah said, Verily a servant utters a word for pleasure of Allah; he does not meet with any disaster for it but Allah raises ranks therefor. And verily a servant who utters a word for displeasure of Allah, does not meet any disaster therefor but goes to Hell on its account. (Bukhari)

٢- عبد الله بن مسعود قال قال رسول الله صلى الله عليه وسلم سباب المسلم فسوق وقتاله كفر (متفق عليه)

Abdullah-b-Mas'ud reported that the Messenger of Allah said, To backbite a Muslim is transgression, and to kill him is infidelity. (Agreed)

٣- عن أبى ذر قال قال رسول الله صلى الله عليه وسلم من دعا رجلا بالكفر أو قال عدو الله و ليس كذلك الا حار عليه (متفق عليه)

Abu Zaar reported that the Messenger of Allah said : Whoever blames a man with infidelity or says "Enemy of Allah" while he is not like that, it goes back to him. (Agreed)

٤- عن حذيفة قال سمعت رسول الله صلى الله عليه وسلم يقول لا يدخل الجنة قتات (متفق عليه)

Huzaifa reported : I heard the Messenger of Allah say : The sower of dissensions shall not enter Paradise. (Agreed)

٥- عن أبى هريرة أن رسول الله صلى الله عليه وسلم قال اتدرون ما الغيبة قالوا الله و رسوله اعلم قال ذكرك اخاك بما يكره قيل افرأيت ان كان فى اخى ما أقول قال ان كان فيه ما تقول فقد اغتبته ، وان لم يكن فيه ما تقول فقد بهته (مسلم)

Abu Hurairah reported that the Messenger of Allah said: Do you all know what is backbiting? They replied: Allah and his Apostle know best. He said: Your talk about your brother with what he dislikes. He was questioned: Inform me what he says be in my brother. He said: If what you say is in him, still you will be backbiting him; and if what you say is not in him, you will be slandering him. (Muslim)

٦- عن عبد الله بن عمر قال قال رسول الله صلى الله عليه وسلم من صمت نجا (احمد - ترمذی)

Abdullah-b-Amr reported that the Messenger of Allah said: He who has kept silence has got salvation. (Ahmed, Tirmizi)

٧- عن عقبه بن عامر قال لقيت رسول الله صلى الله عليه وسلم فقلت ما النجاة ؟ فقال املك عليك لسانك ويسعك بيتك وابك على خطيئتك (احمد - ترمذی)

Oqbah-b-A'mer reported: I met the Messenger of Allah and enquired: What is salvation? He replied: Control thy tongue to thyself, and let thy house keep thee, and weep over thy sins. (Ahmed, Tirmizi)

٨- عن ابی هريرة قال قال رسول الله صلى الله عليه وسلم ان العبد ليقول الكلمة لا يقولها الا ليضحك به الناس يهوى بها ابعد مما بين السماء والارض وانه ، ليزل عن لسانه اشد مما يزل عن قدميه (البيهقی)

Abu Hurairah reported that the Messenger of Allah said: Verily servant does certainly utter a word; he does not utter it but to make men laugh thereby out of vain pleasure, he is more off than what is between heaven and earth, and verily he slips away from his tongue more seriously than what slips away from his feet. (Baihaqi)

٩- عن أبي سعيد وجابر قالا قال رسول الله صلى الله عليه وسلم الغيبة اشد من الزنا - قالوا يا رسول الله وكيف الغيبة اشد من الزنا ؟ قال ان الرجل ليزنى فيتوب الله عليه وفي رواية فيتوب فيغفر الله له و ان صاحب الغيبة لا يغفر له حتى يغفرها له ، صاحبه و فى رواية انس قال صاحب الزنا يتوب وصاحب الغيبة ليس له توبة (البيهقي)

Ibn Sayeed and Jaber reported that the Messenger of Allah said: Backbiting is greater than fornication. They enquired: O Messenger of Allah! How is backbiting greater than fornication? He replied: Verily a man commits fornication and then he repents and so Allah returns to him (And in a narration—so Allah returns to him and forgives him) but the backbiter is not forgiven till the person backbited by him does not forgive him. And in a narration of Anas, he said: The fornicater repents, but (as for) the backbiter, there is no repentance for him. (Baihaqi)

١٠- عن جبير بن مطعم ان رسول الله صلى الله عليه وسلم قال ليس منا من دعا الى عصبية وليس منا من قاتل عصبية وليس منا من مات على عصبية (ابو داؤد)

Jubair-b-Mut'em reported that the Messenger of Allah said: He is not of us who calls for tribal cause, and he is not of us who fights for tribal cause, and he is not of us who dies for tribal cause. (Abu Daud).

١١- عن ثوبان قال قال رسول الله صلى الله عليه وسلم من مات و هو برى من الكبر والغلول والدين دخل الجنة (ترمذى - ابن ماجه - دارمى)

Saobun reported that the Messenger of Allah said: Whoso dies while he is free from pride, deceit and debt, will enter Paradise. (Tirmizi, Ibn Majah, Darimi)

١٢- عن ابن عمر قال قال رسول الله صلى الله عليه وسلم لايكون المومن لعاناً و فى رواية لاينبغى للمومن ان يكون لعاناً (ترمذى)

Ibn Omar reported that the Messenger of Allah said : It is not proper for a believer to become a great curser. And in a narration, it is not meet for a believer to become a great curser. (Tirmizi)

۱۳۔ عن عبد اللہ بن عمرو قال هجرت الى رسول الله صلى الله عليه وسلم يوماً قال فسمع اصوات رجلين اختلفا فى آية فخرج علينا رسول الله صلى الله عليه وسلم يعرف فى وجهه الغضب فقال انما هلك من كان قبلكم باختلافهم فى الكتاب (مسلم)

Abdullah-b-Am'r reported : "One day I went at noon to the Messenger of Allah. He said that he heard the voice of two men who differed over a verse. Then the Messenger of Allah came down to us while wrath could be recognized in his face and said : Verily those who were before you were destroyed owing to their difference about the Book. (Muslim)

REMARKS :

1. The tongue is a piece of flash in the body, and an instrument which expresses and carries the message of mind and heart to others.

2. The tongue is the chief means of going to Heaven or Hell. Its' control is of utmost importance in forming the pious and useful life of a man. It is the vehicle of language through which it expresses itself. If it is properly controlled, like a bridled horse, it can cast pearls and gems ; but if it goes out of control, it becomes the seat of the devil. According to the teachings of the Quran and Hadith, Paradise is for the man who controls his tongue. On the contrary, its looseness may put him into Fire. As the Holy Prophet asked : Do you know what will be the foremost to lead men to the fire ? Looseness of tongue and private parts, he said.

3. On one side, without tongue, no divine service can effectively be made, no witnessing of faith can stand and no advice for doing good and forbidding evil can take place. While on the other and more important side it is the tongue which may give birth to so many calamisties and bad morals such as :-

1. Foul, false, vain, unseemly, immodest or obscene speech and indecent rebukes.
2. Quarrels, controversies, disputes and dissensions.
3. False deposition and oaths or promises.
4. Disclosing of secrets.
5. Jokes.
6. Abusing, curse etc.
7. Deceit.
8. Transgresion.
9. Blame and slandering.
10. Sorcery.
11. Immoral songs.
12. Hypocrisy.
13. Backbiting.
14. Flattery and
15. Evil counsels, etc. etc.

(7) Patience and Resignation

يٰٓاَيُّهَا الَّذِيْنَ اٰمَنُوا اسْتَعِيْنُوْا بِالصَّبْرِ وَالصَّلٰوةِ ۭ اِنَّ اللّٰهَ مَعَ الصّٰبِرِيْنَ (بقرہ - ۱۵۳)

O you who believe, seek assistance through patience and prayer ; surely Allah is with the patient. (2 : 153)

وَاِنْ تَصْبِرُوْا وَتَتَّقُوْا لَا يَضُرُّكُمْ كَيْدُھُمْ شَـيْـــًٔـا ۭ اِنَّ اللّٰهَ بِمَا يَعْمَلُوْنَ مُحِيْطٌ (آل عمران - ۱۱۹)

And if you are patient and keep your duty, their struggle will not injure you in any way. Surelv Allah encompasses that they do. (3 : 119)

لَتُبْلَوُنَّ فِيْٓ اَمْوَالِكُمْ وَاَنْفُسِكُمْ ۣ وَلَتَسْمَعُنَّ مِنَ الَّذِيْنَ اُوْتُوا الْكِتٰبَ مِنْ قَبْلِكُمْ وَمِنَ الَّذِيْنَ اَشْرَكُوْٓا اَذًى كَثِيْرًا ۭ
وَاِنْ تَصْبِرُوْا وَتَتَّقُوْا فَاِنَّ ذٰلِكَ مِنْ عَزْمِ الْاُمُوْرِ (آل عمران - ۱۸۵)

You will certainly be tried in your property and persons. And you will certainly hear from those who have been given the Book before you and from the idolaters much abuse. And if you are patient and keep your duty, surely this is an affair of great resolution. (3 : 185)

يٰٓاَيُّهَا الَّذِيْنَ اٰمَنُوا اصْبِرُوْا وَصَابِرُوْا وَرَابِطُوْا ۣ وَاتَّقُوا اللّٰهَ لَعَلَّكُمْ تُفْلِحُوْنَ (آل عمران - ۱۹۹)

O you who believe, be steadfast and try to excel in steadfastness and guard (the frontiers). And keep your duty to Allah that you may be successful. (3 : 199)

وَاَطِيْعُوا اللّٰهَ وَرَسُوْلَهٗ وَلَا تَنَازَعُوْا فَتَفْشَلُوْا وَتَذْهَبَ رِيْحُكُمْ وَاصْبِرُوْا ۭ اِنَّ اللّٰهَ مَعَ الصّٰبِرِيْنَ (انفال - ۴۶)

And obey Allah, His Messenger and dispute not one with another, lest you get weak-hearted and your power depart ; and be steadfast. Surely Allah is with the steadfast. (8 : 46)

وَلَئِنْ أَذَقْنَٰهُ نَعْمَآءَ بَعْدَ ضَرَّآءَ مَسَّتْهُ لَيَقُولَنَّ ذَهَبَ السَّيِّـَٔاتُ عَنِّىٓ ۚ إِنَّهُۥ لَفَرِحٌ فَخُورٌ ﴿١٠﴾ إِلَّا الَّذِينَ صَبَرُوا وَعَمِلُوا الصَّٰلِحَٰتِ
أُولَٰٓئِكَ لَهُم مَّغْفِرَةٌ وَأَجْرٌ كَبِيرٌ ﴿١١﴾ (هود - ١٠، ١١)

And if we make him taste a favour after distress has afflicted him, he says : The evils are gone away from me. Certainly he is exultant, boastful, except those who are patient and do good. For them is forgiveness and a great reward. (11 : 10, 11)

فَاصْبِرْ كَمَا صَبَرَ أُولُوا الْعَزْمِ مِنَ الرُّسُلِ وَلَا تَسْتَعْجِل لَّهُمْ (الاحقاف - ٣٥)

So have patience, as men of resolution, the messengers, had patience, and seek not to hasten for them (their doom). (46 : 35)

ثُمَّ كَانَ مِنَ الَّذِينَ ءَامَنُوا وَتَوَاصَوْا بِالصَّبْرِ وَتَوَاصَوْا بِالْمَرْحَمَةِ ﴿١٧﴾ أُولَٰٓئِكَ أَصْحَٰبُ الْمَيْمَنَةِ ﴿١٨﴾ (البلد - ١٧، ١٨)

Then he is of those who believe and exhort one another to patience, and exhort one another to mercy. These are the people of the right hand. (90 : 17, 18)

وَالْعَصْرِ ﴿١﴾ إِنَّ الْإِنسَٰنَ لَفِى خُسْرٍ ﴿٢﴾ إِلَّا الَّذِينَ ءَامَنُوا وَعَمِلُوا الصَّٰلِحَٰتِ وَتَوَاصَوْا بِالْحَقِّ وَتَوَاصَوْا بِالصَّبْرِ ﴿٣﴾ (العصر ١-٣)

By the time ! Surely man is in loss, except those who believe and do good, and exhort one another to truth, and exhort one another to patience. (103 : 1-3).

وَعَلَى اللَّهِ فَلْيَتَوَكَّلِ الْمُؤْمِنُونَ
آل عمران ١٥٩

And in Allah should the believers put their trust. (3 : 159)

قُلْ إِنَّ صَلَاتِي وَنُسُكِي وَمَحْيَايَ وَمَمَاتِي لِلّٰهِ رَبِّ الْعٰلَمِينَ (انعام ۱۶۳)

Say : My prayer and my sacrifices, and my death are surely for Allah, the Lord of the worlds. (6 : 163)

وَمَنْ يَتَوَكَّلْ عَلَى اللّٰهِ فَإِنَّ اللّٰهَ عَزِيزٌ حَكِيمٌ
(انفال - ۴۹)

And whoever trusts in Allah, then surely Allah is Mighty, Wise. (8 : 49)

وَقَالَ مُوسٰى يٰقَوْمِ إِنْ كُنْتُمْ اٰمَنْتُمْ بِاللّٰهِ فَعَلَيْهِ تَوَكَّلُوْا إِنْ كُنْتُمْ مُسْلِمِينَ فَقَالُوْا عَلَى اللّٰهِ تَوَكَّلْنَا
رَبَّنَا لَا تَجْعَلْنَا فِتْنَةً لِلْقَوْمِ الظّٰلِمِينَ وَنَجِّنَا بِرَحْمَتِكَ مِنَ الْقَوْمِ الْكٰفِرِينَ (یونس - ۸۴ تا ۸۶)

And Moses said : O my people, if you believe in Allah, then rely on Him if you submit (to Him). They said : On Allah we rely ; our Lord, make us not a trial of the unjust people and deliver us by Thy mercy from the disbelieving. (10 : 84-86)

وَأَنْ لَيْسَ لِلْإِنْسَانِ إِلَّا مَا سَعٰى وَأَنَّ سَعْيَهُ سَوْفَ يُرٰى ثُمَّ يُجْزٰىهُ الْجَزَاءَ الْأَوْفٰى وَأَنَّ إِلٰى رَبِّكَ الْمُنْتَهٰى (نجم ۳۹-۴۲)

And that man can have nothing but what he strives for and that his striving will soon be seen. Then he will be rewarded for it with the fullest reward and that to thy Lord is the goal. (53 : 37-42)

وَمَنْ يَتَوَكَّلْ عَلَى اللّٰهِ فَهُوَ حَسْبُهُ
(طلاق - ۳)

AHADITH :

١- عن ابن مسعود قال كانى انظر الى رسول الله صلى الله عليه وسلم يحكى نبياً من الانبياء ضربه قومه فادموه وهو يمسح الدم عن وجهه ويقول اللهم اغفر لقومى فانهم لايعلمون (متفق عليه)

Ibn Mas'ud reported : I am as it were looking to the Messenger of Allah who was telling a story about a prophet among the prophets. His people scourged him and shed his blood, while he was effacing blood from his face and saying : O Allah ! forgive my people, because they certainly know not. (Agreed)

٢- عن أنس قال مر النبى صلى الله عليه وسلم بامرأةٍ تبكى عند قبرٍ فقال اتقى الله واصبرى قالت اليك عنى فانك لم تصب بمصيبتى ولم تعرفه فقيل لها أنه النبى صلى الله عليه وسلم فاتت باب النبى صلى الله عليه وسلم فلم تجد عنده بوابين فقالت لم اعرفك فقال انما الصبر عند الصدمة الاولى (متفق عليه)

Anas reported that the Holy Prophet passed by a woman who was weeping near a grave. So he said : Fear Allah and be patient. She said : To you from me. Surely you have not been afflicted with my mishap ; nor have you known it. It was said to her that he was the Holy Prophet. Then she came to the door of the Holy Prophet and did not find door-keepers near him. So she said : I did not recognise you. He said : Verily patience is at the first attack of mishap. (Agreed)

٣- عن ابن سعودٍ قال قال رسول الله صلى الله عليه وسلم الصبر نصف الايمان . (مشكواة)

Ibn Mas'ud reported that the Messenger of Allah said : Patience is half of faith. (Miahkat)

٤- عن ابن عباس قال قال رسول الله صلى الله عليه وسلم يدخل الجنة من امتى سبعون الفاً بغير حساب هم الذين لايسترقون ولا يتطيرون وعلى ربهم يتوكلون . (متفق عليه)

Ibn-Abbas reported that the Messenger of Allah said: 70,000 of my followers shall enter Pradise without counts. They are those who do not recite charms, nor consider bad omens; but on their Lord do they rely. (Agreed)

٥- عن عمر بن الخطاب قال سمعت رسول الله صلى الله عليه وسلم يقول لوانكم تتوكلون على الله حق توكله لرزقكم كما يرزق الطير تغدو خماصاً وتروح بطانا (ترمذى - ابن ماجه)

Omar-b-al-Khattab reported: I heard the Messenger of Allah say: If you all had relied on Allah with due reliance, He would have certainly given you provision as He supplies provisions to birds who get up hungry in the morning and return with full belly at dusk. (Tirmizi, Ibn Majab)

٦- عن ابن عباس قال كنت خلف رسول الله صلى الله عليه وسلم يوماً فقال يا غلام احفظ الله يحفظك احفظ الله تجداه تجاهك واذا سالت فاسئل الله واذا استعنت فاستعن بالله واعلم لن الامة و اجتمعت على ان ينفعوك بشى لم ينفعوك الا بشئٍ قد كتبه الله لك ولو اجتمعوا على أن يضروك بشى ٍ لم يضروك الأشيٍ قد كتب الله عليك رفعت الاقلام وجفت الصحف (احمد - ترمذى)

Ibn-Abbas reported: One day I was behind the Messenger of Allah. He said: O boy! protect Allah and Allah will protect you. Protect Allah and you will find Him turning to you. When you beg, beg to Allah; when you seek help, seek help from Allah; and know that if all the people gather together to do benefit to you with anything, they will not be able to do benefit to you except with a thing which Allah ordained for you. Pens have been raised up, and papers have been soaked up. (Ahmad, Tirmizi).

٧- عن أبي هريرة أن النبي صلى الله عليه وسلم قال قال ربكم عزوجل لو أن عبهدي اطاعوني لاسقيتهم المطر بالليل واطلعت عليهم الشمس بالنهار ولم اسمعهم صوت الرعد (احمد)

Abu Hurairah reported that the Holy Prophet said: Thy Lord, the Almighty and the Glorious, said: If my servants had obeyed Me, I would have given them rain at night and made the sun rise on them at day time, and I would not have made them hear the voice of thunder. (Ahmad)

REMARKS :

—● Patience means to deny something to oneself. Patience is an attribute only of man because he has got devilish tendencies in him.

—● The Holy Quran and Hadith are full of exhortations for patience, and great rewards have been promised for it. The Messenger of Allah said that patience is half of faith, and that there is abundant good in it.

—● Patience over physical tortures such as wounds, assaults and diseases is good but spiritual patience is the best because it is patience over passions, evil appetites and other immoral tendencies.

—● **Tawakkul :** Tawakkul comes from *wakl* which means to resign or rely. There are different degrees of resignation as in patience, but the true man is one who resigns himself absolutely to the will of the Lord in all his affairs. Resignation does not mean absolute reliance on Allah in all our affairs divorced from action. It is both reliance and action. It is to toil hard with the belief that the results are in the hands of Allah.

MORAL VALUES

(8) Indecency and Shame.

وَلَا تَتَّبِعُوا خُطُوٰتِ الشَّيْطٰنِ ۚ اِنَّهٗ لَكُمْ عَدُوٌّ مُّبِيْنٌ ۝ اِنَّمَا يَاْمُرُكُمْ بِالسُّوْٓءِ وَالْفَحْشَآءِ (بقرہ-۱۶۹)

And follow not footsteps of the devil. Surely he is an open enemy to you. He enjoins on you only evil and indecency. (2 : 169).

وَالَّذِيْنَ اِذَا فَعَلُوْا فَاحِشَةً اَوْ ظَلَمُوْٓا اَنْفُسَهُمْ ذَكَرُوا اللّٰهَ فَاسْتَغْفَرُوْا لِذُنُوْبِهِمْ ۠ وَمَنْ يَّغْفِرُ الذُّنُوْبَ اِلَّا اللّٰهُ ۠ وَلَمْ يُصِرُّوْا عَلٰى مَا فَعَلُوْا وَھُمْ يَعْلَمُوْنَ ۝ اُولٰۗىِٕكَ جَزَاۗؤُھُمْ مَّغْفِرَةٌ مِّنْ رَّبِّهِمْ وَجَنّٰتٌ تَجْرِيْ مِنْ تَحْتِهَا الْاَنْهٰرُ خٰلِدِيْنَ فِيْهَا ۭ وَنِعْمَ اَجْرُ الْعٰمِلِيْنَ ۝ (آل عمران-۱۳۴،۱۳۵)

And those who, when they commit an indecency or wrong their souls, remember Allah and ask forgiveness for their sins. And who forgives sin but Allah And they persist not knowingly in what they do. Their reward is protection from their Lord, and Gardens wherein flow rivers, to abide in them. And excellent is the reward of the workers. (3 : 134 , 135)

قُلْ تَعَالَوْا اَتْلُ مَا حَرَّمَ رَبُّكُمْ عَلَيْكُمْ اَلَّا تُشْرِكُوْا بِهٖ شَيْـــًٔـا وَّبِالْوَالِدَيْنِ اِحْسَانًا ۚ وَلَا تَقْتُلُوْٓا اَوْلَادَكُمْ مِّنْ اِمْلَاقٍ ۭ نَحْنُ نَرْزُقُكُمْ وَاِيَّاهُمْ ۚ وَلَا تَقْرَبُوا الْفَوَاحِشَ مَا ظَهَرَ مِنْهَا وَمَا بَطَنَ ۚ وَلَا تَقْتُلُوا النَّفْسَ الَّتِيْ حَرَّمَ اللّٰهُ اِلَّا بِالْحَقِّ ۭ ذٰلِكُمْ وَصّٰىكُمْ بِهٖ لَعَلَّكُمْ تَعْقِلُوْنَ ۝ (انعام-۱۵۲)

Say: Come ! I will recite what your Lord has forbidden to you: Associate naught with Him and do good to parents and slay not your children for (fear of) poverty—We provide for you and for them—and draw not nigh to indecencies, open or secret, and kill not the soul which Allah has made sacred except in the course of justice. This is what He enjoins upon you that you may understand. (6 : 152)

وَإِذَا فَعَلُوا فَاحِشَةً قَالُوا وَجَدْنَا عَلَيْهَا آبَاءَنَا وَاللهُ أَمَرَنَا بِهَا قُلْ إِنَّ اللهَ لَا يَأْمُرُ بِالْفَحْشَاءِ أَتَقُولُونَ عَلَى اللهِ
مَا لَا تَعْلَمُونَ ۝ (اعراف - ٢٨)

And when they commit an indecency they say: We found our fathers doing this, and Allah has enjoined it on us. Say : Surely Allah enjoins not indecency. Do you say of Allah what you know not? (17 : 28)

قُلْ إِنَّمَا حَرَّمَ رَبِّيَ الْفَوَاحِشَ مَا ظَهَرَ مِنْهَا وَمَا بَطَنَ وَالْإِثْمَ وَالْبَغْيَ بِغَيْرِ الْحَقِّ وَأَنْ تُشْرِكُوا بِاللهِ مَا لَمْ يُنَزِّلْ بِهِ
سُلْطَانًا وَأَنْ تَقُولُوا عَلَى اللهِ مَا لَا تَعْلَمُونَ ۝ (اعراف - ٣٣)

Say : My Lord forbids only indecencies, such of them as are apparent and such as are concealed, and sin and unjust rebellion, and that you associate with Allah that for which He has sent down no authority, and that you say of Allah what you know not. (7 : 33)

اُتْلُ مَا أُوحِيَ إِلَيْكَ مِنَ الْكِتَابِ وَأَقِمِ الصَّلٰوةَ إِنَّ الصَّلٰوةَ تَنْهَى عَنِ الْفَحْشَاءِ وَالْمُنْكَرِ (عنكبوت - ٤٥)

Recite that which has been revealed to thee of the Book and keep up prayer. Surely prayer keeps (one) away from indecency and evil. (29 : 45)

إِنَّ الْمُسْلِمِينَ وَالْمُسْلِمَاتِ وَالْمُؤْمِنِينَ وَالْمُؤْمِنَاتِ وَالْقَانِتِينَ وَالْقَانِتَاتِ وَالصَّادِقِينَ وَالصَّادِقَاتِ وَالصَّابِرِينَ
وَالصَّابِرَاتِ وَالْخَاشِعِينَ وَالْخَاشِعَاتِ وَالْمُتَصَدِّقِينَ وَالْمُتَصَدِّقَاتِ وَالصَّائِمِينَ وَالصَّائِمَاتِ وَالْحَافِظِينَ فُرُوجَهُمْ وَالْحَافِظَاتِ
وَالذَّاكِرِينَ اللهَ كَثِيرًا وَالذَّاكِرَاتِ أَعَدَّ اللهُ لَهُمْ مَغْفِرَةً وَأَجْرًا عَظِيمًا ۝ (احزاب - ٣٥)

Surely the men who submit and the women who submit, and the believing men and the believing women, and the obeying men and obeying women, and the truthful men and the truthful women and the patient men and the patient women, and the humble men and the hnmble women, and the charitable men and the charitable women, and the fasting men and the fasting women, and the wen who guard their chastity and the women who guard, and the men who remember Allah much and the women who remember, Allah has prepared for them forgiveness and a mighty reward. (33 : 35)

(9) *Anger*

كُلُوا مِن طَيِّبَٰتِ مَا رَزَقْنَٰكُمْ وَلَا تَطْغَوْا فِيهِ فَيَحِلَّ عَلَيْكُمْ غَضَبِى ۖ وَمَن يَحْلِلْ عَلَيْهِ غَضَبِى فَقَدْ هَوَىٰ (طٰه ٨١)

Eat of the good things we have provided for you, and be not inordinate in respect thereof, lest My wrath come upon you ; and he on whom My wrath comes, the perishes indeed. (20 : 81)

الَّذِينَ يُنفِقُونَ فِى السَّرَّآءِ وَالضَّرَّآءِ وَالْكَٰظِمِينَ الْغَيْظَ وَالْعَافِينَ عَنِ النَّاسِ ۗ وَاللَّهُ يُحِبُّ الْمُحْسِنِينَ (آل عمران ١٣٣)

Those who spend in ease as well as in adversity and those who restrain (their) anger and pardon men. And Allah loves the doers of good (to others). (3 : 133)

وَإِذَا لَقُوكُمْ قَالُوٓا ءَامَنَّا وَإِذَا خَلَوْا عَضُّوا عَلَيْكُمُ الْأَنَامِلَ مِنَ الْغَيْظِ ۚ قُلْ مُوتُوا بِغَيْظِكُمْ ۗ إِنَّ اللَّهَ عَلِيمٌۢ بِذَاتِ الصُّدُورِ (آل عمران - ١١٨)

And when they meet you they say, we believe, and when they are alone, they bite (their) finger tips in rage against you. Say : Die in your rage. Surely Allah is knower of what is in the hearts. (3 : 118)

وَالَّذِينَ يَجْتَنِبُونَ كَبَٰٓئِرَ الْإِثْمِ وَالْفَوَٰحِشَ وَإِذَا مَا غَضِبُوا هُمْ يَغْفِرُونَ (شورىٰ - ٣٧)

And those who shun the great sins and indecencies, and whenever they are angry they forgive. (32 : 37)

فَبِمَا رَحْمَةٍ مِّنَ اللَّهِ لِنتَ لَهُمْ وَلَوْ كُنتَ فَظًّا غَلِيظَ الْقَلْبِ لَانفَضُّوا مِنْ حَوْلِكَ فَاعْفُ عَنْهُمْ وَاسْتَغْفِرْ لَهُمْ

(آل عمران - ١٥٨)

Thus it is by Allah's mercy that thou art gentle to them. And hadst thou been rough, hard hearted, they would certainly have dispersed from around thee. So pardon them and ask protection for them. (3 : 158)

Gems of Prophetic Wisdom

AHADITH :

١- عن أبي هريرة قال قال رسول الله صلى الله عليه وسلم الحياء من الايمان والايمان فى الجنة والبذاء من الجفاء والجفاء فى النار

(احمد - ترمذى)

Abu Hurairah reported that the Messenger of Allah said: Shame is from faith and faith is in Paradise, and indecency is from evil and evil is in the fire. (Ahmad, Tirmizi)

٢- عن أنس قال قال رسول صلى الله عليه وسلم ما كان الفحش فى شئ الاشانه ، وما كان الحياء فى شئ الازانه (ترمذى)

Anas reported that Messenger of Allah said: Indecency does not occur in a thing but disagraces it, and shame does not occur in a thing but to adorn it. (Tirmizi)

٣- عن ابن عمر ان النبى صلى الله عليه وسلم مر على رجل من الانصار وهو يعظ اخاه الحياء فقال رسول الله صلى الله عليه وسلم دعه فان الحياء من الايمان

(متفق عليه)

Ibn Qamar reported that the Messenger of Allah passed by a man of Ansars while he was advising his brother about shame. Then the Messenger of Allah said: Leave him, and verily shame is of faith. (Agreed).

٤- عن ابن مسعود قال قال رسول الله صلى الله عليه وسلم ان مما ادرك الناس من كلام النبوة الاولى إذا لم يستحى فاصنع ما شئت

(بخارى)

Ibn-e Mas'ud reported that the Messenger of Allah said: Out of what people adopted from the earlier prophetic sayings, (it is one)—when you are not shameful, do what you like. (Bukhari).

٥- عن زيد بن طلحة قال قال رسول الله صلى الله عليه وسلم ان لكل دين خلقاً وخلق الاسلام الحياء (مشكواة)

Zaid-b-Talha reported that the Messenger of Allah said: Verily there is a characteristic of every religion, and the characteristic of Islam is shame. (Mishkat)

٦- عن أبى سعيد الخدرى قال كان النبى صلى الله عليه وسلم اشد حياء من العذراء فى خدرها فاذا رأى شيئاً يكرهه عرفناه فى وجهه

(متفق عليه)

Abu Sayeed al Khodri reported that the Messenger of Allah was much more bashful than the virgins within their head-veils. When he saw a thing disagreeable to him, we could have recognised it in his face.) (Agreed)

٧- عن عمران بن حصين قال قال رسول الله صلى الله عليه وسلم الحياء لا ياتى الا بخير و فى رواية الحياء خير كله (متفق عليه)

Imran-b-Hussain reported that the Messenger of Allah said: Shame brings nothing but good. And in a narration: Shame is better in its everything. (Agreed)

٨- عن بهز بن حكيم عن ابيه عن جده قال قال رسول الله صلى الله عليه وسلم ان الغضب ليفسد الايمان كما يفسد الصبر العسل

(بيهقى)

Bhaz-b-Hakeem from this father from his grandfather reported that the Messenger of Allah said: Verily anger destroys faith just as aloes spoil honey. (Baihaqi).

٩- عن انس ان رسول الله صلى عليه وسلم قال من خزن لسانه ستر الله عورته ومن كف غضبه كف الله عذابه يوم القيامة ومن اعتذر الى الله قبل الله عذره (بيهقى)

Anas reported that the Messenger of Allah said: whoso takes up his tongue as treasure, Allah will keep his secret concealed ; and whoso restrains his anger, Allah will keep his punishment from him on the Resurrection Day; and whoso ascribes excuse to Allah, Allah will accept his excuse. (Baihaqi)

١٠- عن عطية بن عروة السعيدى قال قال رسول الله صلى الله عليه وسلم ان الغضب من الشيطان وان الشيطان خلق من النار وانما تطفى النار بالماء فاذا غضب احدكم فليتوضا (ابو داؤد)

Atiyyah-b-Urawh As-Saidi reported that the Messenger of Allah said: Verily anger comes from the devil, and the devil was created from fire, and verily fire is extinguished by water. So whoever of you gets angry, let him make ablution. (Abu Daud)

١١- عن أبي زر ان رسول الله صلى عليه وسلم قال اذا غضب احدكم وهو قائم فاليجلس فان ذهب عنه الغضب والا فاليضطجع

(احمد - ترمذى)

Abu Zar reported that the Messenger of Allah said: Whenever one of you gets angry while he is standing, let him sit down. If anger goes out of him (that is good); but if not, let him lie down. (Ahmad, Tirmizi)

١٢- عن أبي هريرة قال قال رسول الله صلى الله عليه وسلم ليس الشديد بالصرعة انما الشديد الذي يملك نفسه عنه الغضب (متفق عليه)

Abu Hurairah reported that the Messenger of Allah said: The strong man is is he who can control himself at the time of anger.

REMARKS:

Shame is a branch of faith, while indeceney is out of faith: Shame and bashfulunes adorn nature and such a man is always respected, while an indecent person is laughed to scorn.

The Holy Prophet has instructed us to guard ourselves from indecency, because Allah does not love it. There are four practices of the Prophets—shame, use of perfume, teeth cleaning and marriage. Verily Allah is shameful and keeper of secrets.

Anger is natural, and cannot be uprooted. If there is no anger in a man, it must be supposed that he has got some defects. Allah and His Prophet disliked the two extremes ; (a) Extreme anger, and (b) Absence of anger.

Anger should be a servant of wisdom and should be completely under its subjugation. The Holy Prophet has said: "And of them there is some one who gets slowly angry and becomes slowly appeased. One of them compensates for the other. The best of you is he who gets slowly angry and becomes appeased very soon, and the worst of you is he who gets suddenly angry and becomes appeased very slowly.

Restraining of anger, pardoning and doing good to each other besides being great moral qualities, strengthen the bond of union which is so necessary for success. These moral values also inspire the noblest thoughts of toleration and charitableness, moderation and generosity, etc.

(10) Patience, Resignation and Gratefulness :

وَاسْتَعِينُوا بِالصَّبْرِ وَالصَّلٰوةِ (بقرہ-۴۵)

And seek assistance through patience and prayer. (3:45)

يٰاَيُّهَا الَّذِيْنَ اٰمَنُوا اسْتَعِيْنُوْا بِالصَّبْرِ وَالصَّلٰوةِ اِنَّ اللّٰهَ مَعَ الصّٰبِرِيْنَ (بقرہ-۱۵۳)

O You who believe, seek assistance through patience and prayer, surely Allah is with the patient. (2:153)

لَتُبْلَوُنَّ فِيْ اَمْوَالِكُمْ وَاَنْفُسِكُمْ وَلَتَسْمَعُنَّ مِنَ الَّذِيْنَ اُوْتُوا الْكِتٰبَ مِنْ قَبْلِكُمْ وَمِنَ الَّذِيْنَ اَشْرَكُوْا اَذًى كَثِيْرًا
وَاِنْ تَصْبِرُوْا وَتَتَّقُوْا فَاِنَّ ذٰلِكَ مِنْ عَزْمِ الْاُمُوْرِ (آل عمران-۱۸۵)

You will certainly be tried in your property and your persons. And you will certainly hear from those who have been glven the Book before you and from the idolaters much abuse. And if you are patient and keep your duty, surely this is an affair of great resolution. (3:185)

وَلَئِنْ اَذَقْنَا الْاِنْسَانَ مِنَّا رَحْمَةً ثُمَّ نَزَعْنٰهَا مِنْهُ اِنَّهٗ لَيَئُوْسٌ كَفُوْرٌ وَلَئِنْ اَذَقْنٰهُ نَعْمَآءَ بَعْدَ ضَرَّآءَ مَسَّتْهُ لَيَقُوْلَنَّ ذَهَبَ
السَّيِّاٰتُ عَنِّيْ اِنَّهٗ لَفَرِحٌ فَخُوْرٌ اِلَّا الَّذِيْنَ صَبَرُوْا وَعَمِلُوا الصّٰلِحٰتِ اُولٰٓئِكَ لَهُمْ مَّغْفِرَةٌ وَّاَجْرٌ كَبِيْرٌ (هود-۹، ۱۱)

And if we make man taste mercy from us, then withdraw it from him, he is surely despairing, ungrateful. And if we make him taste a favour after distress has afflicted him, he says : The evils are gone away from me. Certainly he is exultant, boastful, except those who are patient and do good. For them is forgiveness and a great reward. (11.9-11)

فَاصْبِرْ كَمَا صَبَرَ اُولُوا الْعَزْمِ مِنَ الرُّسُلِ وَلَا تَسْتَعْجِلْ لَّهُمْ (الاحقاف-۳۵)

So have patience, as men of resolution, the Messengers, had patience, and seek not to hasten on for them. (46:35)

وَالْعَصْرِ ۝ إِنَّ الْإِنْسَانَ لَفِيْ خُسْرٍ ۝ إِلَّا الَّذِيْنَ اٰمَنُوْا وَعَمِلُوا الصّٰلِحٰتِ وَتَوَاصَوْا بِالْحَقِّ ۥ وَتَوَاصَوْا بِالصَّبْرِ ۝ (العصر ۱-۳)

By the Time! Surely man is in loss, except those who believe and do good, and exhort one another to truth, and exhort one another to patience. (103:1-3)

وَعَلَى اللّٰهِ فَلْيَتَوَكَّلِ الْمُؤْمِنُوْنَ ۝ (العمران ۱۶۰)

And in Allah should the believers put their trust. (3:159)

قُلْ إِنَّ صَلَاتِيْ وَنُسُكِيْ وَمَحْيَايَ وَمَمَاتِيْ لِلّٰهِ رَبِّ الْعٰلَمِيْنَ ۝ (انعام-۱۶۳)

Say : My prayer and my sacrifice and my life and my death are surely for Allah, the Lord of the worlds. (6 : 163)

وَمَنْ يَّتَوَكَّلْ عَلَى اللّٰهِ فَإِنَّ اللّٰهَ عَزِيْزٌ حَكِيْمٌ ۝ (انفال-۴۹)

And whoever trusts in Allah, then surely Allah is Mighty, Wise. (8:49)

وَمَا مِنْ دَآبَّةٍ فِي الْأَرْضِ إِلَّا عَلَى اللّٰهِ رِزْقُهَا وَيَعْلَمُ مُسْتَقَرَّهَا وَمُسْتَوْدَعَهَا ۚ كُلٌّ فِيْ كِتٰبٍ مُّبِيْنٍ ۝ (هود-۶)

And there is no animal in the earth but on Allah is the sustenance of it, and He knows its resting place and its depository. All is in a clear record. (11:6)

وَأُفَوِّضُ أَمْرِيْ إِلَى اللّٰهِ ۚ إِنَّ اللّٰهَ بَصِيْرٌ بِالْعِبَادِ ۝ (مومن-۴۴)

And I entrust my affair to Allah. Surely Allah is seer of the servants. (40.54)

وَمَن يَتَّقِ اللَّهَ يَجْعَل لَّهُ مَخْرَجًا ۝ وَيَرْزُقْهُ مِنْ حَيْثُ لَا يَحْتَسِبُ ۚ وَمَن يَتَوَكَّلْ عَلَى اللَّهِ فَهُوَ حَسْبُهُ (طلاق ۲-۳)

And whoever keeps his duty to Allah, He ordains a way out for him. And gives him sustenance from whence he imagines not. And whoever trusts in Allah, He is sufficient for him. (65:2,3)

فَاذْكُرُونِي أَذْكُرْكُمْ وَاشْكُرُوا لِي وَلَا تَكْفُرُونِ ۝ (بقرہ ۱۵۲)

Therefore glorify Me, I will make you eminent, and give thanks to Me and be not ungrateful to Me. (2:152)

وَمَن يُرِدْ ثَوَابَ الدُّنْيَا نُؤْتِهِ مِنْهَا وَمَن يُرِدْ ثَوَابَ الْآخِرَةِ نُؤْتِهِ مِنْهَا ۚ وَسَنَجْزِي الشَّاكِرِينَ ۝ (آل عمران-۱۴۴)

And whoever desires the reward of this world, We give him of it, whoever desires the reward of the Hereafter, We give him of it. And We shall reward the grateful. (3:144)

وَإِذْ تَأَذَّنَ رَبُّكُمْ لَئِن شَكَرْتُمْ لَأَزِيدَنَّكُمْ ۖ وَلَئِن كَفَرْتُمْ إِنَّ عَذَابِي لَشَدِيدٌ ۝ (ابراهيم-۷)

And when your Lord made it known: If you are grateful, I will give you more, and If you are ungrateful, My chastisement is truly severe. (14:7)

الَّذِي أَحْسَنَ كُلَّ شَيْءٍ خَلَقَهُ ۖ وَبَدَأَ خَلْقَ الْإِنسَانِ مِن طِينٍ ۝ ثُمَّ جَعَلَ نَسْلَهُ مِن سُلَالَةٍ مِّن مَّاءٍ مَّهِينٍ ۝ ثُمَّ سَوَّاهُ
وَنَفَخَ فِيهِ مِن رُّوحِهِ ۖ وَجَعَلَ لَكُمُ السَّمْعَ وَالْأَبْصَارَ وَالْأَفْئِدَةَ ۚ قَلِيلًا مَّا تَشْكُرُونَ ۝ (سجده ۷-۹)

Who made beautiful every thing that He created, and He began the creation of man from dust. Then He made his progeny of an extract, or worthless water. Then He made him complete and breathed into him of His spirit, and gave you ears and eyes and hearts ; little it is that you give thanks. (32:7-9)

وَقَلِيلٌ مِّنْ عِبَادِيَ الشَّكُورُ (سبا-١٣)

And very few of my servants are grateful. (34:13)

إِنَّا خَلَقْنَا الْإِنسَانَ مِن نُّطْفَةٍ أَمْشَاجٍ نَّبْتَلِيهِ فَجَعَلْنَاهُ سَمِيعًا بَصِيرًا إِنَّا هَدَيْنَاهُ السَّبِيلَ إِمَّا شَاكِرًا وَإِمَّا كَفُورًا (الدهر-٢-٣)

Surely we have created man from sperm mixed (with ovum), to try him, so We have made him hearing, seeing. We have truly shown him the way, he may be thankful or unthankful. (76:2,3)

قُتِلَ الْإِنسَانُ مَا أَكْفَرَهُ مِنْ أَيِّ شَيْءٍ خَلَقَهُ مِن نُّطْفَةٍ خَلَقَهُ فَقَدَّرَهُ ثُمَّ السَّبِيلَ يَسَّرَهُ
ثُمَّ أَمَاتَهُ فَأَقْبَرَهُ ثُمَّ إِذَا شَاءَ أَنشَرَهُ (عبس ١٧-٢٢)

We to man ! How ungrateful is he ! Of what thing did We create him ? Of a small life-germ. He creates him, then proportions him, then makes the way easy for him, then he causes him to die, then assigns to him a grave, then, when He will, He raises him to life again. (80:17-22)

Gems of Prophetic Wisdom

AHADITH :

١- عن ابن مسعود قال قال رسول الله صلى الله عليه وسلم الصبر نصف الايمان (مشكواة)

Ibn-e-Mas'ud reported that the Messenger of Allah said : Patience is half of faith. (Mishkat)

٢- عن ابن مسعود قال كانى انظر الى رسول الله صلى الله عليه وسلم يحكى نبياً من الانبياء ضربه قومه فادموه وهو المسيح الدم عن وجهه و يقول اللهم اغفر لقومى فانهم لايعلمون (متفق عليه)

Ibn-e-Mas'ud reported : I am as it were looking to the Messenger of Allah who was telling a story about a prophet among the prophets. His people scourged him and shed his blood, while he was effacing blood from his face and saying : O Allah forgive my people, because they certainly know not. (Agreed)

٣- عن ابن عباس قال خرج رسول الله صلى عليه وسلم يوماً فقال عرضت على الامم فجعل يمر النبي و معه الرجل والنبي ومعه الرجلان والنبي ومعه الرهط والنبي وليس معه احد فرأيت سواداً كثيراً سد الأفق فرجوت ان يكون أمتى فقيل هذا موسى في قومه ثم قيل لى انظر فرأيت سواداً كثيراً سد الافق فقيل هٰؤلآء امتك ومع هٰؤلآء سبعون الفاً قدامهم يدخلون الجنة بغير حساب هم الذين لايتطيرون ولا يسترقون ولا يكتوون وعلى ربهم يتوكلون فقام عكاشة بن محصن فقال ادع الله ان يجعلنى منهم قال اللهم اجعله منهم ثم قام رجل أخر فقال ادع الله ان يجعلني منهم فقال سبقك بها عكاشة (متفق عليه)

Ibn-e-Abbas reported that the Messenger of Allah came out one day and said : Nations were presented to me. One prophet was passing accompanied by a man, one prophet accompanied by two men, and one prophet accompanied by a host of men, and one prophet accompanied by none. Then I saw many black figures who closed up the horizon and I hope that they must be followers. It was said : He is Moses with his followers. Then I was addressed "Look." I saw many men who closed up the horizon. I was told : Look thus and thus. Then I saw many figures who closed up the horizon. It was said : These are your followers, and with them there are 70,000 (men) whose vanguard shall enter Pasadise without account. They are those who will seek charms, nor count bad omens, nor use canterization, and they will rely on their Lord. Okkasha-b-Mihsan got up and said : Pray to Allah that I may be one of them : He prayed : O Allah ! make him one of them : Then another man got up and said : Pray to Allah that I may be among them. He said : Okkasha preceded you therewith. (Agreed)

٤- عن عمر بن الخطاب قال سمعت رسول الله صلي عليه وسلم يقول
لو انكم تتوكلون على الله حق توكله لرزقكم كما يرزق الطير تغدو
خماصاً وتروح بطانا (ترمذى - ابن ماجه)

Omar-b-al-Khattab reported : I heard the Messenger of Allah say : If you all had relied on Allah with due reliance, He would have certainly given you provisions as He supplied provisions to birds getting up hungry in the morning and returning with full belly at dusk.
(Tirmizi, Ibn-e-Majah)

٥- عن أبي ذر إن رسول الله صلى عليه وسلم قال انى لا علم أية لو
اخذ الناس بها لكفتهم ومن يتق الله يجعل له مخرجاً ويرزقه من
حيث لا يحتسب (احمد - ابن ماجه)

Abu Zarr reported that the Messenger of Allah said : Surely I know a verse. If people would have followed it, it would have sufficed them — "And whoso fears Allah, He will find out a way for him and He will give him provision from where he will not know. (65:30)
(Ahmad, Ibn Majah)

٦- عن أبي هريرة ان النبى صلى الله عليه وسلم قال ربكم عزوجل لو
أن عبيدى اطاعونى لاستقيتهم المطر بالليل واطلعت عليهم الشمس
بالنهار ولم اسمعهم صوت الرعد (احمد)

Abu Hurairah reported that the Holy Prophet said : Thy Lord, the Almighty and the Glorious, said : If My servants would have obeyed Me, I would have given them rain at night and would have made the sun rise on them at day time, and I would not have made them hear the voice of thunder. (Ahmad)

٧- عن أبي هريرة قال قال رسول الله صلى الله عليه وسلم الطاعم الشاكر بمنزلة الصائم الصابر (بخارى)

Abu Hurarah reported that the Messenger of Allah said : A grateful eater is in the position of a patient fasting man. (Bukhari)

٨- عن أبي هريرة قال قال رسول الله صلى الله عليه وسلم من لم يشكر الناس لم يشكر الله (احمد — ترمذى)

Abu Hurairah reported that the Messenger of Allah said : whoever is not grateful to man is not grateful to Allah. (Ahmad, Tirmizi)

٩- عن أسامة بن زيد قال قال رسول الله صلى الله عليه وسلم من صنع اليه معروف فقال لفاعله جزاك الله خيراً فقد ابلغ فى الثناء (ترمذى)

Osamah-b-Zaid reported that the Messenger of Allah said : whoever is done a benefit and then he says to one who has done it "May Allah recompense thee with good," he has indeed reached perfection in gratefulness. (Tirmizi)

١٠- عن ابن عباس ان رسول الله صلى الله عليه وسلم قال اربع من اعطيهن فقد اعطى خير الدنيا و الاخرة قلب شاكر ولسان ذاكرو بدن على البلاء صابر و زوجة لاتبغيه خوفاً في نفسها ولا ما له (البيهقي)

Ibn-e-Abbas reported that the Messenger of Allah said : whoso has been gifted with four things has been given the good of this world and the hereafter : a grateful heart, and a remembering tongue, and a patient body over calamities, and a wife who does not seek breach of trust regarding herself and his property. (Baihaqi)

Remarks :

Patience is an attribute which may be physical or spiritual. Physical patience is over physical tortures such as wounds, assaults, and diseases, etc., while spiritual patience is over passions, evil appetites and other immoral tendencies.

The Holy Quran and Hadith have repeatedly instructed the Muslims for patience. Those who are patient and rely absolutely upon Allah in happiness are said to be truthful and righteous, and have been promised great rewards. Our Holy Prophet has left an un-approachable example in this respect. The Holy Quran had, in the Prophet's utter helplessness at Mecca, and when the Quraish were day and night planning to take away his very life, uttered forcible predictions of his final triumph and the vanquishment of his opponents. This was promised and all the prophecies were fulfilled because the Holy Prophet remained patient before all trials and in all circumstances.

This is the duty of Muslims to proclaim the great spiritual truth with which they have been favoured, to the whole world (كنتم خير امة اخرجت الناس). This duty can not be fulfilled and this important work can not be done without Divine help, patience and perseverance. As the early Muslims or Sahaba were being tried respecting their property and their person at Mecca—they had been deprived of their property and turned out of their homes, they had been severely persecuted and even puts to death only for professing Islam—so the Muslims of the present day should prepare themselves for the sufferings which are yet in store for them. Actually speaking, no great object can be attained and no goal can be achieved without Divine assistance and patience. Patience is the key to every success.

Resignation does not mean absolute reliance on Allah in all our affairs divorced from action. It is to toil hard with the belief that its results are in the hands of Allah.

Absolute reliance has been practised by the Prophets and the truthful who hold the highest position among the virtuous. Due reliance consists in the belief that every thing comes from the Almighty and not even a drop falls down, or a leaf moves or light shines but by His permission. Thus true resignation signifies a belief in the unity, omniprsesence, omnipotence, all-comprehensive knowledge and all other attributes of Allah. As for one who is dutiful and pious, Allah will save him from all calamities and will give him provision from unknown quarters. So He says : whoever resigns to Allah, He is sufficient for him. (15:3 Q)

Gratefulness is an attribute of Allah, as He is Shakoor (شکور). Gratefulness can be expressed by heart, mind and bodily organs; by heart in the form of cherishing good wish for the entire creation of Allah and by outpouring the heart to Allah; by tongue in the form of reciting Tahlil, Tahmid, and Tasbih, and by the limbs of the body in the form of bowing and prostration. Gratefulness of the eyes is to restrain them from the prohibited things of Allah and to shed tears; and gratefulness of the ears is to hear what has been commanded by Allah and not to hear what has been prohibited by Him. Thus for every limb, there is expression of gratefulness to Allah."

See Eng. trans : of "Mishkat-ul-Masabih" by Maulana F. Karim, Part I. Page 157, (NA).

Adab or Manners

(*i*) Greeting or Salutation :

وَإِذَا حُيِّيتُم بِتَحِيَّةٍ فَحَيُّوا بِأَحْسَنَ مِنْهَا أَوْ رُدُّوهَا ۗ إِنَّ اللَّهَ كَانَ عَلَىٰ كُلِّ شَيْءٍ حَسِيبًا ﴿النساء - ٨٦﴾

And when you are greeted with a greeting, greet with one better than it, or return it. Surely Allah ever takes account of all things. (4:86)

يَا أَيُّهَا الَّذِينَ آمَنُوا لَا تَدْخُلُوا بُيُوتًا غَيْرَ بُيُوتِكُمْ حَتَّىٰ تَسْتَأْنِسُوا وَتُسَلِّمُوا عَلَىٰ أَهْلِهَا ۚ ذَٰلِكُمْ خَيْرٌ لَّكُمْ لَعَلَّكُمْ تَذَكَّرُونَ
﴿النور - ٢٧﴾

You who believe, enter not houses other than your own houses, until you have asked permission and saluted their inmates. This is better for you that you may be mindful. (24:27)

وَسَلَامٌ عَلَيْهِ يَوْمَ وُلِدَ وَيَوْمَ يَمُوتُ وَيَوْمَ يُبْعَثُ حَيًّا

And peace on him the day he was born and the day he died, and the day he is raised to life: (19:15)

فَإِن لَّمْ تَجِدُوا فِيهَا أَحَدًا فَلَا تَدْخُلُوهَا حَتَّىٰ يُؤْذَنَ لَكُمْ ۖ وَإِن قِيلَ لَكُمُ ارْجِعُوا فَارْجِعُوا ۖ هُوَ أَزْكَىٰ لَكُمْ ۚ
وَاللَّهُ بِمَا تَعْمَلُونَ عَلِيمٌ ﴿نور - ٢٨﴾

But if you find no one therein, enter them not, until permission is given to you, and if it is said to you. Go back, then go back; this is purer for you. And Allah is known of what you do. (24:28)

لَيْسَ عَلَيْكُمْ جُنَاحٌ أَن تَدْخُلُوا بُيُوتًا غَيْرَ مَسْكُونَةٍ فِيهَا مَتَاعٌ لَّكُمْ وَاللَّهُ يَعْلَمُ مَا تُبْدُونَ وَمَا تَكْتُمُونَ (نور - ٢٩)

It is no sin for you to enter uninhabited houses wherein you have your necessaries. And Allah knows what you do openly and what you hide. (24:29)

يَا أَيُّهَا الَّذِينَ آمَنُوا لَا تَدْخُلُوا بُيُوتَ النَّبِيِّ إِلَّا أَن يُؤْذَنَ لَكُمْ (الاحزاب - ٥٣)

O you who believe, enter not the houses of the prophet unless permission is given to you. (33:53)

Gems of Prophetic Wisdom

AHADITH :

١- عن أبى سعيد الخدرى قال اتانا أبو موسى قال ان عمر ارسل الى
أن أتيه فاتيت بابه ، فسلمت ثلاثاً فلم يرد على فرجعت فقال ما
منعك أن تاتينا فقلت أنى اتيت فسلمت علي بابك ثلثاً فلم تردوا على
فرجعت وقد قال لى رسول الله صلى الله عليه وسلم اذا استاذن
احدكم ثلثاً يوذن له فليرجع فقال عمر اقم عليه البينة قال أبو سعيد
فقمت معه فذهبت الى عمر فشهدت (متفق عليه)

Abu Saeed al-Khudri reported Abu Musa came to us and said: Verily Omar sent for me to come to him. So I went to his house and saluted thrice, but he did not return to me. Then I returned. He enquired: what did prevent you from coming to us? I said : I came and saluted at your door thrice but you did not return to me. So I returned. The Messenger of Allah said to me : when one of you seeks permission thrice for interview but is not given permission, let him return. Omar said : Give proof of that. Abu Sayeed said : I got up with him, went to Omar and bore witness. (Agreed)

٢- عن جابر قال اتيت النبى صلى الله عليه وسلم فى دين كان على أبي فدققت الباب فقال من ذا فقلت انا فقال انا أنا كانها كرها -

(متفق عليه)

Jabar reported : I came to the Messenger of Allah about a debt outstanding against my father. I knocked at the door and he asked. Who are you? I replied : I. He said : "I, I," as if he disliked it.
(Agreed.)

٣- عن جابر ان النبى صلى الله عليه وسلم قال لا تاذنوا لمن لم يبدأ بالسلام (بيهقي)

Jaber reported that the Messenger of Allah said :
Don't give permission to him who does not begin with a greeting.
(Baihaqi)

٤- عن أبي هريرة قال قال رسول الله صلى الله عليه وسلم للمومن على المومن ست خصال يعوده اذا مرض ويشهده اذا مات ويجيبه اذا دعاه و يسلم عليه اذا لقيه و يشمته اذا عطس وينصح له اذا غاب أو شهد (نسائى)

Abu Hurairah reported that the Messenger of Allah said : There are six duties of one believer to another believer; he will visit him when he falls ill; he will be present before him when he dies ; he will respond to him when he invites him ; he will salute him when he meets him; he will respond to him when he sneezes and he will seek his good when he is either absent or present. (Nisai)

٥- عن أبى هريرة قال قال رسول الله صلى الله عليه وسلم يسلم الراكب علي الماشى والماشى على القاعد والقليل على الكثير (متفق عليه)

Abu Hurairah reported that the Messenger of Allah said one riding shall salute one walking, and one walking (shall salute) one sitting, and small party (shall salute) the big party. (Agreed).

٦- عن أبي هريرة قال قال رسول الله صلى عليه وسلم يسلم الصغير على الكبير والمار على القاعد والقليل على الكثير (بخارى)

Abu Hurairah reported that the Messenger of Allah said : The junior shall tender greeting to the senior, and one passing to one sitting, and the small party to the big party. (Bukhari)

٧- عن أبي امامة قال قال رسول الله صلى الله عليه وسلم ان اولى الناس بالله من بدأ بالسلام (احمد - ترمذى - أبو داود)

Abu Omamah reported that the Messenger of Allah said ; The best of men to Allah is he who begins with a greeting.

(Ahmad, Tirmizi, Abu Dawood.)

٨- عن أبي هريرة أن النبي صلى الله عليه وسلم قال إذا لقى احدكم اخاه فليسلم عليه فان حالت بينهما شجرة أو جدار او حجر لم لقيه فليسلم عليه (أبو داود)

Abu Hurairah reported from the Messenger of Allah who said : When one of you meets his brother, let him salute him, and if a tree or wall or stone intervenes between them and then he meets him, let him salute him. (Abu Daud)

٩- عن جابر قال قال رسول الله صلى الله عليه وسلم السلام قبل الكلام (ترمذى)

Jaber reported that the Messenger of Allah said : Greeting is before talk. (Tirmizi).

١٠- عن اسماء بنت يزيد قالت مر علينا رسول الله صلى الله عليه وسلم فى نسوة فسلم علينا (أبو داود - ابن ماجه - دارمى)

Asma'a-bn-Yezid reported : The Messenger of Allah passed by us among some women, and he saluted us.

(Abu Daud, Ibn Majah, Darimi).

١١- عن قتادة قال قال النبي صلى الله عليه وسلم اذا دخلتم فسلموا على اهله واذا خرجتم فادعوا اهله بسلام (بيهقى)

Qatadah reported that the Holy Prophet said : When you enter, greet its inmates, and when you come out, leave it inmates with a greeting. (Baihaqi)

١٢- عن عبد الله عن النبى صلى الله عليه وسلم قال البادي بالسلام برى من الكبر (بيهقي)

Abdullah reported from the Holy Prophet who said : He who salutes first is free from vanity. (Barshaqi)

١٣- عن قتادة قال قلت لانس اكانت المصافحة فى اصحاب رسول الله صلى الله عليه وسلم قال نعم (بخارى)

Qatadah reported: I asked Anas: Was there any handshaking among the companions of the Messenger of Allah ? He replied: Yes. (Bukhari)

١٤- عن البراء ابن عازب قال قال النبى صلى الله عليه وسلم ما من مسلمين يلتقيان فيتصافحان الاغفرلها قبل ان يتفرقا (احمد - ترمذى - ابن ماجه)

Bara'a-b-Azeb reported that the Holy Prophet said : There are no Muslims who meet and they handshake but they are both forgiven before they part away. (Ahmad, Tirmizi, Ibn-e-Majah)

١٥- عن الشعبى ان البنى صل الله عليه وسلم تلقى جعفر بن ا. طالب فالتزمه و قبل ما بين عينيه (ابوداود)

Shabi reported that the Holy Prophet met Jafar-b-Abi-Taleb, embraced him and kissed what was between his eyes.

Remarks :

The Holy Quran and the Holy Prophet not only elevated the scale of world morality and religion, but also taught the ordinary rules of social moral and etiquate observed in the most advanced and civilized society. This was introduced at a time when there was no notion of civilization and social etiquette, nor was there any time to think over these petty matters.

The greeting of a Muslim by another Muslim is "Assalam-o-Alaikum" (اسلام علیکم) Ṣalam means peace. Thus the term signifies, "Be sure that your life, property, and honour are safe in my hand." While the general reply (و علیکم اسلام) also means the same, i.e., you are also secure in my hand respecting your life, property, and honour.

This term of greeting of one Muslim to another gives mutual sense of security and peace at the very first meeting. And, therefore, under sincere mutual assurance of security and peace, there can be no ill-feeling and malice. Another object of greeting in Islam is to demolish the sense of vanity of the high-class gentleman and to raise the position of the lowest. Thus the social distinction, if any, is buried deep and a true and real brotherhood exists among members of the Islamic society. This excellence of greeting is certainly enhanced when we compare it with good morning and good evening or *adab* etc., which cast no blessing on the greeting person or convey no meaning of blessing.

The rule of greeting is that it must proceed from the higher to the lower. The motive is to remove the least sign of vanity in a man.

Greeting is completed by (مصافحہ) or hand-shaking. Hand-shaking and embracing are signs of love, affection and etiquette. Hand-shaking is a *sunnat* (سنت) of the Holy Prophet.

As far as the question of meeting or interview is concerned, interview must be sought previously. Any stranger coming for meeting must wait and seek interview. If he is allowed, he should enter the house after greeting the inmates of the house. Thus permission is necessary for interview as stressed by Holy Quran & Hadith, and before a man actually enters in another's room or house. It is also instructed by Allah & the Holy Prophet that entry into room or house, when permission for interview etc. is granted, should be always attended with greeting and salutation. Permission is not, however, necessary in case of bosom friends and relatives, for whom it is sufficient to take permission once for all days.

Sitting and Walking :

الَّذِيْنَ يَذْكُرُوْنَ اللّٰهَ قِيَامًا وَّقُعُوْدًا وَّعَلٰى جُنُوْبِهِمْ وَيَتَفَكَّرُوْنَ فِيْ خَلْقِ السَّمٰوٰتِ وَالْاَرْضِ
رَبَّنَا مَا خَلَقْتَ هٰذَا بَاطِلًا سُبْحٰنَكَ فَقِنَا عَذَابَ النَّارِ ﴿آل عمران - ١٩٠﴾

Those who remember Allah standing and sitting and (lying) on their sides, and reflect on the creation of the heavens and the earth : Our Lord, Thou has not created this in vain. Glory be to Thee ! Save us from the chastisement of the Fire. (3:190)

وَقَدْ نَزَّلَ عَلَيْكُمْ فِي الْكِتٰبِ اَنْ اِذَا سَمِعْتُمْ اٰيٰتِ اللّٰهِ يُكْفَرُ بِهَا وَيُسْتَهْزَاُ بِهَا فَلَا تَقْعُدُوْا مَعَهُمْ حَتّٰى يَخُوْضُوْا
فِيْ حَدِيْثٍ غَيْرِهٖٓ اِنَّكُمْ اِذًا مِّثْلُهُمْ ﴿نساء - ١٤٠﴾

And indeed He has revealed to you in the Book that when you hear Allah's messages disbelieved in and mocked at, sit not with them until they enter into some other discourse, for then indeed you would be like them. (4:140)

وَاِذَا رَاَيْتَ الَّذِيْنَ يَخُوْضُوْنَ فِيْٓ اٰيٰتِنَا فَاَعْرِضْ عَنْهُمْ حَتّٰى يَخُوْضُوْا فِيْ حَدِيْثٍ غَيْرِهٖ وَاِمَّا يُنْسِيَنَّكَ الشَّيْطٰنُ فَلَا تَقْعُدْ
بَعْدَ الذِّكْرٰى مَعَ الْقَوْمِ الظّٰلِمِيْنَ ﴿انعام - ٦٨﴾

And when thou seest those who talk nonsense about Our messages, withdraw from them until they enter into some other discourse. And if the devil cause thee to forget, then sit not after recollection with the unjust people. (6:68)

يٰٓاَيُّهَا الَّذِيْنَ اٰمَنُوْٓا اِذَا قِيْلَ لَكُمْ تَفَسَّحُوْا فِي الْمَجٰلِسِ فَافْسَحُوْا يَفْسَحِ اللّٰهُ لَكُمْ وَاِذَا قِيْلَ انْشُزُوْا فَانْشُزُوْا
يَرْفَعِ اللّٰهُ الَّذِيْنَ اٰمَنُوْا مِنْكُمْ وَالَّذِيْنَ اُوْتُوا الْعِلْمَ دَرَجٰتٍ وَاللّٰهُ بِمَا تَعْمَلُوْنَ خَبِيْرٌ ﴿مجادله - ١١﴾

O you who believe, when it is said to you, Make room in assemblies, make room, Allah will give you ample. And when it is said Rise up, rise up. Allah will exalt those of you who believe, and those who are given knowledge, to high ranks. And Allah is Aware of what you do. (58:11)

وَلَا تَمْشِ فِي الْأَرْضِ مَرَحًا إِنَّكَ لَنْ تَخْرِقَ الْأَرْضَ وَلَنْ تَبْلُغَ الْجِبَالَ طُولًا ۝ كُلُّ ذٰلِكَ كَانَ سَيِّئُهُ عِنْدَ رَبِّكَ مَكْرُوهًا ۝
(بنی اسرائیل - ۳۷، ۳۸)

And go not about in the land exaltingly, for thou canst not rend the earth, nor reach the mountains in height. (17:37)

وَلَا تُصَعِّرْ خَدَّكَ لِلنَّاسِ وَلَا تَمْشِ فِي الْأَرْضِ مَرَحًا إِنَّ اللّٰهَ لَا يُحِبُّ كُلَّ مُخْتَالٍ فَخُورٍ ۝
وَاقْصِدْ فِي مَشْيِكَ وَاغْضُضْ مِنْ صَوْتِكَ (لقمان - ۱۸، ۱۹)

And turn not thy face away from people in contempt, nor go about in the land exaltingly. Surely, Allah loves not any self-conceited boaster. And pursue the right course in thy going about and lower thy voice. (31:18, 19)

وَعِبَادُ الرَّحْمٰنِ الَّذِينَ يَمْشُونَ عَلَى الْأَرْضِ هَوْنًا وَإِذَا خَاطَبَهُمُ الْجٰهِلُونَ قَالُوا سَلٰمًا ۝ (الفرقان - ۶۳)

And the servants of the Beneficient are they who walk on the earth in humility, and when the ignorant address them, they, say, "Peace!" (25:63)

فَجَاءَتْهُ إِحْدٰىهُمَا تَمْشِي عَلَى اسْتِحْيَاءٍ (قصص - ۲۵)

Then one of the two women came to him walking bashfully. (28:25)

هُوَ الَّذِي جَعَلَ لَكُمُ الْأَرْضَ ذَلُولًا فَامْشُوا فِي مَنَاكِبِهَا وَكُلُوا مِنْ رِزْقِهِ وَإِلَيْهِ النُّشُورُ ۝ (ملک - ۱۵)

He it is Who made the earth subservient to you, so go about in the spacious sides thereof, and eat of His sustenance. And to Him is the rising (after death). 67:15

Gems of Prophetic Wisdom

AHADITH :

١ - عن ابى سعيد الخدري قال قال رسول الله صلى الله عليه وسلم
خير المجالس اوسعها (ابو داؤد)

Abu Sayeed al-Khudri reported that the Messenger of Allah said : The best of sittings is that which is most spacious. (Abu Daud).

٢ - عن جابر بن سمره قال جاء رسول الله صلى الله عليه وسلم و اصحابه،
جلوس، فقال ما لي اراكم عزين (ابوداؤد)

Jabr-b-Samorah reported that the Messenger of Allah came while his companions were seated. He said : What is for me that I see you (sitting) separate ? (Abu Daud).

٣ - عن واثلة بن الخطاب قال دخل رجل الى رسول الله صلى الله عليه وسلم
وهو فى المسجد قاعد فتزحزح له رسول الله صلى الله عليه وسلم فقال
الرجل يا رسول الله ان فى المكان سعة فقال النبى صلى الله عليه وسلم
ان للمسلم لحقاً اذا راه اخوه ان يتزحزح له (بيهقى)

Waselah-b-Khattab reported : A man came to the Messenger of Allah while he was within the mosque in sitting posture. The Messenger of Allah took to a side for him. The man enquired : O Messenger of Allah ! verily there is ample space. Then the Prophet said : Verily there is a duty on a Muslim that when his brother finds him, he should move to a side for him. (Baihaqi).

٤ - عن جابر بن سمرة قال رأيت النبى صلى الله عليه وسلم متكئاً على وسادة على يساره (ترمذی)

Jaber-b-Samorah reported : I saw the Holy Prophet leaning against a pillow on his left side. (Tirmizi).

٥ - عن ابى حريرة ان رسول الله صلى عليه وسلم قال اذا كان احدكم فى الفئ فقلص عنه الظل فصار بعضه في الشمس و بعضه فى الظل فيقم (ابو داؤد)

Abu Hurairah reported that the Messenger of Allah said : When one of you be in shade and then the shade goes away from him exposing some portion of him in the sun and some portion of him in shade, let him get up. (Abu Daud).

٦ - عن جابر بن سمرة قال كنا اذا اتينا النبى صلى الله عليه وسلم جلس احدنا حيث ينتهى (ابو داؤد)

Jaber-b-Samorah reported : Whenever we came to the Holy Prophet, one of us used to sit at the end (of the assembly). (Abu Daud).

٧ - عن عمرو بن الشريد عن ابيه قال مر بى رسول الله صلى الله عليه وسلم وانا جالس هكذا و قد وضعت يدى اليسرىٰ خلف ظهرى واتكات على الية يدى فقال اتقعد قعدة المغضوب عليهم (ابو داؤد)

Amr-b-Sharid reported from his father who said : The Messenger of Allah passed by me while I was seated like this, and while I put my left hand behind my back and leaned against the palms of my hand. He said : Do you sit, a sitting of those upon whom wrath (of Allah) has fallen ? (Abu Daud)

٨ - عن حذيفة قال ملعون على لسان محمد صلى الله عليه وسلم من قعد وسط الحلقة (ترمذی - ابو داؤد)

Huzaifah reported : Whoso takes seat in the midst of an assembly has been cursed by the tongue of Muhammad. (Tirmizi, Abu Daud).

٩ - عن ابی اسید الانصاری انه سمع رسول اللہ صلی علیه وسلم یقول و هو خارج من المسجد فاختلط الرجال مع النساء فی الطریق فقال للنساء استاخرن فانه لیس لکن ان تحققن الطریق علیکن بحافات الطریق فکانت المراة تلصق بالجدار (ابو داؤد)

Abu Osaid Ansari reported that he heard the Messenger of Allah advising while he was coming out of the mosque and while males mixed with females on the way. He said to women : Tarry a little, because it is not for you to assert right of way. You should take to sides of the way. So the females kept to the side-walls so much so that their clothes certainly touched the walls. (Abu Daud).

١٠ - عن ابن عمر ان النبی صلی اللہ علیه وسلم نهی ان یمشی یعنی الرجل بین المراتین (ابو داؤد)

Ibn-e-Omar reported that the Prophet prohibited walking (nearing of a man) between two women. (Abu Daud).

Remarks :

The Holy Prophet had not only brought about the greatest transformation of mankind but also taught such manners and morals, which have a striking contrast with the evils reigning supreme in Arabia and other parts of the world in the 7th Century A.C. He instructed that all activities of our life and all worldly pursuits should be based on the unity of God and the remembrance of Allah. That is why the Muslims are described in the Holy Quran as remembering Allah in the midst of all worldly affairs and it is said that they are all fully conscious of Divine Presence everywhere and in every condition such as standing, sitting or lying on their sides, etc. Thus a great object which Islam sets before its followers is to conquer self by rememberance of Allah. For this reason, Muslims are told to leave the assembly where Truth or the Message of God is derided.

Sitting cross-legged or sitting by resting hand upon the palms is allowed. Sitting in the midst of an assembly for a late comer is disallowed for the sake of decorum and etiquette. If anybody keeps something in his sitting place and then goes out on a call, none should sit there. It is not lawful to sit between two men or friends, so as to make separation between them or to create any sort of disturbance in their private talks. All should sit in such a manner that room should be made for others. This means that the people should not sit too close to each other. It is not allowed to a new-comer to sit in the midst of an asssembly over-stepping others who have already taken their seats.

Walking should neither be too fast nor too slow. It shall not also how any sign of pride and self-conceit. The middle course is always the best.

ADAB OR MANNERS

(3) Company & Friendship

إِنَّ وَلِيِّـۧ اللّٰهُ الَّذِيْ نَزَّلَ الْكِتٰبَ ۖ وَهُوَ يَتَوَلَّى الصّٰلِحِيْنَ ۝ (اعراف-١٩٦)

Surely my Protecting Friend is Allah, who revealed the Book, and He befriends the righteous. (7:196).

يٰٓاَيُّهَا الَّذِيْنَ اٰمَنُوْا لَا تَتَّخِذُوا الْيَهُوْدَ وَالنَّصٰرٰٓى اَوْلِيَآءَ ۘ بَعْضُهُمْ اَوْلِيَآءُ بَعْضٍ ۚ وَمَنْ يَّتَوَلَّهُمْ مِّنْكُمْ فَاِنَّهٗ مِنْهُمْ ۚ
اِنَّ اللّٰهَ لَا يَهْدِي الْقَوْمَ الظّٰلِمِيْنَ ۝ (مائدہ-٥١)

O you who believe, take not the Jews and Christians for friends. They are friends of each other. And whoever amongst you takes them for friends he is indeed one of them. Surely Allah guides not the unjust people (5:51).

اِنَّمَا وَلِيُّكُمُ اللّٰهُ وَرَسُوْلُهٗ وَالَّذِيْنَ اٰمَنُوا الَّذِيْنَ يُقِيْمُوْنَ الصَّلٰوةَ وَيُؤْتُوْنَ الزَّكٰوةَ وَهُمْ رٰكِعُوْنَ ۝ وَمَنْ يَّتَوَلَّ اللّٰهَ
وَرَسُوْلَهٗ وَالَّذِيْنَ اٰمَنُوْا فَاِنَّ حِزْبَ اللّٰهِ هُمُ الْغٰلِبُوْنَ ۝ (مائدہ-٥٥-٥٦)

Only Allah is your Friend and His Messenger and those who believe, those who keep up prayer and pay Zakat, and they who bow down. And whoever takes Allah and His Messenger and those who believe for friend—surely the party of Allah, it shall triumph (5:55,56).

لَا يَتَّخِذِ الْمُؤْمِنُوْنَ الْكٰفِرِيْنَ اَوْلِيَآءَ مِنْ دُوْنِ الْمُؤْمِنِيْنَ (آل عمران-٢٧)

Let not the believers take the disbelievers for friends rather than believers (3:27).

وَالَّذِيْنَ كَفَرُوْا بَعْضُهُمْ اَوْلِيَآءُ بَعْضٍ (انفال-٧٣)

And those who disbelieve are friends one of another (8:73).

وَالْمُؤْمِنُوْنَ وَالْمُؤْمِنٰتُ بَعْضُهُمْ اَوْلِيَآءُ بَعْضٍ يَاْمُرُوْنَ بِالْمَعْرُوْفِ وَيَنْهَوْنَ عَنِ الْمُنْكَرِ وَيُقِيْمُوْنَ
الصَّلٰوةَ وَيُؤْتُوْنَ الزَّكٰوةَ وَيُطِيْعُوْنَ اللّٰهَ وَرَسُوْلَهٗ اُولٰٓئِكَ سَيَرْحَمُهُمُ اللّٰهُ اِنَّ اللّٰهَ عَزِيْزٌ حَكِيْمٌ (توبه-٧١)

And the believers, men & women, are friends one of another. They enjoin good and forbid evil and keep up prayer and pay Zakat, and obey Allah and His Messenger. As for these, Allah will have mercy on them. Surely Allah is Mighty, Wise (9:71).

اِلَّذِيْنَ يَتَّخِذُوْنَ الْكٰفِرِيْنَ اَوْلِيَآءَ مِنْ دُوْنِ الْمُؤْمِنِيْنَ اَيَبْتَغُوْنَ عِنْدَهُمُ الْعِزَّةَ فَاِنَّ الْعِزَّةَ لِلّٰهِ جَمِيْعًا (نساء-١٣٩)

Those who take disbelievers for friends rather than believers. Do they seek power for them? Power surely belongs wholly to Allah (4:139).

اِنَّ الظّٰلِمِيْنَ بَعْضُهُمْ اَوْلِيَآءُ بَعْضٍ وَاللّٰهُ وَلِيُّ الْمُتَّقِيْنَ (جاثيه 19)

And surely the wrongdoers are friends of each other, and Allah is the friend of the dutiful (45:19).

يٰٓاَيُّهَا الَّذِيْنَ اٰمَنُوْا لَا تَتَّخِذُوْا عَدُوِّيْ وَعَدُوَّكُمْ اَوْلِيَآءَ تُلْقُوْنَ اِلَيْهِمْ بِالْمَوَدَّةِ وَقَدْ كَفَرُوْا بِمَا جَآءَكُمْ مِّنَ الْحَقِّ
يُخْرِجُوْنَ الرَّسُوْلَ وَاِيَّاكُمْ اَنْ تُؤْمِنُوْا بِاللّٰهِ رَبِّكُمْ (ممتحنه-١)

O you who believe, take not My enemy and your enemy for friends. Would you offer them love, while they deny the truth that ha come to you, driving out the Messenger and yourselves because you believe in Allah, your Lord? (60:1).

(4) Hospitality and Entertainment :

يٰبَنِيْٓ اٰدَمَ خُذُوْا زِيْنَتَكُمْ عِنْدَ كُلِّ مَسْجِدٍ وَّكُلُوْا وَاشْرَبُوْا وَلَا تُسْرِفُوْا ۚ اِنَّهٗ لَا يُحِبُّ الْمُسْرِفِيْنَ ۝ (اعراف-۳۱)

O children of Adam, attend to your adornment at every time of prayer, and eat and drink and be not prodigal; surely God loves not the prodigal (7:31).

وَنَبِّئْهُمْ عَنْ ضَيْفِ اِبْرٰهِيْمَ ۝ اِذْ دَخَلُوْا عَلَيْهِ فَقَالُوْا سَلٰمًا
(حجر-۵۱/۵۲)

And inform them of the guests of Abraham. When they entered upon him, they said, Peace! (Salam !) (15:51,52).

قَالَ اِنَّ هٰٓؤُلَآءِ ضَيْفِيْ فَلَا تَفْضَحُوْنِ ۝ (حجر-۶۸)

He said : These are my guests, so disgrace me not (15:68).

هَلْ اَتٰىكَ حَدِيْثُ ضَيْفِ اِبْرٰهِيْمَ الْمُكْرَمِيْنَ ۝ اِذْ دَخَلُوْا عَلَيْهِ فَقَالُوْا سَلٰمًا ۭ قَالَ سَلٰمٌ ۚ قَوْمٌ مُّنْكَرُوْنَ ۝ (ذاریات-۲۴،۲۵)

Has the story of Abraham's honoured guests reached thee? When they came to him, they said: "Peace!" he answered, "Peace!" (and thought) : Folk unknown (to me). (51:24,25).

(یونس-۱۶) لَيْسَ عَلَيْكُمْ جُنَاحٌ اَنْ تَاْكُلُوْا جَمِيْعًا اَوْ اَشْتَاتًا ۭ (نور-۶۱)

It is no sin in you that you eat together or separately (24:61).

AHADITH :

١- عن ابي موسٰى قال قال رسول الله صلى الله عليه وسلم مثل الجليس الصالح والسوء كحامل المسك و نافخ الكير — فحامل المسك اما ان يحذيك واما ان تبتاع منه واما ان تجد منه ريحاً طيبة و نافخ الكير اما ان يحرق ثيابك واما ان تجد منه ريحاً خبيثة (متفق عليه)

Abu Musa reported that the Messenger of Allah said: The likeness of a good and a bad companion is like the bearer of musk and one who pumps out filth. As for the bearer of musk, he will either give you a share or you will purchase something from him, or you will get perfumed air from him; and as for one who pumps out filth, he will either burn your clothes or you will find filthy air from him.

(Agreed)

٢- عن ابي ذر قال قال رسول الله صلى الله عليه وسلم افضل الأعمال الحب فى الله والبغض فى الله (ابو داؤد)

Abu Zarr reported that the Messenger of Allah said: The best of actions is love for (cause of) Allah and hate for Allah.

(Abu Daud)

٣- عن عبدالله بن مسعود قال قال رسول الله صلى الله عليه وسلم اذا كنتم ثلثة فلا يتناجى اثنان دون الآخر حتى تختلطوا بالناس من اجل ان يحزنه (متفق عليه)

Abdullah-b-Masud reported that the Messenger of Allah said: When you will be three, no two will hold consultation in secret besides the other till you all mix with the people, because it may grieve him. (Agreed)

٤۔ عن تمیم الدارمی ان النبی صلی اللہ علیہ وسلم قال الدین النصیحۃ ثلثا قلنا لمن قال للہ و لکتابہ ولرسولہ و لائمۃ المسلمین وعامتھم (مسلم)

Tamion Darimi reported that the Holy Prophet said thrice : Religious instructions ! We asked "for whom" ? He said : For Allah, for His Book, for His Messenger, for the leaders of the Muslims, and for the public among them. (Muslim)

٥۔ عن ابی ھریرہ قال قال رسول اللہ صلی اللہ علیہ وسلم الاقتصاد فی النفقۃ نصف المعیشۃ والتودد الی الناس نصف العقل وحسن السوال نصف العلم (بیہقی)

Abu Hurairah reported that the Messenger of Allah said : Moderation in expenditure is half of livelihood, and love for people is half of wisdom, and good questioning is half of learning. (Baihaqi)

٦۔ عن انس قال قال رسول اللہ صلی اللہ علیہ وسلم المرء علی دین خلیلہ ولا خیر فی صحبۃ من لا یری لك مثل ما تری لہ (مشکواۃ)

Anas reported that the Messenger of Allah said : A man is upon the religion of his friend, and there is no good in friendship with one who does not see for you what he sees for himself. (Mishkat)

٧۔ عن ابی ھریرہ قال قال رسول اللہ صلی اللہ علیہ وسلم من کان یومن باللہ والیوم الآخر فلیکرم ضیفہ و من کان یومن باللہ والیوم الآخر فلا یؤذ جارہ من کان یومن باللہ والیوم الآخر فلیقل خیرا او لیصمت وفی روایۃ بدل الجار و من کان یومن باللہ والیوم الآخر فلیصل رحمہ (متفق علیہ)

Abu Hurairah reported that the Messenger of Allah said : Whoever believes in Allah and the Last Day, let him honour his guest :

and whoever believes in Allah and the Last Day, let him not give trouble to his neighbour, and whoever believes in Allah and the Last Day, let him utter good or be silent. (And in a narration in place of neighbour : And whoso believes in Allah and the Last Day, let him keep amity with his relations). (Agreed)

٨- عن ابى شريح الكعبى ان رسول الله صلى الله عليه وسلم قال من كان يومن بالله واليوم الآخر فليكرم ضيفه جائزته، يوم وليلة و الضيافته ثلثه ايام فما بعد ذلك فهو صدقة و لا يحل له ان يثوى عنده حتى يحرجه، (متفق عليه)

Abu Shuraih Ka'abi reported that the Messenger of Allah said: Whoever believes in Allah and the Last Day, let him entertain his guest; and his trouble is for one day and one night, and entertainment is for three days, and what is after that is charity. It is not lawful for him to cling round him so as to put him in discomfort. (Agreed)

٩- عن وحشى بن حرب عن ابيه عن جده ان اصحاب رسول الله صلى الله عليه وسلم قالوا يا رسول الله صلى عليه وسلم انا ناكل ولا نشبع قال فلعلكم تفترقون قالوانعم قال فاجتمعوا على طعامكم و اذكروا اسم الله يبارك لكم فيه (ابو داؤد)

Wahshi-b-Harb reported from his father from his grand father that the companions of the Messenger of Allah asked : O Messenger of Allah ! We take food but not to our satisfaction. He said. Perhaps you eat separate. "Yes", said they. He said : Sit together over your food and take the name of Allah; He will then give you blessing therein (Abu Daud)

١٠- عن ابن عمر قال قال رسول الله صلى الله عليه وسلم اذا وضعت المائدة فل يقوم رجل حتى ترفع المائدة ولا يرفع يده وان شبع حتى يفرغ القوم وليعذر فان ذالك يخجل الجليس فيقبض يده وعسى ان يكون له فى الطعام حاجة (ابن ماجه)

Ibn-e-Omar reported that the Messenger of Allah said: When the food-cloth is served, no man shall get up till the food-cloth is raised up, nor shall he raise his hand though satisfied with food till the people finish, and let him beg excuse, because that will put the companions to shame. He may withhold his hand. It may be that there will be for him more necessity for food. (Ibn-Majah)

١١- عن اسماء بنت يزيد قالت أتى النبى صلى الله عليه وسلم بطعام فعرض علينا فقلنا لانشتهيه فقال لاتجتمعن جوعاً وكذبا (ابن ماجه)

Asmaa-bin-Yazid reported that some food was taken to the Holy Prophet. It was served before us and we said: We don't wish to take it. He said: Don't unite hunger and falsehood together. (Ibn Majah)

١٢- عن عمر بن الخطاب قال قال رسول الله صلى الله عليه وسلم كلوا جميعاً ولا تفرقوا فان البركة مع الجماعة (ابن ماجه)

Umar-b-al-Khattab reported that the Messenger of Allah said: Eat all in a body and be not separate, because blessing is with the united body. (Ibn Majah)

١٣- عن ابن هريره قال قال رسول الله صلى الله عليه وسلم من السنة ان يخرج الرجل مع ضيفه الى باب الدار (ابن ماجه)

Abu Hurairah reported that the Messenger of Allah said: It is Sunnat that a man goes out with his guest up to the door of the house. (Ibn Majah)

١٤- عن جعفر بن محمد عن ابيه قال كان رسول الله صلى الله عليه وسلم اذا اكل مع قوم كان آخرهم اكلاً (البيهقى)

Jafar-b-Muhammad reported from his father who said, whenever the Messenger of Allah took meal with a people, he was invariably the last to begin eating. (Baihaqi)

١٥- عن ابي هريره قال قال رسول الله صلى الله وسلم اذا دخل احدكم على اخيه المسلم فلياكل من طعامه ولا يسئال و يشرب من شرابه ولا يسال (البيهقى)

Abu Hurairah reported that the Messenger of Allah said : when one of you calls on his brother Muslim, let him eat from his food and not ask, and drink from his drink and not ask. (Bailaqi)

Remarks :

The Almighty Allah has prohibited companionship with the unbelievers, the idolators, the illiterate and the great sinners like drunkards, fornicators, etc.

Before choosing companions, one must look to the habits, nature, virtues and views of the companion. The Holy Prophet said : Man is upon the religion of his friend. Therefore let every one of you look with whom he keeps company.

The believers must entertain guests. Even in case of previous bad treatment from a host who is now a guest, good treatment should be meted out to him.

The host must observe all sorts of formal behaviours with his guest. He should join in the food of his guest if possible in the same dish, as it is also practical illustration of inter-dining irrespective of class and social position.

The host must not rise up till his guest finishes his meal, and he must not begin with food till he begins. The host shall entertain guests with meat as far as possible and can afford. It is, however, not for the guest to cling round his host for more than three days without permission and thereby cause trouble or economic oppression upon his host.

The following are abominable in entertainments :

1. To spread beddings of silk and other unlawful things.

2. To place before the guest cups and plates of gold or silver for use, or

3. To serve such kind of food and drinks which have been forbidden by Islam, such as wine and other intoxicating drinks, etc.

4. To lavishly spend for entertainment of guests as it offends the Quranic Law.

The following are the manners observed in entertainment :—

1. No distinction shall be made in invitation between the rich and the poor, high or low, because the worst food is that in which the rich are invited and poor are neglected.

2. Whenever a man is invited, he should accept invitation irrespective of the social status of the host or kind of food to be served.

3. Invitation should be refused in case there is doubt that unlawful food will be served.

4. The host should bid the guests with a smiling countenance and sweet conversation. When they go away, the host must accompany them at least up to the door of his house.

5. The guest shall not leave the house of the host except with his permission.*

* The remarks have been compiled with the help of Eng. tr. of Mishkat by M. F. Karim (N.A.).

(4) **Dress and Clothing.**

فَلَمَّا ذَاقَا الشَّجَرَةَ بَدَتْ لَهُمَا سَوْاٰتُهُمَا وَطَفِقَا يَخْصِفٰنِ عَلَيْهِمَا مِنْ وَّرَقِ الْجَنَّةِ ؕ وَنَادٰىهُمَا رَبُّهُمَاۤ اَلَمْ اَنْهَكُمَا عَنْ
تِلْكُمَا الشَّجَرَةِ وَاَقُلْ لَّكُمَاۤ اِنَّ الشَّيْطٰنَ لَكُمَا عَدُوٌّ مُّبِيْنٌ ﴿۲۲﴾ (اعراف-٢٢)

And when they tasted of the tree their shame was manifest to them and they began to hide (by heaping) on themselves some of the leaves of the Garden. And their Lord called them, (saying): Did I not forbid you from that tree and tell you: Lo ! Satan is an open enemy to you?
(7:22)

يٰبَنِيْۤ اٰدَمَ قَدْ اَنْزَلْنَا عَلَيْكُمْ لِبَاسًا يُّوَارِيْ سَوْاٰتِكُمْ وَرِيْشًا ؕ وَلِبَاسُ التَّقْوٰى ذٰلِكَ خَيْرٌ (اعراف-٢٦)

O children of Adam, We have indeed sent down to you clothing to cover your shame, and splendid vesture, but the raiment of restraint from evil, that is best.
(7:26)

يٰبَنِيْۤ اٰدَمَ خُذُوْا زِيْنَتَكُمْ عِنْدَ كُلِّ مَسْجِدٍ وَّ كُلُوْا وَاشْرَبُوْا وَلَا تُسْرِفُوْا ۚ اِنَّهٗ لَا يُحِبُّ الْمُسْرِفِيْنَ ﴿۳۱﴾ قُلْ مَنْ حَرَّمَ
زِيْنَةَ اللّٰهِ الَّتِيْۤ اَخْرَجَ لِعِبَادِهٖ وَالطَّيِّبٰتِ مِنَ الرِّزْقِ ؕ قُلْ هِيَ لِلَّذِيْنَ اٰمَنُوْا فِي الْحَيٰوةِ الدُّنْيَا خَالِصَةً يَّوْمَ الْقِيٰمَةِ ؕ
كَذٰلِكَ نُفَصِّلُ الْاٰيٰتِ لِقَوْمٍ يَّعْلَمُوْنَ ﴿۳۲﴾ قُلْ اِنَّمَا حَرَّمَ رَبِّيَ الْفَوَاحِشَ مَا ظَهَرَ مِنْهَا وَمَا بَطَنَ وَالْاِثْمَ وَالْبَغْيَ بِغَيْرِ
الْحَقِّ وَاَنْ تُشْرِكُوْا بِاللّٰهِ مَا لَمْ يُنَزِّلْ بِهٖ سُلْطٰنًا وَّاَنْ تَقُوْلُوْا عَلَى اللّٰهِ مَا لَا تَعْلَمُوْنَ ﴿۳۳﴾ (اعراف-٣١ تا ٣٣)

O children of Adam, attend to your adornment at every time of prayer, and eat and drink and be not prodigal; surely, He loves not the prodigals. Say: Who has forbidden the adornment of Allah, which He has brought forth for His servants, and the good provisions? Say: These are for the believers in the life of this world, purely (theirs) on the Resurrection Day. Thus do We make the messages clear for a people who know. Say: My Lord forbids only indecencies, such of them as are apparent and such as are concealed, and sin and unjust rebellion, and that you associate with

Allah that for which He has sent down no authority, and that you say of Allah what you know not. **(7:31-33)**

وَلَا تَقْرَبُوا الْفَوَاحِشَ مَا ظَهَرَ مِنْهَا وَمَا بَطَنَ (انعام-١٥٢)

And draw not nigh to indecencies, open or secret. **(6:152)**

وَاللّٰهُ جَعَلَ لَكُمْ مِنْ بُيُوتِكُمْ سَكَنًا وَجَعَلَ لَكُمْ مِنْ جُلُودِ الْأَنْعَامِ بُيُوتًا تَسْتَخِفُّونَهَا يَوْمَ ظَعْنِكُمْ وَيَوْمَ
إِقَامَتِكُمْ وَمِنْ أَصْوَافِهَا وَأَوْبَارِهَا وَأَشْعَارِهَا أَثَاثًا وَمَتَاعًا إِلَى حِينٍ ۝ وَاللّٰهُ جَعَلَ لَكُمْ مِمَّا خَلَقَ ظِلَالًا
وَجَعَلَ لَكُمْ مِنَ الْجِبَالِ أَكْنَانًا وَجَعَلَ لَكُمْ سَرَابِيلَ تَقِيكُمُ الْحَرَّ وَسَرَابِيلَ تَقِيكُمْ بَأْسَكُمْ كَذٰلِكَ يُتِمُّ نِعْمَتَهُ
عَلَيْكُمْ لَعَلَّكُمْ تُسْلِمُونَ ۝ (النحل-٨٠، ٨١)

And Allah hath given you in your houses an abode, and hath given you (also) of the hides of cattle, houses which ye find light (to carry) on the day of migration and on the day of pitching camp; and of their wool and their fur and their hair, caparison and comfort for a while. And Allah hath given you, of that which He hath created, shelter from the sun; and hath given you places of refuge in the mountains, and hath given you coats to ward off the heat from you, and coats (of armour) to save you from your own fool-hardiness. Thus doth He perfect His favour unto you, in order that ye may surrender unto Him. **(16:80, 81)**

قُلْ لِلْمُؤْمِنِينَ يَغُضُّوا مِنْ أَبْصَارِهِمْ وَيَحْفَظُوا فُرُوجَهُمْ ذٰلِكَ أَزْكٰى لَهُمْ إِنَّ اللّٰهَ خَبِيرٌ بِمَا يَصْنَعُونَ ۝ وَقُلْ لِلْمُؤْمِنَاتِ يَغْضُضْنَ
مِنْ أَبْصَارِهِنَّ وَيَحْفَظْنَ فُرُوجَهُنَّ وَلَا يُبْدِينَ زِينَتَهُنَّ إِلَّا مَا ظَهَرَ مِنْهَا وَلْيَضْرِبْنَ بِخُمُرِهِنَّ عَلٰى جُيُوبِهِنَّ وَلَا يُبْدِينَ
زِينَتَهُنَّ (نور-٣٠، ٣١)

Say to the believing men that they lower their gaze and restrain their sexual passions. That is purer for them. Surely Allah is Aware of what they do. And say to the believing that they lower their gaze and restrain their sexual passions and do not display their adornment except what appears thereof. And let them wear their head-covering over their bosoms. And they should not display their adornment. **(24:30, 31)**

١- عن سمرة ان النبي صلى الله عليه وسلم قال البسو الثياب البيض فانها اطهر و اطيب و كفنوا فيها موتاكم

(ابن ماجه، احمد، ترمذی، نسائی)

Samorah reported that the Prophet said: Put on white dress, because it is most pure and excellent, and bury therein your dead men. (Ibn Majah, Ahmad, Tirmizi, Nisai).

٢- عن انس قال كان احب الثياب الى النبی صلى الله عليه وسلم يلبسها الحبرة (متفق عليه)

Anas reported that the dress most pleasing to the Prophet for use was green-coloured robe. (Agreed)

٣- عن ابی بردة قال اخرجت الينا عائشه كساءً ملبدا و ازاراً غليظاً فقالت قبض روح رسول الله صلى الله عليه وسلم فی هذين

(متفق عليه)

Abu Burdah reported : Ayesha came to us dressed with a single wrapper and a coarse trouser. She said : The soul of the Messenger of Allah was taken in these two. (Agreed)

٤- عن جابر قال نهى رسول الله صلى الله عليه وسلم ان ياكل الرجل بشماله او يمشی فی نعلٍ واحدة وآن يشتمل الصماء او يحتبي فی ثوبٍ واحدٍ كاشفاً عن فرجه (مسلم)

Jaber reported that the Messenger of Allah forbade a man's eating with his left hand, or walking in one shoe, or treading on hard soil, or putting a single dress exposing his private parts. (Muslim)

٥- عن ام سلمة قالت كان احب الثياب الى رسول الله صلي الله عليه وسلم القميص (ترمدی- ابوداؤد)

Umme-Salmah reported that the dress dearest to the Messenger of Allah was long gown.

٦- عن ابی سعیدن الخدري قال سمعت رسول الله صلی الله علیه وسلم
یقول ازارة المومن الی انصاف ساقیه لا جناح علیه فیما بینه
وبین الکعبین ما اسفل من ذلك فی النار (قال ذلك ثلاث مرات)
ولا ینظرالله یوم القیمة الی من جر ازاره بطراً (ابوداؤد- ابن ماجه)

Abu Sayeed-al-Khodri reported : The trouser of the believer is up to half of his legs, there is no sign for what is between it and between the ankles. What is below that is in the fire. (This he said thrice). Allah shall not look to one on the Resurrection Day who allows his trouser to flow out of vanity. (Abu Daud, Ibn-e-Majah)

٧- عن ابن عمر قال قال رسول الله صلی الله علیه وسلم من لبس ثوب
شهرة فی الدنیا البسه الله ثوب مذلة یوم القیمة

(ترمذي - احمد - ابو داؤد . ابن ماجه)

Ibn-e-Omar reported than the Messenger of Allah said : whoever puts on a robe of fame in this world, Allah will dress him with a robe of disgrace on the Resurrection Day.

(Tirmizi, Ahmad, Abu Daud, Ibn-e- Majah)

٨- عن ابن عمر قال قال رسول الله صلی الله علیه وسلم من تشبه بقوم
فهو منهم (احمد - ابوداؤد)

Ibn-e-Omar reported that the Messenger of Allah said : whoever imitates a people, he belongs to them. (Ahmad, Abu Daud)

٩- عن عمرو بن شعیب عن ابیه عن جده قال قال رسول الله صلي الله
علیه وسلم ان الله یحب ان یری اثر نعمته علی عباده (ترمذی)

Amr-b-Shuaib from his father from his grand father reported that the Messenger of Allah said : Verily Allah likes that the signs of His gifts are seen on His servant. (Tirmizi)

١٠- عن جابر قال اتانا رسول الله صلى الله عليه وسلم زائرا فرأى رجلاً
شعثاً قد تفرق شعره فقال ما كان يجد هذا ما يسكن به راسه
و راي رجلا عليه ثياب و سخة فقال ماكان يجد هذا ما يغسل
به ثوبه (احمد - نسائى)

Jaber reported : The Prophet came to see us and found a man of dishevelled hairs, and his hairs were not arranged. Then he said : This man is not finding with what he should smooth his head. And he saw a man with dirty cloth on. So he said : This man is not finding with what he should wash his cloth. (Ahmad, Nisai)

١١- عن عائشة ان اسماء بنت ابى بكر دخلت على رسول الله صلى الله
عليه وسلم وعليها ثياب رقاق فاعرض عنها وقال يا اسماء ان امرأة
اذا بلغت المحيض لن يصلح ان يرى منها الاهذا وهذا و اشار
الى وجهه وكفيه (ابوداؤد)

Ayesha reported that Asma'a, daug ter of Abu Bakr, came to the Messenger of Allah while there was this cloth on her. He approached her and said : O Asma'a! When a girl reaches the menstrual time, it is not proper that any thing on her should remain exposed except this and this. He hinted at her face and palms. (Abu Daud)

١٢- عن ابن عباس قال انما نهى رسول الله صلى الله عليه وسلم عن
الثوب المنضمت من الحرير فاما العلم وسدى الثوب فلا باس به
(ابو داؤد)

Ibn-e-Abbas reported that the Messenger of Allah prohibited from using the cloth woven of silk (in both ways). As for border and corner of cloth, there is no harm in it. (Abu Daud)

١٣- عن ابن عباس قال كل ماشئت و بس ماشئت ما اخطاتك اثنتان
سرف ومخيلة (بخاري)

Ibn-e-Abbas reported: Eat what you like and put on what you like so long as two things do not mislead you—extravagance and pride. (Bukhari)

١٤- عن ابى الدرداء قال قال رسول الله صلى الله عليه وسلم ان احسن ما زرتم الله فى قبوركم و مساجدكم البياض (ابن ماجه)

Abu Darda'a reported that the Messenger of Allah said: Verily the best dress with which you can meet Allah in your graves and mosque is of white colour. (Ibn-e-Majah)

١٥- عن المغيرة بن شعبة ان النبى صلى الله عليه وسلم لبس جبةً روميهً ضيقة الكمين (متفق عايه)

Mughirah-b-Shu'bah reported that the Prophet put on a Roman robe with tight sleeves. (Agreed)

١٦- عن عائشه قالت كان فراش رسول الله صلى الله عليه وسلم ينام عليه آدماً حشوه ليف (متفق عليه)

Ayesha reported that the bedding of the Messenger of Allah on which he used to sleep was of hide, its contents were of date refuse. (Agreed)

١٧- عن حذيفة قال نهنا رسول الله صلى الله عليه وسلم ان نشرب فى انية الفضة والذهب وان تاكل فيها وعن لبسى الحرير والديباج وان نجلس عليه (متفق عليه)

Huzaifah reported that the Messenger of Allah prohibited us from drinking in cups of gold and silver, and from taking food therein, and from putting on silk and coloured silk and from sitting thereon. (Agreed)

١٨- عن سالم عن ابيه عن النبى صلى الله عليه وسلم قال الاسبال فى الازار والقميص والعمامة من جر منها شيئاً خيلاء لم ينظر الله اليه يوم القيامة (ابو داؤد - نسائى - ماجه)

Salem from his father reported from the Prophet who said: Lengthening is in trouser, gown and turban. Whoever lets loose any thing therefrom out of vanity, Allah shall not look to him on the Resurrection Day. (Abu Daud, Nisai, Ibn e-Majah)

١٩- عن ابى سعيد الخدرى قال كان رسول الله صلى الله عليه وسلم اذا استجد ثوباً سماه باسمه عمامة او قميصاً او رداء ثم يقول اللهم لك الحمد كما كسوتينه أسألك خيره وخير ما صنع له و اعوذ بك من شره و شر ما صنع له (ترمذى - ابوداؤد)

Abu Sayeed-al-Khodri reported that whenever the Messenger of Allah put on a new robe, he used to name with its name—turban, or gown, or sheet, and they say: O Allah! all praise to Thee as Thou hast dressed me therewith. I ask Thee good of it and the good of what has been made for it. I seek refuge to Thee from its evil and the evil of what has been created for it. (Tirmizi, Abu Daud)

٢٠- عن عبد الله بن عمرو قال مر رجل وعليه ثوبان احمران فسلم على النبى صلى الله عليه وسلم فلم يرد عليه (ترمذى - ابوداؤد)

Abdullah-b-Amr reported: A man with two red dresses passed by and saluted the Prophet, but he did not return it. (Tirmizi, Abu Daud)

٢١- عن ابى مطر قال ان علياً اشترى ثوبا بثلثه دراهم فلما لبسه قال الحمد لله الذى رزقنى من الرياش ما اتجمل به في الناس فاوارى به عورتى ثم قال هكذا سمعت رسول الله صلى الله عليه وسلم يقول (احمد)

Abu Matar reported that Ali purchased a cloth with three Dirhama. When he put it on, he said: All praise is for Allah who gave me provision of fineries which I adorn myself among men and cover my private parts. Afterwards he said: Thus I heard the Prophet say. (Ahmad)

Dress and clothing are a necessity of life. Dress is essential for covering the private parts of the body (the parts of the person which are indecent to expose in a man are what is between the navel and knee for a male, and the entire body for a female except the face and the hands as far as the wrists) and to protect the body from heat and cold etc.

Although the present civilized world is going to frustrate the very object of dress and has taken the mode of dress reaching almost to nakedness, yet Islam prohibits and warns that if such dress is worn in which private parts can easily be seen, it is quite unlawful. According to Islam dress should be neither too thin nor too coarse. Moreover, it should be simple and not costly.

Clothing at first simply served to cover shame and further to embellish persons with it; but there is yet a third kind of clothing, says the Holy Quran, which is the best, and that is the clothing of piety, literally the clothing that guards one against evil. Thus adorning may be physical, i.e. a man must have his clothes, but what is specially aimed at is adornment in a spiritual sense. A Muslim must attend to inner beautification. Real زينت or adornment is that which does not disgrace a man in any of his conditions either in the present life or in that which is to come.

Islam has got no fixed type or standard of dress, as dress is regulated by necessities according to geographical, social, and religious conditions. But it is decided that the dress should have the basic characteristics which Islam has laid down, and should fulfil the basic needs and objects of dress. Man should dress according to his riches, without squandering and without being a miser. He should wear neat and clean dress, and the dress which does not go towards extravagance and pride.

The Holy Prophet used to wear neat and clean dress. The colour of cloth most favourable to him was white and green, because dirtiness is manifested more vividly in white cloth. The Holy Prophet recommended the use of trouser to the length of the lower portion of the leg, as the lengthening of trousers beyond ankles gives an air of vanity and catches fouls and dirts of the way. The Holy Prophet used single robe, socks, caps, and turbans, etc and in many traditions, recommended them for others.

(5) Cleanliness (or طہارت) :—

(a) Ablution.

(b) Tayamum.

(c) Cleanliness from calls of nature.

(d) Bath.

وَيُنَزِّلُ عَلَيْكُمْ مِّنَ السَّمَآءِ مَآءً لِّيُطَهِّرَكُمْ بِهٖ وَ يُذْهِبَ عَنْكُمْ رِجْزَ الشَّيْطٰنِ (انفال- ١١)

And He caused rain to descend on you from heaven, to clean you therewith, and to remove from you the stain of Satan. (8:11)

وَهُوَ الَّذِىٓ اَرْسَلَ الرِّيٰحَ بُشْرًاۢ بَيْنَ يَدَىْ رَحْمَتِهٖ ۚ وَاَنْزَلْنَا مِنَ السَّمَآءِ مَآءً طَهُوْرًا ﴿۴۸﴾ (فرقان- ۴۸)

And He it is who sends the winds as heralds of glad tidings, going before His Mercy, and We send down purifying water from the sky. (25:48)

اِنَّ اللّٰهَ يُحِبُّ التَّوَّابِيْنَ وَيُحِبُّ الْمُتَطَهِّرِيْنَ ﴿۲۲۲﴾ (بقرہ- ٢٢٢)

Allah loves those who turn to Him constantly and He loves those who keep themselves pure and clean. (2:222)

وَاللّٰهُ يُحِبُّ الْمُطَّهِّرِيْنَ ﴿۱۰۸﴾ (توبہ- ١٠٨)

And Allah loveth those who make themselves pure. (9:108)

يٰٓاَيُّهَا الْمُدَّثِّرُ ﴿۱﴾ قُمْ فَاَنْذِرْ ﴿۲﴾ وَرَبَّكَ فَكَبِّرْ ﴿۳﴾ وَثِيَابَكَ فَطَهِّرْ ﴿۴﴾ (مدثر- ١تا٤)

O thou wrapped up (in a mantle)! Arise and deliver thy warning! And thy Lord do thou magnify ! And thy garments keep from stain ! (74:1-4)

يٰاَيُّهَا الَّذِيْنَ اٰمَنُوْٓا اِذَا قُمْتُمْ اِلَى الصَّلٰوةِ فَاغْسِلُوْا وُجُوْهَكُمْ وَاَيْدِيَكُمْ اِلَى الْمَرَافِقِ وَامْسَحُوْا بِرُءُوْسِكُمْ وَاَرْجُلَكُمْ
اِلَى الْكَعْبَيْنِ وَاِنْ كُنْتُمْ جُنُبًا فَاطَّهَّرُوْا وَاِنْ كُنْتُمْ مَّرْضٰٓى اَوْ عَلٰى سَفَرٍ اَوْ جَآءَ اَحَدٌ مِّنْكُمْ مِّنَ الْغَآئِطِ اَوْ لٰمَسْتُمُ
النِّسَآءَ فَلَمْ تَجِدُوْا مَآءً فَتَيَمَّمُوْا صَعِيْدًا طَيِّبًا فَامْسَحُوْا بِوُجُوْهِكُمْ وَاَيْدِيْكُمْ مِّنْهُ مَا يُرِيْدُ اللّٰهُ لِيَجْعَلَ عَلَيْكُمْ
مِّنْ حَرَجٍ وَّلٰكِنْ يُّرِيْدُ لِيُطَهِّرَكُمْ وَلِيُتِمَّ نِعْمَتَهٗ عَلَيْكُمْ لَعَلَّكُمْ تَشْكُرُوْنَ ۝ (مائدہ - ۶)

O you who believe ! When you prepare for prayer, wash your faces, and your hands (and arms) to the elbows ; rub your heads (with water) and (wash) your feet to the ankles. If you are in a state of ceremonial impurity, bathe your whole body. But if you are ill or on a journey, or one of you cometh from offices of nature, or you have been in contact with women, and you find no water, then take fo r yourselves clean sand or earth. And rub therewith your faces and hands. Allah doth not wish to place you in a difficulty, but to make you clean, and to complete His favour to you! that you may be grateful. (5:6)

يٰاَيُّهَا الَّذِيْنَ اٰمَنُوْا لَا تَقْرَبُوا الصَّلٰوةَ وَاَنْتُمْ سُكٰرٰى حَتّٰى تَعْلَمُوْا مَا تَقُوْلُوْنَ وَلَا جُنُبًا اِلَّا عَابِرِيْ سَبِيْلٍ حَتّٰى تَغْتَسِلُوْا
وَاِنْ كُنْتُمْ مَّرْضٰٓى اَوْ عَلٰى سَفَرٍ اَوْ جَآءَ اَحَدٌ مِّنْكُمْ مِّنَ الْغَآئِطِ اَوْ لٰمَسْتُمُ النِّسَآءَ فَلَمْ تَجِدُوْا مَآءً فَتَيَمَّمُوْا صَعِيْدًا
طَيِّبًا فَامْسَحُوْا بِوُجُوْهِكُمْ وَاَيْدِيْكُمْ اِنَّ اللّٰهَ كَانَ عَفُوًّا غَفُوْرًا ۝ (نساء - ۴۳)

O you who believe ! Approach not prayers with a mind be-fogged, until you can understand all that you say, nor in a state of ceremonial impurity (Except when travelling on the road) until after washing your whole body. If you are ill, or on a journey, or one of you cometh from office of nature, or you have been in contact with women and you find no water, then take for yourselves clean sand or earth, and rub there with your faces and hands. For Allah doth blot out sins and forgive again and again. (4:43)

AHADITH :

١ــ عن ابي هريرة قال سأل رجل رسول الله صلى الله عليه وسلم فقال يا رسول الله انا نركب البحر و نحمل معنا القليل من الماء فان توضانا به عطشنا افنتوضأ بماء البحر فقال رسول الله صلى الله عليه وسلم هوالطهور ماءه والحل ميته

(مالک ترمذی ، ابوداؤد ، نسائی ، ابن ماجه دارمی)

Abu Hurairah reported that a man asked the Messenger of Allah. He said : O' Messenger of Allah ! We sail in the sea and carry little water with us. If we make ablution therewith, we become thirsty. Shall we make ablution with sea-water ?

The Messenger of Allah replied : Its water is pure and its dead things are permissible.

(Malek, Trimizi, Abu Daud, Nisai, Ibn Majah, Darini).

٢ــ عن ابي مالك الاشعرى قال قال رسول الله صلى الله عليه وسلم الطهور سشطر الايمان ـ (مسلم)

Abu Malik al-Ash'ari reported that the Messenger of Allah said : Cleanliness is half of faith. (Muslim)

٣ــ عن عثمان قال قال رسول الله صلى الله عليه وسلم من توضا فا حسن الوضوء خرجت خطاياه من جسده حتى تخرج من تحت اظفاره (متفق عليه)

Osman reported that the Messenger of Allah said: who so makes ablution well, his sins come out of his body, till they come out even from under his nails. (Agreed).

٤ــ عن عثمان قال قال رسول الله صلى الله عليه وسلم ما من امرء مسلم تحضره صلواة مكتوبة فيحسن وضوء ها وخشو عها و ركوعها الآكانت كفارة لما قبلها من الذنوب سالم يوت كبيرة وذلك الدهر كله (مسلم)

Osman reported that the Messenger of Allah said : There is no Muslim Gentleman to whom the prescribed prayer, present themselves and who then makes well their ablution, and their prostration and their bending except that they will be expiations for sins committed before them so long as he did not commit great sins. And that is for all the time (to come). (Muslim)

٥ــ عن عقبة بن عامر قال قال رسول الله صلى الله عليه وسلم ما من مسلم يتوضأ فيحسن و ضوءه ثم يقوم فيصلى ركعتين مقبل عليها بقلبه و وجهه الا وجبت له الجنه (مسلم)

Oqbat-b-A'mer reported that the Messenger of Allah said : There is no Muslim performing ablution and performing his ablution well and then standing up and saying prayer of two bendings with his heart and face turned (sincerely) to them both except that Paradise becomes obligatory for him. (Muslim).

٦ــ عن عثمان انه توضأ فا فرغ على يديه ثلثاً ثم تمضمض واستنشر ثم غسل وجهه ثلاثاً ثم غسل يده اليمنى الى المرفق ثلاثاً ثم غسل يده اليسرى الى المرفق ثلاثاً ثم مسح برأسبه ثم غسل رجله اليمنى ثلاثاً ثم اليسرى ثلاثا ثم قال رايت رسول الله صلى الله عليه وسلم توضأ وضوئى هذاثم يصلى ركعتين لايحدث نفسه فيهما بشئ غفرله ماتقدم من ذنبه (متفق عليه)

Osman reported that he performed ablution and that he thrice poured (water) over his hands. Then he gargled and washed his nose

Then he washed his face thrice, and then he washed thrice his right hand upto the elbow. Afterwards he washed thrice his left hand upto to the elbow and then he rubbed his head. Afterwards he washed his right leg thrice and then the left leg thrice. After wards he said : I have seen the Messenger of Allah performing ablution similar to this ablution of mine. He then said : Whoso shall perform this ablution of mine and then say Prayer of two rak'ats without allowing himself to talk between these two with anything, will be forgiven of what preceeded of his sins. (Agreed)

٧ــ عن جابر قال قال رسول الله صلى الله عليه وسلم مفتاح الجنة الصلواة مفتاح الصواة الطهور (احمد)

Jaber reported that the Messenger of Allah said : The key to Paradise is prayer, and the key to Prayer is cleanliness. (Ahmad)

٨ــ عن ابى هريرة قال قال رسول الله صلى الله عليه وسلم لاتقبل صلواة من احدث حتى يتوضا (متفق عليه)

Abu Hurairah reported that the Messenger of Allah said : The prayer of one whose ablution has broken is not accepted till he makes (fresh) ablution. (Agreed).

٩ــ عن ابن عمر قال قال رسول الله صلى الله عليه وسلم لاتقبل صلواة بغير طهور ولاصدقة من غلول (مسلم)

Ibn-e-Omar reported that the Messenger of Allah said : Prayer without ablution is not accepted, nor charity from unlawful wealth. (Muslim).

١٠ــ عن ابى هريرة قال قال رسول الله صلى الله عليه وسلم لاوضوء الا من صوت اوريح (احمد ترمذى)

Abu Hurairah reported that the Messenger of Allah said : No ablution (becomes necessary) except on account of sound or wind. (Ahmad, Tirmizi).

١١ـــ عن علی قال سالت النبی صلی اللہ علیه وسلم من المذی فقال من المذی الوضوء ومن المنی الغسل (ترمذی)

Ali reported : I asked the Prophet about emission of water semen. He said : Ablution for emission of water semen, and bath for emission of thick semen. (Tirmizi).

١٢ـــ عن ابن عباس قال قال رسول اللہ صلی اللہ علیه وسلم ان الوضوء علی من نام مفطجعاً فانه اذا اضطجع استرخت مفاصله

(ترمذي ، ابو داؤد)

Ibn Abbas reported that the Messenger of Allah said : Ablution (becomes compulsory) over one who sleeps lying on bed, because when he lies on bed, his joints becomes loose. (Tirmizi, Abu Daud)

١٣ـــ عن عمر بن عبد العزیز عن تمیم الداري قال قال رسول اللہ صلی اللہ علیه وسلم الوضوء من کل دم سائل (دارقطنی)

Omar-b-Abdul Aziz reported from Tamim Dari who said that the Messenger of Allah had said : There is ablution on account of every blood flowing. (Darqutni).

١٤ـــ عن سعید بن زید قال قال رسول اللہ صلي اللہ علیه وسلم لاوضوء لمن لم یذکر اسم اللہ علیه (ترمذی ـ ابن ماجه)

Sayeed-b-Zaid reported that the Messenger of Allah said : There is no ablution for one who does not mention the name of Allah over it. (Tirmizi, Abu Majah)

١٥ـــ عن حذیفة قال قال رسول اللہ صلی اللہ علیه وسلم فضلنا علی الناس بثلث جعلت صفوفنا کصفوف الملائکة وجعلت لنا الارض کلها مسجداً وجعلت تربتها لنا طهوراً اذا لم نجد الماء (مسلم)

Huzaifah reported that the Messenger of Allah said: We have been given superiority over the people for three things-our ranks have been made like the ranks of the angles, and the earth, the entire of it, has been made a prayer-place for us, and its dust has been made a means of purification for us when we don't find water. (Muslim).

١٦ــ عن عمار بن ياسرانه كان يحدث انهم تمسحوا وهم مع رسول الله صلى الله عليه وسلم بالصعيد صلواة الفجر فضربوا باكفهم الصعيد ثم مسحوا بوجوهم مسحة واحدة ثم عادو افضربوا باكفهم الصعيد مرة اخرى فسحوا بايديهم كلها الى المناكب والاباط من بطون ايديهم (ابو داؤد)

Ammar-b-Yasar reported that he used to narrate that they used to rub with earth while they were with their palms and then they rubbed one rub over their faces. Afterwards they repeated and struck earth again with their palms, and rubbed their hands, the entire of them, upto elbow and armpits with the outer surfaces of their hands. (Abu Daud)

١٧ــ عن ابي ايوب الانصاري قال قال رسول الله صلى الله عليه وسلم اذا اتيتم الغائط فلا تستقبلوا القبلة ولا تستد بروها ولكن شرقوا او غربوا (متفق عليه)

Abu Ayyub Ansari reported that the Messenger of Allah said: When you come to privy, don't face the Ka'ba, nor keep it back, but face either the East or the West. (Agreed).

١٨ــ عن انس قال كان رسول الله صلى الله عليه وسلم اذا دخل الخلاء يقول اللهم اني اعوذ بك من خبث والخبائث (متفق عليه)

Anas reported that when the Messenger of Allah entered the privy, he used to say : O Allah ! I seek refuge to Thee from impurities and evil spirits. (Agreed).

۱۹— عن ابی هریرة قال قال رسول الله صلی الله علیه وسلم انما انا لکم
مثل الوالد لولده اعلمکم اذا اتیتم الغائط فلا تستقبوا القبلة
ولا تستد بروها وامر ثبلاثته احجار ونهیٰ عن الروث والرمة
ونهیٰ ان یستطیب الرجل بیمینه (ابن ماجه)

Abu Hurairah reported that the Messenger of Allah Said : Surely I am for you like a father for his son. I teach you that when you come to privy, you shall not face the Ka'ba, nor keep it back. He gave direction of three stones and prohibited (purification) by dungs and bones, and he prohibited a man's cleansing with his right hand. (Ibn-e-Majah)

۲۰— عن عبدالله بن مغضل قال قال رسول الله صلی الله علیه وسلم
لایبولن احدکم فی مستحمه ثم یغستل فیه او یتوضا فیه فان عامة
الوسواس منه (ابوداؤد ـ ترمذی نسائی)

Abdullah-b-Mugaffal reported that the Messenger of Allah said : None of you must pass urine in his bath room and then take bath there in or make ablution therein, because most of the evil inclinations arise there from. (Abu Daud, Tirmizi, Nisai).

۲۱— عن عبدالله بن سرجس قال قال رسول الله صلی الله علیه وسلم
لایبولن احد کم فی حجر (ابوداؤد)

Abdullah-b-Sargas reported that the Messenger of Allah said : None of you must pass urine in a hole. (Nisai, Abu Daud)

۲۲— عن معاذ قال قال رسول الله صلی الله علیه وصلم اتقوا الملاعن
الثلاثه البراز فی الموارد و قارعة الطریق وانطل
(ابو داؤد ـ ابن ماجه).

Mu'az reported that the Messenger of Allah said three: Guard causes of curse : Passing impurities in places of water, and in the middle of a path, and shade. (Abu Daud, Ibn-e-Majah).

۲۳ــ عن عمر قال رانی النبی صلی الله علیه وسلم وانا ابول قائماً فقال یا عمر لاتبل قائماً فما بلت قائماً بعد (ترمذي - ابن ماجه)

Omar reported that the Prophet saw me while I was passing urine standing. So he said : O Omar ! don't pass urine standing. So, I did not afterwards pass urine standing. (Tirmizi, Ibn-e-Majah).

۲٤ــ عن ابی ایوب وجابر وانس ان هذه الایه لما نزلت فیه رجال یحبون ان یتطهروا والله یحب المطهرین قال رسول الله صلی الله علیه وسلم یا معشر الانصار ان الله قد اثنی علیکم فی الطهور فما طهر کم قالوا نتوضأ للصواة ونغسل من الجنابة ونستنجی بالماء قال فذلك معیکموه (ابن ماجه)

Abu Ayyub, Jabar and Anas reported that when the following verse was revealed: There are men therein who ever remain pure ones (9:108) The Messenger of Allah said : O congregation of the Ansars ! Verily Allah praised you for cleanliness. That what is your cleanliness? They replied : We make ablution for prayer and wash our impurities and seek purification with water. He said : It is that, so you should take to it. (Ibn-e-Majah)

۲٥ــ عن عائشه ان النبی صلی الله علیه وسلم نهی الرجال والنساء عن دخول الحمامات ثم رخص للرجال ان یدخلوا بالمیازر (ترمذی ـ ابوداؤد)

Aysha reported that the Prophet prohibited males and females from entering the bathrooms. Afterwards he allowed the males to enter with trousers. (Tirmizi, Abu Daud).

۲٦ــ عن عائشه قالت کان رسول الله صلی الله علیه وسلم اذا اغتسل من الجنابة بدء فغسل یدیه ثم یتوضا کما یتوضا للصواة ثم یدخل اصابعه فی الماء فیخلل بها اصول شعره ثم یصب علی راسه ثلث غرفات بیدیه ثم یفیض الماء علی جلده کله (متفق علیه)

Aysha reported that when the Messenger of Allah took bath from impurities, he *began* and washed his hands, then he made ablution as he used to do for prayer. Afterwards he introduced his fingers into water and made picks therewith unto the roots of his hairs. Then he poured three jungs (of water) upon his head with his hands and then allowed the water to flow over his entire body. (Agreed).

٢٧— عن ابن عمر قال كانت الصلواة خمسين والغسل من الجنابه سبع
مرات وغسل البول من الثوب سبع مرات فلم يزل رسول الله
صلى الله عليه وسلم يسال حتىٰ جعلت الصلواة خمساً وغسل الجابة
مرة وغسل الثوب من البول مرة (ابوداؤد)

Ibn Omar reported that the Messenger of Allah said : When any of you comes to "Friday" prayer, let him take bath. (Agreed).

٢٨— عن ابن عمر قال قال رسول الله صل الله عليه وسلم اذا جاء
احدكم الجمعة فليغتسل (متفق عليه)

Ayesha reported that the Holy Prophet used to take bath from four things: from impurities, and on Friday, and from cupping, and from the washing of the dead body. (Abu Daud)

٢٩— عن عائشه ان النبي صلي الله عليه وسلم كان يغتسل من اربع من
الجنابه ويوم الجمعة ومن الحجامة ومن سل الميت (ابوداؤد)

REMARKS

"Cleanliness is half of faith, "declared the Holy Prophet. Cleanliness contributes towards the preservation of the heath of body and the health of body contributes to the health of mind. Islam laid a great emphasis on cleanliness of body alongwith the cleanliness of mind, because the former leads to the latter. It did not rest content by mere sermons on cleanliness but established positive rules. It has made compulsory bath before prayer in case of impurities, and wash of all exposed bodily limbs before each prayer.

Ablution is compulsory before prayer, without which prayer is void. There are certain things which break ablution :—(a) anything coming out from penis or rectum. (b) vomitting so as to fill up the mouth (c) to fall in sleep (d) in case of blood flowing out of the body etc. etc.

Tayamum, technically, means to intend to purify with pure earth. There are three (Farz) things in Tayamum i.e. (i) to make Niyyat (نيت) (ii) to wipe out the face once and (iii) to wip out the hands once upto the wrists with earth, dust or stone. Tayamum is to be done afresh before each time of prayer.

Tayamum is allowed only :—

(a) When water is not available. (b) When touch of water injures health as in illness. (c) When one is on journey and water is not easily available.

In passing urine or stool, the Holy Ka'ba shall not be kept in front or back. It shall not be passed in bathroom, water, hard ground, paths and shades, and under fruitful trees etc.

Bath becomes compulsory (Farz) in the following cases :—

(i) After sexual intercourse, (ii) After ejaculation of semen with lust. (iii) After menstural discharge and (iv) After stoppage of blood on child birth.*

* Remarks have been written with the help of Eng: Tr: of Mishkat by M.F. Karim (N.A.)

(6) Miscellaneous :

(Laughter, Names, Adornment, Hair-dressing, combing etc.)

فَلْيَضْحَكُوا قَلِيلًا وَلْيَبْكُوا كَثِيرًا جَزَاءً بِمَا كَانُوا يَكْسِبُونَ (توبہ - ۸۲)

Then let them Laugh a little and weep much—a recompense for what they earned (9: 82)

وَلَا تَلْمِزُوا أَنْفُسَكُمْ وَلَا تَنَابَزُوا بِالْأَلْقَابِ (حجرات - ۱۱)

Neither find fault with your own people, nor call one another by nick-names. (49:11)

لَتَدْخُلُنَّ الْمَسْجِدَ الْحَرَامَ إِنْ شَاءَ اللَّهُ آمِنِينَ مُحَلِّقِينَ رُءُوسَكُمْ (فتح - ۲۷)

You shall certainly enter the Sacred Mosque (Masjid-e-Haram), if Allah please, in security, your heads shaved and hair cut short. (48:27)

يَا بَنِي آدَمَ خُذُوا زِينَتَكُمْ (اعراف - ۳۱)

O children of Adam, attend to your Adornment. (7:31)

AHADITH :

۱ـ عن عائشه قالت مارايت النبي صلى الله عليه وسلم مستجمعاً ضاحكاً حتى ارى منه لهواته انما كان يتبسم (بخارى)

Ayesha reported : I did not see the Prophet bursting into laughter so much so that when I saw him too glad, he was only smiling (Bukhari)

٢ــ عن جابرؓ ابن سمرة قال كان رسول الله صلى الله عليه وسلم لايقوم من مصلاه الذى يصلى فيه الصبح حتى تطلع الشمس فاذا طلعت الشمس قام و كانوا يتحدثون فياخذون فى امرا الجاهليه فيضحكون ويتبسم (مسلم)

Jaber-b-Samorah reported that the Messenger of Allah used not to rise from his prayer place in which he prayed his morning prayer till the sun rose up. When the sun rose up, he used to get up while they used to hold talk and converse on the affairs of the Days of Ignorance and laugh and he also used to laugh. (Muslim).

٣ــ عن عبدالله ابن الحارث بن جزء قال مارايت احداً اكثر تبسماً من رسول الله صلى الله عليه وسلم (ترمذى)

Abdullah-b-Haris-b-Jazyin reported : I did never see any body smiling more than the Messenger of Allah (Tirmizi).

٤ــ عن قتادة قال سئل ابن عمر هل كان اصحاب رسول الله صلي الله عليه وسلم يضحكون قال نعم والايمان فى قلوبهم اعظم من الجبل وقال بلال ابن سعد ادركتهم يشدون بين الاغراض و يضحك بعضهم الى بعضٍ فاذا كان الليل كانوا رهباناً (مشكواة)

Qatadah reported that Ibn Omer was asked : Did the companions of of the Prophet laugh ? "Yes" replied he, "while faith in their hearts was greater than mountain". Bilal-b-Sa'ad said : I have seen them taking troubles in various works and some of them laughing with others. When night advanced, they becam hermits. (Mishkat)

٥ــ عن جابر ان النبي صلي الله عليه وسلم قال سموا باسمى و لا تكتنو بكنيتى فاني انما جعلت قاسماً اقسم بينكم (متفق عليه)

Jaber reported that the Holy Prophet said : Call me by my name, and don't call me by my surname. I have been made a distributor to make distribution among you. (Agreed).

٦ـ عن ابن عمر قال قال رسول الله صلى الله عليه وسلم ان احب اسماء كم الى الله عبدالله و عبدالرحمن (مسلم)

Ibn Omer reported that the Messenger of Allah said : The most pleasing of names to Allah are Abdullah (servant of Allah) and Abdur Rahman (servant of the Merciful) (Muslim)

٧ـ عن ابن عمر ان بنتاً كانت لعمر يقال لها عاصية فسمها رسول الله صلى الله عليه وسلم جميلة (مسلم)

Ibn Omar reported that Omer had a daughter called Asiyah. The Messenger of Allah named her Jamilah (beautiful). (Muslim).

٨ـ عن شريح ابن هانئ عن ابيه انه لما وفد الى رسول الله صلى الله عليه وسلم مع قومه سمعهم يكنونه بابي الحكم فدعاه رسول الله فقال ان الله هو الحكم واليه الحكم فلم تكنى ابا الحكم قال ان قومى اذا اختلفوا شئ اتونى فحكمت بينهم فرض كلا الفريقين بحكمى فقال رسول الله صلى الله عليه وسلم ما احسن هذا فمالك من الولد قال لى شريح ومسلم وعبد الله قال فمن اكبرهم قلت شريح قال فانت ابو شريح (ابو داؤد نسائى)

Shuraih-b-Hani reported from his father that when he went as a deputationist with his people to the Prophet, he heard them surnaming him as Abul Hakam (father of the just). The Messenger of Allah called him and said : Verily Allah—He is the just, and order is due to Him. Why do you then surname "Abul Hakam." He said : when my people differ about a thing they come to me and I judge among them. Then the two parties get pleased with my order. The Messenger of Allah said : How good it is ! Have you no children? He said : I have got Shuraih, Muslim and Abdullah. He said : who is the oldest of them ? I said : Shuraih. He said : you are then Abu Shuraih. (Abu Daud, Nisai)

۹۔ عن ابی الدرداء قال قال رسول الله صلی الله علیه وسلم تدعون یوم القیمة باسمائکم واسماء ابائکم فاحسنوا اسمائکم (احمد ابوداؤد)

Abu Darda reported that the Messenger of Allah said: You shall be called on the Resurrection Day by your names or by names of your fathers. So make your names good. (Ahmad, Abu Daud).

۱۰۔ عن عائشه قالت ان النبی صلی الله علیه وسلم کان یغیر الاسم القبیح ۔ (ترمذی)

Aysha reported that the Prophet used to change bad names. (Tirmizi).

۱۱۔ عن ابی وهب الجشمی قال قال رسول الله صلی الله علیه وسلم تسموا باسماء واحب الاسماء الی الله عبد الله و عبدالرحمن واصدقها حارث وهمام واقبحها حرب ومرة (ابوداؤد)

Abu Wahab al Joshami reported that the Messenger of Allah said : Name with the names of the Prophets, and names most liked by Allah are Abdullah and Abdur Rahman, and the most true of them are Haris and Hammam, and the worst of them are Harb and Murrah (Abu Daud).

۱۲۔ عن ابی هریرة ان رسول الله صلی الله علیه وسلم قال من کان له شعر فلیکرمه (ابوداؤد)

Abu Hurairah reported that the Messenger of Allah said : who so has got hair let him honour it. (Abu Daud).

۱۳۔ عن ابن عمر ان النبي صلی الله علیه وسلم راي صبیا قد حلق بعض راسه وترك بعضه فنهاهم عن ذلك وقال احلقوا کله او اترکوا کله (مسلم)

Ibn-e-Omar reported that the Prophet saw a boy some portion of whose head was shaved and some of it was left out. So he prohibited them from that and said : Shave the entire of it or leave the entire of it. (Muslim)

١٤ــ عن ابي قتادة انه قال رسول الله صلى الله عليه وسلم ان لى جمة
افا دجلها قال رسول صلى الله عليه وسلم نعم واكرمها قال فكان
ابوقادة ربما دهنها فى اليوم مرتين من اجل قول رسول الله صلى الله
عليه وسلم نعم واكرمها (مشكواة)

Abu Qatadah reported that he said to the Messenger of Allah : Verily I have got a tuft of hairs. Should I comb it ? "Yes" replied the Prophet, "and honour it." On account of the sayings of the Prophet "yes and honour it," Abu Qatadah often oiled it twice a day. (Mishkat).

١٥ــ عن على قال نهى رسول الله صلى الله عليه وسلم ان تحلق المرأة
راسها (نسائى)

Ali reported that the Messenger of Allah prohibited a woman to shave her head (Nisai).

١٦ــ عن عطاء بن يسار قال كان رسول الله صلى عليه وسلم فى المسجد
فدخل رجل ثائر الرأس والحيه فاشار اليه رسول الله صلى الله
عليه وسلم بيده كانه يامره باصلاح شعره ولحيته ففعل ثم رجع
فقال رسول الله صلى الله عليه وسلم اليس هذا خيراً من ان ياتى
احدكم وهوثا ئرالرأس كانه شيطان (مشكواة)

Ata'a-b-Yasar reported that the Messenger of Allah was within the mosque, a man, dishavelled in hairs and beard, entered. The Messenger of Allah hinted at him with his hand as if he was directing him to arrange his hairs and beard. So he did. Afterwards he returned. Then the Messenger of Allah said : Is this not better than that one of you comes while he is dishavaelled in hairs as if he is a devil. (Mishkat).

١٧— عن ابی هریرة قال قال رسول الله صلی الله علیه وسلم الفطرة خمس الختان والاستعداد وقص الشارب وتقلیم الاظفار ونتف الابط (متفق علیه)

Abu Hurairah reported that the Messenger of Allah said : Natural habits are fine : Circumcission, shaving hairs of private parts, shortening of moustache, pairing off nails and shaving of the hairs of armpit. (Agreed).

١٨— عن ابن عمر قال قال رسول الله صلی الله علیه وسلم خالفوا المشرکین اوفروا اللحی واحفوا الشوارب وفی روایة انهکوا الشوارب واعفوا اللحی (متفق علیه)

Ibn-e-Omar reported that the Messenger of Allah said : Act contrary to polytheists, keep beards and shave the moustaches. (And in narration :) shave the moustaches and let the beard flow. (Agreed).

Nisar Ahmed

KNOWLEDGE, LEARNING & EDUCATION.

(1)
Al-Quran.

وَعَلَّمَ آدَمَ الْأَسْمَاءَ كُلَّهَا ثُمَّ عَرَضَهُمْ عَلَى الْمَلٰٓئِكَةِ فَقَالَ أَنْبِئُونِي بِأَسْمَاءِ هٰٓؤُلَاءِ إِنْ كُنْتُمْ صٰدِقِينَ ۝ قَالُوا سُبْحٰنَكَ
لَا عِلْمَ لَنَا إِلَّا مَا عَلَّمْتَنَا إِنَّكَ أَنْتَ الْعَلِيمُ الْحَكِيمُ ۝ قَالَ يٰٓآدَمُ أَنْبِئْهُمْ بِأَسْمَائِهِمْ فَلَمَّا أَنْبَأَهُمْ بِأَسْمَائِهِمْ قَالَ أَلَمْ أَقُلْ
لَكُمْ إِنِّي أَعْلَمُ غَيْبَ السَّمٰوٰتِ وَالْأَرْضِ وَأَعْلَمُ مَا تُبْدُونَ وَمَا كُنْتُمْ تَكْتُمُونَ ۝ (بقرہ : ۳۱ تا ۳۳)

And He taught Adam all the names, then presented them to the angles ; He said : Tell Me the names of those if you are right. They said : Glory be to Thee ! We have no knowledge but that which Thou has taught us. Surely Thou are the knowing, the Wise. He said : O Adam, inform them of their names. So when he informed them of their names, He said : Did I not say to you that I know what is unseen in the heavens and the earth ? And I know what you manifest and what you hide. (2: 31-33)

كَمَا أَرْسَلْنَا فِيكُمْ رَسُولًا مِنْكُمْ يَتْلُوا عَلَيْكُمْ آيٰتِنَا وَيُزَكِّيكُمْ
وَيُعَلِّمُكُمُ الْكِتٰبَ وَالْحِكْمَةَ وَيُعَلِّمُكُمْ مَا لَمْ تَكُونُوا تَعْلَمُونَ ۝
(بقرہ : ۱۵۱)

Even as We have sent among you a Messenger from among you, who recites to you Our messages and purifies you and teaches you that which you did not know. (2: 151)

وَلَئِنِ اتَّبَعْتَ أَهْوَاءَهُمْ بَعْدَ الَّذِي جَاءَكَ مِنَ الْعِلْمِ مَا لَكَ مِنَ اللّٰهِ مِنْ وَلِيٍّ وَلَا نَصِيرٍ ۝ (بقرہ : ۱۲۰)

And if you follow their desire after the knowledge that has come to thee, thou shalt have from Allah no friend, nor helper. (2: 120)

وَلَئِنِ اتَّبَعْتَ أَهْوَاءَهُمْ مِنْ بَعْدِ مَا جَاءَكَ مِنَ الْعِلْمِ إِنَّكَ إِذًا لَمِنَ الظَّالِمِينَ ۝ (بقرہ : ۱۴۵)

And if thou shouldst follow their desires after the knowledge that has come to thee, then thou wouldst indeed be of the wrongdoers.
(2:145)

اقْرَأْ بِاسْمِ رَبِّكَ الَّذِي خَلَقَ ۝ خَلَقَ الْإِنْسَانَ مِنْ عَلَقٍ ۝
اقْرَأْ وَرَبُّكَ الْأَكْرَمُ ۝ الَّذِي عَلَّمَ بِالْقَلَمِ ۝ عَلَّمَ الْإِنْسَانَ
مَا لَمْ يَعْلَمْ ۝ (علق : ۱—۵)

Read in the name of thy Lord who creates—creates man from a clot, Read and thy Lord is most Generous, who taught by the pen, taught man what he knew not. (96: 1-5)

وَالرَّاسِخُونَ فِي الْعِلْمِ يَقُولُونَ آمَنَّا بِهِ
كُلٌّ مِنْ عِنْدِ رَبِّنَا وَمَا يَذَّكَّرُ إِلَّا أُولُو
الْأَلْبَابِ ۝ (آل عمران۔۷)

And those firmly rooted in knowledge, They say, We believe in it, it is all from our Lord. And none mind except men of understanding.
(3:7)

وَأَنْزَلَ اللَّهُ عَلَيْكَ الْكِتَابَ وَالْحِكْمَةَ وَعَلَّمَكَ مَا لَمْ تَكُنْ تَعْلَمُ وَكَانَ فَضْلُ اللَّهِ عَلَيْكَ عَظِيمًا ۝ (النساء : ۱۱۳)

And Allah has revealed to thee the Book and the wisdom, and taught thee what thou knewest not, and Allah's grace/on you is very great. (4:113)

مَا لَهُمْ بِهِ مِنْ عِلْمٍ إِلَّا اتِّبَاعَ الظَّنِّ
(النساء : ۱۵۷)

They have no knowledge about it, but only follow a conjecture.
(4:157)

وَلَا تَقْفُ مَا لَيْسَ لَكَ بِهِ عِلْمٌ (بنی اسرائیل : ۳۶)

And follow not that of which thou hast no knowledge. (17:36)

قُلْ هَلْ يَسْتَوِي الَّذِينَ يَعْلَمُونَ وَالَّذِينَ لَا يَعْلَمُونَ إِنَّمَا يَتَذَكَّرُ أُولُو الْأَلْبَابِ (زمر : ۹)

Say: Are those who know and those who know not alike? Only men of understanding mind. (39:9)

إِنَّمَا يَخْشَى اللَّهَ مِنْ عِبَادِهِ الْعُلَمَاءُ إِنَّ اللَّهَ عَزِيزٌ غَفُورٌ
(فاطر : ۲۸)

Those of His servants only who are possessed of knowledge fear Allah. Surely Allah is Mighty, Forgiving. (35:28)

وَتِلْكَ الْأَمْثَالُ نَضْرِبُهَا لِلنَّاسِ وَمَا يَعْقِلُهَا إِلَّا الْعَالِمُونَ (عنکبوت : ۴۳)

And these parables, We set them forth for men, and none understand them but the learned. (29:43)

الرَّحْمَٰنُ عَلَّمَ الْقُرْآنَ خَلَقَ الْإِنْسَانَ عَلَّمَهُ الْبَيَانَ
(الرحمٰن : ۱ تا ۴)

The Beneficent taught the Quran. He created man, taught him expression. (55: 1-4)

لَهُمْ قُلُوبٌ لَا يَفْقَهُونَ بِهَا وَلَهُمْ أَعْيُنٌ لَا يُبْصِرُونَ بِهَا وَلَهُمْ آذَانٌ لَا يَسْمَعُونَ بِهَا أُولَٰئِكَ كَالْأَنْعَامِ بَلْ هُمْ أَضَلُّ
أُولَٰئِكَ هُمُ الْغَافِلُونَ (اعراف : ۱۷۹)

They have hearts wherewith they understand not, and they have eyes wherewith they see not, and they have ears wherewith they hear not. They are as cattle, nay, they are more astray. These are the heedless ones. (7:179)

إِنَّ شَرَّ الدَّوَابِّ عِنْدَ اللّٰهِ الصُّمُّ الْبُكْمُ الَّذِيْنَ لَا يَعْقِلُوْنَ ۝ (انفال: ٢٢)

Surely the vilest of beasts in Allah's sight, are the deaf, the dumb, who understand not. (8:22)

وَقُلْ رَّبِّ زِدْنِيْ عِلْمًا ۝ (طٰهٰ: ١١٤)

And say: My Lord, increase me in knowledge. (20:114)

مَثَلُ الَّذِيْنَ حُمِّلُوا التَّوْرٰىةَ ثُمَّ لَمْ يَحْمِلُوْهَا كَمَثَلِ الْحِمَارِ يَحْمِلُ اَسْفَارًا (جمعه ٥)

The likeness of those who were charged with the Torah, then they observed it not, is as the likeness of the ass carrying books.
62:5)

وَهُوَ بِكُلِّ شَيْءٍ عَلِيْمٌ ۝ (بقرة: ٢٩)

And He is Knower of all things. (2:29)

———

AHADITH

١ - عن عبد الله ابن عمرو قال قال رسول الله صلى الله عليه وسلم
بلغوا عنى و لو اية و حدثوا عن بنى اسرائيل ولا حرج و من
كذب على متعمدا فليتبوا مقعده من النار (بخارى)

Abdullah-b-Amr reported that the Messenger of Allah said: Circulate from me though (it be) a sentence, and narrate about the children of Israil and there is no harm. And who so fabricates falsehood against me intentionally, let his him seek abode in the fire. (Bukhari)

٢ - عن عبد الله قال يا ايها الناس من علم شيئاً فليقل به و من لم
يعلم فليقل الله اعلم فان من العلم ان تقول لما لا تعلم الله اعلم قال
الله تعالىٰ لنبيه قل ما اسئلكم عليه من اجر و ما انا من المتكلفين
(متفق عليه)

Abdullah reported: O men! Whoso knows any thing, let him communicate it and whoso does not know, let him say : Allah knows best; because it is a part of knowledge that you should say for what you know not : Allah knows best. The Almighty Allah revealed to His Prophet: Say, I do not ask any reward for it and I am not one of those who inflict hardship. (Agreed)

٣ - عن ابى هريرة قال قال رسول الله صلى الله عليه وسلم الناس
معاون كمعاون الذهب والفضة خيارهم فى الجاهلية خيارهم فى
الاسلام اذا فقهوا
(مسلم)

Abu Hurairah reported that the Messenger of Allah said: Men are mines like the mines of gold and silver. The chiefs among you in the Days of Ignorance are the chiefs among you in Islam when they understand religion. (Muslim)

٤ - عن معاوية قال قال رسول الله صلى الله عليه وسلم من يرد الله
به خيراً يفقهه فى الدين و انما انا قاسم و الله معطى (متفق عليه)

Muawayiah reported that the Messenger of Allah said: Whosoevers good Allah wishes, He gives him understanding in religion; and verily I distribute (knowledge) while Allah bestows it. (Agreed)

٥ - عن ابى هريرة قال قال رسول الله صلى الله عليه وسلم اذا
مات الانسان انقطع عنه عمله الآ من ثلثة الا من صدقة جارية
أو علم ينتفع به او ولد صالح يدعواله (مسلم)

Abu Hurairah reported that the Messenger of Allah said: When a man dies, all his actions are cut off from him except three : ever running charity, or knowledge from which benefit is derived, or a virtuous son praying for him. (Muslim)

٦ - عن ابى سعيد الخدرى قال قال رسول الله صلى الله عليه وسلم
ان الناس لكم تبع و ان رجالاً يا تونكم من اقطار الارض
يتفقهون في الدين فا ذا اتوكم فاستوصوا بهم خيرا (ترمذى)

Abu Sayeedal Khudri reported that the Messenger of Allah said: Verily people will be your followers and verily people will come to you from different parts of the world to acquire learning in theology. So when they will come to you, admonish them with good. (Tirmizi)

٧ - عن ابى امامة الباهلى قال ذكر لرسول الله صلى الله عليه وسلم
رجلان احدهما عابد والآخر عالم فقال رسول الله صل الله عليه
وسلم فضل العالم على العابد كفضلى على ادنكم ثم قال رسول
الله صلى الله عليه وسلم ان الله و ملائكة و اهل السموات والارض
حتى النملة فى حجرها و حتى الحوت ليصلون على معلم
الناس الخير (ترمذى)

Abu Omamah al Bahili reported: Two persons were mentioned to the Messenger of Allah, one of the two is a pious worshipper and the other a learned man. Then the Messenger of Allah said: The superiority of the learned man over the pious worshipper is like my superiority over the meanest of you. Then the Holy Prophet said: Verily Allah, His angles and the dwellers of the heavens and the earth and even an ant in its hole and even a fish certainly send blessings upon a preacher of good to the people. (Tirmizi)

٨ . عن ابن عباس قال قال رسول الله صلى الله عليه وسلم فقيه واحد
اشد على الشيطان من الف (ترمذى ، ابن ماجه)

Ibne-Abbas reported that the Messenger of Allah said: To the devil, a learned theologian is stronger that a thousand pious worshippers. (Tirmizi, Ibne-Majah)

٩ - عن انس قال قال رسول الله صلى الله عليه وسلم طلب العلم فريضه على كل مسلمٍ و مسلمة و واضع العلم عند غير اهله لقلد الخنازير الجوهر و اللؤلؤ والذهب (ابن ماجه)

Anas reported that the Messenger of Allah said: Search for knowledge is compulsory upon every Muslim male and Muslim female. To impart learning to one not deserving of it is to put on a necklace of emerald and pearls and gold to the neck of swines. (Ibne-Majah)

١٠ - عن انس قال قال رسول الله صلى الله عليه وسلم من خرج فى طلب العلم فهو فى سبيل الله حتى يرجع (ترمذى)

Anas reported that the Messenger of Allah said: Whoso goes out in search of knowledge, he is in the path of Allah till he returns. (Tirmizi)

١١ - عن سنجرة الأزدى قال قال رسول الله صلى الله عليه وسلم من طلب العلم كان كفارة لما مضى (ترمذى)

Sakhburah al-Azdi reported that the Messenger of Allah said: Whoever searches after knowledge, it will be expiction for his past sins. (Tirmizi)

١٢ - عن ابى هريرة قال قال رسول الله صلى الله عليه وسلم من سئل عن علم علمه ثم كتمه الجم يوم القيامة بلجام من النار (احمد ، ابوداؤد ، ترمذى ، ابن ماجه عن انس)

Abu Hurairah reported that the Messenger of Allah said: Whoso is questioned about knowledge which he learnt and there he conceals it, shall wear a girdle of the Fire on the Resurrection Day. (Ahmad, Ibn Daud, Tirmizi, Ibn-e-Majah from Anas)

١٣ - عن كعب بن مالك قال قال رسول الله صلى الله عليه وسلم
من طلب العلم ليجاري به العلماء او ليماري به السفهاء او يصرف
به وجوه الناس اليه ادخله الله النار (ترمذى - ابوداؤد)

Ka'ab-b-Malek reported that the Messenger of Allah said: Whoso seeks knowledge either to prevail therewith over the learned, or to argue therewith with the fools or to arrest the faces of men towards him. Allah will admit him in the Fire. (Tirmizi, Ibn-Majah from Ibne Omer)

١٤ - عن ابى هريرة قال قال رسول الله صلى الله عليه وسلم من
تعلم علماً مما يتبغى به وجه الله لا يتعلمه الا ليصيب به غرضاً
من الدنيا لم يجد عرف الجنة يوم القيمة يعنى ريحها
(احمد ، ابو داؤد ، ابن ماجه)

Abu Hurairah reported that the Messenger of Allah said : Whoso acquires a learning other than that wherein the pleasure of Allah is sought, does not learn it but for gaining therewith frailties of the world. He will not find on the Resurrection Day the fragrance of Paradise, meaning its air.

(Ahmad, Abu Daud, Ibn-e-Majah).

١٥ - عن ابن مسعود قال قال رسول الله صلى الله عليه وسلم نضر الله
عبداً سمع مقالتى فحفظها و وعها و اولها فرب حامل فقه
غير فقيه و رب حامل فقه الى من هو افقه منه
(ترمذي ، ابو داؤد)

Ibn-e-Masud reported the Messenger of Allah said : May Allah give freshness to a man who hears any saying and then keeps it in memory, and preserves it and fulfils it (communicates). Many a bearer of theology is not a theologian, and many a bearer of theology (takes theology) to one who is more learned than him.

(Tirmizi, Abu Daud.).

١٦ - عن ابن مسعود قال سمعت رسول الله صلى الله عليه وسلم يقول
نضر الله امرأ سمع منا شيئاً فبلغه كما سمعه فرب مبلغ اوعى
له من سامع (ترمذي - ابن ماجه)

Ibne Masood reported: I heard the Messenger of Allah said: May Allah be pleased with a man who heard a thing from us and then broadcast it just as he had heard it. How many a preacher there are who remember much more than the hearer (audience).
(Tirmizi, Ibne-Majah).

١٧ - عن ابن عباس قال قال رسول صلى الله عليه وسلم اتقوا الحديث
عنى الا ما علمتم فمن كذب على متعمداً فليتبوا مقعده من النار
(ترمذى ، ابن ماجه ، على ابن مسعود ، جابر)

Ibn-e-Abbas reported that the Messenger of Allah said: Be careful of (narrating) traditions from me except what you know. Whoso imputes falsehood to me intentionally let him then seek his abode in the Fire. (Ti mizi, Ibne-Majah from Ibn-Masud and Jabar).

١٨ - عن ابي هريرة قال قال رسول الله صلى الله عليه وسلم تعلموا
الفرائض و القران و علموا الناس فانى مقبوض (ترمذي)

Abu Hurairah reported that the Messenger of Allah said: Learn the compulsory doctrines and the Quran, and teach (them to) the people, for varily I am a mortal. (Tirmizi).

١٩ - عن عبدالله بن مسعود قال لو ان اهل العلم صانوا العلم و
وضعوه عند اهله لسادوا به اهل زمانهم و لكنهم بذلوه لاهل
الدنيا لينالوا به من دنياهم فهانوا عليهم سمعت نبيكم صلى الله
عليه وسلم يقول من جعل الهموم هماً واحداً هم آخرته كفاه
الله هم دنياه ومن تشعبت به الهموم احوال الدنيا لم يبال الله فى
اي او ديتها هلك (ابن ماجه)

Abdullah-b-Masud reported : If the learned men guard learning and place it to deserving person, they can become thereby the masters of their time; but they spend it for the worldly men in order to get their worldly things therewith. Thus they become low to them. I heard your Prophet say : Whoso makes the anxieties a single anxiety, the anxiety of his next world, Allah will remove his anxiety of this world, and whoso branches out anxieties around the world, Allah will not care in whatever of it valleys he perishes. Ibn-e-Majah).

٢٠ - عن ابن سيرين قال ان هذا العلم دين فانظروا عمن تاخذون دينكم (مسلم)

Ibn-Sirin reported; certainly this learning is religion. So look from whom you learn your religion. (Muslim),

٢١ - عن عثمان ابن عفان قال قال رسول الله صلى الله عليه وسلم ليشفع يوم القيامة ثلاثة الانبياء ثم العلماء ثم الشهداء (ابن ماجه)

Usman-b-Affan reported that the Messenger of Allah said : On the Resurrection Day, three (persons) will intercede, the Prophets, then the learned, and then the martyrs. (Ibn-e-Majah).

٢٢ - عن علي قال قال رسول الله صلى الله عليه وسلم نعم الرجل الفقيه في الدين ان احتيج اليه نفع و ان استغنى عنه اغنى نفسه (مشكواة)

Ali reported that the Messenger of Allah said : Excellent is the man who is learned in religion. If any body feels necessity to go to him he benefits (him), and if anybody does not feel any necessity to go to him, he benefits his soul. (Mishkat).

٢٣ - عن واثلة بن الاسقع قال قال رسول الله صلى عليه وسلم من طلب العلم فادركه كان له كفلان من الاجر فان لم يدركه كان له كفل من الاجر (دارمی)

Waselah-b-Asqa'a reported that the Messenger of Allah said: Whoso seeks knowledge and then acquires it, there are two rewards for him; and if he does not acquire it, there is only one reward for him (Darimi).

٢٤ - عن عبدالله بن عمرو ان رسول الله صلي الله عليه وسلم مر بمجلسين فى مسجده فقال كلا هما علىٰ خير واحد هما افضل من صاحبه اما هو آلاء فيدعون الله و يرغبون اليه فان شاء اعطهم و ان شاء منعهم و اما هوآلاء فيتعلمون الفقه او العلم و يعلمون الجاهل فهم افضل و انما بعثت معلماً ثم جلس فيهم (دارمى)

Abdullah-b-Amr reported that the Messenger of Allah came across two assemblies in his mosque and said: Both of them are doing good but one of them is better then the other. As for these, they call Allah and pray for help from Him. If He wills, He gives them; and if He wills He denies (it to) them; and as for these, they learn theology or knowledge and teach them to the illiterate. They are therefore better. Verily I have been sent as teacher, Then he took his seat in their midst. (Darimi).

٢٥ - عن انس بن مالك ان النبى صلى الله عليه وسلم قال منهومان لا يشبعان منهوم فى العلم لا يشبع منه و منهوم فى الدنيا لا يشبع منها (بيهقى)

Anas-b-Malek reported that the Holy Prophet said: Two greedy men have got no satisfaction: one who has got greed for learning is never satisfied with it, and one who has greed for this world is never satisfied with it. (Bailaqi).

٢٦ - عن سفيان ان عمر بن الخطاب قال لكعب من ا رباب العلم قال الذين يعلمون بما يعلمون قال فما اخرج العلم من قلوب العلماء قال الطمع (دارمى)

Sufyan reported that Omar-b-al-Khattab asked Ka'ab: who are masters of knowledge? He replied: Those who act upon what they teach. He enquired: What is that which takes out learning from the heart of the learned? "Greed" replied he. (Darimi).

٢٧ - عن ابی الدرداء قال ان من اشر الناس من عند الله منزلة یوم القیامة عالم لا ینتفع بعلمه (دارمی)

Abu Darda'a reported: The worst of men in the sight of Allah on the Resurrection Day will be the learned man who does not derive benefit from his learning. (Darimi).

٢٨ - من الحسن قال العلم علمان فعلم فی القلب فذالك العلم النافع و علم علی االسان فذالك حجة الله عزوجل علی ابن ادم (دارمی)

Hasan reported: Learning is of two kinds: learning by heart and that is the usefull learning; and learning by tongue and that is the proof of Allah, the Exalted and Glorious, to the son of Adam. (Darimi).

٢٩ . عن ابن مسعود قال قال لی رسول الله صلی الله علیه وسلم تعلموا العلم و علموه الناس تعلموا الفرائض و علموها الناس تعلموا القرآن و علموه الناس فانی امرء مقبوض والعلم سیقبض و یظهرا لفتن حتی یختلف اثنان فی فریضة لا یجدان احدا یفصل بینهما (دارمی و دار قطنی)

Ibn-e-Masud reported: that the Messenger of Allah said: Acquire knowledge and teach it to the people. Learn the compulsory doctorines and teach them to the people; learn the Quran and teach it to the people, and verily I am a man who is mortal; and learning will soon be destroyed and trials will soon appear, so much so that two will differ regarding an obligatory doctorine. They will find none who may decided between the two. (Darimi, Darqutni).

۳۰ - عن ابى هريرة قال قال رسول الله صلى الله عليه وسلم مثل علم لا ينتفع به كمثل كنز لا ينفق منه فى سبيل الله

(احمد - دارمى)

Abu Hurairah reported that the Messenger of Allah said : The likeness of learning from which no benefit is derived is as the likeness of a hoarded wealth of which nothing is spent in the way of Allah. (Ahmad, Darimi).

۳۱ - عن ابن عباس قال قال رسول لله صلى الله عليه وسلم اقرب الناس من درجة النبوة اهل العلم و الجهاد (مشكواة)

Ibn-e-Abbas reported that the Messenger of Allah said : The nearest of men in the rank of prophethood are the learned and fighters for religion. (Mishkat).

۳۲ - عن ابن عباس قال قال رسول الله صلى الله عليه وسلم صنفان من امتي اذا صلحوا اصلح الناس و اذا فسدوا فسدوا الناس الامراء و الفقهاء (مشكواة)

Ibne-Abbas reported that the Messenger of Allah said : There are two classes of followers : when they are good, peolple are good and when they are bad, pople are bad—the rulers and the theologians (Mishkat.)

۳۳ - عن انس قال قال رسول الله صلى الله عليه وسلم اطلبوا العلم و لو ان بالصين (بيهقى)

Anas reported that the Messenger of Allah said : Search knowledge though it be in China. (Bailaqi).

۳٤ - عن على قال قال رسول الله صلى الله عليه وسلم العلم خزائن مفاتيحها السوال (مشكواة)

Ali reported the Messenger of Allah said : Learning is treasure-house whose keys are queries.

(Mishkat).

٣٥ - عن الاعمش قال قال رسول صلى الله عليه وسلم افة العلم النسيان واضاعته ان تحدث به غير اهله (دارمی)

A' mash reported that the Messenger of Allah said : The calamity of learning is forgetfulness, and its loss is your talk therewith with those not deserving of it.

(Darimi).

٣٦ - عن ابن عباس قال تدارس العلم ساعة من الیل خیر من احیانها (دارمی)

Ibn-e-Abbas reported ; To seek knowledge for one hour at night is better than keeping it (night) awake.

(Darimi).

٣٧ - عن انس قال كان النبي صلى الله عليه وسلم اذا تكلم بكلمة اعادها ثلثاً حتى تفهم عنه (بخاری)

Anas reported that whenever the Holy Prophet uttered a word, he used to repeat it thrice till it was understood from him.

(Bukhari):